Major Latin American Wars

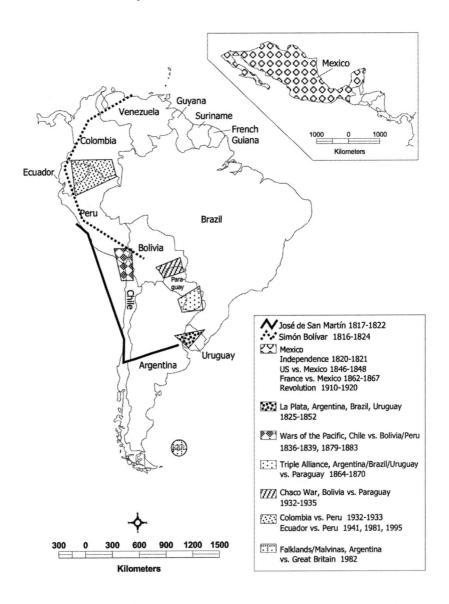

José de San Martín 1817-1822
Simón Bolívar 1816-1824
Mexico
Independence 1820-1821
US vs. Mexico 1846-1848
France vs. Mexico 1862-1867
Revolution 1910-1920

La Plata, Argentina, Brazil, Uruguay
1825-1852

Wars of the Pacific, Chile vs. Bolivia/Peru
1836-1839, 1879-1883

Triple Alliance, Argentina/Brazil/Uruguay
vs. Paraguay 1864-1870

Chaco War, Bolivia vs. Paraguay
1932-1935

Colombia vs. Peru 1932-1933
Ecuador vs. Peru 1941, 1981, 1995

Falklands/Malvinas, Argentina
vs. Great Britain 1982

BLOOD AND DEBT

War and the Nation-State in Latin America

Miguel Angel Centeno

The Pennsylvania State University Press

University Park, Pennsylvania

Library of Congress Cataloging-in-Publication Data

Centeno, Miguel Angel, 1957–
    Blood and debt : war and the nation-state in Latin America / Miguel Angel
Centeno.

    p.   cm.
    Includes bibliographical references and index.
    ISBN 978-0-271-02306-9 (pbk: alk. paper)
    1. Latin America—History, Military. 2. Latin America—Politics and
government. 3. Latin America—Military policy. 4. War and society—Latin
America. 5. Politics and war. I. Title.

F1410.5 .C46 2002
303.6'6'098—dc21   2001036764

For Deborah,
still and always, my best friend

In Italy, for thirty years under the Borgias, they had warfare, terror, murder, bloodshed, but they produced Michelangelo, Leonardo da Vinci and the Renaissance. In Switzerland, they had brotherly love; they had 500 years of democracy and peace—and what did they produce? The cuckoo clock.

—Harry Lime, in *The Third Man* (1949)

Contents

List of Figures

List of Tables

Acknowledgments

I have been tempted to use the phrase "too many people to thank" in reference to this book, but the amount of time and attention others have devoted to my project deserves at least minimal recognition. Of course, the usual caveats about responsibility for errors apply.

First, I should express my gratitude to the wonderful sources of support that made it possible: Princeton University, the National Endowment for the Humanities, the Harry Frank Guggenheim Foundation, and the Universidad Di Tella.

Even more than money, I needed counsel and emotional support, and many friends and colleagues have been far too generous. Marvin Bressler, teacher and friend, first talked me out of a different project and convinced me to try this one. Viviana Zelizer and Paul DiMaggio supported me in much more than merely my writing a book and deserve more than this simple thanks. My colleagues in the sociology department and especially Bruce Western, Alejandro Portes, Patricia Fernández-Kelly, Frank Dobbin, and Michele Lamont gave me intellectual and personal guidance. Cindy Gibson, Blanche Anderson, Donna DeFrancisco, and Barbara McCabe simply put up with me. Jeremy Adelman and Peter Johnson helped me become a better Latin Americanist, while James McPherson, Michael Doyle, and Jeff Herbst also provided much needed information. In Wilson College, Frank Ordiway, Randy Setlock, and Traci Miller have been hearing about this book for far too long and can only hope that it is truly done. William Guthe of the Princeton Educational Technologies Center and T. Wangyal Shawa of the Geographic Information Systems Library made the map.

My students constantly remind me why I chose this profession. I was able to hire several of them while writing this book and their hard work made much of the data gathering possible. Thanks to Alexis Mazon, Sean Rourke,

Susel González, Kit Cutler, Jeff Rinnie, Alex Julca, Eszter Hargittai, Joshua A. Guetzkow, Alexandra Kalev, Margarita Mooney, and Araceli Martínez-Holguin.

Thanking all those outside my various institutional homes may be impossible: Michael Mann, John Womack, Alan Knight, James Dunkerley, Florencia Mallon, Jorge Domínguez, Jaime Rodríguez, Steven Aron, Peter Evans, Mauro Guillen, Doug Massey, Juan Carlos Torre, Randy Collins, Anthony Pereira, Juan Linz, Diane Davis, Dan Chirot, John Markoff, and Dietrich Rueschemeyer. Sandy Thatcher at Penn State Press remains an ideal editor. The friendship with Fernando López-Alves is one of the best results of this book and I hope we can continue to work together for many years. Finally, Charles Tilly's generosity has known no bounds. He deserves his universal reputation not just as a scholar but as one of the good guys.

In September I lost a friend who had helped inspire this book and who will always serve as a professional and personal model. I very much wish Michael Jiménez could read this book and criticize where I went wrong. I would benefit from his lessons and would deeply enjoy our conversation. I (and all of his friends, colleagues, and students) will dearly miss him.

It is typical at this point to comment on how a book cost the author's family innumerable dinners and holidays. I am happy to say that Alex and Maya consistently refused to be ignored and certainly never allowed a bunch of words to displace their father's attention. Thank you both for making me take so long to write this book. Deborah Kaple has put up with all the standard neuroses, bad prose, endless self-centeredness, and just sheer boredom of an academic author and has done so with remarkable grace. She has waited a long time to have me dedicate a book to her. The intervening years have only made my gift even more heartfelt.

1

The Latin American Puzzle

The specter of Leviathan haunts contemporary images of Latin America.[1] A large, unwieldy and all-powerful state, it is said, determines the future of citizens and dictates the thrust of their lives. In the neoliberal paradigm, there has long been an insistence that overreliance on the state trapped Latin America in political and economic mayhem and that the best solution to the continent's myriad problems would be the removal of this institutional dead-

---

1. In the book I focus on eleven cases: Mexico and the ten republics below the isthmus. Except for some occasional comparative comments, I have ignored Central America and the Caribbean. My reasons for doing so were partly driven by geographical reality and partly by the limitations of any scholarly enterprise. Conversations with colleagues have convinced me that Central America represents important exceptions to my arguments. I felt, however, that this region was geopolitically separate, and its inclusion not only would have made the task of this book too daunting, but also would have unnecessarily complicated a narrative already containing significant twists and turns.

weight. For the past two decades, the dominant policy mantra has been "getting the state back out." Once free from the omniscient gaze and monopolistic power of the Leviathan, current wisdom goes, Latin American civil societies and their markets will flower into peaceful, prosperous democracies.

But where is this Leviathan? Where is the institution capable of frustrating and oppressing so many? Is it possible that the Latin American state is capable of so dominating its citizens' lives? Despite a great deal of discussion of a "state-centered matrix,"[2] we still know surprisingly little about the ability of the state in Latin America to do anything.[3] And what we do know points in the opposite direction of the familiar neoliberal beliefs.

What is this institutional creature supposed to look like? Far too many pages have been written in defining this concept to necessitate a long discussion here of its various interpretations and epistemologies.[4] In this book, the state is defined as the permanent institutional core of political authority on which regimes rest and depend. It is permanent in that its general contours and capacities remain constant despite changes in governments. It is institutionalized in that a degree of autonomy from any social sector is assumed. Its authority is widely accepted within society over and above debate regarding specific policies. While the nature of its agency may be problematic, it does possess enough coherence to be considered an actor within the development of a society. That is, even if we may not speak of the state "wanting" or "thinking," we can identify actions and functions associated with it. On the most basic level, the functions of a state include the provision and administration of public goods and the control of both internal and external violence.

How has the Latin American state performed, according to our definition? The results have generally been less than exemplary. Latin American states have regularly failed to establish their institutional autonomy; their scale and scope remain a part of daily political debate; and their legitimacy is often called into question. We consistently also find that the Latin Ameri-

---

2. Cavarozzi, "Beyond Transitions to Democracy."

3. A promising exception is recent work by Peter Evans linking characteristics of state bureaucracies to economic outcomes (Evans and Rauch, "Bureaucracy and Growth." See also D. Smith, Solinger, and Topik, *States and Sovereignty in the Global Economy*).

4. For general discussions, see Barkey and Parikh, "Comparative Perspectives on the State" and literature cited therein. See also Michael Mann's introductory essay "The Autonomous Power of the State," in his *States, War, and Capitalism*. For more recent works in particular fields, see below.

can state has not had the required institutional capacity to perform even a limited set of tasks.[5]

While noting some significant exceptions (for example, Chile and Costa Rica), authors of every report describe a generic failure to provide the basic social services associated with a modern state. Whether one is speaking of health, education, housing, or transportation and communications infrastructures, Latin American states have performed quite badly, even taking into account the resource constraints under which most of these countries operate.[6] The distribution of goods and services across classes, races, genders, and regions is so distorted on most of the continent as to contradict any notion of a political and social collective. For example, whereas the wealthy may obtain the best-quality health care at private institutions, public hospitals in Latin America are notorious even by the standards of their global counterparts. A chasm divides the living conditions of those in the cities and those in the countryside. The vast majority of the rural population does not have access to safe drinking water or sanitation.[7] The relevant states have been largely unable to deal with the subsequent massive urban immigration of the past fifty years, producing public-health nightmares in almost every large Latin American city. A casual walk through any *favela, barrio, colonia popular,* or *villa miseria* horrifies visitors and leads to both engineering and psychological avoidance mechanisms. Even education,

5. Despite the importance of this concept to political sociology, it remains largely understudied. My use of the term focuses on the ability of the relevant political authority to enforce its wishes and implement policies. Perhaps the most extreme manifestation of state authority is as described by James Scott, in *Seeing Like a State.* For a general discussion, see Migdal, *Strong Societies and Weak States;* Evans, Rueschemeyer, and Skocpol, *Bringing the State Back In;* Migdal, Kohli, and Shue, *State Power and Social Forces;* and Callaghy, *The State-Society Struggle.* For Latin America, see Geddes, *Politician's Dilemma,* esp. 15–19; Canak, "The Peripheral State Debate"; Huber Stephens and Stephens, *Democratic Socialism in Jamaica;* Huber, "Assessments of State Strength"; Fishlow, "The Latin American State"; Faletto, "The Specificity of the Latin American State"; Sikkink, "Las capacidades y la autonomía del estado en Brasil y la Argentina"; and Berensztein, "Rebuilding State Capacity in Contemporary Latin America." For historical accounts of the Latin American state, see Oszlak, "The Historical Formation of the State"; Whitehead, "State Organization in Latin America Since 1930"; Coronil, *The Magical State.*

6. Even those with a great deal of wealth have failed to generate anything more than a dramaturgical patina of institutionalized authority and services. See Coronil, *Magical State.* Latin America has of course performed better than Africa. But, it would be stretching the definition of the state to include many of the countries in Africa. In Latin America we have the more puzzling situation whereby states are not stillborn and endure for many years, performing at least the minimum needed for existence, but fail to develop substantial administrative and political capacity.

7. United Nations, Statistics Division.

which was touted as a relative success story for several decades, has left more than a quarter of the population illiterate in many Latin American countries. In most recent times, we have seen even the basic educational infrastructure begin to deteriorate, with the state equally unable to preserve the quality of the leading national universities.

Major cities boast impressive highways and public transport systems today, but all are overused and severely overcrowded. Outside urban centers, travel can be difficult and dangerous. In addition, the telephone remains a luxury in almost all Latin American societies, because of a spotty communications infrastructure outside the main centers.[8] Latin America was an early leader in the cell phone boom, not because of technological sophistication, but because of the absence of adequate public telecommunications.[9] Rather than the market for such electronic toys being hampered by a dominating state, the service vacuum created opportunities.

If the state is supposed to provide the basic foundation that allows for the physical integration of society, the Latin American state has fallen short. It has also failed to create a notion of citizenship, crucial to integrating community.[10] An important function of any modern state has been the "compulsory cooperation" it requires of its subjects as it recognizes their common citizenship.[11] This includes forging basic social equality and collective identity. With the possible exception of the countries of the Southern Cone, no society in Latin America has been integrated to the point that all sectors of the population inherently recognize their common links through the nation.

In one possible area, the Latin American state appears to have exercised considerable authority. Much of the imagery of the overwhelming Leviathan comes from the economic roles the state has assumed. It should first be noted that the actual economic influence of the state has been at times exaggerated and its role in more developed countries minimized. Nevertheless, the liberal state of the nineteenth century played a significant role in the development of the export economy. After 1930, the state was involved in

8. Uruguay boasts the highest level of phone penetration, with 209 lines per one thousand people, while Peru has only 60 per thousand (University of Texas, LANIC, "Trends in Latin American Networking").

9. Subsequently, the continent lags far behind in use of the Internet (University of Texas, LANIC, "Trends in Latin American Networking").

10. Pinheiro, "Democracies Without Citizenship"; Vilas, "Inequality and the Dismantling of Citizenship in Latin America."

11. Mann, "Autonomous Power of the State," 23.

everything from trade to industrial policy. There is no denying that Mexico in the late 1930s and Brazil in the late 1960s had many of the traits associated with so-called developmentalist states. Yet even in those countries where state intervention has been most condemned and where its capacity has been greatest, the ability of the Latin American state to impose its will on a population has been severely limited.[12] The state provided employment for some and protection for others, but it generally failed to force the people it supposedly governed to change their behavior.[13] The bloated public payroll was plagued by corruption and inefficiency, while industry, protected and nationalized, produced shoddy goods. The ability of the state to be generous grew, but not its capacity to be demanding. The resultant state was large but ineffective.

Consider the manner in which the Latin American state has met its fiduciary responsibilities, such as the issuance and governance of a national currency, and the prudent management of national accounts. Once again, the outcome has been an almost unmitigated disaster. Inflation has come to be so associated with the continent that it may even be called a Latin American disease. Over the past thirty years, countries such as Bolivia saw such mind-boggling inflation (11,749 percent in 1985 alone) as to make the notion of a currency meaningless. A million 1979 Argentine pesos would have been literally worthless by 1997. Even such countries as Chile, which were standard exceptions to this kind of problem, have experienced almost perpetual annual double-digit inflation.[14] Over the past decade, several countries have considered surrendering their effective power to issue currency by either establishing parity with the U.S. dollar or making it legal tender.[15]

---

12. Evans, "Predatory, Developmental, and Other Apparatuses"; P. Smith, "The Rise and Fall of the Developmental State," 51–73. The clearest example of failure may be precisely in those cases where attempts were made to create a variant of East Asian authoritarian developmentalism. In an earlier book I described Carlos Salinas's quasi-Leninist technocratic revolution. Note that even this project could not prevent an outbreak of guerrilla war, could not protect basic institutions from the inroads of the drug mafia, could not count on a police force, and certainly could not protect its currency.

13. Some have seen the rise of the informal economy over the past decades as an indication of the suffocating embrace of an all-powerful state-economic apparatus. Yet is not such a huge economic sector free from taxes and regulations an indication of the state's inability to impose its own standards? The percentage of workers not covered by social security or public-health plans does not reflect a wide movement to escape from the grasp of the state, but rather the inability of the state to hold the population in its grip.

14. Data from Committee on Latin American Studies, University of California, Los Angeles, SALA, Table 3322.

15. The almost universal problem of capital flight is another indication of the relatively weak capacity of the Latin American state to control basic economic functions.

Not coincidentally, budgets have consistently been off balance. The Latin American government that is able to pay its own way is rare indeed. The same may be said for many governments worldwide during the past fifty years, but the fiscal fragility of the Latin American state has been extreme. These states have usually had to seek funds outside their own economies, thereby threatening their national autonomy. Moreover, the repayment of these loans has created yet another burden, since it often forces the country to push aside domestic considerations in a frantic search for convertible currency. It may be only a slight exaggeration to describe the fiscal operations of some states as mere transfers of national wealth to international lenders.

The failure of states to pay their own way is also indicative of their constrained capacity to tax their population. Despite their rapacious reputations, Latin American states have historically taxed a much smaller share of their national wealth than other, richer countries. While comparisons of fiscal systems are difficult because of differing definitions, measures, and fiscal jurisdiction, overall trends are indicative. On average, Latin American countries tax their economies at roughly one-third the level of those in the G7.[16] By this measure, then, the Latin American state is far from being a rapacious Leviathan. It would be more accurate to call it a fiscal dwarf.

Political failures have been even more obvious. Much attention has been focused on authoritarianism, less on the actual obedience of orders. The state's capacity to maintain monopoly over the use of violence or territoriality has also always been suspect.[17] With a couple of exceptions, few national capitals could be said to have ruled the hinterlands of the nineteenth or even early twentieth century. Even today, Peru, Ecuador, and Bolivia still lack the ability to control the Sierra; Mexico continues to fight rebels in at least two provinces; Brazil cannot enforce federal policies on regions; and Colombia is quickly disintegrating.

With regard to the maintenance of social or civil order, citizens living in any major Latin American city increasingly find themselves victims to crime

---

16. The average for Latin America is 13.3 percent of gross domestic product (GDP) (median is 12.8 percent). For the G7 (Group of Seven [industrialized nations]) it is 36.8 percent (identical median) (Committee, *SALA*, Tables 3119, 3120 for 1993–1996; OECD, *Revenue Statistics*, 64). Even if we take government expenditure as a percentage of the national economy, the most elaborate state apparatus on the continent pales next to the significance of most OECD states. See also ECLAC, *The Fiscal Covenant*, esp. 65–87.

17. Whitehead, "State Organization."

and are turning to some form of privatized protection.[18] For the rich, these services may be provided by the booming security industry. For the very poor this may involve reluctant membership in gangs or participation in crude protection rackets. For those in the middle class, security may be nothing more than ownership of one of the increasingly available guns or simply the avoidance of any unnecessary exposure in the public arena. In some cities, where the safety of even the most powerful political figures is not assured, daily life has assumed an almost predatory quality. Nowhere, again with the possible exception of Chile, can one rely on the state to provide a reasonable assurance of protection.

Once a crime has been committed, it is equally difficult for the average citizen to take refuge in the justice system. Although scholars have paid little attention to this important aspect of Latin American life, the legal system in those countries is in tatters.[19] Prisoners (except the most privileged) often disappear into the morass of an administrative apparatus that cannot track their whereabouts, much less ensure a prompt trial. Victims of crime rarely bother to report assaults. Depending on the country, business disputes require a third party other than the state to intervene in and manage conflicts and to propose and enforce resolutions. In battles over property, the state's capacity to serve as an even potentially neutral arbiter is highly questionable. The legitimacy of the official judiciary and the level of trust in its capacity to search for legal truths and objective justice are both quite low.

What about the popular conception, then, of the Latin American state as a bloody tyrant? A number of Latin American states have perpetrated their share of mass murder: the Matanza of El Salvador, the anti-Mayan campaign of Guatemala, and the "Dirty War" of Argentina are some examples. Although these were brutal occurrences that brought suffering and death to thousands, even the worst Latin American cases pale in comparison with happenings in much of the rest of the world.[20] In the following several chapters, I demonstrate that taken in context, political violence in Latin America

18. Londoño and Guerrero, "Violencia en América Latina"; ECLAC, "Public Insecurity on the Rise"; Colburn, "Crime in Latin America"; University of Texas, Austin, Department of Sociology, "Rising Violence and the Criminal Justice Response in Latin America."
19. Guillermo O'Donnell has been in the lead with some of the recent concern with the weakness of the judiciary system. See, for example, "The Judiciary and the Rule of Law" and "The State, Democratization, and Some Conceptual Problems." See also Mahon, "Reforms in the Administration of Justice in Latin America."
20. Compare data on Latin America, for example, with the findings detailed in Rummel, *Death by Government*.

has been relatively muted. The state has not been actively responsible for many deaths, relatively speaking. In fact, it has been the *absence* of a state that has been largely responsible for deaths among the greater population.[21]

Many of the deaths produced by political violence have resulted from the inability of the state to impose its authority in a definitive and permanent manner. The hot spots of politically inspired violence in contemporary Latin America, for example, Colombia, are the results not of a Leviathanesque effort to impose new social orders or to dispose of particular populations, but of the persistence of rival claimants to legitimate authority. In other cases, Mexico and again Colombia being the most prominent examples, they are about the inability (or unwillingness) of the central state to impose a rule of law over an international business. The upsurge in crime in nearly every Latin American capital over the past twenty years has come not from officially sanctioned actions, but from rogue police and criminals who feel free to terrorize an increasingly desperate population.

It is also critical to take a look at the motivations for the political violence that has occurred in Latin America. The global holocausts of the past century have been associated with three different forms of political exclusion. The first and most common type defined identity through territory and elevated residence in a particular region to the secular religion of nationalism. A related second form defined identity through ethnicity, sometimes associated with a territory, as in the preceding type, other times with only sections of one or more formal states. A third motivating factor has been ideology, often combined, implicitly or explicitly, with one of the identity claims described above. All these identities claimed the right to impose "the ultimate sacrifice" on their populations. What is peculiar to Latin America is that political violence has rarely been associated with the emotional intensity associated with the first two types, and even the third has not brought about the kind of mass mobilization witnessed in Europe. Again, this is not to deny moments of extreme political violence, but to emphasize that these have been epiphenomenal. We have no evidence of systematic intense violence legitimated by the standard political rubrics.[22]

---

21. If we wish to include the victims of state inaction, the number of premature deaths caused by the absence of basic services has to be at least partly set at the door of political authority. Consider the case of Brazil, widely considered the most unequal industrial society in the world. While the rich and influential of São Paulo avoid traffic snarls by commuting by helicopter, the very poorest have life expectancies that may be decades shorter than the lucky few. Given the existence of great wealth at least potentially available to the state, its failure to appropriate it and redistribute it to prevent some suffering may be judged as criminal as the actual order of violence.

22. Perhaps the most interesting Latin American exception may be found in the Cold War.

Finally, we must discuss the instances of externally oriented violence. This is perhaps the most puzzling aspect of the Latin American state, because there have been very few international wars involving these in almost two centuries of independence. That is, since the early nineteenth century, the continent has been relatively free of major international conflict. Even if we include civil wars, Latin America has enjoyed relative peace. Outside the cases of Paraguay, Mexico, and Colombia, no country has suffered a large number of deaths during *conventional* warfare.[23]

Worldwide, Latin America stands out for the general absence of organized slaughter. Southeast and South Asia, the Middle East, and most of all, Europe have had much bloodier historical experiences. Although the United States has been generally peaceful within its own borders, it has participated in some of the bloodiest contests outside them. Scandinavia, following its bellicose early history, has been peaceful for almost three hundred years, but has also been exceptional in a variety of other ways that make a comparison with Latin America difficult. Africa has been relatively free of international conflict, but most of its countries have enjoyed barely thirty years of independence, in contrast to Latin America's one and a half centuries.[24]

Nowhere is the general peace of the continent more clearly seen than on a map. Examine a map of Latin America in 1840 and the general borders and country configurations look surprisingly like today's. While early units such as Gran Colombia, the Central American Republic, and the Peruvian-Bolivian Confederation have vanished, no politically recognized state has disappeared through conquest. In almost two hundred years of independent political history, Latin America has yet to lose a Poland, a Burgundy, a Saxony, or a Kingdom of the Two Sicilies. In fact, the contemporary states and boundaries resemble quite closely those of the Spanish colonial administration of the eighteenth century.

Academic study of Latin America reflects this lack of war experience.

Consider that notwithstanding its clear authoritarian character, the Cuban regime has never engaged in the mass killing of many other communist countries. Moreover, even the Central American wars of the 1970s and 1980s, while extremely bloody, pale next to the organized slaughter of equivalent struggles in other parts of the world.

23. The Central American wars of the 1970s and 1980s represent another exception, but I am uncertain about where guerrilla wars would fit into the classic models analyzed in the literature on state and war. The recent events along the Peruvian-Ecuadorian frontier and the tensions between Venezuela and Colombia do not represent a break in the pattern of peace, given the relatively small amounts of violence and time involved. See Chapter 2 for more details on numbers of wars.

24. On the African case, see Jackson and Rosberg, "Why Africa's Weak States Persist"; Herbst, *States and Power in Africa*.

Whether measured by bibliographic entries, attention devoted in disciplinary meetings, or space allotted in such works as the *Cambridge Encyclopedia* or the *Cambridge History*, war has warranted little attention.[25] The Latin American state, therefore, appears to have acted in a very different manner from that of other states. Simply put, we cannot make a case for the significance or strength of the Latin American state on the basis of its performance as a protector of territory, since the potential to demonstrate such a capability has been limited. If anything, as I will argue in the coming pages, this international inaction may be the best indicator of the state's fragility.

In summary, using Weber's original language when referring to the state, one cannot speak of states *dominating* their societies. While generalizations are always dangerous, we may classify most of the Latin American states, even well into the twentieth century, as highly despotic, yet infrastructurally weak. They are "despotic" in the ability of state elites to undertake decisions without routine negotiation with civil society. They are weak in the institutional capacity of the state, or its ability to actually implement decisions.[26] Despite its reputation for autocracy and repression, the Latin American state has been far less able to impose itself on its societies than its European counterparts. In reality, the Latin American state cannot be called a Leviathan, or the oppressive equalizer of neoliberal myth, or even the overwhelming centralizer of black legends of Iberian culturalism. What has characterized the Latin American state is not its concentration of power, but the very dilution of power.[27]

As with any multicase generalization, we can place the capacities of the various Latin American states on a spectrum. If we exclude Central America and the Caribbean, we recognize three different general types.[28] On one end of the spectrum we find countries where the state as an institution has succeeded in establishing some administrative norms and where there is relative institutional capacity. The most obvious end point for our spectrum is

25. An important recent exception is López-Alves, *State Formation and Democracy in Latin America, 1810–1900*.

26. Mann, *Sources of Social Power,* vol. 2.

27. Gurr, Jaggers, and Moore, in "Transformation of the Western State," note "the pervasive failure of most Latin American societies to establish coherent, institutionalized political systems of either democratic or autocratic type. . . . When coherent autocracies have been established in Latin America, their institutions usually were too weak to outlast the founding elite" (94).

28. I am borrowing much of this classification from Whitehead, "State Organization," but it follows the standard opinion in the field.

Chile, followed by Uruguay and Argentina. On the other end are those countries where the viability of the state remains in question; Bolivia and Peru are examples of failure in administration and institutionalization, whereas Colombia represents the collapse of authority. In the middle are the two largest Latin American states, Mexico and Brazil.[29] Inside each set of countries we need to take into account regional variation, with state authority concentrated around certain geographical zones and often practically disappearing in less accessible frontiers.[30] The analytical task in this book is to explain both the generic Latin American pattern and its variations.

Latin America thus represents a double empirical puzzle. On the one hand, some of the states have only minimally developed. On the other, we have an equally interesting exception to standard international behavior, in that these countries have mostly avoided large-scale war. A region that has managed to escape both war and the formation of a strong state for the past hundred years calls for analysis and promises important lessons for the development of contemporary political life. The Latin American puzzle also offers a perfect opportunity to explore the relationship between military conflict and subsequent political development in state formation.

Where Do States Come From?

How do we explain the relative lack of development of the Latin American state? How do we account for the variation that does exist on the continent? What is the relationship between the existence of this limited state and the level and forms of political violence observed in the region? After reviewing some possible theoretical answers for the particular development of the Latin American state, I focus on a relatively recent emphasis on what we may call bellicist, or war-centered, accounts of the rise of nation states.[31]

Over the past century, social science has produced myriad theories accounting for the development of the state. While this is not the place for an exhaustive review, an outline of the major theories and their application to Latin America will be useful.

29. Borrowing Charles Ragin's language, we may speak of the first group having fuzzy membership in the set of states of $<.5$; those in the middle may have membership of .5; and those with most developed states may have somewhere around .75 (Ragin, *Fuzzy-Set Social Science*).

30. Indeed, it is often difficult to distinguish between "state" and unofficial authorities. See Nugent, "State and Shadow State in Northern Peru."

31. I borrow the term *bellicist* from Gorski, "Birth of the Leviathan."

In the United States, the most popular account of the state sees it as an arena in which the various members of a community can express their preferences and use previously agreed-upon rules to arrive at a collective decision. This decision, even if it does not satisfy all, represents some optimal distribution of public inclinations. Not coincidentally, the state in this model is something of a market for politics. Like a market, the state has no preferences or inclinations; it is merely an empty vessel that a population may use as it sees fit.

In this view, the most important characteristic of a society is its capacity to participate in the series of deliberations that define the state and to obey the resultant directives. Following the market analogy, this has been expressed as a form of social capital, wherein a state will reflect the collective skills and attributes embodied in its citizenry.[32] The state arises from the cumulative experience of a population's self-government as it grows and requires more and more coordination. As applied to Latin America, this general perspective has generated two very different discussions. In the first, the Latin American state is interpreted as overpowering, centralizing, and coercive, these traits seen as rooted in the Iberian culture brought back by the Spaniards.[33] A very different and less developed view implicitly borrows the notion of "strong societies/weak states" from Migdal and analyzes the manner in which political compromises with social groups disable the state.[34]

While the analysis of the state as a kind of a collective market has enjoyed an intellectual boom of late, it is the degree of autonomy that a state possesses that has most divided contemporary social scientists.[35] That is, to what extent does the state remain independent of the society that it is attempting to integrate and control? From a classic Weberian perspective, the state serves as both impartial police officer and honest clerk.[36] Weber held that the function of the state is to create the conditions under which the various relations between members of a society can develop. Specifically,

32. Putnam with Leonardi and Nanetti, *Making Democracy Work*.
33. Véliz, *The Centralist Tradition of Latin America;* Morse, "The Heritage of Latin America"; Wiarda, *Politics and Social Change in Latin America*.
34. The culprits may be either elites creating repressive protectors of privilege or populist groups creating morasses of clientalism. See, for example, Malloy, *Authoritarianism and Corporatism in Latin America;* Collier and Collier, *Shaping the Political Arena*.
35. For a discussion on Latin America, see Stepan, *The State and Society;* Hamilton, *The Limits of State Autonomy;* and Waisman, *Reversal of Development in Argentina*.
36. The property-rights literature is a related approach; see North and Thomas, *Rise of the Western World* and North, *Institutions, Institutional Change, and Economic Performance*.

the state creates the institutional foundations required by a market economy and a legal bureaucratized order, through domination or the imposition of its control over violence. The perspectives and preferences of the population are in this sense irrelevant. The state exists above and beyond the reach of its citizens; it must or it would not be able to fulfill its functions. Marxists might agree that the state fulfills these necessary roles, but they challenge the notion that it does so neutrally; a capitalist society can only produce a capitalist state. Whether because of structural determinacy or instrumental controls, the state serves the long-term interests of the dominant class. Whatever their arguments, both Weber and Marx adopt a Hobbesian or conflict perspective. The state is needed to cap a set of social, economic, and political struggles.[37]

All the views discussed here emphasize the domestic conditions for the rise of states and determine its autonomy vis-à-vis national actors. A very different set of academic perspectives emphasizes the existence of states within a larger global environment. The most famously associated with Latin America is dependency theory, whose various incarnations share some critical common assumptions about the state in ex-colonial societies. Dependency theory contends that ex-colonial societies can never hope to develop states that will fulfill all the tasks needed to govern and run a country. This results from the understood centrality of external economic relations to these countries, the stunted development of national elites, the overwhelming influence of global powers, and these states' marginal position within a global economy. It also says that postcolonial states will never be impartial arenas, for they were constructed from afar and must constantly look to external actors for approbation and support. In this model, their economies do not require the kind of integration that the Weberian state is meant to provide, nor do their elites provide their acquiescence to political domination, as their external allies are much more powerful and reliable. The result is a dependent state, never fulfilling its own destiny.[38]

During the past few decades, numerous variations on these perspectives have been applied to Latin America. Authors have attempted to document how the state has served the interests of a particular fraction of the domestic elite, how it has served to defend multinational interests, and how it has

37. For a general discussion, see Whitehead, "State Organization"; Oszlak, "The Historical Formation of the State." For a rare explicit application of Weber's theories, see Uricoechea, *The Patrimonial Foundations of the Brazilian Bureaucratic State.*

38. The classic source is Cardoso and Faletto, *Dependency and Development in Latin America.* See also Gereffi and Fonda, "Regional Paths of Development."

suppressed one popular movement or another. Academics have devoted considerable energy to determining who has used state power, how, and for whom. Yet the particular development of the institution of political power has hardly been examined.

To a large extent, students of Latin America have assumed that the state was there to be used; that the tool was available for manipulation. Revolutions have been a much more popular topic than the construction of the states against which they were directed. Consider the number of volumes on the Mexican and Cuban Revolutions and then reflect on the relative scarcity of books on the Cuban Republic and the Porfiriato. With our fascination for how the walls came tumbling down, we have paid scant attention to the rise of buildings, accepting the existence of Latin American states without asking how powerful they really were. Much like the Wizard of Oz, these states seemed all-powerful and full of bombast and smoke. But we have neglected to look for the man behind the curtain.

The study of Latin America has thus reflected a general trend in political sociology; sociologists and their kin have been much more interested in the breakdown of states than in their development.[39] What is startling is that even in analyzing the collapse of states we assume their prior existence. Consider, for example, political sociology's three main conditions for revolution: fiscal strain, elite conflict, and popular revolt.[40] Only the first, fiscal strain, examines the capacity of the state to resist opposition and revolt. But still, the focus of research is on how the apparatus of the already established state became so enfeebled. A related tradition in historical sociology has followed Barrington Moore and sought to explain the forms of rule and social alliances under which the state operates. Once again, however, the administrative capacity of the state is taken for granted.[41]

This paradigm simply does not work for Latin America. The minimalist state is not a product of neoliberalism or of the debt crisis. States in Latin America have never developed the institutional strength of their western European (or even, in some cases, East Asian) counterparts. Latin American

---

39. Peruse a graduate student reading list and note the balance between themes. Some of this may be attributed to the still-relative intellectual influence of Marx over Weber in the academy. The latter has even been drafted to explain state collapse, one of the few themes he did not address exhaustively.

40. Collins, *Macrohistory*.

41. Moore, *Social Origins of Dictatorship and Democracy*; Rueschemeyer, Huber Stephens, and Stephens, *Capitalist Development and Democracy*. A noteworthy exception in that she closely links revolution and state capacity is Skocpol, *States and Social Revolutions*.

state power has always been shallow and contested. The interesting and more insightful question is why.

One source for theoretical guidance is the revival of macrohistorical accounts over the past forty years. From McNeill, in *The Rise of the West,* to Poggi, Moore, Giddens, Mann, van Creveld, Finer, Skocpol, and Tilly, authors have offered a view of the past five hundred years (and often longer) from the veritable mountaintop.[42] As historical narratives, their works are marvelous pieces of scholarship, but they leave little indication of a pattern that can be applied to the Latin American situation. The number of variables and patterns and the complexity of the process make it nearly impossible to apply their work to a non-European case.[43]

Part of this "return to history" has, however, generated yet another, perhaps more useful, internationalist perspective on the rise of the state. Rather than emphasizing the roles state institutions play in the development of a society, this perspective focuses on the most basic of political functions, the defense from violence. In this view, states are mechanisms for defending territories from external threats.[44] Geoffrey Best put it most succinctly: "Human society politically organized, becomes a state; and states distinguish themselves from other states, to put it bluntly, by their abilities to fight or protect themselves from one another."[45] Seen this way, states are above all fighters of wars, and their development has to be understood within the broader context of geopolitical conflict and competition. That is, war partly determines all aspects of states, from their authority structures, administrative capacities, and legitimacy to their levels of inclusion. Each of these in turn helps determine how states fight.

The bellicist perspective represents a potentially rich guide for analyzing the Latin American state. First, more than most theories of state formation, it provides a straightforward historical model that can be abstracted and applied to different locales. The occurrence of war is a relatively clear-cut historical phenomenon that can be dated and from which one can measure

---

42. McNeill, *The Rise of the West;* Poggi, *The Development of the Modern State;* Moore, *Social Origins of Dictatorship and Democracy;* Giddens, *The Nation-State and Violence;* Mann, *Sources of Social Power,* vols. 1 and 2; Skocpol, *States and Social Revolutions;* Tilly, *Coercion, Capital, and European States;* Van Creveld, *Rise and Decline of the State;* Finer, *The History of Government from the Earliest Times.*

43. More problematically, when students and readers do visualize more generic patterns, they tend to forget that these "metanarratives" are still based on a limited set of cases. See Centeno and López-Alves, *The Other Mirror.*

44. For relevant works, see discussion in Chapter 3.

45. G. Best, introduction to M. S. Anderson, *War and Society in Europe,* 8.

institutional effects. Bellicist theory also emphasizes a series of discrete aspects of state formation that can be at least relatively adequately measured and compared. Second, while much of the recent emphasis has been on the institutional development of the state, for example, growth of bureaucracies, related discussion of the effect of war might be found in the literature on nationalism and democracy. The analysis of the consequences of war can thus encompass a wide range of political institutions and major aspects of the nation-state. Third, the study of war allows us to explicitly analyze the international environment's contribution to state development.

Bellicist theory therefore permits us to explore the two puzzles I earlier identified as unique to Latin America. Through it, we can ask about why violence occurs only with certain organizational forms on the continent and is very rare as a geopolitical event, and we can analyze the moments of violence and determine the consequences for the relevant states so as to gauge the possible costs of peace. In turn, Latin America may provide new empirical insights with which to analyze the dynamics between war and state building. The relative absence of wars and the fragility of state formations can serve as a useful counterfactual to the European experience, on which most of our theoretical assumptions rest.

This book is a comparative history of the experience and consequences of war in Latin America. It is an unusual historical puzzle: why have the dogs of war rarely barked in Latin America? It is not that Latin Americans have not tried to kill one another—they have—but that they have generally not attempted to organize their societies with such a goal in mind. These countries have existed with comparatively low levels of militarization.[46] To better understand why this matters, we can look at explanations of violence from both the micro and the macro level.[47] The micro level explores the psychosocial traits and conditions that help explain the barbarity observed in war. It asks a simple yet profound question: how can human beings treat one another this way? On the macro level, a very different question assumes the barbarity, but goes further to analyze the different organizational forms in which it occurs. Latin America does not look very different from Europe from the micro-oriented perspective. However, the reasons for which people

46. "Civil society organizing itself for production of violence [and the] mobilization of resources, material and human, for potential use in warfare" (G. Best, "The Militarization of European Society, 1870–1914," 13). The important exception here is Paraguay under López that will serve for intracontinental comparison.

47. The emphasis on the organizational aspect of violence was suggested in a wonderful seminar led by Kai Erikson during the spring of 2000 at Princeton University.

have killed and the manner in which they have been organized are completely different and extremely illuminating. This difference in development is a focal point of this book.

An analysis of the "long peace" in Latin America makes several valuable contributions to the literature. By studying the dog that did not bark we can better understand the conditions that lead to war. For instance, this book calls into question the often implicit assumption that political violence is organized along territorial lines. Latin America's political violence has occurred largely *within* rather than *between* states. In this volume, I attempt to explain why and to analyze the consequences of this difference.

The forms of violence seen on the continent illustrate one of the key differences between the new postcolonial states and those established before the nineteenth century: For example, the presence of external powers influenced outcomes and helped to ensure (impose?) peace. These external police may have prevented much bloodshed, but they may also have locked regions into political equilibriums unsuited for further institutional development. There is more than a grain of social Darwinism in the warcentric account of state development. What then of a geopolitical ecosystem where adaptation did not necessarily lead to differential success? In light of increased pressures for international intervention in domestic struggles, the answers to this question have clear contemporary importance. The types of violence observed in Latin America are relevant in a world where the "major-theater war" classically seen in Europe may no longer be so relevant, where states may not be the only military actors, and where outcomes may not be decisive.

Further, this book contributes to the scholarship on the still somewhat neglected political history of nineteenth-century Latin America and specifically on the development of state institutions.[48] Why did central authority establish control over the means of violence in Europe, but generally fail in Latin America? The analysis also sheds light on the dynamics of domestic conflicts following independence. Through the prism of war we may also improve our understanding not only of the Latin American state, but also of nationalism and democracy on the continent. The puzzle remains of how Latin American countries have managed to avoid the establishment of order, effective and efficient systems of production, and equitable distribution. Such a magnificent display of institutional failure deserves further attention; and the role of war in it has been understudied.

48. Two significant and recent additions (from radically different perspectives) are López-Alves, *State Formation and Democracy in Latin America* and Adelman, *Republic of Capital*.

Finally, this book is a challenge to a long tradition in historical sociology that has privileged a small number of cases and often generalized a European phenomenon into a universal social fact.[49] For example, Michael Mann can confidently say that the relationship between revolutions and geopolitical pressures is "as consistent a relationship as we find in macrosociology."[50] Yet no such correlation exists in Latin America. The English and French "bourgeois" revolutions have been treated as theoretical models, while the Mexican and Bolivian counterparts are not. The rise of Prussia and its bureaucracy merits attention, but not the solidification of the Chilean state. We can all date Waterloo, but few can do so for the equally decisive battle of Ayacucho. By asking why Latin America is different, I hope to motivate others to ask whether Europe is the true exception.[51] This book is a challenge to assumptions and an encouragement to others to look outside the "usual suspects" for historical paradigms.

The inclusion of more cases might even go a long way toward clarifying the recently heated fight between various practitioners of historical sociology.[52] I hope to offer a challenge to the "implicit claims for essential, invariant universals" that Charles Tilly asserts have become too predominant in the field.[53] By introducing a largely new set of cases to a long-standing debate, I hope to demonstrate that contingency, contextuality, and relationality play too important a role in historical developments to allow for all-encompassing general laws, and certainly when these are based on faulty samples. The book follows what Tilly has called the variation-finding approach to "huge comparisons"[54] and thus favors variability over universals.

First, I have sought to differentiate the region we call Latin America from other parts of the world. I disagree with those who argue against treating the continent as a unit. Certainly from the point of view of geopolitics, it makes a great deal of sense; but these countries have shared critical outcomes as well as heritages and social structures. These commonalties will allow us to study the region as a possible counterfactual to theories of state

---

49. For another wonderful refutation of European universality of state formation, see Barkey, *Bandits and Bureaucrats*. For a broader discussion of this theme, see Centeno and López-Alves, *Other Mirror*.

50. Mann, *Sources of Social Power*, vol. 2, 225.

51. In terms of state development, the "idiosyncrasy" of the European experience has already been noted by Finer in *History of Government*, 5.

52. For a concise and useful critique (with suggestions for a resolution), see Western, "Bayesian Thinking About Macrosociology."

53. Tilly, "To Explain Political Processes," 1597.

54. Tilly, *Big Structures, Large Processes, Huge Comparisons*.

development arising from the European experience. Second, within the region I have sought to find variation from a general pattern. In this way, I am thus also borrowing from two different approaches defined by Tilly. At times, I will claim some level of universality for the region, while at others I will emphasize the very individual characteristics of the relevant countries and descend into the historical details. My dual objective is to generate a better explanation of Latin American reality and to produce a better understanding of the roots of successful state authority. I see this as the ultimate purpose of the Weberian tradition in sociology: to use individual data to regard and analyze the distinctiveness of each case while employing theoretical tools to explain that difference.

I do not intend this book to play any explicit part in the ongoing debate regarding "historicism versus theory-centrism" or "induction versus deduction."[55] I have always considered myself something of an epistemological naïf and have frankly wondered about the utility of sociologists engaging in practices perhaps best left to philosophers. I concur with Jack Goldstone that much of the debate comes down to whether one wishes to emphasize initial conditions versus general laws.[56] I just do not see a reason why we cannot do both. Tales well told should entice an audience with a good story while teaching it a general moral.

There is little question that we may speak of a probabilistic connection between war and state development. My central aim here is to explore and refine this relationship and to analyze how the very different conditions existing in Latin America altered this causal connection. The process of researching and writing this volume has taught me the value of an ongoing and often dialectical interaction between the theory and history. We cannot rely purely on the simple telling of stories. Without the bellicist model, it would be difficult to make sense of the chaos of the cases I have analyzed. Yet without that empirical trail, it would be impossible to go beyond mere theoretical propositions. I have come to understand the story of war and nation-states in Latin America by thinking of it as a series of spiral causalities.[57] We can identify patterns of causes leading from moment A to moment B, and these are often repeated. The pattern, however, is highly dependent on what came before and the conditions at the moment we wish to examine.

55. See "Symposium on Historical Sociology and Rational Choice Theory."
56. Goldstone, "Initial Conditions, General Laws, Path Dependence," 832.
57. I deliberately avoid using the term *path dependence* so not to engage in that particular debate. For an excellent summary of the argument, see Mahoney, "Path Dependence in Historical Sociology."

The trail from our starting point in the eighteenth century to the early twentieth is neither a straight line nor a random disbursement of events. The relevant actions and structures are causally related to each other in what appears to be a circular fashion. We can use the chronology of history to disentangle these knots, but also need to accept the inherent circularity and interaction; in any historical narrative, causal orders are often reversed and interact in feedback loops. Tracing those loops and discovering the general outlines of their curves should be the major tasks of macrohistorical scholarship.[58]

If nothing else, such efforts will allow us to put to rest futile doctrinaire battles about the relative importance of states versus societies in the determination of political development. As I document, it is the empirical interaction of states, as institutions and agents, and societies, as environments and structures, that helps produce the particular Latin American pattern.[59] As in the case of the Ottoman Empire, for example, we cannot speak of a victorious or dominant state or civil society, but can describe the historical creation of a series of compromises that helped define the contemporary condition of the continent.[60]

In general, the lesson to be drawn from this book is that while war may have played a significant role in the development of some European states, its explanatory power wanes on crossing the Atlantic. The particular conditions that defined the process of state creation on the continent precluded the type and consequences of state-making war. Students of peripheral regions in Europe where violence produced results similar to those found in Latin America, for example, the Balkans and Iberia, may have something to learn from these cases. I hope that students of macrohistorical processes will take away the arguably more important lesson that our overreliance on a limited set of cases has encouraged and permitted the formulation of model-like propositions that obscure more-complex historical realities.

Limited War and Limited States

What was the relationship between war and state making in Latin America? Latin America has largely fought what I call *limited* war. To understand

58. Michael Mann notes that "the problem seems to be that for centralized functions to be converted into exploitation, organizational resources are necessary that only actually appeared with the emergence of civilized, stratified, state societies—which is a circular process" ("Autonomous Power of the State," 21).

59. For an extended discussion of a "state in society" approach, see Migdal, Kohli, and Shue, *State Power and Social Forces*.

60. Barkey, *Bandits and Bureaucrats*, 231–32.

what I mean by this, first consider a definition of contemporary *total* war. This form of conflict may be said to have begun with the military revolution of the seventeenth century, to have achieved new levels of destruction and social consequences with the French Revolutionary and Napoleonic Wars, to have developed into their modern counterparts beginning with the Crimean and U.S. Civil Wars, and to have culminated in the two world wars.[61] Total wars may be characterized by (a) increasing lethalness of the battlefield; (b) the expansion of the killing zone to include not only hundreds of miles of frontlines, but also civilian targets; (c) association with a form of moral or ideological crusade that contributes to the demonization of the enemy; (d) the involvement of significant parts of the population either in direct combat or in support roles; and (e) the militarization of society, in which social institutions are increasingly oriented toward military success and judged on their contribution to a war effort.

Such efforts require that states therefore be able to (a) amass and concentrate large amounts of personnel and materiel in a relatively short time, (b) expand their efforts across hundreds if not thousands of miles, (c) prescribe some form of coherent ideological message, (d) convince significant numbers of the population to accept direct military authority over their lives, and (e) transform their societies to be able to meet these challenges.

Limited wars, by contrast, (a) involve short overall duration of conflict with isolated moments of ferocity; (b) are restricted to few and small geographical areas; (c) are between states with shared ideological or cultural profiles and originate in economic or frontier clashes; (d) are fought by either professional mercenary armies, or those made up of a small number of draftees from lower classes; and (e) may be practically ignored by the typical civilian. They do not require dramatic fiscal or personal sacrifices or a strong state to impose these. Most important, they do not require the political or military mobilization of the society except (and not always) in the euphoric initial moments. Because of these limited needs, such conflicts leave little of the historical legacy associated with total wars. The streets are not filled with veterans, the state is not a postbellic Leviathan, and economic wealth is barely touched by fiscal authorities. Life goes on much as before. As I will make clear in the following pages, the limited-war pattern has largely defined the Latin American experience.

---

61. The progress was not linear. The Thirty Years War resembled a twentieth-century conflict much more than did the dynastic struggles of the eighteenth century. In turn, the origins of World War I may be found in precisely the kind of diplomatic gamesmanship that existed in an earlier era.

Wars are not simply products of states, but may also contribute to the development of different authority structures. My aim in this book is not only to understand the nature of war on the continent, but also to comprehend the consequences of this particular pattern of violence. I wish to emphasize that by this I do not mean to imply that the study of war in and of itself holds all the answers to the puzzle of the Latin American state. War simply offers a prism through which the various experiences may be better analyzed. For example, European success in dominating the world after the fifteenth century may have had a great deal to do with greater proclivity toward war and the resulting political and economic developments.[62] The national unity of more than one country has been based on the negation of another's identity and has been forged in battle with that enemy. It has been said that war is the parent of the modern nation-state. To a degree, the notion of a state is impossible without war. Moreover, a mass army of conscripts, each able and expected to shoulder arms, bears more than a passing historical and structural affinity to electoral democracy.

What have been the consequences of peace for Latin America? Would bloodshed earlier and in a more decisive fashion have produced a stronger, more cohesive, and more equitable state? Would earlier instability have created a continent with fewer states? Would the class divisions that permeate these societies have survived long conflicts? Has peace cost more than war? These questions are the subject of the second half of this book.

To understand the possible importance of total war in state building, consider some of its effects in detail. These include (a) increased state capacity to extract resources; (b) centralization of power in national capitals and the gradual disappearance of regional loyalties or identities; (c) stronger emotional links between the population and both a set of state institutions and the often abstract notion of a nation that these are meant to represent; and (d) a qualitative shift in the relationship of the individual to these institutions, which may be summarized as the transition from subject to citizen. Total wars seem to produce richer, more powerful states, with more intimate connections to the majority of the populations living within their territories.

None of these characteristics implies a particular type of regime. They describe a degree of relationship between a set of institutions and the populace living under them, not the manner in which the latter participates in

62. Parker, *The Military Revolution;* Howard, *The Causes of War;* Wallerstein, *The Modern World System.*

their own governance. Both totalitarian and democratic regimes seem able to mobilize their populations and resources in ways unavailable to limited authoritarian regimes that avoid politicizing their population.[63] The variation in institutional outcomes from limited war is much greater than what results from total war. We can, however, safely predict some general patterns. Limited wars are likely to (a) leave some form of fiscal or debt crisis as states have failed to adjust to the extra expenditures; (b) support the development of a professionalized military with little popular participation and possibly the resentment of civilians who have not participated in the struggle; (c) lead to alienation from patriotic symbols, as gains from war will be limited and some element of disenchantment arises; and (d) possibly produce economic downturns resulting from a shift in resources or breaks with the global market. The most generalizable trend may be that limited wars rarely leave positive institutional legacies and often have long-term costs. Instead of producing states built on "blood and iron," they construct ones made of blood and debt. It is precisely this latter pattern that we may observe in Latin America.[64]

Why the Latin American exceptionalism (see Table 1.1)? The geopolitical tendency toward peace and the underdevelopment of the state are closely linked and need to be analyzed within a historical context.

Political autonomy in Latin America resulted largely from the collapse of

Table 1.1   Comparison of bellic models

	Bellic Model	Latin America
Types of war	Mass war	Limited war
External environment	Geopolitical competition	Acceptance of colonial borders
	Absence of external guarantees	Pax Britannica and Pax Americana
Domestic conditions	United elite	Divided elite
	Coherent concept of nation	Race/caste divisions
	Administrative core	Postcolonial chaos

63. This is not to deny the capacity of a wide range of possible institutional forms of conscription. The Austro-Hungarian Empire, for example, was anything but a "total" state, but it still managed to send millions of men to three different fronts during World War I.

64. An early reader of this book urged me to again emphasize that I am not implying a deterministic relationship between forms of war and state institutions. Total war is neither a necessary nor a sufficient condition for the creation of a "total" state, but may contribute to and result from such institutions.

the Spanish Empire rather than from the internal development of new political forces. As the new Latin American nations appeared in the first third of the nineteenth century, they enjoyed little centralized authority and certainly could not enforce a monopoly on the use of violence. It is important to remember that before wars could serve as stimulus for western European development, the protostates had to establish their military dominance. Thus, when these states required the resources with which to fight the new type of wars, especially following the Peace of Westphalia, they were already equipped with the organizational and political capacity to impose these needs on their societies. This was not the case in any Latin American country with the possible exceptions of Chile and Paraguay prior to the last third of the nineteenth century. (The bellicosity of these two states would indicate at least a correlation between greater state capacity and likelihood of war.) The wars that did occur did not provide an opportunity to establish state power over the society precisely because the wars were "limited" and the new states lacked the organizational and political base from which to do so.

Equally important was the domestic social context in which the Latin American republics arose. As in much of the postcolonial world, states preceded nations in Latin America. With limited possible exceptions, we find little evidence of a sense of nationhood paralleling the future state boundaries. While there was a sense of vaguely defined "American-ness," it was generally limited to the miniscule white elite. For the vast majority of the population, belonging to a newly independent state meant very little. While at first some subaltern groups saw the independence movement as a possible avenue for changes in the social and economic status quo, these hopes were dashed by the criollo reaction to early radical claims. By 1820, *American* merely meant the imposition of military duties to complement already heavy fiscal demands. Even such early promises as the abolition of special Indian taxes and tributes were broken.

None of the newly independent states, again with the possible exception of Chile and Paraguay, could easily define the nation that they were supposed to represent. Whether divided by race, caste, class, or a combination of all three, Latin American populations did not possess a common identity. Because the construction of such an identity was so fraught with political conflict, states hesitated to follow the "nation-building" efforts of western European counterparts. The struggle to define the nation and the rights and obligations of citizens consumed most of the nineteenth century in Latin America. And so the region's path was set by wars between and across myriad social boundaries that ultimately defined the Latin American states, and not by struggles between territorially compact, cohesive political units, as in Europe.

The stunted development of Latin American states and the frailty of their respective nations reflect the key, but too often underemphasized, aspect of the development of the continent's nation-states. The wars of independence produced fragments of empire, but not new states. There was little economic or political logic to the frontiers as institutionalized in the 1820s— they merely were the administrative borders of the empire. The new countries were essentially miniempires with all the weaknesses of such political entities. Oscar Oszlak has captured the situation, describing a "national state established in a society that failed to acknowledge fully its institutional presence."[65]

The final element that is key to understanding the Latin American cases is the geopolitical or international context in which these countries arose. The Latin American region was born entire; the countries were each surrounded at birth by states very similar in immediate history and even social structure. Contrast this with the situation in western Europe, where states preceded one another in a complex chronology, producing forms of both competition and emulation not available in Latin America. Moreover, Latin America as a whole arose as a geopolitical entity in a world where the distribution of power was extremely asymmetrical. The ability of any Latin American country to challenge the geopolitical status quo was limited. Unlike Italy and Germany, for example, these states could not even aspire to play a role in imperial competition. They were born in the third rank of nations (at best) with a low probability of moving up. If we think of these nascent nations as city-states, we understand why they had little opportunity to expand beyond their previously assigned zones of influence.[66]

Although I argue in later chapters against an overreliance on external causes, the Latin American peace is in many ways the ultimate expression

65. Oszlak, "Historical Formation of the State," 5.
66. The fascinating comparison (unfortunately beyond the scope of this book) is, of course, between the United States and Latin America, particularly during the nineteenth century. A good start is made by Langley, in *The Americas in the Age of Revolution, 1750–1850*. The United States was equally split by regions and lacked a common national identity. It also suffered from a civil war, with greater violence than anything seen on the southern continent. Its international conflicts during the hundred years were also relatively limited. Yet in this instance, the struggles for independence, territorial consolidation, and national unity contributed to the creation of political authority. Many have argued that the United States is a country made by war.

of *dependencia*. The absence of international conflict in part reflects the irrelevance of immediate neighbors for each country's political and economic development. Latin American states often directed their attention not to their immediate borders, but to metropolitan centers half a globe away. These foreign powers-that-be also provided the continent with a hegemonic balance of strength, thus assuring that no individual regional military giant could arise. This avoided the kind of mutually assured–destruction competition responsible for much contemporary warfare. However, it deprived the region of significant geopolitical autonomy.

The weaknesses of the Latin American state restricted the continent to limited wars and long stretches of peace. This in turn deprived the states of a potentially important impetus for development. A close look at the Latin American cases prompts us to rethink the geopolitical competition between the various European countries and the resultant forms of political authority that developed on that continent. It seems that their development was in no sense inevitable; nor did it reflect a universal political trend. Instead, the interaction of particular societies and a particular set of events best explains the differences observed. It is on that interaction that I focus in the rest of the book.

Plan of the Book

In the following chapter I provide a historical introduction to the nature of war on the continent. I then analyze why Latin American warfare developed in the manner in which it did. I propose a historically bound scenario in which class structures, organizational power, and international constraints enveloped the Latin American states in a peaceful embrace. The underdeveloped administrative capacity of the Latin American state, the divisions within the dominant classes, and the control exercised by European powers helped shape both the occasions of war and their subsequent developments. Latin America was relatively peaceful because it did not form sophisticated political institutions capable of managing wars. No states, no wars. Moreover, given this history, the military as an institution appears to have identified the critical national enemy as an internal one. Given the absence of an external enemy, wars were superfluous.

In Chapter 3, I analyze the contribution of war to the centralization and empowerment of the nineteenth-century Latin American state. While wars did provide an opportunity for greater state cohesion in some circumstances, for example, Chile in the 1830s, these openings were never used to create the institutional infrastructure needed for further development of state capacity. A critical question is why the wars of independence produced anarchy as opposed to a coherent military authoritarianism. I believe that the answer lies in the relatively limited level of military organization and violence involved in the wars of independence. This is not to deny the destruction that these caused. However, although the wars *weakened* the colonial order, they did not kill it. The armed effort was small enough so as to not require the militarization of society throughout the continent. Certainly in comparison with the equivalent wars in European history, such as the Thirty Years War, the independence conflicts left a much more limited institutional legacy. Postindependence wars also produced ambiguous results.

The Latin American cases force us to ask once again how war actually produces order from chaos. How do state demands for money and obedience lead to greater authority instead of internal war and domestic conflict? M. S. Anderson, for example, indicates that efforts to find the money needed could stimulate discontent that was politically dangerous.[67] David Kaiser has demonstrated that the demands of war helped weaken European states in the sixteenth century and clearly helped destroy the Spanish economy.[68] Again, Paul Kennedy has amplified this argument to include the eventual decline of all empires.[69] Yet some states in some situations are able to pay for the greater armies and the more costly wars. A determined government can and has demanded sacrifices, which it was able to then channel in an efficient manner. Why did the expansion of fiscal power succeed in some cases and not in others?[70]

One part of the explanation may be fear of a greater danger from the outside. This was certainly important in the early stages of the Japanese case.[71] Yet Poland faced equal if not more daunting threats. A society's preexisting class structure helps determine the type of coercive and extractive apparatus built by the state. If the key to the feudal state was the monarch's cooperation with preexisting civil society, then later large sections of the powerful elite were also willing to provide quite high tax revenues, because

---

67. M. S. Anderson, *War and Society in Europe,* 20.
68. *Politics and War.*
69. Kennedy, *The Rise and Fall of the Great Powers.*
70. An interesting note here is the apparent claim by Michael Mann that representational government may be best able to extract the required resources (*Sources of Social Power,* vol. 2).
71. Ralston, *Importing the European Army;* Moore, *Social Origins of Dictatorship and Democracy,* 437–40.

they realized that their own interests could be served through a stronger state.[72] In some cases, potential opponents were bought: "Louis XIV did not control his nobility by keeping them idle at Versailles, but by providing state employment for them."[73] In other cases, the state provided a key protection for dominant classes. Capitalism might need militarism, partly because in capitalism "an unusual degree of long distance political regulation backed up by force is required."[74] Similar class structures, however, produced very different centralizing mechanisms. What worked for the Junkers did not work for the Spanish *hidalgos*.

The answer to a successful imposition of authority lies in a conjunction of environmental conditions and domestic political and social structures. The former provide the stimuli, the latter allow a particular state response to that stimulus. In the absence of external threat, the state is deprived of a critical opportunity (but not the only one) to encroach on its society. But war provides no guarantees. For example, despite more than two centuries of unrelieved war, Spain remained dependent on outside income and never developed an adequate domestic fiscal infrastructure. Spain could not survive as a major power because it did not adapt its state-managerial style to the military revolution.[75] Egypt might serve as a contemporary example of how the presence of war in and of itself does not guarantee the development of a coherent state.

The Latin American cases analyzed in Chapter 3 suggest a better and more precise definition of what these specific conjunctions look like. What were the effects of the limited wars of nineteenth-century Latin America on the fiscal capacity of the state? Simply put, they were almost nonexistent, creating only perpetually bankrupt beggar states. The easy availability of external financing allowed the state the luxury of not coming into conflict with those social sectors that possessed the required resources. Whether through loans or through the sale of a commodity, the Latin American state escaped the need to force itself on society. When such loans were not forthcoming, either the state relied on customs (not requiring an extensive administrative commitment) or its institutions simply ceased to play a major role in society.

In this chapter I also describe how the relative absence of war and the limitations of those that did occur did not provide an opening for political

---

72. P. Anderson, *Lineages of the Absolutist State;* Hall, *States in History.*
73. Duffy, introduction to Duffy, *The Military Revolution and the State,* 4.
74. Mann, *States, War, and Capitalism,* 136.
75. Porter, *War and the Rise of the State.*

and subsequent fiscal centralization. The Latin American wars were not long or threatening enough to allow national institutions to override class-based interests. The particularistic interests were always able to survive wars and never felt the need to allow a state strong enough to protect *and* demand. In short, in Latin America, the equivalent of the aristocracy won the Fronde. The closest European model may be Sicily, where one observer has noted that "whenever strong government failed, it was the nobles [who] filled the vacuum of power."[76] The central comparative lesson here is that it is not war in and of itself that provides the "sinews of the state." Rather, it is war *in conjunction with* an already dominant group within a state apparatus that makes it possible to extract resources from a recalcitrant society.

In Chapters 4 and 5, I move away from a discussion of the state itself and emphasize the development of the nations and citizens over which it rules. While it is obviously risky to generalize about the relationship between citizenship and military service, one could see armies as providing modern nation-states with a relatively disciplined and well-educated population ready and able to work within the new industrial order. But such a population now also has at least immediate access to the means of violence and offers the state a needed resource. This forms the basis for a new political contract. Conscription and mass armies also helped to revolutionize the nature of the violence involved in military conflict. The new types of wars temporarily transformed "wolf packs" into coherent and obedient organizations.[77] This did not lead to a decline in aggregate levels of killing, but the manner in which it was accomplished had important ramifications for the state.

Wars encourage a different attitude toward the state—one based on collective identity. The link between military conflict and national loyalty is quite well known.[78] Nothing unites a nation behind a faltering leader like a war; the quickest way to make a nation is to make an army.[79] A total war can help evade social conflict as well as orienting that same struggle toward external enemies.[80] In the nineteenth century, some thought it impossible to create a nation without war.[81]

---

76. Mack Smith, cited in Tilly, *Coercion, Capital, and European States,* 142.
77. Howard, *War in European History.*
78. A. Smith, "War and Ethnicity."
79. Porter, *War and the Rise of the State,* 18.
80. In the perhaps apocryphal words of Cecil Rhodes: "If you want to avoid civil war you must become Imperialists."
81. Howard, *Causes of War.* One may add that it is difficult to become imperialists while in the midst of a civil war.

Although there remains considerable debate about the relationship between "nations" defined by common ethnic characteristics and "states" defined by some legal existence, one could argue that for much of the nineteenth century, the state created nationalism and not vice versa.[82] One mechanism by which it did so was through the army and military activity. Armies and the experience of war helped forge a unified identity that could obscure domestic divisions. Military experience increased the scope of what Mann calls discursive literacy: the set of nationalist assumptions and myths that contribute to the creation of a national identity. Wars may have been the key to the creation of "imagined communities."[83] Through the absorption of elements of the newly arising bourgeoisie and petite bourgeoisie, armies may also have encouraged class cohesion during critical periods of early industrialization.[84] Under these circumstances, armies and war helped transform class societies into armed nations and, according to Palmer, helped break down provincial allegiances and networks and replace them with ones more centered on a national community.[85]

Did armies and war propagate the idea of a nation in Latin America? Did they serve as "institutions of popular education"? In Chapter 4, I analyze the apparently ambiguous findings from the nineteenth and twentieth centuries. Given the reputation for "nationalism" (often ill defined) of Latin American countries, one sees little evidence of the kind of mass identification evident in Europe or the United States. With some exceptions, wars did not provide the mythology on which so much of modern nationalism depends. Latin America lacks the monuments to "our glorious dead" that are ubiquitous in the landscape of Europe and the United States. Once again, the limited international struggles that occurred could not overcome internal divisions.

In Chapter 5, I pinpoint the manner in which conscription contributed (or detracted from) the process of democratization and the creation of citizenship rights. Was there ever discussion of the benefits of conscription? Were leading elites aware of the possible benefits and costs? Would a mass army have served as the surest protection for democratic citizenship? Why did the Latin American state ignore its own population?

The Latin American states were never strong enough to demand full conscription. Perhaps more important, there was never a perceived need for the

82. Hobsbawm, *Nations and Nationalism Since 1780.*
83. B. Anderson, *Imagined Communities.*
84. G. Best, "Militarization."
85. Palmer, *The Age of Democratic Revolutions.*

kind of social upheaval implied by mass armies. The state did not need the population, as soldiers or even as future workers, and thus could afford to exclude it. The state and dominant elites in almost all countries in the region also appeared to prefer passive populations. A too active or fervent sense of nationhood could actually backfire and create conditions inimical to continued elite domination.

Chapters 4 and 5 lead to an improved understanding of the creation of nations' "imagined communities" and the link between these creations and democratic rights. Through data gleaned from a census of national monuments and through analyses of the social makeup of armies I propose to better define the link between military experience and nationalist sentiment. This process may also illuminate the uniqueness of the European pattern and suggest the obstacles faced by countries attempting to emulate it without the respective historical experience.

The concluding chapter provides a summary of the major findings. I discuss how Latin America as a region is different from the rest of the world *and* analyze differentiation inside the continent. Interestingly, the findings from the two sets of comparisons serve to confirm each other.

Next Steps

All books have limitations and the writer becomes increasingly aware of them as the manuscript nears completion. I have already noted some of the geographical limits of my coverage. An analysis of Central America might confirm or contradict much of what is said here. I can only hope that scholars of this region will be sufficiently motivated by this book so as to—if nothing else—prove me wrong. I have focused on a particular period of time: although my discussion of the long peace does touch on contemporary events and trends, most of the historical analysis centers on the nineteenth century, because that is when the foundations of the subsequent states were built. Moreover, in order to analyze the repercussions of war, I had to study the period when these were most relevant. Finally, I have almost exclusively focused on the bellic functions of the state and have largely ignored its role in public welfare. I believe that the former helps explain the latter, but it still requires its own investigation. In this volume, I focus exclusively on the state as warrior and have very little to say about the capitalist state that arises from the late nineteenth century or the developmentalist states that were established in the 1930s. If the classic northwest European states were made by war, they were transformed by the emphasis on public welfare in the 1930s. In the coming years I hope to finish an accompanying volume to this one in which I will compare the construction and limitations of the Latin American welfare state to its European and North American equivalents. If the Latin American state did not fight, it was somewhat more successful in creating new economies and societies. Yet I expect that the legacy of blood and debt was and will continue to be hard to escape.

2
Making War

The military plays an important role in our images of Latin America. Both popular media and academic analyses prominently feature tanks and epaulets. It would be hard to imagine a region more associated with a strong military tradition or one where armed conflict was apparently so central.[1] When told about this book, most colleagues of mine, including experts on the region, have revealed an assumption that Latin America has been at perpetual war. In this chapter I summarize the record of violence and lay a foundation for the analysis that follows.

1. And yet it is the rare book on or guide to general military history that even mentions the continent. See Cowley and Parker, *The Reader's Companion to Military History*; Dupuy and Dupuy, *The Encyclopedia of Military History*; and Keegan, *A History of Warfare*.

Since independence in the early nineteenth century, Latin America has been relatively free of major *international* conflict. In the twentieth century, the record is truly remarkable, especially in light of the experience of other regions of the world. During the same two hundred years, however, Latin America has also experienced a great deal of internal strife ranging from persistent but limited rebellions to almost apocalyptic revolutions and social conflicts. The distinction between these two types of conflict is critical. They are both violent and both involve mobilization of some sort and a great deal of destruction. But their origins and consequences *may be* radically different.

War is not simply acts of military violence or banditry (Latin America has had more than enough of both). Rather, it is a special form of *organized* violence with clear political goals and is different from other violence acts in that it involves the "existence, the creation, or the elimination of states."[2] I would add that wars are different from what we may call "militarized disputes" in that they involve lengths of time and amounts of resources requiring a substantial organizational commitment on behalf of at least one of the actors. That is, wars are concerted efforts requiring a minimal level of organizational and strategic commitment. A simple way of measuring this commitment is through the number of casualties. I will use Singer and Small's threshold of one thousand deaths per year.[3] Below that level, we cannot expect to see the type of state action that is the subject of a large part of this study. Thus, war is "a substantial armed conflict between the organized military forces of independent political units."[4]

The notion of independence does not necessarily require formal international recognition. My definition includes civil wars as long as these are more than armed squabbles; however, incorporating these presents some problems. I consider them in the case of Latin America in part because this increases the relevant sample making systematic study more feasible, but more important, because the distinction between civil and international wars can create problems of anachronistic application. For example, we treat conflict between the king of France and the duke of Burgundy as an international war. Similarly, wars between Italian cities are judged to be interstate. Why not, then, the struggles between the various provinces of early Argentina? Finally, the type of war appears to make an insignificant difference on its *effects,* which constitute the primary focus of this volume.

There is no question that Latin Americans have tried to kill each other.

---

2. Howard, *Causes of War.*
3. Singer and Small, *Resort to Arms.*
4. Levy, *War and the Modern Great Power System,* 51.

There are too many examples of brutal and bloody conflicts for this to be denied. The Creole population of Guanajuato was massacred in 1810, while the Yaquis, Mayas, and Mapuches—to name just three examples—were pursued with practically genocidal fury throughout the nineteenth century. The War of the Triple Alliance almost depopulated Paraguay, and the Chaco War cost nearly one hundred thousand lives. The Mexican Revolution included many of the defining elements of modern war: civilians were not exempt from violence, cities became battlefields, railroads took men to fight, and barbed wire and machine guns killed thousands charging on horseback. On an individual level, wars in Latin America also witnessed the degradation and transformation of humans into wild beasts. How else to explain the atrocities of Colombia's Violencia?

Yet in general, Latin America has experienced low levels of militarization, the organization and mobilization of human and material resources for potential use in warfare. Latin Americans *have* frequently tried to kill one another, but they have generally not attempted to organize their societies with such a goal in mind. The region has experienced what we may call a violent form of peace. It has largely been spared the organized mass slaughter into which modern warfare has developed over the past two hundred years, but it has also been subjected to ferocious chaos.

In this chapter I present a summary of military conflict in Latin America, both international and domestic. In the first section I compare Latin America with other global regions and in the second analyze the distribution of conflicts within the continent. The following two sections contain discussions of specific conflicts and provide a summary narrative of these struggles. A final section concludes with some general observations about organized violence on the continent.

Latin America in the World

There is little question that the past two centuries have seen an unmistakable global acceleration in the ferocity of war (Figs. 2.1 and 2.2). The number of actual conflicts may have declined, and the number of years during which the globe has known peace may have actually increased, but bellic brutality has intensified. All indications of war's destructive capacity—absolute number of deaths, percentages of population affected, military versus civilian casualties—have increased dramatically.[5] Measures such as the number of

5. Keegan, *History of Warfare;* and Tilly, "State-Incited Violence."

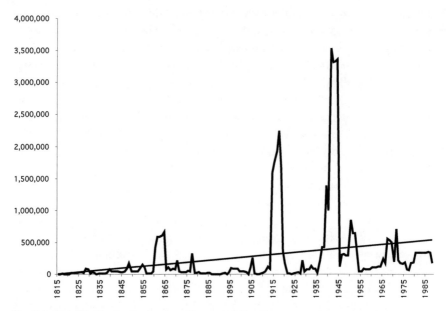

Fig. 2.1 Global battle deaths (source: Singer and Small)

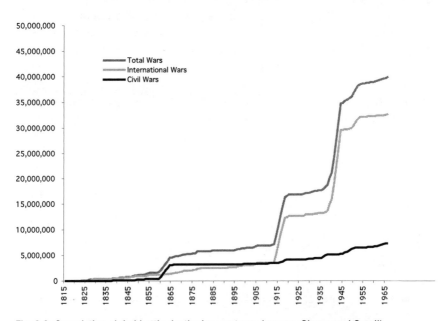

Fig. 2.2 Cumulative global battle deaths by war type (source: Singer and Small)

individuals under arms, expressed either in absolute terms or as percentage of the population, have also increased. Some of these trends reflect the twentieth century's "Thirty Years War," from 1914 to 1945. There is enough evidence from either side of these dates, however, to contradict the notion that this is an isolated phenomenon and the product of a geopolitical quirk.

In this context, Latin America appears unique (Figs. 2.3 and 2.4). The past two centuries have not seen the level of warfare common to other regions. No matter how measured, Latin America appears remarkably peaceful. The nations of Europe and North America, for example, have had nearly four times the number of personnel in their armed forces on a per capita basis and have killed tens of millions more people and at a much faster rate. Latin America, with 150 more years of independence than Africa, has had the same rough order of conflict. The Latin American figures would look even less bellicose but for the demographic disaster of the Paraguayan War of the 1860s. One might say the same about the world wars in Europe, but these conflicts both reflected the history of the region and had much more effect on subsequent societies than did the limited Latin American wars.

The particularity of the continent is most evident if we distinguish between civil and international wars (Figs. 2.5 and 2.6). Latin American states have only rarely fought one another. What is most striking is that Latin America appears to become more peaceful over time—the twentieth century has episodes of warfare, but it is generally nonviolent (Figs. 2.7–2.9). Even when one looks at civil conflicts, moreover, Latin America appears benignly peaceful. By any measure we choose, other regions seem to have been twice as violent.

If we look at the individual wars, we note that they are geographically and historically concentrated (see Fig. 2.10, Table 2.1, and Table 2.2). By far the most numerous and significant international wars occurred in the nineteenth century.[6] The years 1860–80 were particularly bellicose, with almost every country in the region invading a neighbor or defending itself. International conflicts were concentrated in three zones: northern and central Mexico; the section of the La Plata basin shared by Brazil, Paraguay, Uruguay, and Argentina; and the mid-Pacific littoral where Bolivia, Peru, and Chile meet. These wars were largely land grabs by more powerful

6. There was some concern that the region was "heating up" in the 1970s and 1980s, but international stability appears to have returned. See Morris and Millan, *Controlling Latin American Conflicts;* and Little, "International Conflict in Latin America." For a dissenting view, see Mares, "Securing Peace in the Americas," 35–48.

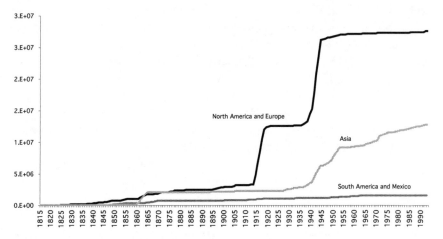

Fig. 2.3 Cumulative battle deaths by region (source: Singer and Small)

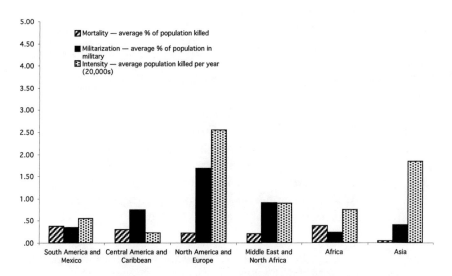

Fig. 2.4 Standardized total wars by region (source: Singer and Small)

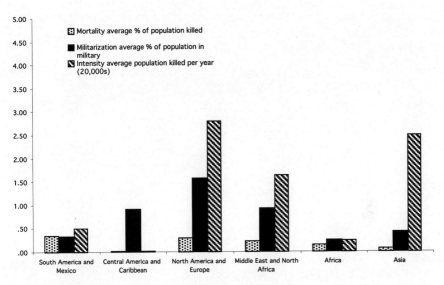

Fig. 2.5 Standardized international wars by region (source: Singer and Small)

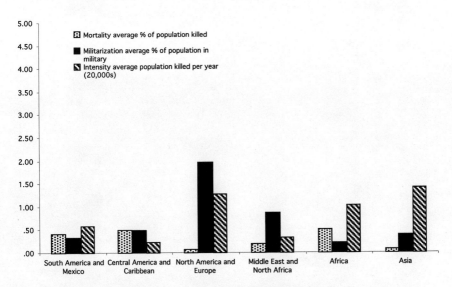

Fig. 2.6 Standardized civil wars by region (source: Singer and Small)

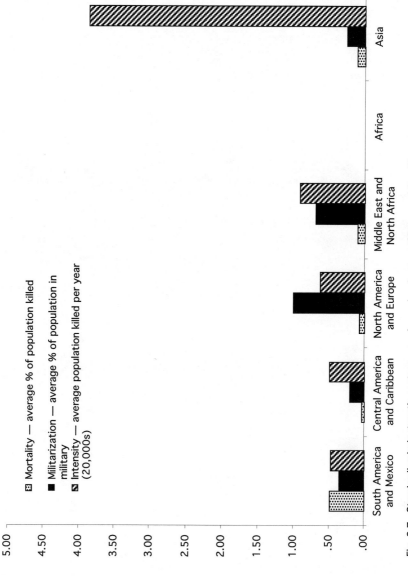

Fig. 2.7 Standardized nineteenth-century wars by region (source: Singer and Small)

Legend (as shown in chart):
- Mortality — average % of population killed
- Militarization — average % of population in military
- Intensity — average population killed per year (20,000s)

Regions (x-axis): South America and Mexico; Central America and Caribbean; North America and Europe; Middle East and North Africa; Africa; Asia

Value axis: .00, .50, 1.00, 1.50, 2.00, 2.50, 3.00, 3.50, 4.00, 4.50, 5.00

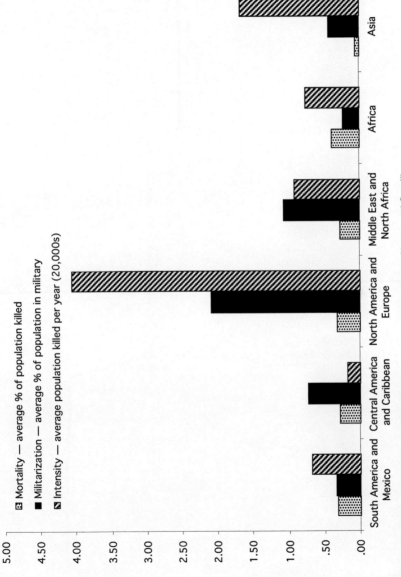

■ Mortality — average % of population killed
■ Militarization — average % of population in military
▨ Intensity — average population killed per year (20,000s)

Fig. 2.8 Standardized twentieth-century wars by region (source: Singer and Small)

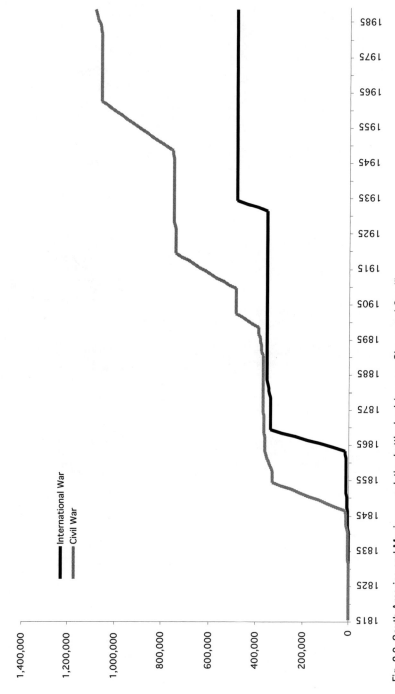

Fig. 2.9 South America and Mexico cumulative battle dead (source: Singer and Small)

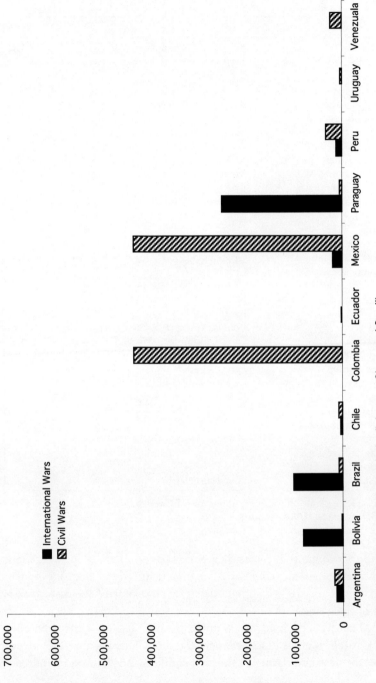

Fig. 2.10 Wars by country (cumulative battle dead) (source: Singer and Small)

Table 2.1 Major international wars in Latin America

War	Countries	Years
Cisplatine	Argentina, Brazil, Uruguay	1825–28
War of La Plata/Guerra Grande	Argentina, Brazil, Uruguay and France and Britain	1836–51
War of Bolivian-Peruvian Confederation	Bolivia, Chile, Peru	1836–39
Texan independence	Mexico, Texas	1836
Pastry War	Mexico, France	1838
Peruvian-Bolivian War	Peru, Bolivia	1841
Mexican-American War	Mexico, U.S.	1846–48
Franco-Mexican War	Mexico, France	1862–67
Ecuador-Colombian	Ecuador, Colombia	1863
Triple Alliance	Argentina, Brazil, Paraguay, Uruguay	1864–70
Spanish Invasion	Bolivia, Chile, Peru, Spain	1865–66
Ten Years War	Cuba, Spain	1868–78
War of the Pacific	Bolivia, Chile, Peru	1879–83
Central American	Guatemala, El Salvador	1885
Independence	Cuba	1895–98
Central American	Guatemala, El Salvador, Honduras	1906
Central American	Nicaragua, El Salvador	1907
World War I	Brazil	1917–18
Chaco War	Bolivia, Paraguay	1932–35
Leticia	Peru, Colombia	1932–33
World War II	Brazil	1944–45
Border dispute	Peru, Ecuador	1941
U.S. intervention	Dominican Republic, U.S.	1965
Football	El Salvador, Honduras	1969
Angola/Ethiopia	Cuba	1975
Ecuador/Peru border dispute	Ecuador, Peru	1981
Falklands War	Argentina, Britain	1982
Ecuador/Peru border dispute	Ecuador, Peru	1995

SOURCES: Kaye, Grant, and Emond, *Major Armed Conflict*; Singer and Small, *A Call to Arms*; Bethell, *Cambridge History of Latin America*.

neighbors seeking to increase their access to resources. None of the international wars experienced by Latin America featured the intensity of ideological, nationalistic, or ethnic hatreds so much a part of the history of other parts of the globe.

Civil conflicts do follow the same pattern of decline in the twentieth century. Overall, there is much less periodization. There is a trend, however, in the reasons for and nature of the civil conflicts. The first one hundred years

Table 2.2 Major civil wars in Latin America

Country/Name	Years
Independence and postindependence conflicts	1810–25
Brazil "Confederation of the Equator"	1824
Argentina	1828–29
Chile	1829
Argentina "Desert Campaign"	1833
Mexico (sporadic rebellions)	1827–55
Brazil (various regional rebellions)	1831–40
Brazil "Farrapos"	1835–45
Uruguay "Guerra Grande"	1838–51
Colombia "War of the Supremos"	1839–42
Argentina Anti-Rojas	1838–51
Ecuador	1845–60
Mexico "Caste War"	1847–55
Colombia	1851
Chile	1851
Peru	1853–55
Colombia	1854
Peru	1856–58
Mexico "Reforma"	1858–61
Venezuela "Federal War"	1859–63
Colombia	1859–62
Argentina	1863
Ecuador	1863
Argentina	1866–67
Peru	1866–68
Venezuela	1868–71
Chile "Mapuches"	1868–81
Argentina	1870–71
Uruguay	1870–75
Argentina	1874
Colombia	1876–77
Argentina "Conquest of the Desert"	1880
Mexico (Indian campaigns)	1880–1900
Colombia	1884–85
Chile	1891
Brazil Rio (Grande do Sul)	1893–94
Peru	1894–95
Ecuador	1895
Brazil (Bahia)	1896–97
Colombia "Thousand Days"	1899–1903
Venezuela	1898–1900
Secession of Panama	1903
Uruguay	1904
Mexico Revolution	1910–20
Ecuador	1911–12

Table 2.2   Major civil wars in Latin America (*cont'd*)

Country/Name	Years
Paraguay	1911–1912
Ecuador	1922–1925
Honduras	1924
Mexico "Cristero Rebellion"	1926–30
El Salvador "Matanza"	1932
Paraguay	1947
Costa Rica	1948
Colombia "La Violencia"	1948–62
Bolivia Revolution	1952
Guatemala Anti-Arbenz	1954
Argentina Anti-Perón	1955
Cuba Revolution	1957–59
Dominican Republic	1965
Guatemala	1966–72
Guatemala	1978–84
Nicaragua Revolution	1978–79
El Salvador	1979–92
Peru "Sendero"	1982–92
Nicaragua "Contras"	1982–90
Colombia	1984–

SOURCE: Kaye, Grant, and Emond, *Major Armed Conflict*; Singer and Small, *A Call to Arms*; Bethell, *Cambridge History of Latin America*.

saw domestic wars largely defined by challenges to central authority and ideological or commercial disputes between elite factions. The twentieth century has seen many more "popular" revolts involving class struggles and a general intensification of the level of violence. Geographical concentration is again quite pronounced. Colombia, Mexico, and Argentina have suffered the most from this type of conflict, but no country has been immune.

I have made several attempts at testing whether any formal statistical relationship existed between the level of civil and international conflicts and have found no strong evidence. That is, we cannot speak of a clear pattern of propensity in one type of conflict affecting the likelihood of the other. Yet I argue in this book that the degree of internal conflict that continues to dominate Latin America is both a cause and an indication of the relative inability of these states to fight one another. Internal violence was a reflection of both the absence of international enemies and political powerlessness. Alternatively, there was not enough external conflict to draw attention away from internal divisions. Perhaps the best evidence of this condition is the relative importance of civil as opposed to international wars during the twentieth century. Moreover, in a notable exception from the European pattern, we see little evidence of internal struggles enveloping neighbors.[7] Violence rarely crossed borders.

Latin America at War

Clearly, Latin America has been violent, but most political conflict occurred *within* states, not between them. In the following pages I provide a summary of the major conflicts in Mexico and South America over the past two centuries, an overview that both serves as background for the analysis to follow and foreshadows some of the central arguments of this book.

The Wars of Independence

The most significant wars in Latin American history occurred almost at the very birth of the new states.[8] It is impossible to classify these as international or civil; they contained elements of both. Formally fought against an external power, Spain, the wars were often conflicts between different elite groups or even—at their bloodiest—between different social classes and different castes. It is significant that the most momentous wars for the continent were fought prior to the establishment of states. Violence was not between states, but oriented toward the creation of a new political order. This pattern would be repeated over the next century.

The wars of independence originated both in the internal conditions of the colonies and in events in Europe. In part, they were the culmination of centuries-old tensions between the colonies seeking greater autonomy and a weakened empire that had only recently attempted to reestablish centralized control. Social divisions paralleled institutional ones. Within the elite, whites born in the colonies (*criollos,* or Creoles) suffered from systematic discrimination in favor of Spanish-born subjects *(peninsulares)*. Attempts to reform economic policies or political institutions were often read as benefiting one or the other of these two elite factions. The alliance of subaltern

---

7. The obvious exceptions here are U.S. interventions and more recent Cold War struggles.

8. For the best narrative of the military campaigns, see Lynch, *The Spanish-American Revolutions, 1808–1826.* For more analytical depth, see Rodríguez O., *The Independence in Spanish America.* See also Kinsbruner, *Independence in Spanish America.* For a fascinating comparison of the independence wars in the United States, Haiti, and Latin America, see Langley, *Americas in the Age of Revolution.*

groups to one side or another of the elite depended on region and specific circumstances.

The confusion produced by the Napoleonic invasions of Spain in 1808 provided the spark as well as the opportunity for Latin American independence. The legitimacy of the empire resided in the person of the King. With his abdication, the already strained political apparatus fell apart. By 1810, colonial juntas had been declared in Caracas and Buenos Aires, and with the exception of Peru and Cuba, the entire continent witnessed the rise of independence movements. The wars can be distinguished by three major fronts: Mexico, the Southern Cone, and the northern Andes.

The Mexican independence movement was paradoxical. It began with the most socially radical agenda of any in the Americas and ended in the collapse of central authority after 1824. As such it is emblematic of the generic fate of all the successful independence movements: none sought to reshape society (except to shift elite privileges toward American-born whites), and all failed to quickly institutionalize authority.

The independence struggle began in 1810 in the Bajío region.[9] There, Father Miguel Hidalgo led a poorly armed mass of largely Indian and mestizo soldiers through some spectacular early victories and infamous massacres and to an early defeat as the discipline of the colonial army wore the insurgents down. Hidalgo's successor, José María Morelos, was more successful at creating a viable military and even called on the Congress of Chilpacingo to draw up a model for the new postindependence Mexico. Once again, however, the greater resources and organization available to the Spaniards was decisive, and Morelos was captured and executed by 1815. The rebellion was largely dormant for the following five years. When independence did come in 1821 it was thanks to the reformist efforts of Agustín Iturbide's Army of the Three Guarantees, whose emphasis on maintaining links with Spain and the Catholic Church marked a clean break with the much more radical movements of Hidalgo and Morelos.

Critical to an understanding of the failure of the first stage of the Mexican revolt and subsequent events is the fact that Hidalgo's and Morelos's armies did not merely oppose Spanish political rule; they also expressed hatred of all of the institutional legacies of the conquest. The fight against

9. For Mexico, see Tutino, *From Insurrection to Revolution in Mexico;* Anna, *The Fall of Royal Government in Mexico City;* Hamnett, "The Economic and Social Dimension of the Revolution of Independence, 1800–1824"; *Roots of Insurgency;* Archer, *The Army in Bourbon Mexico;* "The Royalist Army in New Spain"; and "The Army of New Spain and the Wars of Independence, 1790–1821."

the rebellion soon evolved into much more than a defense of colonial rule. Many criollos originally sympathetic to independence chose to fight against any threat to their social position. The defeat of Hidalgo's and Morelos's forces led to several critical developments. First, it marginalized the Indian masses from what was to become increasingly an intra-elite struggle. Second, the white elite came to fear the potential for social violence and sought to limit opportunities for such explosions to flare again. In a lesson to be repeated again and again throughout the continent, criollos appreciated that whatever differences may exist between whites necessarily came second to the need for preserving the colonial social order.

In the Southern Cone, the independence wars began in Buenos Aires in May 1810 and in Santiago in September the same year with the establishment of juntas claiming to replace royal authority from Spain.[10] Unlike in the Mexican case, these events did not generate calls for radical changes in social structures. (This was not the case in Uruguay, where José Artigas led a much more popular rural force.) Although the Buenos Aires junta was unable to hold on to Paraguay, which established its autonomy by 1812, or Upper Peru (now Bolivia), which was reconquered by loyal troops from Peru, it never faced a serious royalist threat to its own independence. Instead, in a pattern that was to be repeated for the following fifty years, its main military efforts were oriented toward maintaining other provinces under its control. Revolutionary Santiago had no such luck with weak royal forces, being retaken by loyalists in 1814.

On the northern coasts, the pattern was the same as in Chile.[11] Original enthusiasm in Caracas faced provincial resistance, fears of social upheaval, and determined royalist opposition. Control over the area shifted, but by 1815, Bolívar was exiled in Jamaica and royalists were exacting their revenge in all the major cities.

The lessons from the first five years of the independence struggles on the continent serve as a perfect introduction for the themes to be later elaborated in this book. First, there is a contradictory pattern of substantial de-

10. For the Southern Cone, see Halperín-Donghi, *The Aftermath of Revolution in Latin America; Politics, Economics, and Society; Guerra y finanzas en los orígines;* Collier, *Ideas and Politics of Chilean Independence;* Street, *Artigas and the Emancipation of Uruguay;* and Williams, *The Rise and Fall of the Paraguayan Republic, 1800–1870.*

11. The literature for this area is sparser at least in English. Unfortunately, the Spanish-language literature is dominated by hagiography or mind-numbing military detail. See Masur, *Simón Bolívar;* Lynch, "Bolívar and the Caudillos"; Bushnell, *The Santander Regime in Gran Colombia;* Anna, *The Fall of the Royal Government of Peru;* Lecuna, *Bolívar y el arte militar;* and general works cited above.

struction with limited logistical complexity. The armies that fought in these wars were not large (see Chapter 5), but they left in their wake considerable death and destruction. Second, everywhere one sees squabbling elites. The first cut was clearly between *peninsulares* and criollos, but even beneath these divisions we see ever shrinking factions and battles between supposed allies. Sides are switched, loyalties betrayed, ideologies overturned in a dizzying cadence. Finally, we detect the terror of race and class war hanging over all the battles and motivating elites to go to one side or another depending on local conditions. The subtext running through the independence wars was the fear that a political battle would be transformed into a social one. Only when enough of those in power felt secure in their future (or Spain began to represent a potentially greater threat to the social status quo), could the revolutions proceed.

José de San Martín and Simón Bolívar led the rebellion's comeback. San Martín had been an officer in the royal army, but had joined the rebellion upon his arrival in Buenos Aires in 1812. Convinced that the key to the success of the war lay in capturing loyalist Lima, he lobbied for an invasion through Chile as opposed to the already failed route through Upper Peru. San Martín's campaign is notable on several counts. There is of course the sheer military bravado of the Andes crossing, and the strategic intelligence that San Martín displayed at Chacabuco, Maipu, and later the siege of Lima. For our purposes, the most important aspect of the campaign is one that makes it practically unique in the independence wars. Prior to crossing the Andes in the winter of 1817, San Martín gathered forces and materiel in Mendoza, Argentina. There he established the kind of organizational and logistical center typical for armies in the contemporary period. His forces were not a semiorganized rabble, but a disciplined and relatively well-supported army. With it, he was able to defeat loyalist troops left in Chile, invade Peru by sea, and capture Lima in 1821. The administrative and financial support enjoyed by San Martín prior to and during his Chilean campaign meant that the final conquest of that country was not undertaken by semiautonomous and divided bands, but by a centralized power that used the occasion to reassert its authority. In future chapters we will note the legacy of this experience.

Bolívar's war was equally triumphant, if somewhat more complex. Returning from exile in 1816, Bolívar benefited from popular resentment of the newly victorious *peninsulares* and their draconian policies. He won his first victory in the small port town of Angostura, allowing him access to supplies and volunteers arriving by sea. With this new victory in hand,

Bolívar allied himself with the *llaneros* cavalry of José Antonio Páez and together they began the difficult invasion of New Granada across the northern tip of the Andes. Following the victories of Boyacá and Carabobo, Bolívar now ruled a combined "Gran Colombia," which would soon also include Ecuador. Conquering Quito in 1822, Bolívar and his lieutenant Antonio José de Sucre moved on to Peru and the decisive defeat of the Spanish at Ayacucho on December 9, 1824.

Several aspects of Bolívar's campaigns deserve attention. First, in an early hint of tensions that would characterize the next century, efforts to recruit nonelites and nonwhites into the army met with various obstacles and produced resentment among local criollos and within the army itself. The question of who could be trusted with the citizenship implied by military service was never resolved. Second, the various congresses and meetings organized by Bolívar during the campaign betrayed the ambivalence between what would come to be called Conservative and Liberal views on the formation of the new states and their relationships with the societies under their rule. The extent to which the population could be trusted with its own affairs, the state's relationship with the church, and the autonomy of the various parts of the newly liberated continent were never adequately determined. In the absence of a hegemonic political vision with an accompanying enforcement capacity, claimants arose in each of the distinctive regions. They did not necessarily reflect the respective social and political status quo, but relied on their military resources to establish their rule. The Bolívarian project produced neither the unitary state that the Libertador had sought, nor coherent smaller political entities.

The most important consequence of the wars was the fracturing of political power. Not only did the Spanish-American Empire dissolve into several nations (a process that continued through the 1820s), but even within the new borders, governments exercised little authority and had even less control. Civilian administration was destroyed throughout the continent. Its opposition to the wars of independence weakened the other major institution, the church. The wars also did a great deal of sheer physical damage to the economic infrastructure of the Latin American economy, especially the mining sector. Unlike in the case of Europe, where the end of the Napoleonic Wars provided a political base for one hundred years of political consolidation and economic growth, the independence struggles in Latin America left a legacy of violence and destruction that still haunts the region.

Yet although I will argue in the following chapters for the central importance of the independence wars in explaining subsequent developments in

Latin America, the case of Brazil reminds us to tread cautiously among any deterministic theories. Brazil largely escaped the dislocations of a military struggle. The Royal House of Portugal had moved there from Lisbon in 1808 in order to avoid the fate of the Spanish crown. Even after João VI moved back to Portugal in 1821, his son Dom Pedro remained in Rio de Janeiro. The immediate cause of independence came, not from within Brazil (where the dominant landowners felt well represented by the crown), but from changes in Portugal and that country's feeble attempts to return to the status quo ante. The Brazilians were able to establish their independence in late 1822 with little violence.[12] Brazil escaped colonial rule without militarization and with an enviable administrative and political continuity. Largely because of this, it also managed to maintain its geographical integrity and did not suffer from the kind of economic collapse experienced by other parts of the continent. But as we will see, Brazil did not differ radically from the rest of the continent in many of the aspects analyzed in this volume, and we will need to explore the particular relationship of Latin America with war with reference to more than the simple result of a single struggle, no matter how protracted.

International Wars

All the major Latin American wars[13] may be characterized as involving territorial swaps motivated by fairly simple geopolitical competition.[14] While the territorial adjustments made to the colonial map have been relatively small, the acquisition and defense of territory has been the dominant historical trope. This may seem unsurprising or even universal, but it is critical to recognize the kinds of international wars that Latin America has avoided. No countries have fought one another as representatives of an ideology or a religious faith. That is, the Latin American nation-states, with the possible exception of Cuba after 1959, have never mounted crusades on behalf of an

12. In 1823, there was an encounter between Brazilian forces and a Portuguese fleet in Bahia, but this was the extent of military activity.

13. For summary accounts of the wars, see Loveman, *For la Patria;* Halperín-Donghi, *The Contemporary History of Latin America;* Bushnell and Macaulay, *The Emergence of Latin America in the Nineteenth Century;* and Bethell, *The Cambridge History of Latin America,* especially vol. 3. For an excellent discussion of the geopolitics of the continent during the transition into the long peace, see Resende-Santos, "Anarchy and the Emulation of Military Systems."

14. See Ireland, *Boundaries, Possessions, and Conflicts;* Child, *Geopolitics and Conflict in South America;* and Clissold and Hennessey, "Territorial Disputes."

abstract principle. Invasions and wars have, of course, been defended with rhetorical claims to justice (and even here we find surprisingly little of the political self-justifications associated with international conflict), but the flags carried by the respective armies were theirs alone. This is particularly interesting in light of the legacy of the independence wars when armies of one region sought to export their notions of liberty and autonomy. To a surprising extent, though with some exceptions, noted later, the individual countries have respected one another's autonomy—even when lusting after or pursuing a neighbor's property.

The wars have also been relatively short and with simple linear narratives. Most have been settled by one or two decisive battles, and in almost all cases, the French invasion of Mexico being an exception, the stronger country winning at the start of the struggle was victorious at the end. Bibliographic accounts are remarkably simple. There is often no need for more than one strategic map, battles can be described in a single paragraph, and whole wars summarized in a few pages. Not surprisingly, by contemporary standards, the wars involved relatively few men and minimal equipment. What is surprising is the almost complete absence of tribalistic hatred (Paraguayan views of Brazilians and Peruvians of Ecuadorians excepted). Soldiers fighting one another—often for the first and last time—do so without the form of collective hatred so prevalent in other parts of the world. They meet and kill one another with an apparently desultory attitude. It often appears as if participants and observers had already accepted the marginality of their actions. Looking back on nearly two hundred years of global violence, one can find few incidents as apparently meaningless.

The Battle for La Plata

From the 1820s to the 1850s, the Río de la Plata saw a series of struggles over which country would control the river and dominate the regional economy.[15] The conflict had a long history going back to the contests between Portugal and Spain. The early development of Buenos Aires and the establishment of the Viceroyalty of La Plata in 1776 were at least partly a result of this rivalry. Within the Spanish territories, Buenos Aires and Montevideo competed for dominance. Upriver, the future territory of Paraguay was al-

---

15. See López-Alves, *Between the Economy and the Polity;* and "Wars and the Formation of Political Parties"; Halperín-Donghi, *Historia Argentina;* Luna, *Historia integral de la Argentina,* vol. 5. A good start on this topic is Halperín-Donghi, *Politics, Economics, and Society.* For the Brazilian side, see Seckinger, *The Brazilian Monarchy and the South American Republics.*

ready a land apart, with the heritage of Jesuit missions and the demographic survival of the Guaraní Indians. In the north, cattle ranchers in southern Brazil sought greater pastures and, like all the players, access to the River Plate. The region was the site of a classic geopolitical as well as some of the bloodiest wars in the continent's history.

During much of the first part of the nineteenth century, Brazil was the strongest player, either occupying the eastern bank of the river, what it called the Cisplatine Province and is now Uruguay, or controlling the politics of that country after its independence. In 1825, a revolt by a group of Uruguayan exiles from Argentina (the famous "33 orientales") soon led to the official incorporation of the "Banda Oriental" into the Argentine Republic. The Brazilians responded with a blockade of the river. Two years of considerable naval and land warfare followed, exhausting the fiscal and military capacity of both sides. By 1827, Argentina seemed to have the upper hand, but the collapse of the Rivadavia government and the pressure of the British, whose merchants were suffering from the interruption in trade, led to the acceptance of the independent buffer state of Uruguay. At least in the case of Argentina, the war accelerated the disintegration of central authority while simultaneously initiating the long-term financial dependence on British capital. In Brazil, however, the wars arguably helped consolidate centralized rule.

Ten years later, the conflict resumed. Internal divisions in Uruguay drew in Juan Manuel de Rosas, dictator of Buenos Aires. The resulting complications produced—in rough order—a French intervention, revolts in the Argentine littoral, a ten-year siege of Montevideo, a British intervention, the entry of Brazil, and the fall of Rosas. While arguably signaling the beginning of the process that would lead to Argentine consolidation, and again strengthening the Brazilian state, the war was a disaster for Uruguay and sentenced that country to fifty more years of caudillos and chaos. The end of this conflict sealed the entente between Argentina and Brazil, which is perhaps one of the most remarkable aspects of intraregional relations in Latin America. Despite the continuing tensions between the two most obvious potential superpowers, they never fought a war against each other after midcentury.

The War of the Triple Alliance

The origins of this war may be traced to a variety of sources: the colonial legacy of imperial rivalry and vague borders, international competition for trade, geopolitical struggles for control over the La Plata River system, long-standing Brazilian-Argentinean intervention in Uruguayan politics, British support for the creation of a new economic system in the Southern Cone, domestic instability in both Argentina and Uruguay, and the personal dementia of the Paraguayan leader Francisco Solano López.[16] While Brazil and Argentina were clearly the more powerful states, Paraguay had developed an independent manufacturing capacity in small arms and ship repair. Using all the resources available to a state monopolizing the country's economy, López sought to finish the long-standing quarrels with his neighbors and create a new South American empire. He believed that in conjunction with his internal allies in both Uruguay and Argentina, and with the likely Argentinean opposition to bloodshed on behalf of the slave monarchy in Brazil, the alliance between the two regional giants would not survive a single Paraguayan victory.

As in the earlier conflicts along the River Plate, the weakness of the Uruguayan state was the immediate cause of the war. The possible entry of Paraguay into the geopolitical mix was not welcomed by either Brazil or Argentina. It was in the interest of the Brazilian Empire that Uruguay and Paraguay remain pliant and weak in order to ensure free passage on the Paraguay River to the increasingly important province of Mato Grosso. Argentina saw the continued existence of Paraguay, a breakaway province from the former Viceroyalty of La Plata, as an incentive for separatist caudillos. López hated and feared both larger neighbors. Uruguay was essentially a passive observer in a war ostensibly fought over it.

In 1864, Brazil marched into Uruguay to support its clients in the Colorado Party. López responded by commandeering an imperial steamer and then successfully invading Brazil. But then he made the critical error of entering Argentina to "improve" his strategic position. This brought Argentina into the war on the side of Brazil (despite the expected distaste at finding itself allied with a slave state). Within a few months, Paraguay had lost two major battles and most of its navy. Lacking support from potential allies such as Bolivia and Chile, Paraguay soon faced a completely defensive struggle. López by increments committed the entire Paraguayan society to the defense of the republic and allowed for the continuation of the war even after disastrous military defeats in 1866. These battles usually consisted of

16. See Williams, *Rise and Fall*; Box, *The Origins of the Paraguayan War*; Kolinski, *Independence or Death*; J. M. Rosa, *La guerra del Paraguay*. For an example of the more polemical treatment, see Pomer, *La guerra del Paraguay*. For a discussion of the demographic results of the war, see Reber, "The Demographics of Paraguay"; Whigham and Potthast, "Some Strong Reservations"; "The Paraguayan Rosetta Stone."

notoriously courageous Paraguayan soldiers assaulting strong allied positions and suffering massive casualties. Paraguayan resistance shocked the allies, but the country soon began to run out of bodies that could be thrown at the cannons. In part because of the allies' overestimation of Paraguayan resources, in part because of the cholera epidemics that caused havoc, in part because of López's ability to mobilize the entire society in a defensive struggle, the war dragged on for three more years and did not end until López was killed in 1870.

The War of the Triple Alliance is unique in many ways. In its length, intensity of passion, logistical challenges, and consequences, it has no equal on the continent. In Latin America, this is as close as we come to the modern notion of total war. The destruction caused by the war removed Paraguay from the geopolitical map—and almost removed the entire country and its population from the globe. It was the most difficult postindependence military challenge faced by Brazil and Argentina and the consequences of their campaigns were significant. As the one dog of war that definitely did bark, the War of the Triple Alliance sets off the rarity of the continental experience in a clearer light and, if nothing else, allows us to better appreciate the good fortune of the continent.

Wars of the Peruvian-Bolivian Confederation and of the Pacific
The Pacific littoral was the other site of protracted military struggle.[17] Given their very close economic and administrative links during the colonial era, the early separation of Bolivia and Peru was in many ways a political fiction. In part because of their historic and economic connection and in part because of the rising strength of the Chilean state, the Bolivian president General Andrés Santa Cruz sought to establish closer connections between two halves of the old Viceroyalty of Lima. In alliance with a number of Peruvian caudillos, he invaded Peru in 1835, and in October 1836 he proclaimed the existence of the Peruvian-Bolivian Confederation. This union did have some popular support, but the division of Peru into two provinces and the selection of Lima as the capital alienated elites in both countries. More important, the union threatened the geopolitical position of Chile and Argentina. Both countries viewed a strong Peru as a challenge to their predominance. The first declared war in December 1836, the latter in May 1837. Despite some early failures, the Chilean army, in alliance with Peruvian forces op-

17. See Sater, *Chile and the War of the Pacific* for an exhaustive analysis. There is no equivalent for the Peruvian side, but one may consult Bonilla, "The War of the Pacific"; Mallon, *The Defense of Community in Peru's Central Highlands;* and *Peasant and Nation.*

posed to the union, were able to defeat Santa Cruz in the battle of Yungay in January 1839, leading to the dissolution of the confederation.

Chile's victory over Peru and Bolivia in the 1830s established its reputation as the regional "Prussia" and further solidified the political institutionalization begun under Diego Portales (who was assassinated at the very beginning of the war). If any war "made" Chilean exceptionalism, it was this one, as it provided a rare legitimacy while also establishing a stable civil-military relationship. For Peru and Bolivia, defeat appears to have accelerated the process of economic and political fragmentation begun with independence.[18]

Beginning in 1840, various international companies began the exploration of the Bolivian coast in order to make use of the guano and nitrate deposits there. The exploitation of silver beginning in 1870 led to an economic boom. During this decade Chile and Bolivia appeared to resolve a series of quarrels by increasing the influence of the former in the disputed region. But disagreements over taxes and the nationalization of Chilean mines in the Peruvian desert in 1875 fueled the tension. Following diplomatic efforts to resolve a new set of crises, Chile declared war in April 1879. Given a Peruvian-Bolivian alliance, this involved Chile in a war with both northern neighbors. The war quickly became a contest for plunder.

None of the countries was prepared for war, although Chile had a significant advantage in naval forces. More important, the Chilean state retained its institutional solidity, whereas both Peru and Bolivia suffered from internal divisions. Chile occupied the Bolivian littoral, then Tarapaca in 1879, and Tacna and Arica and most of the northern coast in 1880. By this stage the Chilean army had increased significantly with an invasion force of twelve thousand men. International pressure from both the U.S. and European powers forced the two sides into negotiation, but the Chileans sought a complete victory. In 1881, with an army now numbering twenty-six thousand, the Chileans entered Lima. They did not leave until 1884, extracting the province of Tarapaca permanently and the provinces of Tacna and Arica, which they retained until 1929. Chile also took the entire Bolivian coast (Atacama).

The victory helped determine the future institutionalization of both the Chilean and Peruvian militaries, as well as partially defining the develop-

---

18. Peru did have one successful military adventure in the nineteenth century. Following the Spanish invasion of the Chincha Islands, Peru defeated the Spaniards in the war of 1864–66.

ment options of the three countries. Chile enjoyed an economic boom as well as unprecedented patriotic euphoria, both of which helped dispel the gloom of the 1870s. Despite the relative shortness of the war, Peru suffered severe casualties and the destruction of much of its coastal infrastructure. The war may also be seen as the best example of a military impetus for a new national identity, as the Peruvian and Bolivian memory of their defeat continues to play a large role in their respective nationalisms. The Bolivian defeat deprived that country of a great part of its wealth and left it contained within the Altiplano, in which Chile had no interest. The war did help decrease the political influence of the military and helped consolidate the rule of a civilian oligarchy dominated by mining interests.

The War of the Chaco

In many ways this was the most tragic of all the international conflicts involving as it did two extremely poor and autocratic societies in which the military already played important roles, Paraguay and Bolivia.[19] The war arguably originated in earlier defeats suffered by the two participants. For Bolivia, whose access to the sea had been lost to Chile, the Chaco promised access through the Paraguay River. For Paraguay, control of the Chaco served to ameliorate the pain of the López catastrophe. Unfounded hopes of natural wealth only served to heighten the competition.

The two countries had been in a low-intensity conflict over the region since the early twentieth century. Thanks to military autonomy, sheer political inertia, and rumors of oil, clashes in 1928 were followed by all-out war in 1932. At first, the Bolivians appeared to lead with their early assault on Fort López, but under the leadership of José Felix Estigarribia, Paraguay united behind the war effort, its army growing to more than twenty times its peacetime strength. Over the following three years, the armies fought in some of the most inhospitable terrain in the world. By 1935, the Bolivian army had collapsed and Paraguay was awarded the disputed territory.

Both victory and defeat produced long-term changes. The failure of the Bolivian army embittered a whole generation of junior officers who were to lead a series of pseudoradical experiments in the following years. More important, it weakened the political legitimacy of the mining oligarchy that had run the country for so long. In Paraguay, victory led to the end of the

---

19. See Farcau, *The Chaco War;* Klein, *Bolivia;* Zook, *The Conduct of the Chaco War;* and Warren, *Paraguay.* The Chaco War may also be responsible for much of the international imagery of war and the military in South America. For a fascinating (and telling) depiction, see Tintin's adventure *The Broken Ear.*

Liberal regime, which had dominated in the twentieth century and prepared the setting for a civil-military alliance through the Colorado Party that would culminate in Alfredo Stroessner. Yet, although it was one of the bloodiest wars in Latin American history, the Chaco conflict was relatively marginal to the continent. Much as geopolitical events in Latin America made little difference to the larger world, the results of a squabble between Bolivia and Paraguay mattered little to even their own neighbors.

The Invasions of Mexico

In terms of geography and global historical impact, the U.S.-Mexican War was no doubt the most important of the conflicts fought by a Latin American country.[20] The war may have been largely unavoidable, given the economic and ideological pressure of U.S. expansion as well as the particular political needs of slavery. While it is undeniable that Mexico could not have been worse served than by the leadership of General Antonio López de Santa Anna, it is difficult to imagine any other outcome, in light of the very different military and political capacities of the two states.

The origins of the war may be partly traced to the political instability of postindependence Mexico, particularly after 1827. This instability, and the aborted Spanish invasion of 1829, paved the way for the rise to power of General Santa Anna. His attempted imposition of greater centralized control from Mexico City led to revolt in the northern province of Texas. Despite his opening bravado and early victory in San Antonio, Santa Anna was unable to defeat the rebellion. Following his capture by the rebels, he had to recognize the independence of the new Texan Republic. The southern province of Yucatán also tried to escape increased centralized control—and obtain more effective military support for its system of caste slavery—later in the decade, but was unable to secure its independence.

Santa Anna remained a key player in the increasingly chaotic Mexican political scene in the early 1840s, often relying on military bombast and threats to declare war on the United States should it attempt to annex the Texan Republic. Despite European efforts to mediate the dispute, the momentum of "manifest destiny" and Southern slavery politics led to the American annexation of the province in February 1845. The United States

20. Brack, *Mexico Views Manifest Destiny;* Schroeder, *Mr. Polk's War;* Hale, "The War with the United States"; and Ruiz, *The Mexican War.* For an excellent narrative, see Bazant, *A Concise History of Mexico;* and Cosío Villegas, *A Compact History of Mexico.* See also the Web site for the excellent Public Broadcasting Service (PBS) documentary on the war: http://www.pbs.org/kera/usmexicanwar/mainframe.html.

made it clear that its ambitions would not be satisfied with Texas and that it desired all the territory north of the Rio Grande as well as California. Despite early efforts to avoid a war—few Mexicans had any delusions about the capacity of the army to withstand an invasion—public opinion and military pride led to Mexican refusal to accept annexation.

By May 1846, three months after the beginning of hostilities, the U.S. army had occupied most of northern Mexico. In part because of continuing instability requiring the participation of the Mexican army in civil unrest in Mexico City, the United States was able to land in Veracruz in March 1847. Proving that war does not necessarily unite, much of the Mexican military effort was expended on domestic struggles. States would not support the federal government, which in turn did not trust the cities, which had to bear the brunt of the American invasion. When the Mexican government was able to produce an army to fight the U.S. invaders, it was defeated largely by the absence of logistical support. Artillery was outdated, powder was limited, the soldiers were untrained, and the officers seemed to care little and know less of strategy. By September 1847 U.S. troops were overcoming the last Mexican resisters in Chapultepec Castle, the famed "Halls of Montezuma" of the U.S. Marines.

The Treaty of Guadalupe Hidalgo left Mexico without half its territory. It may have also contributed to the rise of the new Liberal party that under Benito Juárez would begin the construction of contemporary Mexico. For the United States, the war brought both glory and heartache. The acquisition of so many resources and the transcontinental expansion provided the basis for future power. The control over vast territories also intensified the competition between the Southern and Northern views on the union.

A decade later, Mexico had to defend itself again.[21] The Wars of Reform, the culminating conflict between Liberals and Conservatives, had left not only a continued divided elite and weakened government, but also an economic disaster. Finding himself bankrupt, President Benito Juárez refused to immediately pay back some of the debts and claims held by European citizens. The French emperor Napoleon III was not merely interested in payment, but also sought to re-create an empire in the Americas. In December 1861, his troops, temporarily accompanied by those of Britain and Spain, began the occupation of Veracruz.

The French were generally welcomed by the defeated Conservatives and

21. For the background to the French wars, the best source is Barker, *The French Experience in Mexico, 1821–1861*. Again, see Bazant, *Concise History of Mexico* and Cosío Villegas, *A Compact History of Mexico*.

particularly by the church. Despite an early Mexican victory in Puebla—the famous Cinco de Mayo of 1862—by early 1863 the French and their Conservative allies had occupied Mexico City. They were followed by the new court of Maximilian and Carlota. The French-Conservative royal government appeared to succeed in finally destroying the Liberals, and for two years the Habsburg court attempted to establish its legitimacy. But the withdrawal of French troops beginning in 1866 and the end of the American Civil War meant that Maximilian had lost his protector whereas Juárez gained new support. The end was relatively quick, with the Liberal army easily defeating the now isolated Conservatives and finally capturing the emperor in May 1867. With the fall of Queretaro, Mexico's independence as well as the liberal hegemony were firmly established.

Two characteristics of the international wars fought by Mexico deserve special attention. The first was the absence of any sense of elite unity prior to the ultimate victory by Juárez. Whether arguing among themselves as the U.S. troops conquered huge territories or cooperating with a foreign invader, the Mexican political elite was unable to either bring about a general consensus regarding the form of government or securely establish its control over the entire country. This resulted in the second key aspect of the wars: despite the bloodletting—the war against the French consumed fifty thousand lives—the armies that fought over Mexico were never logistically complex. The Liberals won in 1867 with rifles and the flesh of soldiers, and the government of Mexico was never able to muster enough authority or will to field anything approaching a modern army.

Civil Wars

Latin America has experienced much internal or civil conflict.[22] The number of wars and the complexity of their historical and social origins make it difficult to give any summary description here. As Loveman notes, it is impossible to exhaustively list all the civil conflicts. This is especially true if we wish to count coups, *cuartelazos,* and *pronunciamientos.* Bolivia, for example, suffered thirteen military uprisings in four months in 1840, Colombia had eleven major rebellions in the nineteenth century, and Mexico forty-nine administrations in just thirty-three years.[23] Table 2.2 is a list of merely the most prominent struggles. We may distinguish five general types of civil wars that students of Latin America need to consider.

22. A wonderful new book on the nineteenth century is Earle, *Rumours of Wars.*
23. Loveman, *For la Patria,* 43.

Regional Rebellions
This first type of conflict dominated the nineteenth century and largely involved struggles over the establishment of central authority or provinces
rebelling against control by the capital. Nearly every country suffered such
wars. In Argentina, the fight within and between provinces (or between *unitarios* and *federalistas*) lasted much of the century. The first twenty-five
years after independence witnessed innumerable battles between the various
independence generals, and then between Rosas and autonomous caudillos.
In the 1850s, the confederation and Buenos Aires continued to fight. Even
after the victory of Bartolomé Mitre, central authority was not absolutely
secured and would not be until 1880. Uruguay was for many years almost
two countries, Montevideo and the rural hinterland, each fighting the other
for either control or autonomy. During the 1830s, only two of the Brazilian
Empire's eighteen provinces did *not* rebel. Particularly serious were uprisings in Maranhão (1831–32), Bahia (1832–35), Minas Gerais (1833), Mato
Grosso (1834), Pará (1835–37), and Rio Grande do Sul (1835–1845). Regionalism continued as a political force well into this century. Mexico's version of the Federalist-versus-Centralist battle took up much of the first half
of the century and arguably still played a role in the twentieth. Peru was
divided into north and south, coast and sierra, while Ecuador was torn between Guayaquil and Quito, and Bolivia's Altiplano was isolated from the
rest of the country. Finally, recent events in Colombia indicate that that
country's traditionally weak state has not been able to impose assumed centralized control even after almost two hundred years of independence. The
central government has essentially recognized the sovereignty of two guerrilla armies over country-sized swaths of its territory.

   Although these conflicts were often quite bloody, in part because racial
and class elements frequently entered geographical disputes, they usually
involved small armies and irregular troops. In many cases, it would be difficult to distinguish between civil wars and police actions against banditry. In
this way, regional struggles are the prototypical Latin American wars: nasty,
brutish, and short.

Ideological Battles
Often indistinguishable from the regional rebellions, these conflicts have
persisted well into this century. The nineteenth century consists of almost
universal squabbles between Liberals and Conservatives (often paralleling
divisions between federalists and centralists respectively). Liberals believed
in free trade, the elimination of special *fueros* or corporate rights and prop-

erty ownership, and favored an expansion of citizenship rights—at least theoretically. Conservatives were protectionist, favored the church, and looked
back to the colonial past for some of their inspiration. Mexico may be the
extreme example of this kind of conflict. The Conservatives dominated during much of the first thirty years of independence and the Liberals in the
following twenty, but each group had to expend huge amounts of time,
energy, and resources to fight the other. Ecuador experienced similar divisions, as did Colombia continuing into the twentieth century. In the last
case, the struggle began with the War of the Supremes in 1839 (in part a
regionalist squabble), continued through fifty years of almost perpetual conflict, and culminated in the extremely bloody War of the Thousand Days
(1899). This struggle became so institutionalized that competition between
political parties and their adherents became more important than the original points of dispute. Histories of conflict bred their own ferocity, resulting
in the infamous Violencia of the 1940s and 1950s. In some cases, the ideological divisions focused on relations with the church. This was clearly an
element in the Mexican case—not resolved until the 1920s—as well as in
Chile, where the fight over anticlericalism belied the notion of a perfect
Portalian consensus. More recently, the doctrine of national security and
subsequent "dirty wars" against "communist subversion" may be seen as
the heirs of such splits.

Clearly, both what I am calling ideological and regional wars reflected
underlying social and economic conditions and inequalities. Regional struggles in Brazil in the nineteenth century were often less about where power
resided and much more about which social sector wielded it. Often, concerns over trade policy, protectionism, and the status of slavery were more
important than the call for local autonomy. The Brazilian Farroupilha was
arguably more about class than geography. Both types of civil wars reflected
the inability of postindependence governments to establish the hegemony of
a single political and ideological regime. These wars arose not because the
state was so important or so powerful, but precisely the opposite. It was the
marginality of state power and the absence of a clear elite project that
brought forth so many struggles.

Caudillo Wars
The type of civil conflict most prevalent in the nineteenth century, caudillo
wars, remained part of the political landscape well into the twentieth.[24]

24. Chasteen, *Heroes on Horseback;* Lynch, *Caudillos in Spanish America;* Krauze, *Siglo
de caudillos.*

These conflicts, unlike the two types described earlier, did not reflect social divisions on the ground, but rather were the product of simple squabbles over government privileges or booty. This is not to say that caudillos were completely endogenous to their respective societies, but it is important to distinguish between social conflicts that were led by military strongmen and hostilities that were about little but personal ambition. Although these may constitute the most popular image of military struggles in Latin America, I would argue that they were the least significant. Rather than being a cause of the political instability that they symbolized, they were the products of the failure to institutionalize political authority. Perhaps the prototypical examples are the careers of Generals Agustín Gamarra and Ramón Castilla of Peru or that of General Santa Anna in Mexico.

Race/Ethnic Wars

The most important conflicts over racial and ethnic differences occurred before independence, during which time the vast majority of the pre-Columbian population either was killed or died from disease and overwork.[25] While the conquest is outside of the purview of this book, its legacy overshadows the centuries discussed. The very success of the conquest and the fact that it occurred centuries before the formation of the independent states led to ethnically divided populations and ambiguous national origins. It may be obvious, but is too often forgotten, that much more so than any other case outside of South Africa and the United States, the states that arose in the nineteenth century had a clear racialist component.[26] To a large extent, the new governments were seen as white institutions maintaining control over an Indian, black, or mixed population. As we shall see in subsequent chapters, the history of Latin American wars cannot be understood without reference to this fundamental division.

In the eighteenth and nineteenth centuries, rebellions in Peru and Mexico were attempts to win back the region from the European population. These uprisings contributed to an atmosphere of white fear that helped determine how wars were fought and against whom and how they would involve their

25. See Mallon, *Defense of Community* and *Peasant and Nation;* and Reed, *The Caste War of Yucatán.* For a discussion of race and state creation and comparisons, see Marx, *Making Race and Nation;* Thurner, *From Two Republics;* Ada Ferrer, *Insurgent Cuba.*

26. Of course, what may be called "racial" hierarchies existed in Europe. Examples may be the Norman/Saxon distinction in medieval England (and later ones between English, Welsh, Scots, and Irish) or the special caste claims of the Polish and Magyar nobility.

respective societies. The genocide of the Indians continued as well, as frontier wars culminated with the expulsion, killing, or subjugation of native populations in Chile, Argentina, and Mexico. It may not be coincidental that these three states, along with Brazil arguably the most institutionalized polities in the region, led assaults on Indian territories and populations precisely at critical points in the consolidation of centralized authority. These campaigns not only served to unite white opinion, but also often provided new resources and territories that could be distributed so as to consolidate consensus. More recently, the civil war in Guatemala has at times taken on characteristics of a race war as the government identified Indians as automatic enemy sympathizers. The rebellion in Chiapas and recent insurgencies in Peru indicate that this war will continue well into the twenty-first century.

Revolutions

A final type of civil war is that generated by revolution.[27] These conflicts may combine aspects of the first three discussed earlier with an organized effort to remake the social and economic rules of the respective countries. These wars are not so much over territory, but rather, over the distribution of a social and economic pie. As a military struggle, the Mexican Revolution deserves pride of place. In length (ten years), destruction (a million dead, or more than 5 percent of the population), tactics and logistics (barbed wire, railroads, artillery), and sheer narrative complexity, this conflict ranks as one of the great wars of the twentieth century. It also arguably heralds the next half century of "great" revolutions throughout the globe.[28] For contemporary Latin America, however, the Cuban Revolution of the 1950s, despite its military marginality, may be the most important case. Other examples include Bolivia in 1952, and El Salvador and Nicaragua in the 1970s.

Latin American revolutionary wars tend to have a similar origin and structure. They begin with the conjunction of long-term subaltern discontent, rising middle-class political aspirations, and perhaps most important, weakened repressive regimes. An early "honeymoon" when all those in revolt can agree on the need, if not the form, of change is followed by the collapse of reformist governments and battles between those wishing to pre-

---

27. For Mexico, see Knight, *The Mexican Revolution;* for Cuba, see Thomas, *Cuba, or The Pursuit of Freedom;* for Bolivia, see Dunkerley, *Rebellion in the Veins;* and for Central America, see Dunkerley, *Power in the Isthmus.*

28. But note how that "honor" is usually assigned to 1917.

serve aspects of the status quo ante and more radical forces. These conflicts share a great deal with the independence wars. Despite a great deal of violence, rarely does the postbellic social order not look much like its predecessor.

Explaining the Peace

How do we explain the particular form and distribution of war in Latin America? Why is it that Latin America appears to have largely escaped the scourge of international war? Why has its state system enjoyed such incredible stability? How do we explain the much more standard degree of domestic conflict as compared with other regions? In the following section, I address these questions.

The coexistence of international peace and domestic strife may seem contradictory. One might expect that states would be either peaceful or bellicose. Latin America seems paradoxical in that political battles were quite common, but only of a particular type. My central hypothesis is that these two phenomena, international peace and domestic strife, are causally linked. Simply put, *Latin American states did not have the organizational or ideological capacity to go to war with one another.*[29] The societies were not geared toward the logistical and cultural transformations required by international conflict. Conversely, *domestic conflict often reflected the inability of the nascent states to impose their control over the relevant societies.*[30] Equally important, the definition of the enemy in the Latin American context has rarely been along territorial lines. The enemy, as defined by state elites, has been *within,* defined racially, along class lines, and by critical ideological struggles.[31] We might even argue for a negative correlation between international bellicosity and internal violence. Chile, the so-called Prussia of Latin America, has enjoyed relative domestic tranquility. Mexico

29. This is the polar opposite of the thesis presented in Holsti, *The State, War, and the State of War* claiming that increased state strength explains the decline in war from the nineteenth century on.

30. Here I am applying the same logic employed by Kenneth Waltz in *The Theory of International Politics* to explain international wars: the absence of governmental authority. Wolf Grabendorff, in "Interstate Conflict Behavior," sought to explain the increase in international hostility in the 1970s and 1980s by reference to increased political and military capacity.

31. The most significant exception has been in the case of anticommunism, but again the threat was largely perceived as coming from inside the society, not from outside.

and Colombia, while enjoying international peace for more than one hundred years, have endured murderous domestic conflict.[32]

This pattern reproduced itself historically. On the international front, states that have traditionally been peaceful or fought only limited wars may in time find it practically impossible to ever consider fighting total wars. As the technological, social, economic, and organizational demands of total war have increased, those states that have not participated in any of its preliminary stages would require an even larger transformation than usual to participate in such conflicts. In societies where military service has never been institutionalized, the removal of entire cohorts of young men is inconceivable. In economies where the ability of the state to enforce its tax laws has always been constrained, the ability of central authorities to pay for or borrow the goods of war may be severely limited. Moreover, by having avoided previous ideological mobilizations, states that have avoided holocausts may lack the historical memories required for mobilization. They may lack what we could call the "cultural repertoires" of war. Patriotic calls may sound shallower than in other societies and calls for sacrifice may go unheeded. As we will see, the limitations of history may go far in explaining the Latin American peace.

Similarly, the pattern of civil war reproduced itself for much of the nineteenth century. Few of the domestic wars produced unequivocal victors who used the conflicts as opportunities to develop solid institutional frameworks for governance. Instead, mutual exhaustion and compromise decided many of the civil wars, and these left the seeds for future conflicts. Organizations remained to enable recruitment of soldiers, and partisans retained enough resources to feed a rebellious military machine. A history of domestic strife often left a legacy of regional and partisan hatreds. People may not have been willing to kill or die for Colombia (to use one obvious example), but they seemed more than able and ready to do so on behalf of the Liberal or Conservative parties. In that country's case, each wave of violence appears to have laid the foundation for the next. These divisions also made it ever more difficult for the central state to establish its authority or consensual legitimacy, thereby leaving the opportunity open for further bloodshed.

States and nations, then, fight the wars they have been taught to fight. All peaceful states may be alike, but each warring state fights in its own

32. Attempts to test this relationship statistically were inconclusive, but given the quality of data and the difficulty in modeling these events, such results should not be taken as absolute resolutions of the issue.

way. Wars reflect the political and social idiosyncrasies of the states that fight them. Since wars originate from a form of social organization,[33] it would make sense that they reflect it. The structures and habits of political life obviously help shape the manner in which a society practices war. Consider the contrast between the hoplite armies of the Greek city-states and those of imperial Persia. The first was characterized by individual prowess woven into a powerful strategic weapon by the discipline of shared citizenship and constant training. The second, while physically impressive, was often rotten at the core and unable to withstand adversity. A millennium later, Machiavelli despondently compared the mercenary armies of the Italian city-states with those larger and more homegrown varieties that appeared to enjoy an unbeatable advantage on the battlefield. In the 1790s, the French Revolution gave birth to the first true national army of citizens, which militarily and politically transformed the rest of Europe. The world wars of the twentieth century may be seen as products and producers of the contemporary regulatory welfare state. In short, armies reflect their societies and help in turn to shape them through their demands and socializing influences.

In the European, and by extension North American, geopolitical environment, states and nations solved their international conflicts through violence and came to create institutions that allowed for peaceful resolution of internal conflicts. In Latin America, we detect the opposite pattern. Why?

Causes of War

In looking for the causes of war,[34] we need to begin by distinguishing between explanations of war, of wars, and of a particular war.[35] The first is largely the province of anthropologists and philosophers.[36] For this volume, I am assuming that human beings make war and that such conflicts are an inherent part of an international system. On the other side of the explanatory spectrum, I am also not proposing an analysis of a particular war. That

33. Nye, "Old Wars and Future Wars."
34. Given the massive literature on this theme, I cannot do it justice within the purview of this chapter. See Levy, "The Causes of War and the Conditions of Peace"; and Rotberg and Rabb, *The Origin and Prevention of Major Wars* for reviews.
35. Black, *Why Wars Happen.*
36. Some recent examples of the discussion include Ehrenreich, *Blood Rites;* Kagan, *On the Origins of War;* Keeley, *War Before Civilization;* O'Connell, *Ride the Second Horseman;* and Bourke, *An Intimate History of Killing.*

is much more the province of historians discussing the specific events and circumstances that produced conflict, or for that matter prevented it. The subject of this section is in the middle range between generalities about the nature of violence and the specifics of a particular struggle. I seek to explain an apparent historical pattern, not a universal one or a single phenomenon. We may begin by distinguishing between short- and long-term developments, or what Wright calls immediate versus general causes of wars.[37] Levy prefers distinguishing between systemic, societal, and individual levels of explanation.[38] The following analysis borrows from both schema.

Accounts that would focus on the immediate conditions of peace and that would emphasize the characteristics of individual policy makers or states would include diplomatic history, analyses of negotiation, and (more recently) different game-playing scenarios. Such explanations would appear particularly attractive for explaining how Latin America has escaped from many possible *individual* conflicts without resorting to arms. Latin America, for example, appears to have had a significant number of border disputes, in large part due to the vagueness of the colonial territorial legacy. But few evolved into war (5 percent versus 62 percent for Europe).[39] Recent examples such as the relatively quick resolution of the Peruvian-Ecuadorian border conflict or the even more complex territorial disputes between Argentina and Chile would support such an emphasis. Yet, unless we are prepared to accept perpetual exceptional diplomatic skill or almost omniscient game playing on the part of all the relevant actors, such explanations are inadequate to explain the long pattern of international peace for more than a century. Moreover, we would have to ask why such diplomatic skill seems to disappear when there are attempts to resolve domestic conflicts.

A related explanation, but focusing on systemic characteristics, would include theories of balance of power or those emphasizing hegemonic cycles of rise and decline.[40] This approach has been used to explain the outbreak of war in specific circumstances in Latin America.[41] Perhaps the most promising of these approaches is a geopolitical analysis that claims that the alliance structure of the continent provides an explanation for the long

37. Wright, *A Study of War.*
38. Levy, "Causes of War."
39. Gochman and Maoz, "Militarized Disputes"; Diehl and Goertz, "Territorial Changes and Militarized Conflicts."
40. Morgenthau, *Politics Among Nations;* Waltz, *Theory of International Politics;* Gilpin, *War and Change in World Politics.*
41. Burr, *By Reason or Force;* Abente, "The War of the Triple Alliance."

peace.[42] Latin America, for example, is a classic geopolitical *checkerboard* in which "my neighbor is my enemy, but my neighbor's enemy is my friend." These patterns have prevented the development of hegemonic rivalries and have ensured that a balance of power was maintained even as the capacities of the players changed. *Shatterbelts,* by contrast, are where international rivalries are transformed into local squabbles. Except in the special case of Cuba and in the internal wars of Central America, the continent has not seen those kinds of proxy conflicts to any significant degree. Much of the recent literature on regional security has focused on the creation of systematic mutual interdependence and security,[43] and it is undeniable that Latin America constructed an intercontinental system of conferences and treaties long before these became standard international practice.[44]

Overall, however, these systemic models appear to have limited value in explaining the long period of peace that has prevailed on the continent. The geopolitical explanation requires that we accept a century of military and political stability as an exogenous factor without investigating the origins of that stability. Why has the system remained dominant and why has it fostered such a peaceful resolution of conflicts?

We might perhaps turn to an "inverted" form of the classic Marxist explanation for war. In the accepted Leninist view, the outbreak of war can be traced to the machinations of capitalist elites or imperial powers that stand to benefit from such a struggle. The "long peace" would require that we posit that the elite or relevant imperial powers sought to prevent war to maximize return on their investments. In this view, since war is bad for trade[45] it must be deterred. A related explanation would focus on the military as an international caste seeking to minimize damage to itself through useless slaughter or respecting the social prerogatives of the various national officer corps.

As relevant as these concerns may be for exploring the outbreak of individual wars, it is difficult to imagine how such an interpretation could be applied to a hundred years of relative peace. A century-long continental "conspiracy of peace" would require that Latin American elites exhibit a

42. Child, *Geopolitics and Conflict in South America;* Kelly, *Checkerboards and Shatterbelts.*

43. Hurrell, "Security in Latin America"; "An Emerging Security Community?"; Varas and Caro, *Medidas de confianza mutua;* Fuentes Saavedra, "Chile-Argentina: El proceso de construir confianza"; *SER en el 2000.*

44. Calvert, *The International Politics of Latin America,* esp. chap. 6.

45. Polachek, "Conflict and Trade."

classwide rationality for which there is little evidence. The existence of a continental military alliance may be more probable, but such a caste also existed in pre–World War I Europe with no discernible contribution to the peaceful resolution of conflict. Moreover, such a view would ignore critical differences in the social origins of the various national militaries. As I will argue later, however, there is something to be said for a form of elite race consciousness that would preclude conflicts across borders and focus attention on internal social struggles.

We also cannot ignore the role of external powers, which may have guaranteed borders and the status quo, thereby removing many of the immediate stimuli of conflict. The Latin American peace may thus be the ultimate expression of *dependencia*. The presence of the European powers prevented a series of military events that may have created a very different geopolitical balance.[46] We should be careful, however, with resorting to explanations that might deny Latin American societies any control over their own fate. We might even reverse the causal order and suggest that it was the absence of war that produced a weak state, which in turn made intervention possible. To paraphrase Perry Anderson's comments on Italy, since Latin America was unable to create an empire from within, it had to suffer one from without.

There is no doubt that Latin America has been under a neoimperial umbrella for most of its independent history. For most of the nineteenth century, the continent belonged to what has been called the informal British Empire.[47] That the British played a decisive role in the resolution of the La Plata conflicts in the first half of the century is unquestionable. After 1850, the British imperial influence is much more debatable. In the twentieth century, the United States had an overwhelming role. The 1948 Rio accords to a large extent helped shape the foreign relations of the continent. Nevertheless, it would seem that outside Central America and the Caribbean and at least *in terms of intracontinental relations,* the United States has respected the autonomy of the various republics.

Locating systematic evidence of foreign intervention—or the absence thereof—is difficult, as the significance of such efforts will vary a great deal by context, among other things. While not exhaustive records, the *Foreign Relations of the United States* and the *British Documents on Foreign Affairs*

---

46. Andreski, *Military Organization and Society.*
47. Ferns, "Britain's Informal Empire in Argentina"; Winn, "British Informal Empire in Uruguay"; A. Thompson, "Informal Empire?"

can provide insights into the attitudes of the two powers toward continental conflicts.[48] As revealed in correspondence dealing with the War of the Pacific, the Chaco War, and the 1941 border conflict between Peru and Ecuador, the consistent position of both governments is a (a) concern that other countries not become involved; (b) reluctance to be seen as an arbitrator or mediator (even when such a role is requested by belligerents); and (c) sponsorship of Latin American neutrals becoming involved, particularly Brazil. The only clearly interventionist trend is the consistent effort to protect the property interests of nationals caught in the hostilities. The very absence of records of explicit intervention could merely reflect the depth and scope of the hegemonic control exercised by the imperial powers. It would be difficult, however, to explain such a long pattern of peaceful relations through reference to a hegemony that left no indications of its existence. That is, one would have to assume that imperial controls were so insidious as to leave no trace.

A typical exchange on the War of the Pacific described the consistent U.S. position: "We aim to be regarded as a disinterested friend and counselor, but we do not assume to impose our wishes upon [Chile and Peru], or to act as arbiter or umpire in their disputes."[49] At one point British and French interest in stopping the fighting appears to have been successfully discouraged by the United States.[50] Efforts by neutral nations to draw the United States into a peaceful resolution of the Chaco conflict were consistently rebuffed.[51] The 1941 conflict between Peru and Ecuador appears to have been largely resolved through continental efforts. Most tellingly, in the case where one would have expected the greatest U.S. influence, and for which we have the best documentation, the Falklands/Malvinas conflict, the United States had relatively little direct influence over Argentine decision making.[52] Again, this is not to deny the powerful U.S. and even U.K. influence on Latin American politics in general. Nor should we neglect the potentially decisive effect of these two countries serving as the guarantors of a geopolitical status quo. But it does not appear that we can attribute responsibility for the absence of conflict solely to these two countries.

48. United States Department of State, *Foreign Relations;* Bourne and Watt, *British Documents.* But note the problems discussed in Schoultz, *Beneath the United States* with the U.S. source (390). His wonderful book, however, does not contradict my reading of American noninterference in Latin American wars.

49. United States Department of State, *Foreign Relations,* 1882, 76.

50. Bourne and Watt, *British Documents,* pt. I, ser. D, vol. 2, doc. 130.

51. For example, United States Department of State, *Foreign Relations,* 1933, 341, 376.

52. Piñeiro, *Historia de la guerra de Malvinas.*

Even if we can make an argument for a pacifying influence from imperial powers, they also directly or indirectly caused other conflicts. While they helped to impose a peace on the Cisplatine War in 1828, later British interference, along with that of France, arguably prolonged the Guerra Grande and associated conflicts in the 1840s. Both of Mexico's major wars in the nineteenth century involved invasions by great powers. In the twentieth, much of the political instability of Central America can be directly attributed to U.S. intervention. The one Latin American country that has been mobilized for war for several decades, Cuba, has seen the northern neighbor as its principal adversary. In the end, empires may bring peace, but they also generate their share of internal and external conflicts.

Even if they cannot adequately account for the "long peace," the insights from systemic-stability, elite-driven, and "neoimperial" theories may serve to explain the significant degree of domestic conflict we observe during the same time period. Instead of treating the set of nation-states as the relevant actors, we might better focus on domestic or internal social sectors and political groups. If we reversed these sets of explanations we would then posit that it was the absence of a domestic hegemon, the instability of the national balance of power, and the lack of elite agreement that may best explain the almost constant state of civil war somewhere on the continent during this period. The evidence is ample for all three. Again and again, the civil wars in Latin America appear to arise from the failure of an institutionalized authority to impose a set of governing rules over squabbling elites. Certainly during most of the nineteenth century, there was neither consensus regarding the legitimate scope and scale of government nor any agreement on how disputes should be solved. This created precisely the kind of situation envisioned in many of the balance-of-power theses: in the absence of a clear distribution of power, each side would be tempted to act in its own interests before others could do the same. These theories essentially come down to the capacity of a system, an actor within it, or an external force to police agreements and maintain the status quo. With relatively few exceptions, the Latin American states were unable to play such a role during much of the period in question.

Given the limitation of these system-driven theories to account for the long international peace, we can therefore turn to explanations focusing on the characteristics of the specific countries in the region. Why is it that some nations appear to be more and others less prone to warlike behavior?

In her systematic review of a variety of regime, socioeconomic, and situational variables, Zinnes finds little evidence for any consistent structural correlation. Levy reports similar results in his survey.[53] One exception may be the apparent causal link between democratic regimes and nonbellic behavior.[54] In the 1990s, authors speculated about the creation of a Kantian "Pacific Union" on the continent, based on shared Liberal democratic values and free trade.[55] Yet given that in Latin America, militaristic, authoritarian, and conservative countries have been so successful at avoiding conflict with one another, such a relationship does not take us very far toward an explanation.

Michael Howard among others has emphasized what he calls "a cultural predisposition to war."[56] Thus, particular societies, regions, and/or epochs might be culturally predisposed to interstate conflict. As in many of the other generalizing theories of war, this view can easily degenerate into tautology, as measures of bellicosity may be products of war itself. Moreover, it is difficult to imagine a continent where cultural predisposition to political violence has been more emphasized than in Latin America. While we should always be careful with culturally deterministic arguments, it is undeniable that the general political culture in Latin America is not peaceful. The pervasiveness and extent of *internal* violence do not indicate some essentialist quality that would prevent Latin Americans from killing one another. Civil conflicts in the region have featured the same kind of brutality and terror associated with similar wars in other parts of the world. The ferocity of the War of the Triple Alliance and of the Chaco War are also well documented.[57]

A related explanation might rely on the relatively homogenous culture of the continent. Without the struggles between different elite cultures, there was no subsequent conflict between political claims over territory. Yet similar cultures did not make Renaissance Italy or seventeenth-century Germany particularly peaceful. Further, as we saw recently in the Balkans and in East Africa, competing political institutions can forge inimical heterogeneity out of the most apparently uniform populations. In any case, given the extent of civil conflicts, cultural affinity would not explain the divergence in the different types of political violence. In the following pages, I suggest a series of factors that might better account for the Latin American exception.

53. Zinnes, "Why War?"; Levy, "Causes of War."
54. Ray, "Does Democracy Cause Peace?"
55. Peceny, "The Inter-American System as a Liberal Pacific Union?"
56. Howard, *Causes of War.*
57. For a related approach noting the contribution of a Latin American political culture to foreign policy, see Ebel, Taras, and Cochrane, *Political Culture and Foreign Policy in Latin America.*

Physical Constraints

Borders often make for uneasy neighbors, and that has been the case in Latin America.[58] There is a clear correlation between sharing a frontier and likelihood of conflict.[59] Yet even here, the level of conflict is less than might be expected, given global patterns.[60] What accounts for the pacificity in light of the "availability" of conflict? First, with some limited exceptions, most frontier zones feature forbidding conditions. John Keegan suggests that large-scale military operations can only be conducted in certain physical environments.[61] In Latin America, much of the interstate violence has been concentrated in the La Plata River system and the south-central Pacific Coast, both of which are much more hospitable to military logistics than the Andes or the Amazon.[62] Second, it is also possible that international conflict did not occur because the region was large enough to allow the creation of sufficient buffer zones. In general, frontiers have not abutted significant population centers or areas of great economic potential. Moreover, the economic and political gaze of elites has usually been oriented not toward neighbors, but toward the metropoles of the United States and Europe. Thus, international conflict was precluded because competing elites never came into contact with one another. It was precisely in those areas of concentrated resources or potential for wealth (for example, La Plata or the Andean deserts) where we see the greatest conflict.[63] That is, uncertainty in borders only translated into fighting when there was something to fight about. Attention to the actual conditions of the frontiers may also help explain the shift in the likelihood of war between the nineteenth and twentieth centuries. As discussed earlier, many of the wars in the nineteenth century were precisely the kind of land grabs I suggest were no longer relevant by the twentieth. The victors of the earlier wars were able to establish their control over the areas that were worth having or, as in the case of Argentina

58. See McIntyre, "The Longest Peace."
59. Kelly, *Checkerboards and Shatterbelts*, 135–38.
60. Gochman and Maoz, "Militarized Disputes"; Diehl and Goertz, "Territorial Changes and Militarized Conflicts." For accounts of borders where conflicts have been avoided, see Martz, "National Security and Politics"; George, "Realism and Internationalism"; and Garrett, "The Beagle Channel Dispute."
61. Keegan, *History of Warfare*.
62. The persistent Peruvian-Ecuadorian dispute would seem to contradict this explanation. Yet, a consistent characteristic of these semiregular conflicts is their relatively short duration and limited logistical impact.
63. My thanks to Tom Rudel for first suggesting this point.

and Brazil, were forced to accept buffer states. To the extent that the nineteenth-century wars secured these borders, systemic theories of the regional peace are relevant. This situation may be changing, however, as the expansion of sea frontiers and the location of new resources, such as hydroelectric power, has created the potential for conflict.

A purely "physical" explanation is unsatisfactory, however, given that a prominent feature of Latin American diplomatic relations has been the peaceful resolution of the many frontier disputes that do exist. How do we account for the fact that these states do not fight even when they have something about which to disagree?

Fears and Threats

There are two conditions that seem absolutely necessary for conflict to occur. First, some significant segment of the elite must see war as a favorable option. Even more fundamental, war must be part of the policy repertoire of leading decision makers. If war is never considered or is judged as too extreme a solution or as not providing enough chances for some "return" to the country, then even the most intense rivalries or disagreements are less likely to lead to armed conflict. Second, a significant part of the population must be supportive of the notion of war or at least be willing to accept the government's decision. This is not to deny the coercive capacity of states or that many soldiers would rather be anywhere but the frontline. But in order to incur the expense and sacrifice of war, states must be able to count on a base of popular support or at least acquiescence.

I argue that neither condition has applied in Latin America (with some exceptions) during the past century. The absence of war over time creates conditions in which countries can avoid the type of behavior, such as arms races, that is correlated with conflict. The long peace of the twentieth century may be thus explained by the absence of revanchist myths[64] or long-standing cultures venerating interstate conflict. As discussed in Chapter 4, Latin American political iconography is surprisingly peaceful and lacks both bellicose themes and collective identifications associated with mass warfare. In order to explore this issue I concentrate on both military and civilian attitudes toward war.

---

64. On the impact of previous conflicts on subsequent relations, see Hensel, "One Thing Leads to Another," 287–97.

Focusing on attitudes toward war and expressions of nationalism is not to return to the cultural determinism dismissed earlier. The point here is not to argue that these are "peaceful" societies or that they shared too many similarities to fight. Rather, I want to emphasize that both elite and popular perspectives on intracontinental relations to a large extent did not include war as a feasible policy. This represents a critical shift from the nineteenth century, when state elites did treat war as a much more feasible outcome of disputes. Even then, however, with the exception of Paraguay during the War of the Triple Alliance and (possibly) Mexico during the civil wars of the 1860s, no government had to rely on the kind of mass mobilization associated with contemporary war.

The Military Mind

Attempting to define, much less understand, the mindset of a particular institution or its leading members is always difficult. For the inherently secretive military, it is even more so. Scholars with privileged access, such as Potash in Argentina, Nunn in Chile, and Stepan in Brazil, have done an admirable job of describing these attitudes.[65] To replicate such efforts with a sample of eleven countries across a century would be nearly impossible. Yet to answer the question of why so little war, we need to at least peer into the professional perspective of the respective militaries. Was there a proclivity for war that was frustrated by the lack of resources? Conversely, can we speak of an inherent abhorrence of interstate conflict that placed limits on the bellicosity of civilian authorities? What did the military think about the possibility of interstate war on the continent?

To answer this last question, I looked to the contents of the relevant countries' leading professional military journals. These often serve as the professional platforms for up-and-coming junior officers, as well as a bully pulpit for retired personnel. Since these are public documents, they will not reveal the secret life of the military, but they do serve as a rough indicator of the spirit of the institution—What themes does it discuss? What enemies does it worry about?

Given the size of the potential sample, I limited myself to an analysis of the article titles. I was able to find a significant number of title pages or

65. Potash, *The Army and Politics in Argentina, 1928–1945; The Army and Politics in Argentina, 1945–1962;* Nunn, *The Time of the Generals; Yesterday's Soldiers;* Stepan, *The Military in Politics.*

sumarios for ten of my eleven countries. For Brazil, I was able to locate 6,954 titles for an almost unbroken period from 1882 to 1996 and analyzed this group separately. The titles for the remaining nine countries totaled 16,139 in a variety of periods stretching from the late nineteenth century to the present day.[66]

Several trends are noteworthy. First, it does not appear that the respective militaries devote a great deal of attention to interstate war. Of the more than 2,500 articles in the Argentinean *Revista del Círculo Militar* examined, only 2 could be regarded as dealing with a strategic analysis of a future interregional war. Of the nine countries discussed here, Chile had the highest number, with 4 articles out of 2,790 studied. The pattern is consistent and remarkably similar across countries and over time. When speaking with one another through these journals, the military like to dwell on (a) technical issues (for example, ballistics, machinery); (b) organizational problems (for example, how to train noncommissioned officers, pension plans); (c) historical reenactments (for example, triumphs of San Martín); and (d) scholarly exercises (for example, thoughts on Napoleon). Beginning in the late 1950s and early 1960s we do see the appearance of discussions of domestic issues (the economy) and especially concerns with "national security" and the threat of global communism (Fig. 2.11a). The one topic that is rarely dealt with is explicit strategic discussions about the region and possible battles between neighboring countries.[67]

The more historically detailed Brazilian analysis provides an interesting progression (Fig. 2.11b). In the late nineteenth and early twentieth century, the military journals emphasize practical matters such as technical and organizational concerns. Historical pieces appear to be fairly common. Beginning in the 1930s, geopolitics becomes a popular topic (and would remain a

66. For a much more exhaustive use of similar sources and a more detailed analysis of the ideologies of contemporary militaries, see Nunn, *Time of the Generals.* My sample includes *Revista del Círculo Militar* (Argentina), *Revista Armas y Servicios del Ejército* (Chile), *Ejército y Fuerza Aerea Mexicana* (Mexico), *Revista de las Fuerzas Armadas* (Venezuela), *Gaceta Académica de la Academia Boliviana de Historia Militar* (Bolivia), *Revista del Ejército* (Colombia), *Revista de las Fuerzas Armadas Ecuatorianas* (Ecuador), *Revista Militar de las Fuerzas Armadas de la Nación* (Paraguay), *Gaceta Militar y Naval* (Uruguay), *Revista do Exercito Brasileiro, Revista Militar, Boletim Mensal do Estado Maior do Exército, Nação Armada, Revista do Clube Militar* (Brazil). The material available for Peru was limited, but came from the *Revista Militar del Perú.*

67. This does not necessarily contradict the work of Kelly and Child, in *Geopolitics of the Southern Cone and Antarctica,* who see a great deal of geopolitical thinking on the continent. This may go on, but it appears to take a very abstract form and does not seem to include "middle range" strategic planning.

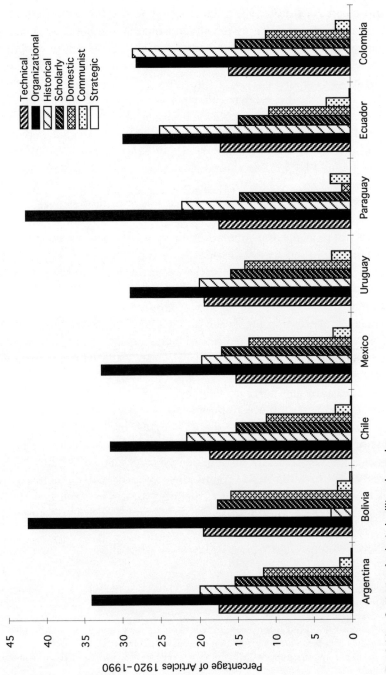

Fig. 2.11a Contents of selected military journals

significant component of the Brazilian military intellectual tradition). More interesting, beginning in the 1940s, the Brazilian military, and its continental counterparts, emphasize its internal roles, such as economic development and the defense of "national identity." The threat to national security—a term with increasingly ominous implications in the 1960s—was viewed as internal. This point is critical: *the enemy was within.* One could argue that such a perspective led to even more violence and bloodshed than if the militaries had concentrated on their international mission.[68] The link between a focus on internal threat and the existence of external peace is a tempting one and it would be possible to argue for causal orders flowing both ways. As far as this chapter is concerned, however, the main point is to note the relatively limited role international conflict plays in professional military discourse.

This is not to argue that standard military considerations never play an important role in internal discussions, that each military might not have prepared contingency plans for a variety of scenarios, or that the military has not considered in excruciating detail the logistical needs of such operations. Tensions have existed. In the 1970s, relations were particularly strained across several fronts. Perón thought war with Brazil likely[69] while Bolivia's Hugo Banzer, Chile's Augusto Pinochet, and Peru's Juan Velasco rattled sabers at one another. Not surprisingly, Chile's *Revista Militar y Naval* during this period did feature aggressive articles on possible conflicts with eastern and northern neighbors. It is important to note, however, that these tended to be exceptions and that interstate conflict was not part of the normal professional discourse.[70] An open, even if academic, discussion of such a contingency is not an accepted part of the public dialogue. Contrast this with the much more frank debate in North Atlantic Treaty Organization (NATO) militaries concerning the likelihood of a conflict with the Soviet Union and possible strategies to deal with the threat or with the again "open secret" of planning for the next Franco-German war after 1870.[71]

Different countries do express their own strategic interests in these maga-

---

68. Thus the argument for Spanish entry into NATO at a critical point in the democratization of that country.

69. *Foreign Broadcast Information Service,* LAT-96–207.

70. González, in "The Longer Peace in South America, 1935–1995," would even question the extent to which the militaries would be interested in fighting each other at all.

71. I make this comparison on the basis of my familiarity with such journals and conversations with military historians of these countries.

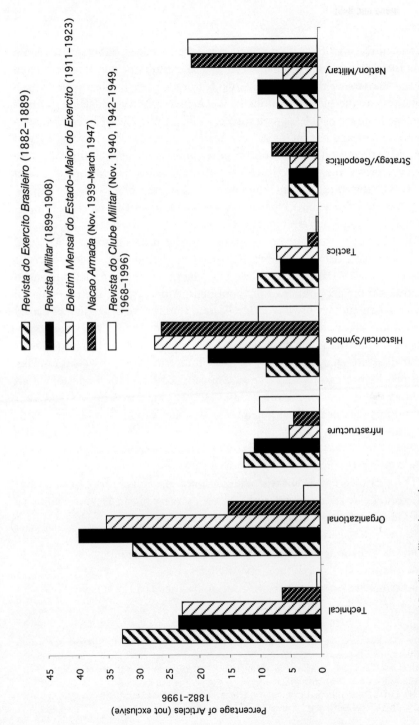

Fig. 2.11b Contents of Brazilian military journals

Legend:

Revista do Exercito Brasileiro (1882–1889)

Revista Militar (1899–1908)

Boletim Mensal do Estado-Maior do Exercito (1911–1923)

Nacao Armada (Nov. 1939–March 1947)

Revista do Clube Militar (Nov. 1940, 1942–1949, 1968–1996)

Categories: Technical, Organizational, Infrastructure, Historical/Symbols, Tactics, Strategy/Geopolitics, Nation/Military

Percentage of Articles (not exclusive) 1882–1996

zines, but the possibility of war is rarely acknowledged.[72] Argentina's main military journals, for example, were, are, and probably will remain fixated on the Malvinas/Falklands. They also feature articles on "los hielos continentales" or the glacier frontier between that country and Chile. Others discussed similar problems with the Beagle Channel. Their Chilean counterparts were fixated less on the Argentinean frontier than on the possibility of general "subversion," but in recent years, much greater attention has been paid to protecting Antarctic claims. Peruvians discuss historical consequences of the wars between them and Ecuador and Chile. Given the continuing territorial tensions, the Peruvians may have the most developed tradition of explicitly recognizing likely enemies and discussing relevant strategies. Ecuador focuses on its claims to the Amazonian territories and on fear of Peru. Uruguayans express some trepidation about being squeezed between the two giants on their borders. The Brazilians formulate advanced treatises on the geopolitics of the continent. Alone among their neighbors, the Brazilian military possess an intellectual tradition of discussing potential territorial expansion (usually regarding a link to the Pacific) and of geopolitical paranoia (stemming from Spanish/Portuguese colonial animosities).[73] What does not characterize any of these militaries, however, is an intellectual proclivity to go to war. It would appear that war is not considered an obvious viable option in strategic analysis. Again, this is not to deny that the military is concerned with neighbors and seeks to protect borders. Walter Little reports on various militaries' concerns with frontiers and frontier regions in the 1980s.[74] But none of these, with the exception of the Ecuador-Peru conflict, resulted in war.

This picture is consistent with the self-image provided through other military sources. A recent glossy publication by the Chilean Defense Ministry lists the following as "objectives of national defense":[75]

- Conserve the independence and sovereignty of the country.
- Maintain the territorial integrity of Chile.
- Contribute to preserving the institutional order and the state of law.
- Conserve and promote historical and cultural identity.

72. There are exceptions, of course. Chile, for example, offered the British communication facilities during the Malvinas/Falklands War and Brazil has explicitly stated its commitment to political stability in Paraguay and its willingness to intervene in order to preserve it.
73. Kelly, *Checkerboards and Shatterbelts,* 53–54, 84–134.
74. Little, "International Conflict in Latin America," 598 n. 22.
75. Ministerio de Defensa, *Libro de la Defensa Nacional,* 29.

- Create the conditions of external security necessary for the well-being of the nation.
- Contribute to the development of national power ("that which supports the capacity of the nation to express its will").
- Strengthen the citizens' commitment to defense.
- Support the international standing of Chile.
- Contribute to the maintenance and promotion of international peace and security in accord with the national interest.

Two points are worth noting from this list: first, the key role domestic issues play in defining the role of the armed forces; and second, the absence of bellicose sentiment. This is even clearer in a section devoted to war and crisis in which the discussion is kept on a purely abstract basis with no indication of where an external source of danger could or may originate. The section devoted to the rest of the continent emphasizes a system of "mutual confidence" by which the nations have institutionalized a process that is designed to lower perceived threats. In regard to neighboring countries, the document emphasizes Chile's defensive posture and the importance of recent steps toward integration. Even when referring to frontier zones with high economic potential, but low population density, the emphasis is on potential economic development and even peaceful integration of immigrant populations, not on the construction of a military wall.[76] This emphasis on "internal conquest" of peripheral zones runs throughout geopolitical discussions in the continent, as do concerns with "internal frontiers."

Again, the apparently nonbellicose professional military mind is an important, indeed vital, aspect of the explanation for the long peace. War was not featured on the strategic menu. It was not one of the first options discussed. It may even have been difficult to imagine as a policy outcome, and that conceptual impossibility may go far in explaining the long peace.[77]

76. Ministerio de Defensa, *Libro de la Defensa Nacional,* 126.
77. The reading of military experts supports the military's view of the situation. According to the Institute of International Strategic Studies, "The main challenge facing the security forces in the Caribbean and Latin America remains guerrilla groups, but with a less ideologically driven agenda and one more linked to organized crime and drug trafficking. Inter-state disputes remain few and are unlikely to provoke more than skirmishes over borders and illegal immigration" (IIS Studies Web site, http://www.isn.ethz.ch/iiss/mb10.htm). In a discussion of security in the Americas in a conference cosponsored by the chief of staff of the U.S. army, barely any mention is made of international conflict while internal policing is a constant theme (Mainwaring, "Security and Civil-Military Relations in the New World Disorder").

Conversely, the contemporary focus on internal threats is a reflection of a historical fear that the real threat to the safety of the state lies within its own frontiers. As many others have already pointed out, the Latin American military has always seen itself as especially qualified and required to defend the essence of the nation-state from any perceived threat, whether foreign or domestic.[78] The actual nature of that threat has always been ambiguous and flexible, but the role of the military as an internal police force has been a constant.

Public Nationalism

Whether democratic or authoritarian, regimes need some element of support before engaging in war. As important as military proclivities may be for determining the likelihood of conflict, popular attitudes may be just as critical. To what extent have the various populations of Latin America learned to hate their neighbors? To what extent are they prepared to kill them or die trying? Is there a public reservoir of bellicosity that regimes could tap to launch aggressive actions?

The first possible source for a systemic analysis of such attitudes would be public opinion polls. Unfortunately, there is little data on how citizens of each country feel about the others and nothing that uses the same method in various locations.[79] The very absence of such data would indicate that intracontinental affairs, friendly or otherwise, are not a significant factor in most domestic politics. When asked to name the most significant problem facing their respective countries, no Latin American population listed a foreign policy issue.[80] The similar absence of questions dealing with nationalism or patriotism may be equally indicative. One recent survey did ask respondents to name a country that they felt was their nation's best friend. While some popular responses were not surprising, the positive attitudes toward the United States were. More important was the almost total absence of other Latin American countries from the list.[81] In examining responses to questions about specific Latin American countries, we note that several of the expected hostile pairs actually do not seem to have a great

---

78. Loveman and Davies, *The Politics of Antipolitics;* Stepan, *Military in Politics;* Nunn, *Yesterday's Soldiers;* Potash, *Army and Politics, 1945–1962.*

79. This is based on an analysis of polls available through the Roper Archive and publications such as *Polling the Nations.*

80. Survey conducted by *Wall Street Journal* reported in *Polling the Nations,* no. 4698.

81. Survey conducted by *Latinobarometer* reported in *Polling the Nations,* no. 205.

deal of antipathy. A similar question asking for levels of trust as criteria for economic partners reveals the same pattern. Respondents in almost all the countries report positive feelings of trust in other Latin American countries in economic matters. (We unfortunately do not have a parallel set of responses to questions asking about enemies or distrust.) Another indication of popular opinion is the continentwide rejection of arms races. In 1998, two-thirds of those polled objected to the sale of high-tech weapons by the United States to any country in Latin America.[82] While this evidence is not a perfect indicator, it does not point to any strong popular antagonism or jingoism (exceptions will be noted later). If anything characterizes continental views it is mutual apathy.

In the absence of systematic public opinion data, I have used newspapers as reflectors of public moods. There are several obvious limits to such a strategy. First, newspapers reflect their own editorial policies much more than popular sentiment. Second, they are often more concerned with elite opinions than with the views of the masses. Third, they are often voices for the regime and may espouse a stronger patriotic line than might actually be felt by the majority. Nevertheless, they do serve as a mirror, albeit imperfect, for the nationalistic ethos of the relevant countries.[83]

The most significant finding culled from this reading of the newspapers is the general and almost universal absence of nationalist sentiment expressed in *statecentric terms*. That is, although there are some clear examples of competition between countries reflected in speeches, public attitudes, and festivities, these are not marked by the expression of nationalist hatred. The only exception I was able to locate was in the case of the Peruvian-Ecuador conflict (see below).[84] This is not to deny racist attitudes or unflattering characterizations of other nations. Almost all Latin American countries tell Argentinean jokes; and racist comments about Bolivians and Paraguayans abound in the Southern Cone. I would argue, however, that these rarely if ever take the form of "Bolivians must be eliminated" or "Kill Chileans before they kill you," and so on.

82. Survey conducted by *Wall Street Journal* reported in *Polling the Nations,* no. 6220.
83. I used the following: *La Prensa* (Buenos Aires), *O Estado de São Paulo* (São Paulo), *La Tribuna* (Asunción), *El Telégrafo* (Quito), *El Mercurio* (Santiago), *El Comercio* (Lima), *El Día* (Bogotá), *Marcha* (Montevideo), *Excelsior* (Mexico City). The choice was largely determined by the availability of newspaper archives. For each country, I selected a series of patriotic holidays during which one might expect the greatest public nationalistic sentiment. These were checked at five-year intervals beginning with the earliest available issue. I augmented these with coverage of moments of crisis in the history of the relevant countries.
84. We may also include the racist propaganda in Paraguay during the War of the Triple Alliance, but this seems to have had little contemporary relevance.

The analysis reveals several trends. First, there is a consistent mention of other Latin American countries as "sister republics" or use of similar language, indicating considerable diplomatic and interregime contact. The continent is seen as a larger community over and above the nation-state. One expression of this is sharing of heroes and the tradition of giving to other cities statues commemorating one hero or another. An important subelement is the use of Latin American republics as co-guarantors of treaties and deals on frontiers, and so on. There is often some resentment of this by the "losing" country (for example, Ecuador's complaints concerning the 1942 Rio Protocol), but there remains remarkable willingness to accept such meddling. Celebrations of pancontinental unity are particularly strong on days of independence or celebrations of founding fathers that often emphasize the commonalties of the countries established by them. These celebrations and conferences often include ex-enemies—for instance, Peru participates in Bolívarian festivities in Ecuador. As is the case with monuments described in Chapter 4, the major celebrations are of the independence wars, not of interstate conflicts.

Coverage of national feast day celebrations—even in the nineteenth and early twentieth centuries—is relatively limited: "These days are reduced to simple holidays, to mere days of rest. Today should be what the 14th of July is in France, or what the 2nd of May is in Spain. Sadly, it is only an official holiday and the people do not come together to celebrate it."[85] Another Brazilian journalist fifteen years later noted that at a time when European countries were evoking the grand figures of their past, "it is good to remember a few of ours."[86] The view of historical moments is also much more problematic. In 1887, a newspaper could make negative comparisons between Brazilian independence and that of the United States—to the effect that in the United States "liberty was planted with the blood of patriots," while in Brazil a monarchy was established.[87] This clearly reflects republican sentiment prior to the end of the monarchy. The key issue here is that a normally sacrosanct date would be problematized. Similarly, the celebration of the feats of Tiradentes in Brazil was abolished and reinstated depending on the extent to which such celebration fit with the political profile of the regime. Even when the moments to commemorate are not very distant, the celebration seems muted, as for the role of the Brazilian Expeditionary Force in World War II. Even in 1945, there appears to have been little effort to glorify this moment.

85. *O Estado de São Paulo*, September 7, 1899.
86. *O Estado de São Paulo*, September 7, 1914, 7.
87. *O Estado de São Paulo*, April 21, 1887, 1–2.

Those celebrations that do exist often do not involve the masses but are seen as moments when the urban elite could demonstrate their patriotism. One could also discern popular resentment of forced military service or patriotic propaganda: "we are fed-up [hartos] with being told that one has to serve the fatherland, of heroism, of the national colors. . . . It is all nonsense."[88]

Victory in wars is not always celebrated. In Brazil and Argentina, for example, there is a remarkable silence about the Triple Alliance. One newspaper says: "[The war] interrupted once again the regular march of national progress."[89] In neither country are the dates of exceptional battles celebrated. Paraguay, however, devotes considerable attention to "the National Epic" and to López, particularly after the Chaco wars. At that time, the Panteón de Héroes becomes the site for celebrations of López's heroism, of patriotism, and of honoring the sacrifices of "los caídos." Yet even in Paraguay, ex-enemies can establish good relationships. A writer reporting on a Paraguayan independence celebration noted a cocktail party held at the Brazilian embassy in Asunción attended by members of the government and armed forces, while Bolivia held a similar feast to celebrate the end of the Chaco War.[90]

In general, foreign policy is absent as a central political issue. It is common to read speeches given at major patriotic dates that make no references to external affairs or do so in the most general manner. Potential conflicts are generally muted. At least from the Colombian side, for example, the frontier differences with Venezuela are not phrased in particularly nationalistic ways. Some conflicts do receive attention. For example, we see evidence of tensions between Argentina and Chile going back to the beginning of the twentieth century. There is considerable discussion of Patagonia, but rhetoric is largely about the Beagle Channel and *hielos continentales*. The 1900s and 1970s represent the heights of this tension. Yet neither country seems to engage in demonization of the other, and that references are made to Chile and Argentina and rarely to *los chilenos* or *los argentinos*. One reads some hyperbolic language, for example, "La cesión de las islas australes a Chile tendrá el significado de una deslealtad para la nación argentina, de una traición a su historia."[91] The conflict over the Beagle Channel was particularly problematic and required the intervention of the Vatican. In the Chilean press, there is a regular discussion of the central importance of the Beagle Channel and its key role in the Antarctic claim. There is also conflict

88. *Marcha,* August 23, 1940, 5.
89. *O Estado de São Paulo,* September 7, 1913, 7.
90. *La Tribuna,* May 16, 1945, 2; and June 13, 1945, 2.
91. Almirante Rojas of Argentina, *La Prensa,* January 4, 1984, 3.

over the "Laguna del Desierto." There is a well-documented record of the national dementia that accompanied the announcement that Argentine forces had occupied the Malvinas/Falklands. This was followed by exhibitions of Anglophobia in a country that had previously prided itself on its "Englishness." Even national icons and monuments were not spared. Yet despite the defeat and the horrible cost paid by Argentina, popular hatred of things British dissipated almost immediately after the end of hostilities and were largely transferred to the military, who had created the absurd situation in the first place.[92]

The triangle of Chile, Peru, and Bolivia has had moments of tension, for example, in the mid-1920s. The language here is often about the injustice of the Chilean conquest—Peru resenting the loss of Tacna (later recovered) and Arica, Bolivia the loss of access to the sea. In the late 1970s, there was some escalation of the "cold war" between Peru and Chile. In part this was a reflection of Peruvian military's use of the anniversary for a buildup of armed forces and fears on the part of the Chileans that Velasco would use the anniversary to strengthen his regime. Ambassadors were sent home, and Peru executed a noncommissioned officer accused of treason.[93] Bolivia and Peru also remained tense during this period. Throughout the twentieth century, Bolivia has expressed continued frustration with the absence of an outlet to the sea, which is established as the "principal objective of the nation."[94] In the 1970s, there was a heightening of popular interest and public protest, including a "march to the sea" by various groups of Bolivian women.

In terms of nationalist liturgy (see Chapter 4), Chile actively celebrates the battle of Yungay, which caused the defeat of the Peruvian-Bolivian Confederation in 1839. The central symbol here is the monument to the Roto Chileno, one of the very few monuments that celebrates the common soldier's bravery—and of course martyrdom. There is regular concern in Chile about Peruvian arms buildups, specifically with Peru's greater population and ability to recruit a much larger army.[95] But there is also awareness of the cost of war and an often expressed hope that it will not occur again.[96]

---

92. The absence of such hatred took surprising forms. While living in Buenos Aires I never felt any tension when people on the street or bus would overhear my family speaking English. In a kiosk I bought some toy soldiers for my son that not only had British uniforms, but also included a Union Jack. When my son played with these in a nearby sandbox, no children commented on the obvious nationality of the soldiers, but only asked to be included in the game.

93. *El Mercurio,* January 20, 1979, 1.

94. President Paz Estensoro, *El Comercio,* August 7, 1963, 7.

95. *El Mercurio,* January 21, 1915, 3.

96. *El Mercurio,* September 20, 1929, 3.

There is also an interesting mutual recognition of each other's heroes. The Chilean media, for example, constantly praise the Peruvian hero Grau, as seen in the general celebration of Arturo Prat's martyrdom at Iquique, the central symbol in the commemoration of the War of the Pacific. Two things are of interest here: the emphasis on martyrdom and the willingness to recognize the heroism of the other side.[97] For Peru, the martyrs are Grau and Bolognesi, whose line "tengo deberes sagrados y los cumplire hasta quemar el último cartucho" is taught to every Peruvian schoolchild.

In the Peru-Ecuador conflict we do see perhaps the most extensive and intensive case of popular participation. For February 1995, for example, there are reports in all the continental newspapers of "bellicose fervor" and popular demonstrations. Even the relatively limited conflict of 1995 is portrayed as an apocalyptic battle. Yet at least on the Ecuadorian side (prior to 1941), one could find expressions of hope that an agreement could be found in the border dispute.[98] By 1940, one can detect a clearer martial air and claims that national territory will be defended, but still without the kind of racial language often seen in other conflicts. Yet consistent mention is made of the fact that Ecuador and Peru share so much "history and blood."[99] Even when calling for a buildup of the army in response to the Peruvian crisis, the emphasis is on using the military to support development on the frontier rather than on eliminating the enemy. The emphasis in anniversary speeches is not on martial posturing, but on the need to pursue diplomatic efforts. Only a few years after the struggle, the Peruvian president could visit the frontier and be applauded by Ecuadorian citizens.[100]

Nevertheless, this is one of the few examples where the discussion of war brings in "el pueblo" and there is talk of a nation at arms.[101] In the 1930s, wealthy citizens in Ecuador offered jewels to pay for arms with which to defend their territory.[102] July 1941 saw student demonstrations in both capitals in support of war and the Ecuadorian president announced that "in each Ecuadorian there is a soldier, a hero."[103] Anniversaries of the Rio Protocol (generally unfavorable to Ecuador and seen as "atrociously mutilating national territory") are celebrated with popular demonstrations, including

97. "[L]as glorias de Iquique, que cubrieron por igual a peruanos y chilenos, en aquel entonces en lucha fratricida," *El Mercurio,* May 21, 1969, 2.

98. President Isidro Ayora, *El Telégrafo,* August 11, 1930, 3.

99. *El Telégrafo,* August 10, 1940, 15; August 11, 8–10.

100. *El Tiempo,* December 18, 1944.

101. *El Telégrafo,* January 29, 1945, 1.

102. *El Comercio,* June 8, 1938, 9.

103. *El Comercio,* July 8, 1941, 3.

student marches in Quito.[104] Critiques of the military junta in the 1960s and 1970s were often based on the supposed cost of military governments to the chances that Ecuador could reclaim lost territory.[105] We also find an outstanding and perhaps unique use of chauvinist pejorative, especially on the Peruvian side. Popular newspapers in Peru *(El Chivo, Aja!)* refer to Ecuadorians as "monos" and articles about Ecuador feature photographs of gorillas and other apes.[106]

What do these press accounts tell us about war in Latin America? In general when wars are celebrated, the liturgy is the same. First, the enemy had great superiority in numbers[107] and the national army was a clear underdog. Second, national forces had courage, honor, dignity, and so on (the enemy, however, is not demonized and similar characteristics may be found in them). But because of the imbalance in resources, the national forces were not able to triumph, producing many martyrs. Even for wars that are won, martyrs are celebrated; when emotional appeals are made it is often to express sadness at the loss of these heroes. I found no celebration of the "beauty of war," and overall, the population is not indoctrinated in a cult of war. Certainly we see nothing like the racialist culture one can observe in almost every major European and North American struggle from the nineteenth century on.

Defining the Enemy

In Chapter 4, I argue that most Latin American countries have lacked the identification of an external enemy that encourages the development and solidification of a national identity. As far as state elites are concerned, the greatest threat to their power has not come from a competing elite across a border, but from the masses below. In some ways the internal-war orientation of the military is partly a product of this ethnic division. The enemy of "la patria" was perceived not as the nation next door, but as those in the population who threatened the social and economic status quo. This perception is particularly relevant in countries with significant Indian populations.

104. *El Telégrafo,* January 30, 1945, 3; January 29, 1950, 1.
105. *El Telégrafo,* December 17, 1965.
106. The only other blatantly racist reference I have seen comes from the Paraguayan assault on Brazilian soldiers during the War of the Triple Alliance. Newspapers and broadsides consistently emphasized black soldiers, using a variety of insults (Williams, *Rise and Fall*).
107. This is particularly evident in comparisons of Peruvian and Chilean accounts of the War of the Pacific, as both sides claim to have had old, decrepit ships, whereas the enemy was armed with modern dreadnoughts.

It is important to recall that the defining "ethnic war" of the continent occurred prior to state formation. The conquest and its results left deeper divisions within countries than could ever develop between them. Certainly in the case of Guatemala and perhaps in Peru, ideological and racial/class threats were clearly perceived as correlated. The external peace was therefore bought with internal hatred and divisions. Simply put, each nation's military remained too busy killing its own peasants to bother with someone else's. (Conversely, the absence of wars may have also retarded national integration.)

The absence of an elaborate discourse of international hatreds has its inverse counterpart in the history of domestic or internal wars. Examples include the Rosista literal call for death to the *unitarios;* the depth of hatred in Mexico during the various Liberal-Conservative civil wars, culminating in the harsh policies of the French War; the spectacular violence of the Mexican Revolution; the level of animosity in the fight over clericalism in Chile; and, perhaps most extreme, the brutality of la Violencia in Colombia. In each instance, the relevant publics and armies were taught to hate their opponents and to see them as threats to a national destiny. In contemporary Latin America, the violence inflicted upon the victims of the dirty wars cannot be explained by a simple overrepresentation of psychopaths, but must take into account an atmosphere of terror and Manichean ideology. When we compare tracts associated with each of these struggles with the level of discourse aimed at international enemies, the direction of hatred in the continent becomes patently clear.

In summary, whether analyzed from the viewpoint of the military professionals or the general populace we see little of the culturalist basis for a creed of war. Latin American societies have not been trained to fight one another and to see in such war the ultimate expression of their patriotism. We now turn to the institutional capacity of states to fight wars.

Material Limits

In explaining the Latin American peace, we need to question the assumption that all states are capable of war. Singer and Small have explored the importance of "military capability" and found a strong correlation between political and economic power, and bellicose behavior.[108] War requires basic

108. Singer and Small, *Resort to Arms.*

organizational competence and access to resources that only certain states have. From this point of view, Latin America has been peaceful because the states in the region never developed the political capacity to have prolonged wars. No states, no wars.

The degree of internal violence that continues to dominate Latin America is both a cause and an indication of the relative inability of these states to fight one another. Again, some of this reflects the definition of the internal enemy alluded to earlier. But I would also argue that the search for an internal threat had something to do with the military's need to define a mission it could handle. Whether one speaks of race warfare in Guatemala or the disappearances of Argentina, the organizational and logistical demands placed on the respective militaries pale in comparison with what would have been required by external war. Faced with material constraints and already oriented toward suspecting the mass of the population, the military defined a mission it felt comfortable with and, equally important, felt that it could meet.

Given that the states had even less military capacity in the nineteenth century, how do we explain the frequency of war during that period? What has changed is the form of warfare. The kind of international conflict in which the countries engaged during most of that century did not require great logistical sophistication. Even the limited operations involved in the "great" wars of the 1860s to 1880s severely taxed the relevant governments. By the twentieth century, however, limited international struggles have become much more difficult to manage. The "start-up" costs of war have increased dramatically, while the capacity of these states to carry them has not. Such a perspective helps explain why the two poorest countries on the continent—Paraguay and Bolivia—fought the longest war in the twentieth century. In many ways, the Chaco was fought as a nineteenth-century struggle and did not include the expensive and complicated machinery of modern war. The other major conflict, between Peru and Ecuador, has been fought with modern equipment. One of the consequences of this, however, is that the actual disputes have been extremely short, in part because the military capacities of the belligerents were rapidly exhausted

Paying for War

We may begin with a rough measure of state capacity to engage in war, already discussed in the previous chapter. Despite Latin American states' reputation for dominating economies, they have *not* taxed their populations at levels approaching those of western Europe and the United States. If we con-

sider that the ability to tax is also representative of a state's capacity to penetrate and impose its will on a society, the likelihood of a Latin American state
being able to impose draconian measures is severely limited (see Chapter 3).
Contemporary examples of interstate war such as the Falklands/Malvinas
War and the Ecuador-Peru border conflict indicate that this is still the case.

Since they have limited access to fiscal revenues, Latin American countries
can spend much less on creating the type of military apparatus necessary for
contemporary warfare. Certainly in comparison with other regions, the Latin
American countries have spent much smaller amounts by any measure. Ex-
pressing budgets as percentages of gross national product (GNP) or central
government expenditure (CGE) serves to control for the massive differences
in resources available in population or capital. The propensity to allocate
moneys to the military is relatively low in Latin America even if we control
for the availability of resources. The gulf between the continent and other
global regions is more extreme when viewed as absolute amounts or on a per
capita basis. Here, the combinations of smaller economies and fewer military
concerns produce relatively minuscule military budgets (Fig. 2.12).

The pattern during the past twenty years shows remarkable stability in
terms of relative importance of the military.[109] We see some fluctuations in
the military budgets as a percentage of government expenditures, but this is
extremely sensitive to policy regimes, which increase or decrease overall
public spending. The biggest change seems to be the decline in overall military expenditures over the past few years, with an ominous rise in the mid-
1990s (Fig. 2.13). While the correlation between form of regime and military expenditure is difficult to measure exactly (but military governments
appear to favor their own sectors), we have seen an apparent decline in the
relative attention paid to the military after the democratic wave of the
1980s.[110] Argentina may be the most extreme case, with a 30 percent decline
in expenditures over the decade and an even more drastic reduction in the
number of soldiers, 60 percent. Even where civilians have been constrained
by an institutionalized military "veto" such as in Chile, expenditures appear
to have declined through the 1990s as a percentage of the GNP and government budgets, although they have increased in absolute terms.[111]

109. There was a significant increase in the 1960s and 1970s along with increased emphasis on high technology weapons and the creation of arms manufacturing industries in the
Southern Cone (Little, "International Conflict in Latin America," 598).

110. For an analysis of geographical and historical variance, see Looney and Fredericksen,
"The Effect of Declining Military Influence on Defense Budgets in Latin America."

111. Ministerio de Defensa, *Libro de la Defensa Nacional de Chile,* 194–96.

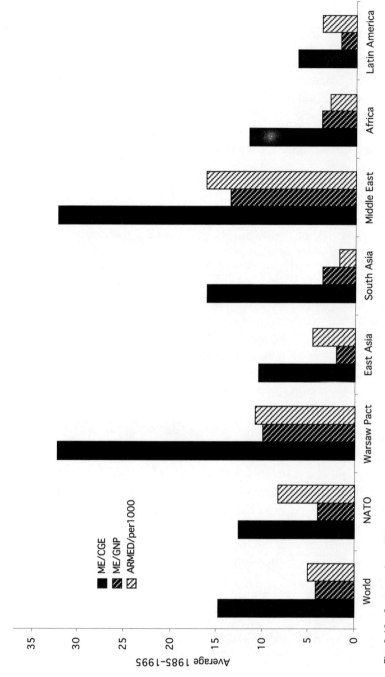

Fig. 2.12 Comparative military capacity (source: Stockholm International Peace Research Institute)

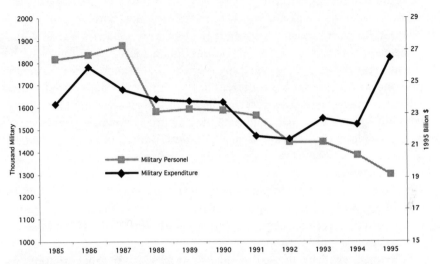

Fig. 2.13 Latin American military capacity (source: Stockholm International Peace
Research Institute)

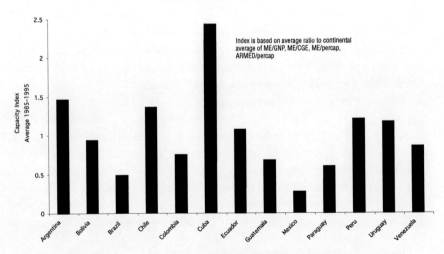

Fig. 2.14 National military capacity (source: Stockholm International Peace
Research Institute)

There is some logic to the geographical distribution of defense expenditures. The Southern Cone, which has seen the most intense geopolitical rivalries, has spent more money on their respective militaries—at least as a percentage of their total economic output (Fig. 2.14).

Given the comparatively small size of the relevant economies, the amount of moneys available for armed forces has remained severely limited. These militaries often spent close to three-fourths of their budgets on current and pensioned personnel, further limiting their ability to purchase sophisticated military gadgets.[112] Publications such as Jane's *Annuals* provide detailed description of the weaponry and technology available to the Latin American militaries; evidently, they are incapable of fighting for prolonged periods in any broad front.[113] Simply put, wars cost money, and the Latin American militaries have not had access to the massive infusion of resources required to equip themselves for anything but the most limited border clashes or police actions (Table 2.3).

The forces available to use this equipment present a parallel situation. As discussed in Chapter 5, Latin America has traditionally employed a much smaller percentage of its population in its military. Even Chile in the 1980s, with its armed forces enjoying full support of the government, with a significant historical adversary (Peru), and with a long tradition of military prowess, had an army of only fifty-seven thousand—hardly enough to mount a limited defense of the national territory. No matter the sophistication of equipment, war requires men (the gender specificity is especially relevant for Latin America) to physically move into and hold territory. The Latin American militaries simply do not have the human resources to fulfill even the most basic missions. Perhaps equally important, relatively small parts of the population have been exposed to a martial culture and subsequently there may be less inherent support for such adventures. In personnel and hardware, again there is a geographical concentration of resources. Brazil clearly has the largest armed forces, but given the discrepancy in size, it appears to have devoted relatively less attention to military growth. Argentina, Chile, and Peru appear to have the most developed military capacity, which may be explained either by the recent history of military involvement or by the geopolitical tensions between these countries and their neighbors.

The most important finding here is that these relatively small amounts of

112. Dietz and Schmitt, "Militarization in Latin America."
113. This situation was recognized even in the midst of the recent "war scare" among observers of Latin American relations (Dietz and Schmitt, "Militarization in Latin America," 48).

Table 2.3 Military capacity in Latin America, 1995

	Active Armed Forces (000)	Tanks	Combat Helicopters	Destroyers	Submarines	Fighters	Bombers
Argentina	36	460	41	6	4	100	6
Bolivia	25	36	18	0	0	22	0
Brazil	195	394	72	5	7	85	0
Chile	52	200	54	4	4	67	0
Colombia	121	12	0	0	4	27	0
Ecuador	50	153	54	0	2	37	3
Peru	85	410	59	1	8	67	19
Venezuela	34	261	20	0	2	62	0

SOURCE: Jane's Information Group, *Jane's Sentinel* (1996)

resources translate into severely constrained military capacity.[114] Even for the countries with the most developed military, both the numbers and quality of materiel would make prolonged warfare difficult if not impossible. The composition of the military hardware indicates that it tends to be of less than mint vintage with severely limited operational ranges. Without exception, for example, the navies are designed primarily to guard the coast.[115] Moreover, with few exceptions, no country could afford the typical attrition one might expect in a naval or air battle.

This situation, however, may be shifting. While the region remains one of the smallest arms markets, spending rose in 1996 to $1.6 billion, its highest level since 1991.[116] Through a major trade development, U.S. arms-sales policy has changed, allowing U.S. companies to sell major conventional weapon systems to the region. Other competitors are also moving into the market. For example, Peru and Colombia have placed orders for combat aircraft and helicopters from Belarus and Russia.[117] Pressures to use the military for new tasks such as drug enforcement may have the unforeseen effect of creating arms races, for example, between a Chile alarmed by its neighbors' growth and a Peru partly financed by U.S. Drug Enforcement Agency money. A significant increase in the logistical and institutional capacity of the military unaccompanied by a clear delineation of a mission could produce a functional need to define potential conflicts outside the borders and challenge the long peace. The great concern that continental neighbors have expressed about "Plan Colombia" is noteworthy.

Exceptions

In the Central America of the past three decades, we have seen a militarization of society and an often violent intrusion of the state into everyday life. I would argue, however, that these cases represent important deviations from the western European norm. Perhaps most important is the role played by the United States as financier and organizer of last resort. I have not been able to locate evidence on the extent to which the Salvadoran or Guatemalan upper classes, for example, autofinanced the protection of their position—aside from the employment of private gangs. Moreover, the wars did

---

114. Jane's Information Group, *Jane's Sentinel, South America 1998.*
115. Kelly, *Checkerboards and Shatterbelts,* 29.
116. See discussion of U.S. policy in the *New York Times,* July 21, 1996, 3.
117. International Institute of Strategic Studies Web site, http://www.isn.ethz.ch/iiss/mb10.htm.

little to unify their countries, as discussed earlier. Instead of their obscuring internal divisions through the demonization of an enemy, they worsened these. Finally, they certainly did not contribute to the economic well-being of the governments or their societies as a whole. As in the other cases, some argument might be made that they did in fact help establish the domination of centralized political authority, but even that may be debatable.

Perhaps the most interesting exception to the overall trend is contemporary Cuba, which has twice been able to operate in a strategic theater thousands of miles from its home base and has deployed significant numbers of personnel and used large amounts of sophisticated equipment. But Cuba is precisely the exception that proves the rule, as it has achieved a permanent mobilization of society that is alien to the Latin American political tradition. This pattern may offer the best clue for explaining the relative peace on the continent. Total wars require mobilization and this in turn requires some degree of integration and even inclusion.

Contemporary Cuba also differs from the other Latin American countries in having developed a conflictive international discourse. One could argue that the conflict with the United States is at the very heart of the political project of the Cuban Revolution. As has become increasingly apparent in the 1990s, the "permanent state of war" under which Cuba lives may also be critical to the preservation of state power, to the centralization of its authority, and to its ability to mobilize the population. None of this necessarily implies democratic participation, but it does involve the creation of equal societies not yet seen anywhere on the continent.

Conclusions

What are the lessons offered by the Latin American cases? I would argue that it is the absence of a consistent socially created hatred—whether inside the military or as an element of civilian culture—and the limited capacity of the states that best explains the long peace. These are not societies taught to go to war, nor those in which extreme efforts have been made to facilitate military activity. They have not been taught to hate or given the capacity to destroy. We return again to the importance of distinguishing between a psychological predisposition to violence and the form of political organization that shapes and directs this violence.

Precisely because of the long peace, by early in the twentieth century, war was no longer a part of the political vocabulary of either the populations or their respective governments. In such an atmosphere, the kind of jingoistic mobilization and militarization required by total war would be almost impossible.[118] Latin American states and their populations do not appear to have had the historically forged institutional or political appetite for the type of organizational insanity of modern war. The violence that many of these countries have experienced internally would indicate that it is not a generic cultural characteristic that helps explain the Latin American peace, but the very concrete manifestations of cultural and fiscal preparations for war.

Limited administrative and political capacities also restrain Latin American states from waging war. Given their resource and personnel endowments, Latin American countries have not been able to pursue total-war strategies. This last point may be specifically worth noting, as it would suggest that the benefits of modern states may have even more severe costs than had previously been considered.

The particular forms of military conflict seen on the continent may be especially relevant in the contemporary world, where wars increasingly involve limited conflicts between nonstate actors. The origins and results of these may be quite different from those of our traditional notion of war and will require the adoption of a new perspective. More specifically, the relationship between political authority as traditionally embodied in states and organized violence may need to be redefined as the rest of the world comes closer to a Latin American pattern.

118. Note, for example, that despite the early euphoria that accompanied the Argentinean invasion of the Falklands/Malvinas, the population soon tired of the affair and accepted defeat with remarkable ease.

3
Making the State

The destructive capacity of war is self-evident. Less so is the manner in which war, or more accurately, the process of going to war, can be constructive. War is rejuvenating. The demands of war create opportunities for innovation and adaptation. Wars help build the institutional basis of modern states by requiring a degree of organization and efficiency that only new political structures could provide; they are the great stimulus for state building.[1] States, in a sense, are by-products of rulers' efforts to acquire the means of war; war is inherently an organizing phenomenon from which the state derives its administrative machinery. According to Hintze,

1. Huntington, *Political Order in Changing Societies.*

all state organization is principally military in nature. The shape and size of the state may even be seen as deriving from the managerial potential and limits of military technology.[2] So, for example, the advance of bureaucratic forms may be in part a result of increasing demands for administrative efficiency generated by the needs of growing armed forces and the escalating costs of waging war.[3]

The notion that war supports the institutional development of the state is widely accepted in political sociology.[4] This is not a recent discovery, but reflects the importance assigned to war by Weber and Hintze.[5] Wars help build the institutional basis of the modern state by requiring a degree of organization and efficiency that only new political structures could provide. Charles Tilly has best summarized this process with his statement "States make wars and wars make states."

This at least is the scholarly consensus on the European experience. On that continent, wars served as a crucial causal mechanism behind the growth of the state. The rise of the modern European state may be traced to the military revolution of the sixteenth and seventeenth centuries.[6] During this period, three critical organizational developments changed the nature of military struggle: control over the means of violence shifted from private to public control; the size of armies increased dramatically; and their composition became less varied and more based on a specific national identity.[7]

War made the territorial consolidation of a state more feasible and more imperative. Only those states that could wield great armies *and* guarantee control over their own territories could play the great game. Only those

---

2. Bean, "War and the Birth of the Nation State."
3. M. S. Anderson, *War and Society in Europe.*
4. Andreski, *Military Organization and Society;* Finer, "State and Nation Building in Europe"; Tilly, "Reflections"; Downing, *The Military Revolution and Political Change;* Porter, *War and the Rise of the State;* Ertman, *Birth of the Leviathan.*
5. Weber, *General Economic History;* Hintze, "Military Organization."
6. Outside Europe, the American Civil War both provided the major impetus for state expansion and allowed the industrial North to reshape the antebellum agenda (Bensel, *Yankee Leviathan*). Karsten describes the links between the rationalization of the armed services in the United States and similar organized efforts in other government sectors ("Militarization and Rationalization"). Bendix suggests that the effective rule of early Japanese shogunates may originate in the aristocracy's military experience (*Kings or People*).
7. Finer, "State and Nation Building in Europe"; Porter, *War and the Rise of the State;* Roberts, *Essays in Swedish History;* Parker, *Military Revolution;* Duffy, introduction to Duffy, *Military Revolution and the State;* Ralston, *Importing the European Army;* Kaiser, *Politics and War.*

states able to impose that central control could survive the military revolution. Countries unable to do so—Poland being one example—disappeared. The decline in the number of European states after the fifteenth century (from fifteen hundred to twenty-five by 1900) is an obvious indicator of the centralization of power wrought by military conflict. Wars pushed power toward the center.[8] War provided both the incentive *and* the means with which the central power was able to dominate. Peter Paret explains that "military force performed the essential task of defeating particularistic rivals to the crown, lending authority to the expanding process of government."[9] Whether in the France of Louis XIII, seventeenth-century Prussia, or Restoration England, violence was used to impose the rule of the center. The means for this violence were provided by war.

The key to the relationship between war and state making in western Europe is what Finer calls the "extraction-coercion" cycle.[10] We begin with the obvious fact that wars require capital: by the sixteenth century, combat became so expensive that the mobilization of an entire country was required. Professional armies clearly outperformed any rivals, but these needed "ample and continuous amounts of money."[11] These changes causally linked military and political development. On the one hand, states penetrated their societies in increasingly complex forms in order to obtain resources. The organizational innovations that occurred during wartime did not disappear with peace, but often left an infrastructural residue that Ardant calls the "physiology" of the state.[12] On the other hand, the new form of the post-Westphalian state was particularly well suited to the organizational task of managing this penetration and channeling the resources thus obtained into "productive" violence directed at some external enemy. Thus, wars both built and were an expression of political power.

Taxation is the best measure of effective political authority and institutional development, both representing and augmenting the strength of the state as measured by the capacity to enforce centralized rule on a territory and its population.[13] Taxes partly determine the very size of states' institutions and shape relationships between these and society; they help mold the

---

8. Howard, *Causes of War.*
9. *Understanding War,* 41.
10. Finer, "State and Nation Building in Europe."
11. Howard, *War in European History,* 37.
12. Ardant, "Financial Policy and Economic Infrastructure."
13. Peacock and Wiseman, *The Growth of Public Expenditure in the U.K.;* Organski and Kugler, *The War Ledger.*

eventual form of the state.[14] War is widely perceived as increasing the capacity of a state to tax its population.[15] Combat simultaneously generates greater need for resources and temporary declines in the state's social constraints; it also provides a focus around which the state's organizational capacity may improve. Finally, armies raised for war might also serve as a means with which to collect resources.

The evidence for the positive link between war and the rise of taxes in early modern Europe is exhaustive.[16] The pattern is also evident in the United States.[17] In all these cases, not only does state revenue increase after war; the structure of taxation also changes. For example, wars led both the British state in the eighteenth century and the American in the nineteenth and twentieth to increase both the amount of revenue (which never returned to prebellic levels) and the relative importance of domestic and direct taxes (Fig. 3.1). Military conflicts allow—and force—the state to depend less on the administratively simple, but inelastic, custom taxes and to rely on the more politically challenging, but potentially more lucrative, domestic sources of revenue. The greater bureaucratic complexity required is at the heart of the institutional legacy of war.

Yet how automatic is the relationship between war and increased state strength? Appreciation of historical specificity and structural conditions is vital for the production of truly generalizable models of state development. Only some wars built states, only some states were built by wars. The European experience indicates that warfare in and of itself does not necessarily lead to state making. Until the sixteenth century, several centuries of prior warfare had not produced states in Europe. Rather, as Tilly has emphasized, particular circumstances found in parts of Europe between 1600 and 1800 promoted conflict-led state development.[18]

14. Tilly, "Reflections on the History of European State-Making"; and Ardant, "Financial Policy and Economic Infrastructure"; Schumpeter, "The Crisis of the Tax State"; Gallo, *Taxes and State Power;* von Stein, "On Taxation"; Levi, *Of Rule and Revenue.*

15. Peacock and Wiseman, *Growth of Public Expenditure;* Mann, *Sources of Social Power,* vols. 1 and 2; *States, War, and Capitalism;* Tilly, *Coercion, Capital, and European States;* Rasler and Thompson, *War and Statemaking;* J. Campbell, "The State and Fiscal Sociology."

16. Ames and Rapp, "The Birth and Death of Taxes"; Mathias and O'Brien, "Taxation in Britain and France"; Stone, *An Imperial State at War;* Brewer, *The Sinews of Power;* Aftalion, "Le financement des guerres."

17. Bensel, *Yankee Leviathan;* Skowronek, *Building a New American State;* David and Legler, "Government in the American Economy"; Hooks and McLauchlan, "The Institutional Foundation of Warmaking."

18. Tilly, *Coercion, Capital, and European States.*

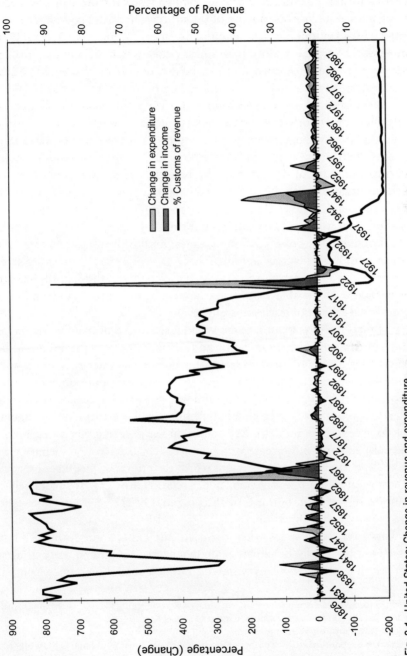

Fig. 3.1 United States: Change in revenue and expenditure

To an extent, this transformation remains a historical black box. We possess myriad references to the rise of the modern state and countless monographic descriptions of the specific historical sequences. Yet political sociology has generally failed to produce a coherent model of how violence was transformed into order. Sociological and comparative accounts of the relationship between war and state building have also not sufficiently emphasized historical order in their analysis. There is a causal ambiguity in Tilly's famous aphorism: Which came first, states or wars?[19]

I argue in this chapter that wars in and of themselves do not make anything. Rather, they merely provide a *potential* stimulus for state growth. Wars can only make states if they are preceded by at least a modicum of political organization. Without institutional cohesion, wars will make for chaos and defeat. Wars only provide an opportunity for those political organizations that are able to capitalize on them; they cannot create institutions out of thin air. The consolidation of central authority and the creation of a modicum of a bureaucracy appear to have preceded the state-making stage of war in England, France, and Prussia. The venality of the Spanish bureaucracy and the financial leakage of tax farming in a variety of other countries represented critical obstacles to state development.

It is vital to fully appreciate the social resistance that may be offered to state penetration. The combination of coercion and capital symbolized by the military draft and direct taxation, the defining characteristics of a war-made modern state according to Tilly,[20] does not come about simply because a bureaucratic apparatus is in place and wishes it so. The capacity of a state to extract resources will be closely linked to the willingness of the population to accept these burdens. Reluctance on the part of either an economic oligarchy to part with its cash or a populace to move closer to penury may make expansion of taxes simply not worth the effort.[21] Thus, state capacity is not an absolute phenomenon, but a relational one. It is not merely a question of strength, but also of the potential of the relevant societies to resist (or welcome) intrusion.

Wars only make states when there already exists some form of union between a politically or militarily dominant institution and a social class that sees it as the best means with which to defend and reproduce its privi-

---

19. Tallett, in *War and Society in Early Modern Europe* (citing I. A. A. Thompson's work on Spain), calls war less a stimulant than a test of state strength.

20. Tilly, *European Revolutions*, 32.

21. On the political costs of pushing too far, a wonderful recent addition is Markoff, *The Abolition of Feudalism*.

lege. That is, following Perry Anderson, there has to be a prior agreement that the state will be responsible for collecting and disposing of social surplus.[22] European cases demonstrate that the fragmentation of sovereignty, be it through the persistence of local autonomies (Spain), powerful but divided aristocracies (Poland), or direct external control (the Balkans), can and does prevent the solidification of states even when they are surrounded by conflict. In contrast, more successful war-making states established a coalition between central authority and potential aristocratic challengers either through alliance (England) or through coercion (France, Prussia).[23]

Following the methodological logic of the counterfactual, the failure of Latin American wars to generate similar state-building forces as seen in Europe after the seventeenth century can serve to improve our understanding of the relationship between conflict and institutional development. The findings from this exercise could then be used to explain both geographic and temporal variation outside of Latin America. Not only do these cases expand the relevant sample; they also allow us to discover whether the specific postcolonial conditions under which these states initially developed helped determine their further evolution. In this way at least, the Latin American experience may be much more relevant for contemporary analysis than western Europe in the early modern era.

In this chapter I analyze the contribution of war to the process of centralization and empowerment of the nineteenth-century Latin American state. I identify the critical elements that transform (or fail to transform) the anarchy of war into the imposition of order through monopolized violence and argue that war in Latin America was never able to break the disastrous equilibrium that existed between various powers and social interests. We must trace successful state developments not to war in itself, but to the presence of a united elite, willing—or forced to—accept the loss of individual prerogatives for a (still elite-defined) collective good, and leading a society not already torn asunder by ethnic or racial divisions. Europe has been exceptional not only in the immense amount of organized violence that has characterized continental geopolitics, but also in enjoying preconditions that allowed it to transform this bloodshed into modern political institutions.

This is not to imply that war is the only possible catalyst for state devel-

22. P. Anderson, *Lineages of the Absolutist State.*
23. Again, by this I do not mean to imply that such coalitions or alliances are either sufficient or necessary, but only that they increase the probability of being able to establish a successful central authority.

opment or that the Prussian model is the only one available from the European experience. The empirical question of whether war assisted the development of the state in Latin America allows us to isolate theoretically critical aspects of the continent's experience and to better highlight the crucial differences between the historical development of particular regions. In such an exercise we must engage in generalizations about both regions and about individual cases within them. Nevertheless, the general pattern of what I describe should be of interest even for those whose individual cases do not exactly fit the descriptions found in what follows.

War and the Latin American State

What was the effect of war on Latin American institutional political capacity? Measuring state strength, particularly without reliable comparative data, is a risky enterprise. One of the most critical aspects of a modern state is its ability to create and enforce what Frederic Lane and later Charles Tilly have called a "protection racket."[24] From this vantage point, the state is often little more than the stereotypical Hollywood goon warning store owners of the potential disasters awaiting them should they fail to purchase his particular brand of insurance. For all its flags, anthems, and other symbolic paraphernalia, the state offers its citizens a simple proposal: in exchange for obedience to a set of laws, state institutions offer protection from both internal and external violence; the Weberian monopoly over legitimate use of violence.[25] In the first section that follows, I discuss the creation of that monopoly, after which I turn to the political ability to extract rents.

Providing Protection

In order to maintain its racket, the state has to be able to defend preset frontiers and ensure obedience to its laws within those frontiers. It has to defend its right to exist and to demand internal recognition of its domination internally. The internal element involves two aspects (and they may be related, but it is important to keep them separate): (a) Only state officials

---

24. Tilly, "War Making and State Making as Organized Crime."
25. "[The state] is thus a compulsory organization with a territorial basis. . . . the use of force is regarded as legitimate only so far as it is either permitted by the state or prescribed by it" (M. Weber, *Economy and Society,* 56).

may have access to means of violence; and (b) the central state institutions (those claiming national coverage) have priority over any other regional or local competitors. The first is about controlling lawless violence, for example, banditry; as well as the elimination of rival claimants to the national territory, for example, Indians in Latin America or the North American West. The second is about the number of governments inside the territory who are claiming the right or duty to stamp out the violence. We will refer to the first as a process of *pacification* and to the second as *centralization*.

There is no precise measure that we may use to absolutely establish the date when centralization or pacification was achieved in Latin America. For the first, we may use the last date of significant regional revolts. For the second we might consider the effective end of banditry or the elimination of a viable Indian military threat. In some cases, defining the threshold is relatively easy. In Argentina, 1880 marks the last major *regional* rebellion within the political class and also the final conquest of the southern Indian tribes. Chile is effectively centralized by the early 1830s, and we see no explicitly regionalist rebellions after that date. Pacification is finally accomplished with the final assault on the Mapuches in the early 1880s. As the subsequent history of both of these countries makes clear, neither centralization nor pacification implies the end of social or even political struggle, but rather the establishment of central authority as a final arbiter or goal for a political project.

Paraguay represents something of an outlier in that despite the extreme degree of external violence it has suffered, the domestic architecture of political power was essentially settled in the early years of Dr. José Francia's rule. By contrast, Uruguay had to wait almost a century for this denouement, but has enjoyed relative stability since then. Other cases are more difficult to pinpoint. Major regional rebellions are a regular part of Brazilian history through the 1850s, but after that date the specific geographical aspect of uprisings becomes less clear. Regionalism still matters (witness Paulismo), but, again the contest is about who will control the center rather than attempts to redefine national borders. With the victory over the Canudos rebellion, the government effectively established its authority over most of the country.

We are clearly left with some judgment calls that can be debated. In Venezuela, Guzmán Blanco established centralized control and the fifty years of Andinos established political peace. In Mexico, Porfirio Díaz both centralized authority and pacified the countryside (often meaning killing those in it). The revolution and its consolidation in the 1920s finished the process.

Yet recent events have indicated that even the apparently solid *pax priiana* may not have been as permanent as many would have guessed. Finally, one could argue that Peru, Bolivia, Ecuador, and Colombia have not yet accomplished the basic task of pacification. In two of these countries, guerrilla movements held the government at bay for years. In three, Indian communities oftentimes remain beyond the purview of central control and may represent a challenge to national unity. In all, the capacity of the government to guarantee safety and defend its authority is questionable. Note, moreover, that neither process of pacification nor centralization has been historically linear and each has involved often alternating trends.

Table 3.1 includes two possible proxies for state centralization/pacification. One is the date of the first national census. Such efforts require that government representatives not only have authority to ask sometimes difficult questions, but also can be protected from random violence while performing their jobs. An alternative measure is the development of a communications and transportation infrastructure here indicated by railroad mileage in 1900. If we use either measure as an indicator of infrastructural development we note the gap that existed between even the most developed Latin American countries and the United States. Extensive railroad development does not begin on the continent until the 1880s, while few countries were able to thoroughly count their populations before the end of the century. Not coincidentally, it is also around this time that we note the disappearance of regional or local currencies and the establishment of a monopoly over legal tender by the central government. A final indicator of centralization would push the relevant date further into the twentieth century. Using the "governmental scope" measure in the POLITY II data set,[26] we note that the social intrusion of the government is minimal until after World War I and only escalates during the Depression (Fig. 3.2).

Any of these time lines make it difficult to argue for the causal significance of war, as the most important conflicts had occurred at least a decade prior to the key dates. Even if we accept a historical lag in order to account for the possible influence of the Pacific and Triple Alliance Wars their immediate effect was limited. The relationship between even international wars and state building is largely spurious, as these wars did not play an important role in the centralization and pacification of these countries.

The Paraguayan War did provide Mitre and later Domingo Sarmiento with a much stronger instrument with which to crush continued regional

26. Gurr, "Polity II."

Table 3.1 Centralization and pacification

Country	Centralization*	Pacification*	Date of First National Census**	RR km in 1900***	Relevant War
Argentina	1880	1881	1869	16,767	Triple Alliance
Bolivia	1900[a]	1952	1900 (1831?)	972	Confederation and Pacific
Brazil	1850	1890s	1872	15,316	Triple Alliance
Chile	1833	1881	1831/1835	4,354	Confederation and Pacific
Colombia	1880s[a]	1950s	1912 (1825?)	568	Thousand Days
Ecuador	1916	1950s	1950	92	?
Mexico	1880s	1920s	1895	13,585	French Invasion
Paraguay	1820s	1820	1899 (1847?)	240	Triple Alliance
Peru	1895	1940s	1876 (1836?)	1,800	Confederation and Pacific
Uruguay	1903	1900s	1908 (1852?)	1,730	Guerra Grande
Venezuela	1870s	1930s	1873	858	?
United States	1865	1800s	1790	311,160	Civil War

*Estimates based on federalization of capital, end of major regional revolt, or effective end of banditry and Indian attacks of major centers.

**First date is for recognized national census fulfilling basic criteria. Second date is for possible earlier effort with significant limitations. SOURCE: Goyer and Domschke, *Handbook of Censuses.*

***SOURCE: Mitchell, *International Historical Statistics.*

[a]Regression in 1990s.

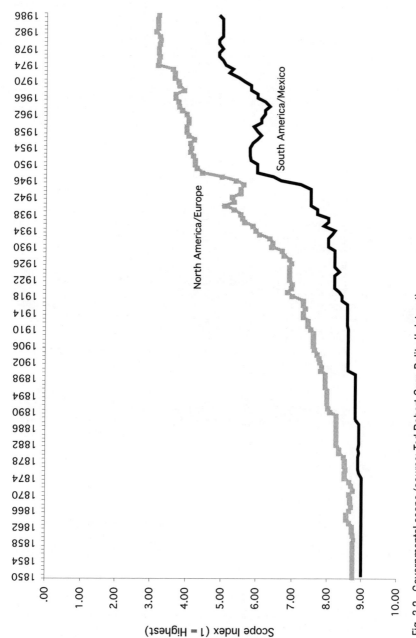

Fig. 3.2 Governmental scope (source: Ted Robert Gurr, Polity II dataset)

revolts in Argentina.[27] The 1860s saw the last of the *montoneras*. But the war may have actually encouraged many of these regional revolts. During the five-year period of conflict there were eighty-five rebellions, twenty-seven mutinies, and forty-three military protests![28] The army that returns from Paraguay is much better equipped to suppress internal revolts. Both these presidents also used the army and local garrisons as a means with which to impose their authority on the provinces. Yet one could argue that it was not the war itself but the development of national institutions, of which the army was but one, under Sarmiento and his successors that consolidated rule from Buenos Aires. It was this success rather than the War of the Triple Alliance that killed regional autonomy. These developments were not born from military victories, but from a series of political contracts and defeats within elite circles. The war arguably had even less effect in Brazil. The army shrank and suffered from the very same political divisions and conflicts as the state; it certainly did not impose a solution until much later.

Paraguay's experience is perhaps closest to a typical "unifying" war, but the relevant struggle was not in the 1860s, when the country was left destroyed, but many decades earlier. By 1811, not only had the Paraguayans already defeated an army from Buenos Aires attempting to maintain the capital's control over the province, but even more important, the *porteño* threat and the possibility of a Brazilian intervention forced the local elite to unite behind a single program and junta. Having established a unitary government with all power centered on Asunción, Francia was able to dominate the ruling junta and finally make himself dictator in 1816. It is interesting to note that Francia was able to use hatred of a white elite to unite an Indian and mestizo population in support of the central state.

It has often been said that war made Chile, and it is true that the war against the Peruvian-Bolivian Confederation was accompanied by efforts to create a more solid and effective central authority. The first Peruvian war "provided a basis for solidarity and legitimacy, as well as the leadership that spared Chile the political disorder and caudillismo."[29] But one could argue that by the time Chile went to war in the 1830s, the Portalian Constitution had already established the mechanisms required to maintain central control. Moreover, it was the assassination of Portales that served to consoli-

27. Although Argentina's central authority really consolidated in 1880 when Roca defeated the Buenos Aires Guardia Nacional led by Carlos Tejedor.
28. Pomer, *La guerra del Paraguay,* 246.
29. Loveman, *Chile,* 141.

date support for the war and the regime.[30] If by 1859 Manuel Montt could declare that "political parties have disappeared in Chile,"[31] this had more to do with geography and elite interaction than with military developments. The "second" war of the Pacific increased government legitimacy and encouraged economic development. The large army created to defeat Peru was then available for the last conquest of the Indians to the south. Nevertheless, it would be difficult to argue that the 1879–83 war made the Chilean state that much more centralized or pacified.

Overall, infrastructural and political development in the late nineteenth century appears more closely related to the expansion of the primary export economy than to the logistical needs of war (Fig. 3.3). Argentina's railroads, for example, were not designed by a General Staff seeking to accelerate mobilization, but for and by the agricultural export economy. The growth in state capacity or centralization noted as beginning in the late 1880s matches exactly a continentwide expansion in the export of basic commodities. Of course, causal order is ambiguous here. To what extent did the increase in trade fuel state centralization and to what extent was it made possible by the prior political stabilization? The question is far too complex to settle here.[32] For our purposes the critical issue is that state growth was linked more to the development of capital and trade than to military exploits and conflicts.[33]

Even such a cursory overview indicates that precisely in the period of its history when Latin America was most bellicose, the state was still struggling to establish its authority. During an extremely bloody century we can speak of stable regimes in Brazil after 1840, Chile between 1830 and 1891; and Venezuela, Colombia, and Ecuador until the 1840s. Up to the last decade of the nineteenth century, violence was endemic, power was fractured, and authority was fragile in much of the continent.[34] Despite a great deal of

30. Collier and Sater, *A History of Chile, 1808–1994,* 66.
31. Collier and Sater, *History of Chile,* 118.
32. Isolated evidence would indicate that trade produced the state. In Bolivia, for example, the state was seen as a necessary police officer acting to defend investments and direct the needed infrastructural development (Klein, *Bolivia,* 148–52; Paz, *Historia económica de Bolivia,* 111).
33. Nearly simultaneously and across the entire continent, a variety of foreign missions led efforts to discipline national militaries and create more professional forces. These arguably produced more efficient, but much less internationally active, militaries (Nunn, *Yesterday's Soldiers;* Loveman, *For la Patria*). The link between these two trends is weak at best. Neither one was an expression of nascent states born out of war, but independent responses to Latin America's emerging role within a global economy and polity.
34. There were other exceptions. Castilla brought a semblance of order to chaotic Peru in the 1850s and Santa Cruz to Bolivia in the 1830s.

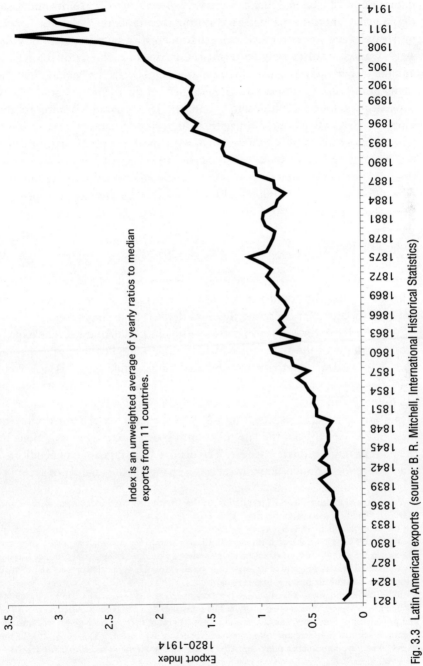

Index is an unweighted average of yearly ratios to median exports from 11 countries.

Fig. 3.3 Latin American exports (source: B. R. Mitchell, International Historical Statistics)

military conflict, Latin America remained something of a continental frontier; a place where no one had an enduring monopoly on violence.[35]

The relevant model is much more that of Austria-Hungary than of Prussia.[36] Wars seemed to only highlight the intrinsic weakness of the regime
and the fragility of any sense of nationhood. Only with the beginning of the
"long peace" do we observe the development of the forms of state capacity
supposedly associated with military conflict. The apparent paradox is even
more puzzling when we recognize that the forms of Latin American states
with the most characteristics associated with "modern" political institutions
(extensive bureaucracies, closer interaction with larger parts of the population) did not appear until the 1930s and 1940s under corporate and populist
guises and were hardly influenced by the kind of geopolitical competition
supposedly responsible for European development (see Fig. 3.2).

Collecting Rents

If the capacity to "protect" was weak and apparently not significantly influenced by war, it should not surprise us that Latin American states were
not very successful at collecting the rents derived from the racket.

War did have some of the expected results in Latin America. The expenditure patterns of the states for which we have a modicum of information
look a great deal like the classic bellicist state (Table 3.2).[37] These were
countries *apparently* devoted to war. Expenditures were concentrated on
the military and paying the debt derived from war.[38] (The overall decrease
in military expenditures after the 1870s does reflect a general decline in
interstate violence from the late nineteenth century on.) The exceptions to
the pattern tend to prove the rule. The decline in Paraguayan expenditures
after 1840, for example, actually reflects a change in the manner of account-

---

35. Borrowing from Lane's formulation of the frontier as cited in Duncan Baretta and
Markoff, "Civilization and Barbarism," 590.
36. With thanks to Steve Topik.
37. I have avoided the use of formal statistical methods for two reasons. First, given the
vagaries in the data, formal cross-national comparisons would be deceptive. Second, qualifying
any individual year as peaceful or at war would be an extremely subjective process and involve
distinctions beyond the purview of this book.
38. Conflict did not necessarily mean large organized armed forces (see Chapter 5). Colombia had a very violent nineteenth century, yet its army was down to eight hundred men in 1854
and 511 in 1858. The army was in fact almost nothing more than a palace guard well into the
twentieth century (McGreevey, *An Economic History of Colombia, 1845–1930*, 87). In the
1830s, the entire Venezuelan army consisted of one thousand men (Bethell, *Cambridge History*, vol. 3, 520).

ing adopted in order to disguise an increase in the attention paid by the state to military development.[39] The low Uruguayan numbers come almost fifty years after formal independence; in those fifty years (1830–80) the state did little but fight internal and external enemies.

Among winners, such as Argentina and Brazil in the 1870s, war led to an increase in the size of government. Wars also provided the expected economic stimulus. Military procurement and the slightly higher war tariffs encouraged domestic industrial development in Brazil during the War of the Triple Alliance.[40] The need to supply the Chilean expeditionary forces in Peru during the War of the Pacific increased the demand for domestic production of basic products such as textiles and foodstuffs. More factories were founded in Chile between 1880 and 1889 than had existed prior to the war.[41] Recruitment and increased demand also lowered unemployment.[42]

But at least as measured by taxation, the Latin American states did not penetrate or extract from their societies in the expected manner. Comparisons of relative extractive capacities in the nineteenth century are difficult, given the lack of comparable national economic data and the questionable use of official exchange figures. The two countries for which we have the most reliable information that can be translated into an international currency are Chile and Brazil. During the entire period in question, neither Latin American state could extract even half the revenue per capita available to the British state, arguably the least rapacious European power at the time, despite the fact that these countries experienced considerable conflict.[43] Moreover, both Latin American countries were much more dependent on customs revenues than were the United Kingdom or France during this time period. While such taxes accounted for roughly one-third of British revenues and were marginal for France, in Brazil and Chile they represented at least two-thirds and often more (Fig. 3.4).[44] As discussed earlier, the upward trend in tax receipts of the Latin American countries reflects increased connection to the global economy, not a stronger state.

Even if the state grew, and this was not universally true,[45] it did not de-

39. Thomas Whigham, private communication with the author.

40. Bethell, *Cambridge History*, vol. 3, 768.

41. Loveman, *Chile*, 169; Zeitlin, *The Civil Wars in Chile*, 77–78.

42. Cariola and Sunkel, *Un siglo de historia económica de Chile*.

43. Flora, *State, Economy, and Society in Western Europe*; Mitchell, *International Historical Statistics*; Dirección de Contabilidad (Chile), *Resumen de la hacienda pública de Chile*; Buescu, *História administrativa do Brasil*.

44. Cariola and Sunkel, *Un siglo de historia económica de Chile*.

45. No matter whether at war or peace, Colombia had one of the lowest levels of government expenditure per capita in Latin America (Tovar Pinzón, "La lenta ruptura con el pasado

velop the fiscal musculature associated with the warring state. The stimulus of war did not produce the dramatic increase in the institutional complexity of extraction associated with the theoretical model. Despite rises in expenditures, revenues lagged far behind. As in the European cases, war produced immediate deficits, but with one prominent exception, the Latin American states did not respond to these with increased extractions, at least not in the form of domestic taxes. Customs and royalties from the export of primary goods remained the mainstay of the most Latin American states (Table 3.3).

The internal and external wars experienced by the Brazilian Empire did not elicit the kind of fiscal intrusion seen in western Europe or even the United States.[46] Overall, taxes on wealth and production contributed less than 4 percent of ordinary revenue even during the war years.[47] In Chile, domestic taxes played an even smaller role. The most significant was a colonial tithe used to support the church, which represented less than 3 percent of all revenues by the 1860s. Early Argentinean governments attempted to impose a capital tax *(contribución directa)* with rates of 1–8 percent, but this never functioned and was not obeyed.[48] Land rents never accounted for more than 3 percent of total receipts.[49]

Three important exceptions serve to clarify the pattern. Mexico's relatively low dependence on customs receipts reflects continual state dependence on domestic loans and the printing press. The central government was generally incapable of imposing domestic taxes prior to the Porfiriato. By contrast, Bolivia maintained the oppressive colonial Indian tribute and relied on these sources for a large part of its revenues through the mid-nineteenth century. Two aspects of this tax bear notice. First, it was not sensitive to the stimulus provided by external conflict, but rather reflected internal caste divisions. Second, such a tax did not rely on central government infrastructural development, but rather on the retention of special social privileges and localized fiefdoms.

---

colonial," 115). In 1871 Colombia gathered one-half of Mexico's revenues and one-fifth of those of Chile. During the same period one local authority estimated that the government received only 2 percent of the national product (Deas, "The Fiscal Problems of Nineteenth Century Colombia," 289, 310, 326).

46. During the War of the Triple Alliance a tax was instituted on buildings with a 3 percent surcharge on their value, but this excluded the most valuable rural properties. Moreover, an attempt to establish a tax on industry and the professions was never enforced and the rates remained minimal.

47. Buescu, *Evolução econômica do Brasil*, 89–91; Cavalcanti, "Finances," 326.

48. Alemann, *Breve historia de la política económica argentina*, 61.

49. Rock, *Argentina, 1516–1987*, 99.

Table 3.2 Combined military and financial expenditures as share of budget

	Argentina	Brazil	Chile	Ecuador	Mexico	Paraguay[a]	Peru	Uruguay	Venezuela
1820						0.81			
1821									
1822	0.92				0.96	0.80			
1823	0.93					0.85			
1824	0.85				0.81				
1825					0.95	0.84			
1826	0.98				0.66		0.84		
1827						0.91			
1828		0.90			0.92				
1829	0.90	0.88			0.94	0.89			
1830	0.85	0.85		0.74	0.93				0.83
1831	1.00	0.82			0.92	0.86	0.70		0.79
1832	0.74	0.62		0.57	0.91	0.87			0.84
1833	0.78	0.88	0.57		0.81	0.85			0.80
1834	0.78	0.86	0.58		0.70	0.76			0.83
1835		0.86	0.60		0.90	0.85			0.41
1836		0.85	0.56		0.80				0.65
1837		0.86	0.51		0.93	0.92			0.73
1838		0.87	0.48			0.94			0.68
1839		0.88	0.47	0.58	0.86	0.89			0.53
1840	0.98	0.84	0.41		0.88	0.89			0.64
1841	0.96	0.86	0.34		0.85				0.72
1842	1.00	0.83	0.83		0.95				0.57
1843	1.00	0.82	0.83		0.94	0.43			0.73
1844	0.98	0.81	0.73		0.93				

Table 3.2 Combined military and financial expenditures as share of budget (*cont'd*)

	Argentina	Brazil	Chile	Ecuador	Mexico	Paraguay[a]	Peru	Uruguay	Venezuela
1845	0.98	0.79	0.72		0.98		0.51		0.69
1846	0.93	0.78	0.70	0.77	0.93	0.81	0.58		0.63
1847	0.94	0.78	0.72				0.66		0.66
1848	0.95	0.79	0.71		0.89		0.74		0.84
1849	0.93	0.77	0.71		0.90		0.75		0.72
1850	0.95	0.78	0.70		0.40		0.76		0.76
1851		0.81	0.77		0.55		0.82		0.83
1852		0.77	0.73	0.74	0.86		0.83		0.83
1853		0.76	0.66	0.60	0.85	0.56	0.85		0.82
1854		0.74	0.60	0.62	0.73		0.86		0.35
1855		0.72	0.53	0.61	0.84		0.87		0.32
1856		0.74	0.55	0.62		0.27	0.88		
1857		0.74	0.57	0.60			0.84		
1858		0.70	0.44			0.40	0.79		0.83
1859		0.70	0.68				0.77		
1860		0.68	0.67	0.80	0.57	0.32	0.74		0.74
1861		0.71	0.66	0.62	0.75		0.80		
1862		0.72	0.64	0.69			0.73		
1863		0.72	0.67	0.62					
1864	0.80	0.73	0.70	0.57		0.72			
1865	0.88	0.84	0.71	0.66		0.71		0.94	
1866	0.73	0.83	0.79	0.58	0.85		0.69		
1867	0.72	0.87	0.77		0.87		0.60		0.79
1868	0.64	0.86	0.67		0.65		0.47		
1869	0.66	0.84	0.70	0.54	0.55		0.57		
1870	0.71	0.72	0.64	0.38	0.55		0.57		
1871	0.63	0.69	0.57				0.57		0.93

Year								
1872	0.88	0.69	0.58	0.51	0.51	0.58		0.60
1873	0.82	0.67	0.57		0.51	0.53		0.82
1874	0.80	0.67	0.52		0.49	0.57		0.67
1875	0.54	0.65	0.54	0.61	0.70	0.74		
1876	0.51	0.62	0.60		0.76	0.78		
1877	0.61	0.52	0.67		0.63	0.57		0.77
1878	0.58	0.43	0.64	0.28	0.69	0.61		
1879	0.54	0.57	0.78		0.82	0.53		
1880	0.57	0.62	0.68					0.69
1881	0.49	0.62	0.76					
1882	0.56	0.61	0.78					
1883		0.58	0.74					0.45
1884		0.57	0.68	0.43			0.35	0.29
1885		0.61	0.64	0.25			0.35	0.46
1886		0.59	0.72	0.41			0.32	
1887			0.68	0.50			0.31	
1888			0.44	0.47			0.32	
1889			0.41	0.35			0.31	
1890			0.37	0.40				

aFor Paraguay, the figures are military expenditures alone. Apparent drop after 1840 reflects changes in government accounting that appear to disguise continued military expenditure.

SOURCE: Cortés Conde, *Dinero deuda y crisis*; Burgin, *The Economic Aspects of Argentine Federalism, 1820–1852*; Halperín-Donghi, *Guerra y finanzas en los orígines del estado argentino*; Mercea Buescu, *Organização e administração do Ministério da Fazenda no Império*; Dirección de Contabilidad, *Resumen de la hacienda pública de Chile, 1833–1914*; Rodríguez, *The Search for Public Policy*; Aguilar, *Los presupuestos mexicanos*; Arbulu, *Política económico-financiera y la formación del estado*; Vera Blinn Reber, unpublished tables; República de Uruguay, *Anuario Estadístico*; Tomás Enrique Carillo Batalla, *Historia de las finanzas públicas en Venezuela*.

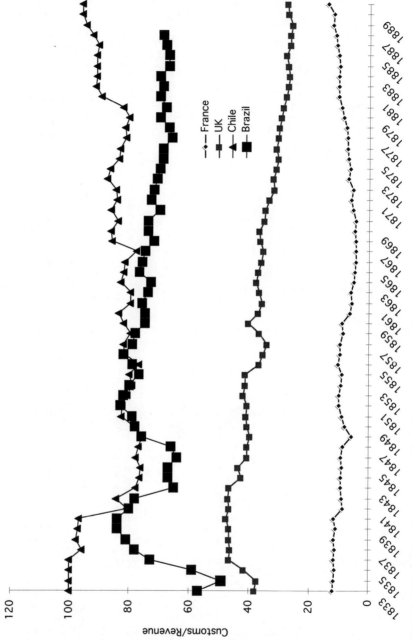

Fig. 3.4. Reliance on customs (source: Direccion de Contabilidad, Buescu, Flora)

Legend:
- France
- UK
- Chile
- Brazil

Y-axis: Customs/Revenue (0, 20, 40, 60, 80, 100, 120)

X-axis years: 1833, 1835, 1837, 1839, 1841, 1843, 1845, 1847, 1849, 1851, 1853, 1855, 1857, 1859, 1861, 1863, 1865, 1867, 1869, 1871, 1873, 1875, 1877, 1879, 1881, 1883, 1885, 1887, 1889

Table 3.3 Customs and royalties as share of ordinary income

	Argentina	Bolivia	Brazil	Chile	Colombia	Ecuador[a]	Mexico	Paraguay	Peru	Uruguay	Venezuela
1820								0.18			
1821											
1822	0.84						0.54	0.02			
1823								0.09			
1824	0.80						0.41				
1825							0.55				
1826							0.46				
1827		0.13	0.50				0.42		0.33		
1828			0.32				0.45				
1829	0.85		0.29				0.34				
1830	0.87		0.29			0.51	0.45				0.39
1831	0.83	0.15	0.33				0.37	0.01	0.52		0.63
1832	0.82	0.11	0.57		0.30	0.43	0.42	0.02			0.55
1833	0.87	0.12	0.49	0.51			0.49				0.52
1834	0.76		0.59	0.56		0.51	0.20				0.49
1835		0.09	0.73	0.56			0.21	0.01			0.52
1836		0.09	0.78	0.57	0.33	0.57	0.25				0.61
1837		0.10	0.81	0.57		0.57	0.25				0.50
1838			0.84	0.57		0.57	0.19	0.01			0.59
1839		0.07	0.84	0.57		0.57	0.35	0.03			0.65
1840	0.70		0.80	0.62	0.32		0.25	0.06			0.74
1841	0.93	0.07	0.78	0.59			0.17				0.88
1842	0.92	0.07	0.66	0.60			0.22				0.73
1843	0.90	0.06	0.67	0.55			0.23				0.62
1844	0.90	0.06		0.51							0.68

Table 3.3 Customs and royalties as share of ordinary income (*cont'd*)

	Argentina	Bolivia	Brazil	Chile	Colombia	Ecuador[a]	Mexico	Paraguay	Peru	Uruguay	Venezuela
1845	0.89	0.09	0.67	0.53		0.54			0.35		0.67
1846	0.69		0.64	0.56	0.21	0.60		0.05	0.40		0.69
1847	0.84	0.07	0.65	0.53		0.62			0.44		0.57
1848	0.90	0.07	0.76	0.49			0.25		0.37		0.33
1849	0.93	0.09	0.77	0.51			0.35		0.53		0.45
1850	0.93		0.79	0.57	0.47		0.34	0.04	0.57		0.49
1851			0.84	0.57			0.55		0.74		0.57
1852		0.07	0.82	0.57		0.60	0.26		0.82		0.72
1853		0.11	0.80	0.43		0.59	0.45		0.86		0.66
1854		0.09	0.77	0.60	0.52	0.59	0.50	0.06	0.91		0.77
1855		0.10	0.79	0.56		0.59	0.43		0.91		0.74
1856		0.09	0.81	0.50		0.61		0.11	0.95		0.74
1857			0.79	0.58		0.61		0.22	0.94		0.74
1858			0.78	0.51		0.65		0.18	0.86		0.53
1859			0.76	0.41					0.94		0.63
1860			0.75	0.56				0.25	0.95		0.56
1861			0.76	0.49		0.70			0.86		0.62
1862		0.10	0.74	0.43		0.59			0.56		0.60
1863		0.15	0.73	0.47	0.32	0.52			0.62		
1864	0.81		0.78	0.36		0.50			0.74		0.57
1865	0.92		0.76	0.23	0.21	0.50			0.87		0.74
1866	1.00	0.05	0.75	0.18		0.64			0.70		0.75
1867	0.86	0.06	0.72	0.28	0.40	0.62	0.53		0.72		0.80
1868	0.95	0.04	0.74	0.47		0.77	0.53		0.47		0.89
1869	0.97	0.05	0.74	0.45		0.73	0.48		0.75		0.99
1870	0.94		0.70	0.34		0.73	0.53		0.96		
1871	1.00	0.12	0.73	0.45	0.47	0.64	0.45		0.62		
1872	0.83		0.72	0.53	0.45	0.53	0.45				0.76

Year									
1873	0.83		0.71	0.33	0.52	0.66	0.48	0.76		0.85
1874	0.80	0.35	0.70	0.50	0.59	0.61	0.47	0.94		0.79
1875	0.72		0.69	0.38	0.69	0.48	0.63	0.72		0.80
1876	0.89		0.70	0.40	0.69	0.67	0.57	0.73		0.74
1877	0.96		0.66	0.36	0.62	0.53	0.44	0.85		0.57
1878	0.82		0.67	0.37	0.62	0.64	0.36	0.90		
1879	0.72		0.69	0.25	0.62	0.49	0.36	0.85		0.75
1880	0.79	0.42	0.68	0.34	0.61	0.72				0.71
1881	0.89	0.31	0.70	0.58	0.61					0.70
1882	0.78	0.26	0.69	0.70	0.68	0.75				0.65
1883			0.70	0.65	0.63	0.70			0.53	0.72
1884			0.67	0.67	0.68	0.68			0.57	0.70
1885			0.67	0.62	0.60	0.57			0.50	0.63
1886			0.68	0.39	0.48	0.62			0.57	0.69
1887				0.44	0.47	0.74			0.60	0.73
1888				0.71		0.68			0.59	0.70
1889				0.66	0.52	0.61			0.61	0.74
1890				0.65		0.80			0.55	0.76

aEcuador figures are for indirect taxes largely consisting of customs.

SOURCE: Cortés Conde, Dinero deuda y crisis; Burgin, The Economic Aspects of Argentine Federalism, 1820–1852; Halperín-Donghi, Guerra y finanzas en los orígenes del estado argentino; Erwin P. Grieshaber, Survival of Indian Communities in Nineteenth-Century Bolivia; Buescu, Organização e administração do Ministério da Fazenda no Império; Dirección de Contabilidad, Resumen de la hacienda pública de Chile, 1833–1914; D.A.N.E., Boletín Mensual de Estadística; José Antonio Ocampo and Santiago Montenegro, Crisis Mundial, Protección e Industrialización; Rodríguez, The Search for Public Policy; Carmagnani, "Finanzas y estado en México, 1820–1880"; Arbulu, Política económico-financiera y la formación del estado; Vera Blinn Reber, unpublished tables; República de Uruguay, Anuario Estadístico; Raman Veloz, Economía y finanzas de Venezuela; Rafael Cartay, Historia económica de Venezuela.

The third exception is the most interesting. Because of its location and the almost continual threats to its existence as well as the ideological proclivities of the dictator Francia, Paraguay could not rely on external financing for much of its early history. That is, unlike other Latin American countries, it could not count on either customs or loans to balance its books, but had to live on its own resources.[50] The state financed itself through sales to soldiers and the populace as well as through confiscation of property. The structure of Paraguayan finances appeared to change immediately after Francia's death as the importance of customs increased to nearly half of state revenues. Unlike most Latin American countries, however, Paraguay ran a consistent trade surplus during this period.[51] The state remained largely in charge of external trade (mostly of *yerba maté*) either through its own administration or through the patronage network of the Lópezes.[52] Direct sales continued to play an important role as well. What is most significant is that Paraguay depended on foreign trade (directly or indirectly) for only 40 percent of its government revenue.[53] Paraguay also did not rely on debt, that other great source of international financing; when the War of the Triple Alliance began, it did not have any external debt.[54] Given the chaos found in Paraguay during the War of the Triple Alliance, there are no records of how López financed it. It would appear, however, that he paid for the war through the complete mobilization of the country.[55] How much of this was voluntary patriotism and how much it reflected the reach of the state is impossible to tell. The relevant point, however, remains the same: unlike other Latin American countries, Paraguay autofinanced its war.

Even in these cases, however, wars did not produce the expected institutional transformation in state civil relations or the structure of the political apparatus. The fiscal infrastructure was established independent of interstate conflict and remained relatively constant in peace and war. In general, Latin American states were not able to escape the "cycle of levies, bankruptcies and mutinies" that characterized warring states prior to the revenue revolution of the late seventeenth century;[56] they were not "built" by war.

50. Pastore, "Trade Contraction and Economic Decline," 539.
51. Rivarola and Bautista, *Historia monetaria de Paraguay,* 104.
52. Whigham, *The Politics of River Trade,* 69–70.
53. Pastore, "State-Led Industrialization," 304.
54. Rivarola and Bautista, *Historia monetaria de Paraguay,* 119.
55. Williams, *Rise and Fall,* 217–21; Pastore, "State-Led Industrialization," 306, 318.
56. Kaiser, *Politics and War,* 35.

Blood and Debt

What were the effects of the wars of nineteenth-century Latin America on the political capacity of the state? They produced blood and debt and not much more. If stability requires acts of force, authoritarian impositions, exercises in power justified by internal and external danger, why did the Latin American violence of the nineteenth century not produce a coherent state? What explains the limited significance of war on state development in Latin America? Certainly the eighteenth and nineteenth centuries saw enough organized violence that a concomitant evolution in state capacity could be expected. If the relationship between organized violence and institutional development were automatic, we might expect Latin America to follow the European pattern.

The easy availability of external financing allowed the state the luxury of not coming into conflict with those social sectors that possessed the required resources. In the 1820s and from the 1870s through the 1890s, loans were relatively easy to obtain. Increasingly throughout the nineteenth century, almost all the Latin American economies became integrated into a global economy through the export of a mineral or agricultural commodity. In any case, whenever the state did try to extract greater domestic resources, it was universally defeated. The European pattern includes a basic organizational capacity that was missing in Latin America. The wars occurred too soon after independence and were fought by countries not capable or responding in the pattern described by Tilly and others.

In the following sections I discuss the effect of the form and timing of the warfare that predominated on the continent. I then turn to focus more on the societies in which they were fought.

Wrong Kind of Wars?

It is important to first distinguish between the different kinds of wars and their respective state-building effects. For example, Latin America has not experienced one of the most significant forms of warfare producing centralized authority. In many of the European cases, war contributes to state formation not as an unintended by-product, but as a direct result of conquest.[57]

---

57. The sixteenth-century Conquest did produce an elaborate political institution and fostered separate identities (both between it and other imperial claimants and within it, between ruling whites and dominated Indians and blacks).

The two most obvious examples here are the Italian and German cases. These unifications essentially involved not a central authority systematically expanding control over provinces, but a regional contender for supremacy defeating all other claimants. Prussia and Piedmont essentially conquered Germany and Italy. The same could also be said for England, Ile-de-France, Castille, or Muscovy.[58] One could say the same of the Northern victory in the U.S. Civil War.

The combination of colonial heritage and the particular military experience of South America produced a very different variant of state making than that seen in Europe, where states were built from the inside out; a region or province would carve its dominance over others. The state was built at the same time as the territory was acquired. In Latin America, the fight was about assuming control over what was left of a patrimonial state (the descendant of the crown) even if it did not exercise meaningful authority over large parts of the formally defined nation.[59] Wars, therefore, were counterproductive for state building. They were either internal squabbles that left domestic territory pillaged or fights between political lightweights that did not produce the necessary stimulus for organizational and institutional evolution. Unlike in Europe, the military did not conquer territory in order to make a state, but had to impose order over a fractious set of local interests, each irrevocably married to the other. Wars were likely to remain within the family, with the particular destruction and divisiveness that civil struggles tend to leave behind.

Civil wars in Latin America were at times defined territorially, but more commonly involved competing claims to central power. These conflicts were rarely about delimiting internal or external frontiers, but instead about deciding who controlled the already defined national territory. Unlike in Europe, we have few examples—two being the creation of Uruguay and the War of the Peruvian-Bolivian Confederation—where international war combined with the process of regional conquest. The principle of *uti possidetis* (right of possession) consecrated colonial boundaries. This disallowed the kind of Darwinian geopolitics that arguably fueled state development in Europe. There are no Latin American equivalents to Sadowa or Sedan. The closest equivalent to the unification-through-conquest model would be Bue-

58. This is not to deny how non-Conquest wars may have contributed to the capacity of a region to establish itself as first among equals. Again, Prussia, Piedmont, and England were made the powerful regions they were partly through the experience of war. It is this process rather than explicit conquest that we need to analyze.

59. Morse, "Heritage of Latin America," 162.

nos Aires and the half-century-long struggle for mastery over the confederation. But even here one could argue that the provinces conquered the capital
as much as vice versa. Moreover, it is arguable to what extent the final union
was a product of war. Urquiza was not vanquished at Pavón and the union
of 1861–62 was really the result of elite pacts arrived at politically, not
militarily.

Most commonly, wars resulted from attempts of states to consolidate
their authority. The final set of conflicts between Liberals and Conservatives
in Mexico, for example, is partly a product of attempts by the central government to finance itself through the appropriation of church property. The
first war between Chile and Peru and Bolivia was in part a response to the
efforts of Santa Cruz to consolidate his rule. A fear of the influence of Paraguay on still semiautonomous regions helps explain some of the unity of the
Triple Alliance.

Interestingly, given the relative low level of technical capacity available to
the combatants, the Latin American wars were also extremely destructive—
arguably more so than most European wars between Westphalia and Sara-
jevo. The ruinous consequences of war were often not limited or far
removed from population centers, but involved the destruction of one side.
Losing a war was often disastrous for political order. Unlike in Europe,
where the victor's rule would succeed that of the loser, the pattern in Latin
America was closer to the creation of a vacuum. In the late 1880s, for example, the Peruvian countryside was not accessible to the state.[60] The Paraguayan case is even more extreme.

The historical record certainly supports analytical emphasis on war type.
The two wars of the Pacific, the War of the Triple Alliance, and the Mexi-
can-French War of 1862—in part an internal conflict that became a nationalist one—all appear to have played at least a *limited* role in the subsequent
consolidation of the *winning* nation-states (but still smaller than might be
expected). The much more common Conservative-Liberal conflicts of Mexico and Colombia, the regionalist rebellions of Brazil and Argentina, and
the caudillo wars of Peru did little but destroy. Losing a war was universally
a disaster.

Looking back at the critical contributions made by wars to state making
in Europe, we find that Latin American conflicts did not generally embody
the three critical characteristics of wars associated with "military revolution." First, they often did not accompany a shift from private to public

60. Mallon, *Defense of Community*, 102–3.

control of violence. In many cases, the chaos that followed them meant that powerful private actors remained in de facto control of their respective lands. Moreover, as wars often were about establishing claims to power, they were perceived as private battles over public goods. Second, armies generally remained small and logistics severely constrained. None of the Latin American conflicts, with the exception of the Paraguayan experience in the 1860s, were "total wars" requiring the militarization of every aspect of social and economic life. Third, the vast majority of the wars did not emphasize or support the development of a national identity, but consisted of struggles in which either such questions were irrelevant or the very definition of that identity was at stake.

Artificial Wealth

For the "coercion-extraction cycle" to begin, the relevant states must not have alternative sources of financing, while the domestic economy must be capable of sustaining the new fiscal and bureaucratic growth. Conflict-induced extraction will only occur if easier options are not available. Even then, the relevant societies might not be able to produce enough surplus to make the effort productive. Thus, for example, the availability of Latin American silver and the willingness of bankers to risk massive sums freed the Spanish Habsburgs from imposing greater fiscal control over their provinces as a means to pay for their wars. Conversely, the relative scarcity of such external supports drove the expansion of the early English state.

It is not clear how much even the most voracious state could have extracted from such extremely poor societies. The independence wars left little base on which to build a state and destroyed much of the economy on which it might have relied. The Mexican economy experienced a significant decline after independence.[61] During the first forty years of the century, Bolivia saw the decapitalization of its mining industry—in 1840 there were ten thousand abandoned mines—and the depopulation of its cities. Venezuela was "left a wasteland" by a war that was "cruel, destructive, and total," with armies regularly destroying the property of enemies and paying their soldiers with

---

61. Per capita income declined from 35–40 to 25–30 pesos between 1810 and 1820 and did not attain colonial levels until the Porfiriato of the last quarter century (Bethell, *Cambridge History: Independence*, 91). One indication of the fall is Mexico's changing position relative to the U.S. economy. By John Coatsworth's estimates ("Obstacles to Growth in Nineteenth Century Mexico," 82–83), Mexico had 44 percent of the U.S. per capita income in 1800, but only 13 percent by 1910, with most of the comparative decline coming prior to 1845.

plunder.[62] The Peruvian economy was crippled by the need to support loyal armies throughout the continent.[63] The situation was made even worse by the collapse of the continental "customs union" maintained by Spanish mercantilism.[64] Material goods were not the only thing destroyed by the wars of independence. An entire system of economic, juridical, and social relationships was also their victim.[65] For most, the wars brought misery, hardship, and penury.

This did not change during most of the period in question. The Colombian economy, for example, was small and undeveloped, while difficult transport constrained the growth of taxable market exchange.[66] In general, squeezing the rich did not yield very much because even this social group had relatively small amounts of capital available.[67] In the late 1830s, Ecuador's exports totaled the equivalent of two hundred thousand pounds sterling.[68] Even a thoroughly rapacious state would have produced per capita extractions much lower than those in Europe. Those states that did impose a direct tax on their populations could expect little. Even with an onerous Indian tribute, for example, Bolivia's government revenues per capita in the 1840s, following a war against Chile, were one-fortieth those of Britain.[69]

This poverty made it extremely difficult to use excise taxes as a form of income. Aside from relatively few commodities, large parts of the population did not consume very much that could be easily taxed. In any case, the hatred of the colonial *alcabala* would have made it practically impossible for the newly independent governments to impose such a tax. Equally important, there were few wage laborers whose income could be measured and taxed in any systematic manner. Even the landed oligarchy, while rich in land, in most cases did not possess large amounts of directly extractable resources.[70] In several cases, the church did have considerable wealth, but even successful appropriations, as in Mexico, produced disappointing results.

---

62. Lynch, *Spanish-American Revolutions,* 202–18; Halperín-Donghi, *Aftermath of Revolution,* 8.
63. Lynch, *Spanish-American Revolutions,* 162.
64. Bulmer-Thomas, *The Economic History of Latin America Since Independence,* 29.
65. Bethell, *Cambridge History,* vol. 3, 307.
66. Bushnell, *The Making of Modern Colombia,* 76.
67. Deas, "Fiscal Problems," 314.
68. Bethell, *Cambridge History,* vol. 3, 511.
69. Dalence, *Bosquejo estadístico de Bolivia,* 316.
70. Nevertheless, it is possible to build a considerable state apparatus on the basis of a land tax. See Bird, "Land Taxation and Economic Development."

How then did the Latin American states pay for their wars? A common experience—and one not dissimilar to that of the European cases—was to print money. During its war with Brazil in the 1820s, Argentina resorted to currency emissions that produced a monetary cataclysm: the price of an ounce of gold on the Buenos Aires stock exchange went from 17 pesos in January 1826 to 112 pesos in December 1830.[71] During the same war, the amount of available Brazilian currency doubled, and subsequently the reis lost half of its value.[72] Even more dramatic was the endless printing of money in Brazil during the War of the Triple Alliance. In 1864 there were 29 million milreis in circulation; by 1870, there were 151 million.[73] Between 1859 and 1901, the Uruguayan state issued 342 million pesos, of which 124 million were still outstanding. To give an idea of the degree of printing insanity, the customs house of Montevideo was producing an average of only 10 million pesos per year.[74] Thus, the vast majority of Latin American governments resorted to a form of inflation tax in order to pay at least partially for their wars.

This profligate reliance on an inflation tax may represent a possible institutional and administrative legacy of war. Such a tax would require that the central government be able to establish a monopoly on the issue of currency. Thus war would provide an incentive to expand centralized authority as a way to tax through a printing press. It may be worthwhile analyzing the link between war and monetary development in Europe; the Latin American experience also would deserve further analysis. This form of taxation also serves as an indication of the relative power of social groups. Inflation taxes would favor rural over urban populations and exporters over importers. They were generally extremely regressive.[75]

States also borrowed from both domestic and international sources. In Mexico, the government increasingly relied on the *agiotistas,* who would provide funds during fiscal emergencies—an almost everyday occurrence as ministers often found empty tills upon assuming office. In exchange for the considerable risk, domestic lenders were often given very favorable terms, with rates in the range of 300–500 percent.[76] Since borrowing was constant

71. Burgin, *The Economic Aspects of Argentine Federalism,* 69.
72. Cardoso, ed., *México en el siglo XIX,* 105; Barman, *Brazil,*140; Nogueira, *Raízes de uma Nação,* 313.
73. Castro Carreira, *História financiera,* 743.
74. Acevedo, *Notas y apuntes,* 457.
75. Rock, *Argentina, 1516–1987,* 107; Oszlak, *La formación del estado argentino,* 183; Halperín-Donghi, *Guerra y finanzas,* 161; Aldo Ferrer, *The Argentine Economy,* 61.
76. Bazant, *Historia de la deuda exterior de México,* 44.

and loans were continuously rolled over, the debt ballooned to 102 million pesos by 1840, 120 million in the 1850s, and 165 million by 1867.[77] The Argentine government also borrowed: by 1840, the debt stood at 36 million pesos, while the total income for that year was 1,710,491 pesos.[78] The response to later wars was no different. Between 1865 and 1876, Argentina acquired almost 19 million pounds of debt.[79] By 1885, the figure was 26 million.[80] Currency conversions make comparisons difficult, but this represented at least four times the revenue of the state during these years. The *total* public debt by 1888 was more than 60 million sterling, and indebtedness per capita tripled.[81] The War of the Triple Alliance brought similar results in Brazil. Real net debt increased from 4.5 million pounds in 1863 to 9.3 million in 1871. Debt as a percentage of exports increased from 58 percent to 82 percent during the same decade.[82] By the time an independent Uruguay appeared in 1830, the government had already accumulated a debt of 2 million pesos.[83] It continued to spiral: by 1853, when the first attempt was made to organize and systematically manage public finances, it reached 40 million pesos. By 1854, the estimate was 60 million, and by 1858 it was 106 million. To put these numbers in context, the estimate for the annual budget of these years is 2 million pesos.[84]

In and of itself, however, relying on debt and the printing press does not explain why the Latin American countries did not impose domestic taxes *after* the wars. Many European countries initially used debt to pay for wars and later imposed taxes to meet their obligations. What distinguishes Latin America is that the fiscal reckoning never came. Moreover, government debt did not encourage the creation of a *stable* domestic financial market, a criti-

77. These are considerable sums, considering that the metal peso was officially set at practically dollar parity (López Cámarra, *La estructura económica y social de México,* 171–72; López Gallo, *Economía y política en la historia de México,* 98).

78. Halperín-Donghi, *Guerra y finanzas,* 213.

79. Pomer, *La guerra del Paraguay,* 238.

80. Randall, *A Comparative Economic History of Latin America,* vol. 2, 215.

81. Oszlak, *La formación del estado argentino,* 217; Dirección de Contabilidad (Chile), *Resumen de la hacienda pública de Chile,* section VII.

82. Buescu, *Evolução económica do Brasil,* 119, 126; Nogueira, *Raízes de uma Nação,* 313; Castro Carreira, *História financiera,* 429.

83. Reyes Abadie and Vázquez Romero, *Crónica general del Uruguay,* 337.

84. Percentage of GDP or of export income would be much better measures of the relative size of these debts. Numbers on the size of the national economy even well into the twentieth century are notoriously unreliable. Export revenue and debts are often expressed in different currencies (e.g., paper vs. gold, or in different international currencies) making a more precise measure practically impossible. Reyes Abadie and Vázquez Romero, *Crónica general del Uruguay,* 339.

cal contribution of war in the cases of Britain and the Netherlands. Rather, government paper fueled unproductive cycles of speculation and ruin. Because of the risk involved, interest rates remained usurious, further hampering domestic development and increasing external dependence.

The availability of external resources freed the state from having to exploit the domestic economy. The relationship between the state and the global economy had three legs: foreign debt, the sale of commodities, and customs.

Much of the debt discussed earlier was to foreign banks.[85] From the beginning, postindependence governments sought to supplement their inadequate domestic sources with foreign loans.[86] Unlike the United States, for example, the new countries lacked allies and external aid, which meant that they had to pay hard cash for all the supplies that reached them. By 1820, the Gran Colombian government had already accumulated European debts of five hundred thousand pounds. Chile similarly contracted in 1822 for 1 million pounds to buy a navy. Peru had to obtain loans in order to pay back wages and a bonus to the victors of Ayacucho as well as some loans to the Gran Colombian government. Mexico borrowed 2.5 million pounds in 1824, 65 percent of which went to direct military expenses. Argentina borrowed in London beginning in 1824. Most of these proceeds went to the creation of a domestic financial system that was largely destroyed by the Argentine-Brazilian War of 1826–28.[87] The first Brazilian loan of 1824 was used to pay for Portuguese loans from Britain. More money followed in 1825 and 1829. By 1830, Brazil had already borrowed 4.8 million pounds, or approximately four times its annual revenues.[88] While Latin America was out of the international financial markets for nearly forty years following this early boom, it made a significant comeback after 1860. For example, during the War of the Triple Alliance, Brazil borrowed 5 million pounds in 1865. In 1867, the state needed another loan from Rothschild for 71 million milreis.[89]

If they could not borrow on international markets (as was the case from roughly 1830 to 1870), Latin American states could sell access to a com-

85. Rippy, *British Investments in Latin America;* Marichal, *A Century of Debt Crises.*

86. These included some intracontinental debts, which usually represented payments for armies or military materials during the independence struggles. By the late 1820s, Bolivia owed Peru 725,000 pesos, Peru owed Colombia 6,000,000 pesos and Chile 3,000,000 pesos (Seckinger, *Brazilian Monarchy,* 51).

87. Marichal, *A Century of Debt Crises,* 27–36.

88. Cardoso, *México en el siglo XIX,* 105.

89. Nogueira, *Raízes de uma Nação,* 378–380; Castro Carreira, *História financiera,* 429.

modity. Guano allowed Peru to become what Shane Hunt has called a "rentier state."[90] The availability of guano revenues retarded the development of the state by allowing it to exist without the remotest contact with the society on which it rested and without having to institute a more efficient administrative machine. Guano did allow the removal of the regressive *contribución* (in 1855), but it also permitted the state to avoid modernizing its fiscal structure while borrowing large amounts of money. A contemporary British observer noted that "a wise government would have treated this source of revenues as temporary and extraordinary. The Peruvians looked upon it as if it was permanent, *abolishing other taxes,* and recklessly increasing expenditure" (my emphasis).[91] Much like the guano bonanza in the Peruvian case, the conquest of nitrate territories allowed the Chilean state to expand without having to "penetrate" its society and confront the rampant inequality.[92] By 1900 nitrate and iodine accounted for 50 percent of Chilean revenues and 14 percent of GDP.[93]

Custom taxes represented an ideal solution to fiscal problems, given the organizational ease with which they could be collected. A few soldiers in the main ports could provide considerable income. More important, given their indirect nature, these taxes were the least likely to provoke popular protest.[94] A revenue tariff was a characteristic feature of a society dominated by landed proprietors, who diverted taxation away from property toward the consumer.[95] A reliance on customs also reflected the sectoral distribution of the continent's economies. For some countries, such as Peru, a large share of the national product was concentrated on the export of a commodity. Thus, government taxed that part of the economy that was most visible. Others having a less developed export market would target imports as well as exports. The distribution between these two often reflected the relative influence of importers over exporters. In the case of Brazil, for example, the heaviest taxes were on manufactured imports. This strategy, in turn, may have made this form of taxation even more regressive, depending on the distribution of goods within the typical import basket.

Argentina is an extreme example of this pattern. From the 1820s, the

90. Hunt, "Growth and Guano."

91. Markham, *The War Between Peru and Chile, 1879–1882*, 37.

92. Loveman, *Chile*, 169; Sater, *Chile and the War of the Pacific*, 227.

93. Mamalakis, *The Growth and Structure of the Chilean Economy*, 19–21; Sater, *Chile and the War of the Pacific*, 275.

94. Marichal, *A Century of Debt Crises*, 17.

95. Lynch, *Spanish-American Revolutions*, 150.

various incarnations of the Argentine state depended on customs duties for the vast majority of its income. The dictator Rosas continued the policy of allowing customs revenues to replace the more politically costly excise or land taxes.[96] The fragility of such dependence was demonstrated by the European naval blockades of 1827, 1839, and 1846, which produced fiscal crises. Despite the massive changes in the Argentine economy during the last quarter of the century, including a fivefold increase in exports from 1862 to 1914, the fiscal system remained largely dependent on import taxes.[97] Even by Latin American standards, this dependence is striking, as customs often accounted for more than 90 percent of ordinary revenues. Trade taxes were seen as the only way of maintaining some semblance of peace between the various politically relevant factions.[98] All knew that this fiscal system was inadequate, but it was the only way of maintaining the social status quo.[99] Tariffs were particularly attractive to the elite. They required no sacrifice, helped finance the expansion of the frontier from which the elite benefited disproportionately,[100] and demanded few administrative resources.

The particular links between Latin America and the global markets had important domestic repercussions. First, they often linked the fiscal health of the state to the world economy and the price of a single commodity. In the well-known pattern, declines in trade or demand for a good could halve government receipts in a single year. Long-term planning and investment were impossible. Depending on the state apparatus as a political patron was also extremely risky. Precisely because the new governments were so fiscally strained and could not impose domestic taxes, they also could not risk losing foreign trade, from which they garnered such a huge part of their income. The fiscal use of trade thus contradicted any possibility of protectionist economic policy.[101]

96. Halperín-Donghi, *Guerra y finanzas,* 242–243.

97. Oszlak, *La formación,* 173.

98. Oszlak, *La formación,* 186.

99. Gorostegui de Torres, *Historia Argentina,* 120–21.

100. Oszlak, *La formación,* 189.

101. This, combined with the already significant ideological bent toward laissez-faire, devastated what little domestic industry existed and worsened the already considerable tensions between urban centers and the interior. For example, the dependence on the guano receipts (either through loans or through customs) allowed the Peruvian government to follow an open-market policy, since there was no fiscal requirement for tariffs. This "scorched earth free trade" further devastated what was left of a domestic producer class (Gootenberg, *Between Silver and Guano,* 134). In Peru, unlike in Europe, economic liberalism was not used to help the victory of an industrial bourgeoisie over a rural oligarchy, but was employed by foreign capital to establish its dominance (Yepes del Castillo, *Perú, 1820–1920,* 38). The low tariffs enforced by the British on Brazil until 1844 had the expected devastating impact on domestic industry. A

Simultaneously, the availability of foreign capital prevented the government from challenging elite groups and forging with them a national alliance. In fact, rather than war leading to greater central control, the absence of such sovereignty may have led to conflict. The War of the Pacific may best demonstrate the consequences of the external orientation of these states and the lack of domestic domination. It was "at heart a bald struggle over exports among jealous Chile, Bolivia, and Peru."[102] "All three countries were hard up, and run by oligarchies which disliked paying taxes and looked to revenue from these fertilizers [nitrate] as a substitute."[103] Each country was competing with the others for those resources that would allow it to maintain its "rentier" status and not challenge the domestic status quo.[104] War came because the states were too weak to fight their respective elites. For example, because the elites of the Altiplano were too powerful to tax, the Bolivian state saw the littoral and the nascent nitrate industry as the best source of fiscal support.[105] This brought it into conflict with Chile. But, precisely because it did not have adequate support from its home base, Bolivia could not hope to win.[106]

Wrong Timing

Rather than focusing on the importance of the "wrong kind" of wars or resources, it might be more accurate to say that the "right kind" of war came too soon. The Spanish Conquest in the sixteenth century had already subjugated the most powerful enemy of the criollos, the Indians. Arguably, where that fight continued well into the nineteenth century, it provided an important impetus for state making. Frontiers were areas of continuous warfare.[107] On the northern Mexican frontier, for example, the fight against the Indians did generate a social consensus on the need to develop an extensive military force and the subsequent need for the ability to pay for it.[108] The state of Nuevo León established relationships with its merchant and

---

similar decimation of the colonial artisanal and "manufacturing" class occurred in most other countries. Thus, Latin America delayed developing a national bourgeoisie around which a modern state apparatus could evolve.

102. Gootenberg, *Imagining Development*, 182.
103. Kiernan, "Foreign Interests in the War of the Pacific," 14.
104. Bonilla, "La crisis de 1872," 179.
105. Mörner, *The Andean Past*, 140–43.
106. Klein, *Bolivia*, 144–46.
107. Duncan Baretta and Markoff, "Civilization and Barbarism."
108. Cerrutti, *Economía de guerra y poder*, 29–30.

landowning classes much more along the lines of the European model than
what we see in the central government. The final Argentinean war against
the Indians, also known as the "Conquest of the Desert," in 1879–80 perhaps made a more significant economic contribution than the War of the
Triple Alliance, as it freed the frontier of the often expensive Indian raids
while allowing vast expansion of agribusiness and the promotion of greater
immigration. The war also helped to solidify the legitimacy of the state and
made President Julio Roca's political career.[109] The Conquest of the Desert
was partly financed by land sales, which further established the power of
the landowning elite.[110] This territorial expansion, combined with developments in the international economy, helped consolidate the oligarchic control that was to allow the Argentinean state some measure of coherence
during the following five decades. In Chile, the army that was to defeat its
northern neighbors during two critical wars was largely born and trained
on the frontier. Given the important role of the "frontier" in the development of the European state[111] and the United States, as well as the experience of Argentina, Chile, and Mexico, the presence of an easily defined
ethnic enemy *outside the borders* of a state could also have played an important role in Latin American political development.[112]

No matter the form of war, the Latin American states were not structur-
ally, politically, or ideologically ready to exploit the political opportunities
provided. The birth of the Latin American state, despite being announced
by gunfire, did not produce the expected political apparatus. Liberation
from Spain produced a much weaker institution (at least as measured by
fiscal structure) and one much more dependent on the international economy. The independence wars wrecked the economy and indebted the countries, making the rise of the structural equivalent of a national bourgeoisie
much more difficult. Thus Latin America was deprived of both a political
and a social anchor on which to base institutional development. The Latin
American state was never able to impose the internal unity required for the
extraction process, even in the face of military threats. As strange as it might
appear, given the oppression so endemic to the continent, the Latin Ameri-

109. Puigbo, *Historia social y económica Argentina*, 125–27; Gasio and San Román, *La conquista del progreso*, 115–25; Alemann, *Breve historia de la política económica argentina*, 101.
110. Rock, *Argentina, 1516–1987*, 154; Ferns, *The Argentine Republic, 1516–1971*, 70.
111. Robert Bartlett, *The Making of Europe*.
112. I owe much of this point to conversations with Michael Jiménez, Stephen Aron, and Jeremy Adelman.

can state may have suffered from an incomplete process of internal domination. In the European cases, representatives of the monarchy, the landed oligarchy, or the newly developing bourgeoisie were either willing to bear part of the burden in order to protect themselves, or were able to impose that obligation on recalcitrant social sectors. In Latin America, control of the state remained in contention.

It may be that wars can only make states within an ideological framework of enlightened despotism.[113] If so, independent Latin America provided an inauspicious setting. The postindependence period was not ideologically predisposed to state growth, in part a reaction to the expansion of the Spanish colonial state during the eighteenth century.[114] This met significant resistance; after the 1770s, rebellion against colonial authority became increasingly commonplace. Thus it was particularly difficult for postindependence governments to impose new tax measures, as these were associated with the absolutism that had just been defeated. Old taxes were abolished before new ones could be instituted.[115]

The dominance of liberal economic thought throughout the continent also went against the idea of a powerful and intrusive state.[116] The acceptance of classic liberalism set the ideological stage for the challenges to follow. Perhaps most important, none of the successful independence rebellions involved radical social reforms and most represented leading economic sectors. Those movements that did call for changes in the distribution of wealth, such as Hidalgo and Morelos in Mexico, may have actually contributed to the conservative bias of postindependence government by raising the specter of race war.

Latin America was not alone in this attitude toward taxation and government penetration, and certainly the United States had a very different institutional development despite similar ideological constraints. But Latin America faced obstacles not found further north. Even had the fiscal spirit been willing, it would have been difficult for the body to follow. Taxes do not collect themselves, but require a considerable administrative apparatus.

113. Kaiser, *Politics and War*, 206.

114. Similar to the experience of absolutism in western Europe, this generated a remarkable increase in resources available to the colonial governments. Mexican revenues, for example, increased fourfold during the eighteenth century (Bethell, *Cambridge History: Independence*, 10).

115. Burkholder and Johnson, *Colonial Latin America*, 330.

116. Collier, *Ideas and Politics of Chilean Independence*; Hale, *Mexican Liberalism in the Age of Mora, 1821–1853*; Burns, *Poverty of Progress*; Peloso and Tenenbaum, *Liberals, Politics, and Power*; Love and Jacobsen, *Guiding the Invisible Hand*.

The states facing war simply did not have the administrative capacity to respond with increased extraction. There was not enough "there" there to follow the coercion-extraction cycle.[117] For example, the administrative backwardness of the Ecuadorian bureaucracy was such that double-entry bookkeeping was not successfully imposed even after the 1850s and 1860s.[118] In 1851 and 1852, the Brazilian government attempted a census, to considerable opposition from members of almost all social sectors, who saw it as an effort to establish a list for either new taxes or conscription. As a result, the idea was abandoned.[119] In addition, despite the obvious benefits of a land tax, the sheer task of a cadastral survey would have been beyond the capacity of the Brazilian state.[120]

In the following section I discuss the reasons why the state was so unable to make use of the opportunities presented by war. It was not only the number or type of wars that distinguished Latin America, but also the social context in which these were fought.[121] Understanding the impact—or lack thereof—of war on the continent, requires analysis of both the conflicts themselves and the societies that fought them. While to some extent the institutional product of European war was technologically determined by the greater expenses involved in post-seventeenth-century warfare, the important break had more to do with the social and economic contexts in which the wars took place than with what happened on the battlefield.[122] In Latin America, the institutional and political stimulus of the drums of war fell on deaf ears. The structures or authority required to make use of these opportunities were not consolidated. Thus, even if the subsequent history had looked much more like that of western Europe, the starting conditions were too different for the same outcome to result.

117. Lofstrom, "From Colony to Republic."

118. Rodríguez, *The Search for Public Policy.*

119. Barman, *Brazil,* 236.

120. For an interesting contrast with the Japanese case, see Bird, "Land Taxation and Economic Development." The key comparative issue here would be that the military revolution in Europe was also accompanied by a bureaucratic revolution that dramatically increased the administrative capacity of the state.

121. It should be clear that I am addressing questions of state building from above. That war may have contributed to nationalism from below or that it fostered different types of communities is now fairly well accepted (Mallon, *Peasant and Nation*). The question still stands of why it did not seem to affect the construction of authoritative and inclusive political institutions at the level of the nation-state.

122. Kaiser, *Politics and War;* Tallett, *War and Society in Early Modern Europe;* Wallerstein, *Modern World System.*

Shadow States and Divided Societies

Wars provide opportunities for institutional development, but centralization requires a preexisting elaborated political logic. This can come from an already united elite that sees the growth of the state as in its interest, or alternatively, from a nascent class seeking to augment the territory under which it may function. Whether nationalist aristocracy or expanding bourgeoisie, these groups use war to defeat rivals or competing claimants. Latin America did not posses either group during its century of wars. There were too many divisions and claims to power. Unlike in Europe, wars did not provide opportunities for a single elite faction or family to impose its will on others, but rather functioned to perpetually maintain the possibility of rebellion.

We might wish to recall the distinction between a dominant and a ruling class.[123] Latin America possessed the first, but arguably not the second. In general, Latin American countries lacked a single class able to impose its will and organize the capacities of the state toward war. At best, military caudillos, urban merchants, and large landowners made temporary and unstable alliances. The independence wars failed to produce the hegemony required for the conjunction of military action and internal extraction. No faction of the dominant class was able to establish a strong enough hegemony to prioritize *national* collective interests (even if still defined in class terms). Because of the absence of this dominion, the state apparatus was not truly fiscally sovereign.

The key to understanding the Latin American failure to "benefit" from war lies in the myriad divisions that characterized these societies, detectable even prior to independence, when Latin America underwent an attempt at centralization of authority partly fueled by military concerns: the Bourbon reforms. The Seven Years War, which ended in 1763, and the Spanish involvement in the campaigns against France beginning in 1793 challenged the status quo relationship that had developed between Iberia and America.[124] The reforms initiated by Charles III, involving attempts to re-centralize authority and increase revenue, could be interpreted as an effort to transform the unwieldy Bourbon Empire into something resembling a

123. I owe this point to John Womack.
124. Bethell, *Cambridge History: Independence;* Lynch, *Spanish Colonial Administration; Bourbon Spain, 1700–1808;* Fisher, *Government and Society in Colonial Peru;* Brading, *Miners and Merchants in Bourbon Mexico; Haciendas and Ranchos.* See also Stein, *Silver, Trade, and War.*

cross-Atlantic state. The Bourbon army was essentially created to deal with these external challenges.[125] The reforms were considerably successful, although met with opposition, including violent protest.[126] Could these reforms have produced a state closer to the European model? Following Rodríguez one could imagine the development of such a political entity, or more likely, the consolidation producing three or four larger states than arose out of the independence wars.[127] In any case, the Bourbon reforms indicate that the role of war as a stimulus or incentive for institutional development and political consolidation was relevant to the continent prior to the nineteenth century.

This experience provides a hint of the future role of war in state building.[128] Thanks to the increased need for armed force, the military was granted greater institutional autonomy through the *fueros*. The result was that the military played a more important role in the region, but remained outside society and above the state, establishing a pattern that would continue for years to come. Most important, while the greater military and administrative capacity may have developed as a response to international threats, armed force was increasingly directed inward. The colonial state came to be oriented not to protecting the society from an external menace, but to repressing internal threats.[129]

It is these real and perceived threats that best explain the particular relationship between state and war making on the continent. The Bourbon reforms produced a more efficient political apparatus, but they also brought to a head the internal divisions that would haunt Latin America over the following one hundred years. Military tensions and concerns created administrative and fiscal crises that encouraged the state to impose its authority, but the last quarter of the eighteenth century already saw the conflicts that would plague attempts to create more solid political structures. The society on which the state rested was not sufficiently united to provide an adequate arena for institutional consolidation. Institutional developments fueled by military conflict were frustrated by the strength of geographical, social, and racial divisions. These appeared in slightly different forms across the conti-

125. Rodríguez, introduction to *Rank and Privilege*, x.

126. Phelan, *The People and the King*; Stern, *Resistance, Rebellion, and Consciousness in the Andean Peasant World, Eighteenth to Twentieth Centuries*.

127. Rodríguez O., *Independence in Spanish America*.

128. Archer, *Army in Bourbon Mexico*; L. G. Campbell, "The Army of Peru and the Túpac Amaru Revolt," 1; McAlister, *The "Fuero Militar" in New Spain, 1764–1800*.

129. It was largely unsuccessful in the face of external menace. For example, the British were thrown out of Buenos Aires in 1806 by forces organized and led by nonofficial actors.

nent (Table 3.4), but the result was generally the same. War led not to increased order and unity, but to chaos and division. In the following pages I discuss each of these divisions in turn.

Regionalism

Despite the efforts of Charles III, Latin America entered the nineteenth century arguably more divided than ever. The Americas as a whole resented the imposition of an order dictated in Madrid. The various subunits of the Bourbon domains wished to protect and expand their autonomy vis-à-vis the central power. The viceregal seats in turn resisted efforts to create small, more autonomous governments from their individual parts (for example, the captaincy-generals and *intendencias*). Granting greater local autonomy to one group, as in the creation of the Viceroyalty of Río de Plata, often meant diminishing that of others, such as Paraguay, or forcing others to shift their administrative allegiances, as in Charcas. Thus, efforts to create a greater whole—whatever the benefits to be derived from this—were met with resistance from those who felt that their individual part would suffer. Autonomist rebellions consistently brought to head salient social divisions within the various regions.

The notion of a fragmented sovereignty had a long history on the continent. The colonial regime had already recognized considerable regional diversity and autonomy and even had floated a plan of dividing the continent into three kingdoms—Mexico, Peru, and Nueva Granada.[130] The conflicts over sovereignty were not simply between province and capital, but also within the provinces themselves, between regional and municipal governments.[131] In any case, the colonial state barely controlled large parts of the empire. Most of northern Mexico was beyond its control, as was the southern area of the continent. In part because of geographical and logistical challenges, and in part because of Spain's fears of transatlantic autonomy, the Bourbon reforms established at least a semicentralized state, *but not a unitary one*.[132] Each part of the empire was connected to the center, but the separate regions were not linked with one another. The resulting political entity that had to face the challenge of the Napoleonic invasion in 1808 thus lacked a solid territorial cohesion. The crown was the real source of

130. Jaramillo Uribe, "Nación y región,"
131. Annino, "Soberanías en lucha," 250.
132. Kossok, "Revolución, estado y nación," 163.

Table 3.4 Internal divisions in Latin America

	Regionalism	Racism/Class Conflict	Elite Division
Argentina	Buenos Aires vs. provinces	Indian conflict; gauchos	Unitarios vs. Federalistas; different caudillos
Bolivia	La Paz vs. Sucre	Minuscule elite with disenfranchised Indian masses	No dominant group
Brazil	Rampant through 19th century	Concern with postslavery inclusion	Declines after regency
Chile	Santiago soon dominant	Becomes more relevant with mining development	Later 19th-century ideological divisions
Colombia	Rampant through 19th century	Centered on class divisions	Liberals vs. conservatives
Ecuador	Coast vs. Sierra	Indian vs. white elite	Liberals vs. conservatives
Mexico	Provinces at margin	Very strong in postindependence	Liberals vs. conservatives; caudillo politics
Paraguay	Asunción dominates	State co-opts Indian identity	None left after Francia
Peru	Lima vs. Sierra vs. Coast	Fear of Indian uprising	Caudillo and follows geography
Uruguay	Montevideo vs. rural	Urban class conflict	Blancos/Colorados
Venezuela	Llanos vs. coast	Very strong in postindependence	Caudillos

sovereignty, and when the political order came under strain and the crown lost much of its inherent legitimacy, there were relatively weak links keeping the various parts together.

The early experiences with the wars of independence exacerbated these conflicts of sovereignty. In large part because of both sides' need to acquire resources, rebel and loyal administrations each sought to centralize power over areas under their control. Such efforts continued after the 1820s because of fear of postbellic chaos. Since both the royal governments and their successors were generally too weak to enforce their constitutional claims, attempts to at least formally increase their authority merely exacerbated local fears without resolving the conflict in their favor. Instead of a true federalism with enough assurances to ensure provincial loyalty, or an autocratic centralism resolving regional differences, efforts at centralization merely produced resentment and rebellion. The result was the worst of all possible worlds: the threat of central authority kept the provinces and local powers restive, while the limits on the state prevented a final resolution.

The wars of independence witnessed the dispersion and dissipation of political authority. In New Granada, the authority of the autonomist government in Bogotá did not extend much past that city as Cundinamarca and Santa Marta, among others, claimed different allegiances, and *patrias bobas* survived repeated attempts to centralize authority. In Ecuador, the longstanding rivalry between coastal Guayaquil and highlands Quito moved to new levels as the latter became politically dominated by Venezuelans from the invading liberators. In Bolivia, Sucre provided the Charcas elite with the military protection it needed to separate itself from Peru and establish its own independent nation. The very same logic that would allow La Plata to break from the rest of the empire seemed to permit each of the provinces to divorce itself from Buenos Aires. Each new subunit produced further claims to autonomy. The state of Tucumán faced secession from Santiago de Estero and La Rioja broke off from Córdoba. The failure of Buenos Aires to stop this process is most critical to understanding the following fifty years. Forces in both what would become Bolivia and Paraguay defeated *porteño* attempts to keep them in the old viceroyalty. These failures served as an inspiration to other regions. Moreover, the military and political effort expended by the various expeditions made it difficult to gather the resources needed to keep other provinces in line.

The discrepancy in resources available to the provinces actually abetted regionalism, since it often made the richer regions, often associated with the capital, reluctant to enter into political contracts that necessitated sharing their wealth. The Argentine situation was emblematic of a pattern found across the continent. The income of Tucumán, for example, was one-thousandth of that available to Buenos Aires, while that of Jujuy was almost nonexistent. In 1827, the province of Córdoba had an income of seventy thousand pesos whereas Buenos Aires had 2.5 million.[133] If unwilling to share its bounty, Buenos Aires might have yet conquered the rest of the country. But poverty did not mean military incompetence, and the poorer regions were able to hold the richer ones at bay while never being able to conquer them.

In Mexico, the pattern continued after independence, when the country essentially dissolved into a "series of satrapies dominated by caudillos."[134] Throughout the nineteenth century, the central Mexican state could not even eliminate interstate barriers to national commerce. The Texas War, which began in 1835 and arguably continued until 1847, certainly did not aid the institutional development of the Mexican state. The many civil wars actually impeded efforts to impose central authority, as individual provinces could usually find a general or pretender to challenge any dictates from Mexico City or attempt to change the government. Ironically, Mexico City was accused of attempting to establish a new Tenochtitlán even as it could not control the road to Veracruz.[135] In fact, no single authority possessed the capacity to impose its project on the whole country.[136] Political regionalism arguably survived the Díaz era and was only stamped out after 1910.[137]

The independence project also suffered from a critical contradiction at its core.[138] On the one hand, the independence of each region was always subordinated to the independence of the continent. No province was allowed to concentrate on its purely protonational interests. The struggle was to free America. On the other hand, however, the sovereignty of each region was never sacrificed to a central entity. Conquest was not allowed. San Martín could not conquer Chile for La Plata. But Chile did not completely control the armies within its borders. This resulted in a disastrous combination of a supranational military with regional political authority, in turn, producing a disjunction between military might and territorial limits that fatally weakened the centralizing effect of war.

133. Scobie, *Argentina,* 94; Burgin, *Economic Aspects of Argentine Federalism,* 126.
134. Coatsworth, "Obstacles to Growth in Nineteenth Century Mexico," 95.
135. This was not a unique situation. In the 1820s and 1830s, the road from Lima to Callao was often unusable because of bandits (Dobyns and Doughty, *Peru,* 171).
136. Cardoso, *México en el siglo XIX,* 60.
137. G. Thompson, "Federalism and Vantonalism in Mexico."
138. Kossok, "Revolución, estado y nación."

As Halperín-Donghi has often noted, the independence wars established a particularly vicious connection between regional identities and divisions and military force. Thanks to the duration and savagery of the independence struggle, by the 1820s the continent had literally dozens of armed groups contending for control. Perhaps more important, military power was essentially autonomous. With few exceptions, armies did not evolve past a provincial militia mode, with a few professionals leading local masses.[139] The military was not the armed representative of the state, but fought for either an individual leader or some vague notion of "liberty." Partly because of relatively low technical requirements, partly because of the absence of competition, leaders of irregular armed forces could easily become independent of the governments that organized them. Armies were not regulated by any central authority, but were often under the control of precisely those who wished to be left alone by such powers. Armies, in this case, were not a way of establishing political authority, but keeping it at bay. Military mobilization was not accompanied, much less preceded, by political mobilization.

Even countries that were spared ruinous independence wars found regionalism an almost insurmountable obstacle. The first thirty years of the Brazilian Empire witnessed yearly efforts to bring a recalcitrant region or social group under the control of Rio. While the army did serve as a unifier during much of this period, particularly during the 1830s and 1840s, it also suffered from regional divisions. Military camps and barracks, for example, would often be divided according to the geographical origins of the troops.[140] The empire never established a strong central authority. Instead it could be interpreted as a patrimonial state operating a network of favors, guaranteeing some legitimacy, and serving as the police of last resort for elite squabbles.[141]

Rather than mitigating regionalism, war often made geographical divisions even more detrimental to centralized authority. To survive in often difficult logistical situations or to obtain needed resources, armies (whether claimants to power or representatives of official authority) often had to negotiate deals with local powers. As recruitment was often geographically concentrated, significant parts of armies also reflected their provincial origins and replicated their loyalties to their towns through their chiefs.[142]

139. Annino, "Soberanías en lucha," 252.
140. Nunn, *Yesterday's Soldiers,* 58–59.
141. Graham, *Patronage and Politics in Nineteenth-Century Brazil.*
142. Annino, "Soberanías en lucha," 252.

Racism

One could argue that some early military conflicts helped create a nascent *Latin American* identity. The militias and even formal armies established by the Bourbon reforms were largely staffed by colonials.[143] The military was arguably the first truly American institution and one that helped develop and consolidate a separate identity of criolloism. Yet a more salient response to the Bourbon reforms, and again one that would haunt Latin America into contemporary times, was increasing conflict between races, classes, and castes. The Tupac Amarú and Quito revolts grew from foundations much older and more complex than the Bourbon reforms. In the case of the Peruvian rebellion, we should take into account the frustrations of the old Inca aristocracy, the heavy weight of the *mita* forced labor, regionalist pressures to create a separate intendancy for Cuzco, and most important, racial strife. What is most relevant for our purposes, however, is that the specter of race war hampered the progress of the rebellion and helped shape attitudes toward the loyalist victory in 1783.

Much more than in Europe and or even the United States, Latin American elites lived in constant fear of the *enemy below*. More than any competing elite across a border, nonwhite subalterns represented the most significant threat to the social status quo. Such fears need to be understood in light of the demographics facing the white elite at the beginning to middle of the century. In Brazil, for example, slaves made up one-third of the population.[144] New Spain at independence consisted of 20 percent whites, 20 percent mestizos, 40 percent Indians, and 20 percent *castas*.[145] New Granada at independence was 33 percent whites, 43 percent mestizos, 17 percent Indians, and 6.5 percent slaves while Venezuela had sixty thousand slaves.[146] Quito was 90 percent Indian.[147]

Racial conflicts were particularly critical to the historical impact of the war of independence in Mexico. The Hidalgo and Morelos revolts of the first part of the decade convinced a significant part of even autonomist criollo opinion that the dissolution of the political status quo would produce a race war in which they would suffer the fate of their equivalents in Guanajuato or, the true specter, Haiti. The criollo elite united in supporting the authori-

143. Loveman, *For la Patria,* 15.
144. Bushnell and Macaulay, *Emergence of Latin America,* 150.
145. Torre Villar, "El origen del estado mexicano," 128.
146. Jaramillo Uribe, "Nación y región," 342–47.
147. Ocampo López, "La separación de la Gran Colombia," 370.

ties, and by 1814, loyalist control was assured. Rather than an assertion of liberal sentiment, the eventual independence of Mexico came as a reaction to the Cadiz Mutiny of 1820 and the threat it represented to vested interests and ideologies. The almost bloodless Iturbide revolt that produced an independent Mexico in 1821 was a classic rebellion from above meant to slow social change through political restructuring.[148]

Racism and fear of armed nonwhites also hampered Bolívar's early campaigns. The royal government successfully exploited these tensions. By 1812, a royalist army allied with blacks, Indians, and *pardos* was able to impose its authority over Venezuela. Bolívar's next attempt did include an alliance with the *pardos,* and more important, with the *llanero* cowboys under José Antonio Páez. Later campaigns in Peru, in turn, appeared to have been hampered by perceptions of the independence army as Indian dominated.

Throughout the following century the prospect of armed Indians alarmed white elites (much as the prospect of armed ex-slaves and freedmen alarmed both Northern and Southern whites in the American Civil War). This was not only because of the immediate access to violence that guns provided, but also because of the perhaps more dangerous and insidious notion that participation in battle bestowed equality on Indians. Peasants who fought *did* begin to believe in their own equality as soldiers and demanded to be treated accordingly.[149] Thus, the very fact that the military was at least perceived as a ladder for social and ethnic mobility made its role as a national unifier problematic. The "tool" was tainted by the very problems it was meant to solve.

This contradiction was complicated by the army's central mission in most of Latin America: protection of "civilization" either from revolts by internal subalterns or through defense of frontiers from "savages." Yet large numbers of those in the army were ethnically (as well as socioeconomically and geographically) related to the "enemy." The military was composed of the very same threat from which it was to protect the nation.

Racism also often limited the potential authority of promising leaders, even when faced by war. Andrés Santa Cruz attempted to unite Peru and Bolivia and faced war with Chile. Yet he received little support from the Lima elite, who despised him for his race and class origins. Members of the

---

148. Sometimes, however, racial fears could actually assist central authority. Creole Yucatecos' willingness to obey Mexico City certainly increased when they realized that they needed the central government's help to put down local Indian revolts in the 1840s.
149. Mallon, *Defense of Community,* 88.

Peruvian elite (along with future presidents Agustín Gamarra and Ramón Castilla) fought on the side of the Chileans against Santa Cruz.[150] Rather than consolidating a sense of nation and Lima's sovereignty, the war maintained the isolated fiefdoms defined by geographical regions. Gamarra and Castilla subsequently faced the same discrimination against their mixed origins when they assumed power.

Racial divisions enjoyed some institutional sanctions. Well into the nineteenth century, for example, there existed *repúblicas indias* where the national government did not rule, as well as pockets of territorial loyalties or *patrias chicas* often associated with indigenous groups. Liberal critiques of these separate nations were not completely off the mark in suggesting that no nation could arise as long as these communities existed. This is not to deny the disastrous consequences for the Indian populations when liberals later in the century dismantled these protections. Yet, while they did serve to protect segments of the population against the commercial onslaught that was often to leave them landless, their existence made the consolidation of a single nation very difficult. The idea of two—if not more—nations haunted the nineteenth century.

While all the major European nations created their nationalities as they were developing their territories, they were not as internally divided as Latin America. If making Italians, Germans, Britons, or the French involved the forceful imposition of the culture of a single region or creation of a compromise national language, it did not require the mending of centuries-long racial gulfs closely correlated with the distribution of political and economic power. The very composition of "the nation" was fraught with conflict. Under these circumstances, wars were not occasions for institutional unity, but represented opportunities for groups to opt out of the national project. In the end, the *official* military was not organized to protect or even co-opt the people, but to coerce them.[151]

Elite Divisions

Despite, or perhaps because of, their extremely privileged position, elites in most Latin American countries have been internally divided.[152] This took a

---

150. Dobyns and Doughty, *Peru,* 158.
151. I emphasize the form of military, since we need to distinguish it from more popular armed organizations such as resisted the Chileans or fought against the French (Mallon, *Peasant and Nation*).
152. My argument here of course follows the work of Halperín-Donghi.

variety of forms during the Bourbon period. One was the struggle between state and church. The Bourbon reforms sought to increase the power of the former at the cost of the latter. In some places, most prominently in the case of the Jesuits of Paraguay, this involved removing church influence altogether. In others it simply meant a shift in control of resources. A second form of intra-elite struggle exacerbated by the Bourbon reforms was that between American-born criollos and *peninsulares,* born in Spain. The latter had the most to benefit from attempts to delocalize administration and associated efforts to increase immigration from Spain. Although often dressed in the Enlightenment guise of liberty and rights, American opposition to the reforms frequently had more to do with the protection of sinecures and social positions. The imposition of mercantilist policies, which again might have benefited the Iberian-American Empire as a whole, met with a similar response.

There were also divisions within the elite regarding the benefits of remaining within the imperial system. The Spanish crown offered some American elites a series of important advantages, protection from external threats and internal security being perhaps the most important. While large portions of the American population might chafe under the control of Madrid—such as it was—significant groups saw it as preferable to a situation in which they would not be able to maintain their social, political, and economic control. It is not surprising that some elites (and nonelites) were loyal to the crown and that the independence struggle took nearly two decades to complete.

Elite divisions made it difficult to unify coercive capacity and use it constructively. At least theoretically, Argentina and Chile should have enjoyed the best of all possible worlds in their experience with the wars of independence. While both (but especially Argentina) provided important logistical support for the liberation of other regions, neither suffered significant destruction. Yet in both cases, the wars of independence did not produce the consolidated state we might have predicted and in one, such an institution would not arise until fifty years later. How do we explain this pattern?

In the case of Argentina, the first decade following May 1810 was characterized by elite divisions not simply along *peninsular*/criollo lines, but also between groups wishing different levels of separation from the government in Spain. By the Congress of Tucumán, Argentina had seen "two juntas, two triumvirates, one assembly, one directorate with four office holders, and a constituent congress."[153] In part this may be explained by the very absence

153. Navarro de García, "El orden tradicional," 156.

of a believable threat to Buenos Aires, but it also reflected real divisions in the Argentinean elite along both instrumental and ideological lines. A fateful decision in this regard was to allow Buenos Aires's best general and considerable troops and resources to be devoted to the defeat of Loyalist forces in Chile and Peru. A San Martín in Entre Ríos or Santa Fe *might* have given a Buenos Aires–dominated union a better chance. In this case, it would appear that external war (if so we can count the Chilean and Peruvian campaigns) sucked strength out of the nascent state. Had San Martín been needed to fight a believable Spanish threat in Montevideo after 1814, he might have been able to impose a unitary order on the other provinces.

The initial Argentinean involvement in Uruguay and fears of Brazilian reaction in the late 1820s produced greater support for a stronger president. Bernardino Rivadavia certainly benefited from some of the victories against the Brazilians. He even envisioned using the army that had fought Brazil in Uruguay for local consolidation: "haremos la unidad a palos."[154] But his inability or unwillingness to exploit the peace created tension and actually led to the subsequent political dissolution.

On the other side of the river, the Cisplatine war was a disaster for Pedro I. The defeat—and Uruguayan independence was perceived as such—weakened his authority and complicated the political balance between centrists and federalists. In both cases, divisions inside the ruling elites led to the waste of the opportunity presented by international conflict.[155] In general, however, Brazil after 1840 may represent an important exception to this pattern of elite division, as it was able to develop something resembling a governing class whose professional and political interests were linked to the preservation and even expansion of state authority.[156] In this instance a war may have assisted in the imposition of a governmental directive. The War of the Triple Alliance provided the government with a better opportunity than it had ever enjoyed to challenge the slave owners' power and impose at least gradual manumission.

Elite divisions also helped shape the independence struggle on the northern coast of the continent. In the early stages of the struggle, some of the

154. Rock, *Argentina, 1516–1987*, 102.
155. Wars in the Platine region did provide resources for central authorities to purchase political loyalty. Rosas's campaign against the Indians in the early 1830s gave him a great deal more land with which to reward allies. Similarly, Brazilian success in Uruguay following Rosas's defeat improved relations between the emperor and the elites of the southern states.
156. Merquior, "Patterns of State-Building"; Graham, *Patronage and Politics;* Carvalho, "Political Elites and State-Building."

elite feared that the collapse of the royal government in Spain would provide an opportunity for the nonwhite majority to threaten the social status quo, but a more radical segment wished to move toward full independence. The resulting power struggle quashed both hopes. Criollos killed criollos under a variety of flags. Not even Bolívar's considerable military successes could stop the infighting. By 1819, Bolívar once again controlled most of what would become Colombia and Venezuela. But the wars had left the region devastated; various groups (most important, Páez's army) remained largely beyond the control of the central government; and regional antagonisms remained. When Bolívar moved his army south, his representative Francisco Santander was not able to hold the various parts together.

Postindependence Peru continued to suffer from elite divisions, often correlated with regions. Members of the Lima elite were divided in their attitudes to Bolívar and San Martín and their successors. In turn, Lima was split from the merchants and miners of the highlands, who did not see eye to eye with sugar planters on the coast.[157] With the possible exception of Ramón Castilla, no single political entrepreneur could establish a monopoly over national power. From 1826 to 1865, thirty-four different men served as Peru's chief executive.[158] These divisions played a major role in the eventual defeat of Peru in the War of the Pacific. In the words of Florencia Mallon, "[N]o measure of heroic exploits or symbols could compensate for the lack of unity and national purpose of the Peruvian elite."[159] In Bolivia, the independence army was soon torn apart in a struggle between those who sought union with southern or western neighbors and those who wanted full independence.[160]

Further, the Mexican war of independence failed to provide the opportunity to consolidate authority in a postcolonial setting. On the one hand, elites were united enough to resist a popular insurrection that might have created a more socially revolutionary national government. On the other, once the threat of race war was removed, no individual segment was strong enough to impose its will on the others. Even more than in Argentina and Chile, independence destroyed what political authority had existed without leaving the framework for domination by a central government. The construction of a new nation-state was begun without the existence of a hege-

157. Halperín-Donghi, *Contemporary History,* 99.
158. Dobyns and Doughty, *Peru,* 158.
159. Mallon, *Defense of Community,* 82.
160. Buisson, Kahle, König, and Pietschmann, *Problemas de la formación del estado y de la nación en Hispanoamérica,* 502.

monic power bloc; instead of durable alliances, Mexico had hard battles.[161] Santa Anna's disastrous, decades-long rebellions began in 1822—merely a year after his helping Iturbide come to power. Perhaps worse than Santa Anna's meddling was his failure (or lack of interest?) in establishing a permanent domination over the Mexican state. Neither domineering autocrat nor obedient subject, Santa Anna made Mexican political stability impossible.

Latin America was torn in a half-century struggle between what would be called, despite localized differences, Liberal and Conservative views of the role of the state.[162] Liberals—arguing for greater political inclusion and intellectual and commercial freedom—had dominated the independence struggles. But in the immediate aftermath of victory they faced a dilemma: how to protect individual rights while also constructing a new political order.[163] In opposition, Conservatives sought to protect what they saw as worthwhile inheritances from the colonial period: protection of property, the church, and some economic sectors. The two strands were associated (in varying ways) with federalist versus centralist projects. Divisions also persisted during much of this period over notions of citizenship, sovereignty, and the relation between state and society. For much of the nineteenth century, Latin America was stuck between a liberalism that did not guarantee order and a form of nationalism that would inherently exclude a large part of the population. Supporters of opposing visions "prolonged the military phase of the independence movements and virtually guaranteed that chaos would be an inescapable legacy of newly formed states."[164] Much as in fifteenth-century Italy, the prevalence of factions and their myopic preoccupation with local battles retarded the creation of a political union capable of acting on the international stage and expanding its domestic authority.[165]

The nature or outcome of disputes was not as important as the fact that for many years neither tendency was able to completely dominate political

161. San Juan Victoria and Velázquez Ramírez, "La formación del estado," 67.

162. There were also cases where the struggles were more openly between elite factions not encumbered with much ideological baggage, as was the case with Blancos and Colorados in Uruguay. In this instance elite divisions appeared to have been at least partly the product of international squabbles and subsequent conflicts. In this sense, wars were very much responsible for the underdevelopment of the Uruguayan state (López-Alves, "Wars and the Formation of Political Parties").

163. Adelman and Centeno, "Law and the Failure of Liberalism in Latin America"; Botana, *La tradición republicana*.

164. Knight, "State of Sovereignty and the Sovereignty of States," 18.

165. Morse, "Theory of Spanish American Government," 79.

life. The "German" road to nationhood was not open, given the ethnic divisions, but the state was not strong enough to enforce a "French" road.[166] Nor could any one camp construct systems acceptable to the others. Without either consensus or hegemony, many Latin American states could not consolidate their rule. One war did help resolve these struggles and arguably played a role similar to that of conflicts in Europe. The Mexican war against the French (in many ways a continuation of the Reforma) destroyed the classic conservative elite. It also necessitated the creation of a truly national army garrisoned throughout the country. This army and the elimination of *some* elite divisions provided the basis for the Porfiriato.

Because these divisions played themselves out militarily all over the continent, armies, for all intents and purposes, *were* the state, and they certainly consumed the largest part of its resources.[167] But unlike in Europe, the military did not serve a single master. First, it was willing to be bought by whichever actor promised the best reward for its services. Equally important, because of the lack of technical sophistication, it could not impose a monopoly on the means of violence. The costs of entry into the military-political competitive market were generally low. Throughout the continent, provinces and local caudillos raised and maintained militias that protected their interests. Militias served to defend property, not governments.[168] The militarization of Latin America during this period represented the worst of all possible worlds: armies fought without being able to dominate and they coerced without extracting. Although draining large amounts of money, the military did not provide a means with which to pay for itself. Here we come to the crux of the Latin American puzzle that may explain not only the state's relationship with war, but also that of the military with civilian authority. Through a series of historical events beginning with the independence war, the military assumed a political autonomy separate from the state as such. Much has been written about how this encouraged the military to set itself up as the ultimate judge of national virtue. We have appreciated less the fact that this divorce between state and military robbed the former of an assured means with which to impose its will.

The absence of an institutional consensus and the difficulties facing the establishment of order often forced the most successful rulers to ignore constitutional principles. That is, order was too often based on the disregard of

166. Brubaker, *Citizenship and Nationhood.*
167. Halperín-Donghi, *Aftermath of Revolution,* 74–75.
168. Halperín-Donghi, *Aftermath of Revolution,* 9.

law that made the long-term consolidation of a political system and the creation of an elite consensus still more difficult. Vincente Rocafuerte best expressed this contradiction when he declared himself "a true lover of enlightenment and civilization," adding, "I consent to pass for a tyrant."[169]

But it was not tyranny as such that represented a problem for the growth of the state, but on what forms of authority that tyranny rested. Here it is important to analyze the role of political entrepreneurs in Latin America. For much of the first seventy-five years of independence, the region's critical political actor was not the institutionalized authority of the state, but the much more personalized rule of the caudillo.[170] Arising from the destruction of colonial institutions, the emergence of local power centers, and the need for some form of order, the caudillos sought to alternatively appropriate the power of the central state, as in the case of Páez or Santa Anna; or challenge it, as in the classic Argentine regional caudillos such as Estanislao López or Facundo Quiroga.[171] If the "worst" were full of passionate intensity and political prowess, the "best" were unable to defend their authority. Santa Anna's antagonist, Lucas Alamán, for example, never served a government strong enough to impose a permanent centralized republic.

The more interesting cases are the caudillos who could have become much more. Páez gave Venezuela two decades of peace by successfully constructing an alliance between the military and pre-independence elites and Rosas temporarily managed an equilibrium of various regional leaders' interests. Such gifted caudillos sometimes were able to construct the semblance of states, but these were hardly institutional orders and rarely, if ever, survived their founders. Perhaps the most mysterious of cases is Rosas. There is no question that he pacified the province of Buenos Aires or that he was at least first among equals in the confederation. Once he had established his position, however, he seemed uninterested in expanding the region under his direct control. Rosas's nearly constant warfare, especially his conflicts with Britain and France, helped to consolidate his popular legitimacy, but he never used this to do anything but reinforce his control over Buenos Aires Province. The forty years of civil war following independence brought little more than superficial change to an Argentina still dominated by caudillos.

Neither Argentina nor any of the other nations produced by indepen-

---

169. Bethell, *Cambridge History*, vol. 3, 369.
170. Lynch, *Caudillos in Spanish America*.
171. Lynch, *Caudillos in Spanish America*.

dence experienced a post-Thermidor, which would have institutionalized the changes brought about through political revolution and re-created the state in a new bureaucratic form. The result was a disastrous combination of local autocracy with little weak central domination; a continent of repressive islands with few links between them.

Nor was the appearance of the Latin American state accompanied by the rise of a hegemonic class willing and able to ride it to social and political dominance. The wars of independence were produced by the collapse of the Spanish crown's legitimacy, not by *internal* changes in the colonial societies. The wars disrupted the old order, but they did not establish an alternative system of domination. When the colonial apparat disappeared, no social group had an interest in replacing it with one equally strong. What the criollos wanted was as little interference as possible in their immediate profit making. The availability of international moneys allowed elites an exit, thereby inhibiting the development of class loyalty to the state.

In an almost complete reversal of the European pattern, the appearance of the modern state strengthened the political power of the landowning class. It was a Fronde in reverse. Those who possessed resources were completely successful in protecting their wealth. The only exception came, perhaps, in the immediate period of the independence wars. When San Martín finally arrived in Peru in 1821, for example, he gave a great deal of Spanish-held property to those who fought in his army. It is important to note, however, that the criollo landowning class was largely spared these sacrifices, as they were borne by the Spanish *peninsulares* and, in some cases, the church. When the criollo elite was asked to pay for its independence, it almost always refused, a pattern that was to be repeated for the following hundred years, if not longer. Given that the criollos were unwilling to pay even for the elimination of the old masters, we should not be surprised that they would be reluctant to pay for a new one.

The response to subsequent wars was similar. While the Chilean armies were marching on Lima, Peruvian finance minister Quimper suggested a small tax on capital to pay the troops in the field. These measures were defeated.[172] The government also asked for an internal loan of 10 million soles. This request generated 1 million, largely from the "popular classes," as the rich did not want to risk their money.[173] During the same war, the

172. Ugarte, *Historia económica del Perú*; United States Department of State, *Foreign Relations*, 165–68.

173. Bonilla, "War of the Pacific," 99. The British ambassador noted with surprise that "Peru appears struck with paralysis; the people themselves seem as indifferent to the future as

Chilean legislature was repeatedly unable to impose a wealth or an income tax.[174] When Mexican finance minister Lorenzo Zavala attempted to impose a direct tax to finance a defense against the possible Spanish invasion of 1829, he was defeated and his government overthrown by an elite-sponsored coup.[175] Similar efforts during the so-called Pastry War with France produced identical results. Even as the U.S. army marched toward Mexico City in 1847, the government frantically negotiated with the church and domestic lenders for funds.[176] In Brazil the Chamber of Deputies consistently refused to give any funds to Pedro I to fight in Uruguay.[177]

Taxes and the avoidance thereof made it very clear where the line marking off the dominant from the dominated was to be drawn.[178] In Brazil, the *fazenderio* was systematically avoided as an object of taxation. Discussions regarding land or income taxes had no result; the landowning elite was considered fiscally untouchable.[179] Bolivia's Sucre attempted to impose a direct tax on wealth in the 1820s; within a year, this tax had been abolished. Resistance was both economically and racially based. Along with the rich resisting the new imposition, whites resented being placed under a *contribución* and being placed on the same level as Indians.[180] Argentinean attempts to expand the tax base faltered because of the successful opposition of powerful social interests already well represented in the legislature.[181] The *contribución directa* was a farce, as the legislature would not allow the creation of an independent system of assessment.[182] In the 1830s, a ranch with nineteen thousand head of cattle paid a total of 540 depreciated pesos.[183]

While the avoidance of taxes is perhaps one of the few truly universal traits, the absolute regressivity of the Latin American cases compares unfavorably with some European cases. The resistance of the French is famous, but the British and German propertied classes were made to pay in one form

the governing classes, who are thinking more of their personal ambition than the welfare of their country" (quoted in Bonilla, "War of the Pacific," 98).

174. Sater, *Chile and the War of the Pacific,* 131–54.
175. Tenenbaum, *The Politics of Penury,* 34–35.
176. Tenenbaum, *Politics of Penury,* 79.
177. Haring, *Empire in Brazil,* 35 n. 17.
178. Gomes, *The Roots of State Intervention in the Brazilian Economy,* 93–94.
179. Buescu, *Evolução econômica do Brasil,* 142; Leff, *Underdevelopment and Development in Brazil.*
180. Lofstrom, "Attempted Economic Reform," 282–86; Paz, *Historia económica de Bolivia,* 52.
181. Halperín-Donghi, *Guerra y finanzas,* 155.
182. Friedman, *The State and Underdevelopment in Spanish America,* 185.
183. Burgin, *Economic Aspects of Argentine Federalism,* 189.

or another.[184] In Latin America, what little was paid appears to have come from those on the bottom, caste taxes being perhaps the most glaring example. While there are differences depending on the import basket and the specific rates, the general view is that customs taxes were also extremely regressive.[185]

An important factor here is that the relevant elites did not see the wars as threatening their social positions and thus did not have the incentive to permit greater political penetration. That is, the relevant elite did not appear to care which state ruled them as long as it was not markedly stronger than its predecessor. No state was alien to the elites' immediate interests.[186] A transfer of political allegiance did not imply a change in property. Certainly in most cases, their concern appears to have been with protection from internal enemies, either ideological or, more commonly, class and racial ones. The maintenance of such internal control did not require an expansive and expensive state. In this, as in perhaps many factors, the Latin American elites were much closer to their Italian and Polish counterparts than to the English gentry or the Dutch bourgeoisie. For both these last two, fear of external threats, be it the Spaniards or "Popery," drove the elites to support high levels of taxation.

Interestingly, losing wars appeared to have created the base not for a more powerful state, but at least for a closer union between political goals and the interests of the dominant elite.[187] Following the defeat by Chile, Bolivian elites appear to have been more open to paying for a state that could protect as well as build the infrastructure needed for the exploitation of natural resources. Mexico's defeat in 1848 and the subsequent Treaty of Guadalupe produced a split among the *agiotistas* regarding the need for stronger government. Some members of the elite began to recognize the advantage of a better-integrated national economy and the need for a government to nurture it.[188] For the first time, the state was perceived as something other than a massive feeding trough. The Liberals who took

---

184. Stone, *An Imperial State at War.*

185. Further research needs to be done on the composition of imports during the nineteenth century to determine the class distribution of payment of customs taxes.

186. I owe this point to Michael Mann.

187. The consequences of war could be disastrous. From 1870 to 1894, Peru went from having 18 millionaires, to none; from 11,587 classified as rich to 1,725; from 22,148 classified as well off to 2,000. Yet despite this looming disaster, the Peruvian elite seemed more concerned with resistance by peasants than invasion by Chileans (Mallon, *Defense of Community,* chap. 2).

188. Tenenbaum, *Politics of Penury,* 83–85, 116–17.

power in 1855 had the support of some of the wealthy who had begun to understand the potential benefits of a stronger state and they looked to the considerable wealth of the church for funds. The most interesting aspect of the ecclesiastical reforms is that in its battle with the church, the government enjoyed the support of a faction of the *agiotistas* who sought a securer basis for their loans. Thus, for the first time, the government had social allies supporting its encroachment on a part of civil society.[189] In this way, at least, wars constituted the foundational first steps toward a state.

Toward the end of the century, several key figures who in previous times might have remained personalistic caudillos began to build the institutional basis for a state (Díaz in Mexico, Guzmán Blanco in Venezuela, or even Roca in Argentina). I would argue that this was the result of a different institutional context of caudilloism. If during the first part of the century caudillos had secured their material and political base by controlling regions in conflict with central authority, toward the end of the century the road to power and wealth lay in expanding the capital's domain. The causes of this shift were rooted not in war or military competition, but in the requirements of capital and export production. As long as a hacienda economy writ large dominated the continent, it made political sense for the state to be weaker than its most powerful subjects.[190] When that changed so did the goal of the armed political actors.

Differences at the Margin

Within the Latin American pattern there are, of course, relative exceptions, and these serve to prove the rule. The violence of the wars between 1860 and 1880 clearly resulted in a much more powerful Argentine state. The key difference is that unlike in the 1810s and 1820s, the later Argentina did possess a semblance of a central government that could and did use the war both against Paraguay and the Indians to stamp out provincial opposition and impose uniform control over the entire country. More important, by the second half of the century, the central state had found its social ally whose interests it could serve: the export of meat and wheat to European markets required much more political and institutional infrastructure than

189. Tenenbaum, *Politics of Penury*, 162–66.
190. I am borrowing the language from Bethell, *Cambridge History*, vol. 3, 663, but the original only refers to Uruguay.

the sale of salted beef to the slave owners of Brazil. Although the rural oli-garchs of Argentina remained unwilling to pay for the new state, they were also unwilling to accept challenges to its authority. With this narrow sup-port, Mitre and his successors were able to establish their domination.

The key to Brazil's relative unity would seem to lie in its avoidance of the struggles for independence. Neither the Brazilian economy nor its polity were destroyed by years of civil war, nor did the empire have to maintain an absurdly large military in order to establish its authority. Conflicts during the reign of Dom Pedro I helped resolve the intra-elite struggle between the "native" aristocracy and the Portuguese courtiers brought by Pedro's father and thereby consolidated the creation of a Brazilian political class. While there is considerable debate regarding the autonomy of this sector,[191] there is no doubt about the existence of an "imperial" class that gave Brazil a particular coherence. The secessionist wars in the 1830s and 1840s helped consolidate this group. By the time of the War of the Triple Alliance, Brazil possessed enough institutional coherence to survive, if not necessarily prosper.

Although Chile experienced considerable political dislocation during the independence wars, its economy was not crippled by them, and may have even grown.[192] More important, even before the rule of Diego Portales and certainly afterward, the Chilean elite displayed a remarkable cohesion.[193] To what extent this was the result of the small size of the country, the concen-tration in a single city, the pervasiveness of dense interfamilial networks, or just sheer luck is the subject of debate. For our purposes, what is most im-portant is that the Chilean state preceded war and thus was able to extract some benefits from it. Yet it is important to note that even the Chilean "ex-ception" still fits the general Latin American pattern discussed earlier. Even as the state expanded, it did so without extracting from the domestic econ-omy. Overall, the wars helped make Chile, not by a combination of blood and iron, but by allowing a fiscal improvisation fueled by duties on exports of commodities.[194]

Paraguay represents perhaps the most interesting exception to the Latin American pattern. Following the requisite period of instability following independence in 1814, the country was ruled by three dictators: José Francia until 1840, followed by Carlos Antonio López, and then his son

191. Graham, "State and Society in Brazil."
192. Cariola and Sunkel, *Un siglo de historia económica*, 25.
193. Collier, *Ideas and Politics of Chilean Independence*.
194. Bethell, *Cambridge History*, vol. 3, 610.

Francisco Solano López until Francisco's death in 1870. Francia created an all-encompassing state that dominated every aspect of public life and was completely controlled by him. The state owned all the land and largely managed all external trade. During the rule of the first López, the state was involved in economic development, building some infrastructure and attempting to achieve self-sufficiency through the production of several industrial goods. López *fils* encouraged military development to the point that the small country had arguably the strongest army in South America.[195]

The early Paraguayan state enjoyed a rare degree of autonomy. Unlike in the other Latin American countries, there existed an agent within the state that drove it to impose itself on the society.[196] Francia served as the structural equivalent of an absolutist monarch, which helped ensure the continuance of Paraguayan autonomy.[197] Francia's centurions allowed him to funnel all social resources toward his political apparatus.[198] If we follow White, who claims that the rise of the military was a direct response to external threat, it would then appear that early Paraguay was perhaps the only example of the classic European variant of war-led state development. Paraguay could maintain this independence in part because the revenue that it could gather covered the state's needs. Unlike its neighbors, the Paraguayan state ran a consistent surplus during the entire postindependence period prior to the War of the Triple Alliance. This reflected the limited demands placed on it, but also the monopoly that the state enjoyed over almost all economic activity.

It is no longer possible to speak of Paraguay as the best example of antidependency and of a successful state-led development.[199] Nevertheless, it is

195. Williamson, *The Penguin History of Latin America*, 273.
196. Pastore, "Trade Contraction and Economic Decline," 587.
197. White, *Paraguay's Autonomous Revolution*, 101–2.
198. The one consistent demand on the Paraguayan state during Francia's rule was the military budget. Despite the fact that the army never included more than two thousand men, the military absorbed an average of at least 64 percent of government expenditures during this period (White, *Paraguay's Autonomous Revolution*, 104). Much of the cost was associated with maintaining the military industries that supplied the armed forces. This relative self-sufficiency also helped protect Paraguay's international autonomy. While there are obviously different interpretations of the role of the Paraguayan army (107; Pastore, "Trade Contraction and Economic Decline," 591–92; Williams, *Rise and Fall*, 60–61), it is clear that it served to protect the state (or perhaps better said, Francia) from both external and internal enemies. Note that the apparent decline in military expenditure after 1840 in Table 3.2 may simply reflect a change in accounting practices (Thomas Whigham, private communication).
199. Whigham, *Politics of River Trade*, 83–84; Pastore, "State-Led Industrialization," 321–24.

clear that the Paraguayan state was a very different institutional animal from its continental counterparts. The Paraguayan experience in building a much more powerful state apparatus than those of its neighbors even in the absence of war prior to the 1860s indicates again that while conflict does provide a stimulus and an opportunity, what matters is the organizational and political base of the state and its sources of support.

Conclusions: How Context Matters

In the end, wars did not make states in Latin America. The best that states could do was to survive wars or gain enough of their neighbors' territory to finance expansion. Nowhere did military action generate the kind of societal penetration seen in Europe. Latin America was caught in an inertial equilibrium: no class was powerful enough to impose its domination and no state was strong enough to enforce its control. The path to the modern state required one or the other.

Having argued that Latin America fought different wars and suffered from social, racial, and geographical barriers that precluded state development, the question then becomes why these were particularly acute on the continent. Europe also had divided elites, regional identities, and ethnic and class divisions. Why did these represent a more daunting obstacle in Latin America?

As discussed earlier, the forms of warfare were drastically different in the two regions. I would add, however, that differences in societal contexts were more important and that the analysis of these can make a more important contribution to our understanding of state making on the continent than any adjustment to the bellicist theory of political development.

First, regionalism in Latin America was encouraged by an important natural ally. The physical geography of the continent presented logistical and administrative obstacles only replicated in selected parts of Europe.[200] Communications from the capital were uncertain and military support was irregular. Because of these problems, efforts to impose central authority in much of Latin America might be better compared with those of empires rather than of nation-states. The United States also faced geographical challenges,

200. One could even find a rough correlation between the success of state making in those regions and suitability of terrain. Certainly the plains of France made it easier to impose central authority than the mountains of southeastern Europe.

but in that country territory expanded much more in line with the capacity of the central state to administer. Imagine a United States having to fight an independence war across the Appalachians or trying to procure revenue from California to pay for the War of 1812. In Latin America, political institutions suited for a city-state were given empires to rule. We should not be surprised that they failed to do so.

The apparent (if illusory) cultural homogeneity of the continent also supported regionalism albeit in a perverse fashion. Given the absence of clear, strong distinctions across regions, the natural centrifugal attraction of the nation-state appeared less obvious. Thus, Latin American countries faced more significant natural obstacles while not enjoying the intrinsic attraction of differentiated pockets of cultural cohesion.

Ethnic divisions were also much more significant in Latin America, as they were not only accompanied by visible racial characteristics, but also supported by a legal and social system that institutionalized the minutest differences. Paris had to absorb Bretons and Provençal speakers, but it was much less successful with Basques. One can only imagine Spain's history with a sizable Morisco population, even with no ethnic differences involved. Once again, the relevant European model is Austria-Hungary, where internal ethnic/national divisions overpowered most notions of shared legacy or destiny. The presence of significant ethnic divisions, and their legal recognition, is perhaps the characteristic that most distinguishes the experience of Latin America from that of Europe.[201] Again, we might best understand the birthing pains of independent states in Latin America by imagining them not as nations, but empires.

Finally, few elites could be as unruly as the European aristocracy that constructed states after the sixteenth century. Could the Argentinean or Peruvian elites really claim to be more fractious than their French or English counterparts? One major difference was the long European association of elite status with military prowess (broken in Latin America soon after the conquest). This relationship established a close link between martial competition and the viability of any elite group, which never existed in Latin America. The control of violence was an intrinsic part of elite functions in Europe; considering the state irrelevant was never an option. In Latin America, by contrast, political power was often secondary to economic con-

---

201. The experience of the United States is clearly relevant here. The counterfactual comparison might be an independent Confederacy having to construct a democratic state in the aftermath of slavery.

trol, and this made the necessity to construct a state less urgent. European protostates were also helped by the institution of monarchy, which gave at least one family and its political network a very strong stake in the development of political capacity. Not even the Brazilian monarchy developed the congruence between individual and collective interests that may be so crucial at early stages of political growth.

Violence pervaded Latin American and European life during the development of these regions' respective states. There was violence between elites, between classes, between races, and between regions. Yet this did not generate the institutional development one might have expected from the European experience. The various regions of Europe competed with one another for supremacy and sovereignty, but they did so while re-creating a political map and not attempting to conform to a colonial geography. Ethnicities clashed, but they rarely were as hard to disentangle through territorial division. Elites might fight, but political entrepreneurs with monarchical legitimacy could impose institutional orders. With limited exceptions, Latin America did not possess the institutional or social kernel from which nation-states might have arisen, and wars did little to encourage their development. Where local conditions more closely approximated the European cases, war did provide the necessary institutional cement to secure the development of more powerful and stable states. In general, however, the military road to political development was not available on the continent.

The combination of weak central power and external economic direction is the defining characteristic of postcolonial states. The delegitimation of political authority as associated with the colonial power, the fragility of elite coalitions and lack of national cohesion or even identity, and the orientation toward a metropole and away from the interior and regional neighbors—all have characterized, in one form or another, the experiences of independent countries in Latin America, Africa, and Asia. Many have also experienced considerable violence without the benefits of the organizational development seen in western Europe. This pattern should make us wonder about the advisability of using such an idiosyncratic experience as the early modern western European one for the construction of universalistic paradigms. At the very least, the experience of Latin America should make us more curious about the particular circumstances that allowed states to flourish following the "Military Revolution" of the sixteenth and seventeenth centuries.

As discussed earlier, several special conditions allow wars to make states. The first of these is pressure on the state to respond to the financial challenge of war through increased domestic extraction. There is no reason to expect states to undertake the political and organizational challenge of penetrating their societies if resources can be found more easily. Second, enough of an administrative core must already be in place that the state can use as a base on which to develop its strength. The chaos and violence of war do not provide the appropriate incubation for underdeveloped polities. Third, no political body can amass enough authority to coerce and extract without social allies. Domestic threats to sovereignty have to be resolved prior to "productive" conflict. Further research might test the relative significance of these three factors through their application to a variety of geographical and historical cases. Certainly these might help explain why it took nearly a millennium of violence for war to produce states in Europe. The case of Poland and the Balkans, suffering from both war and relatively weak states, would also merit attention.

The central lesson to be drawn from the Latin American experience is that we cannot assume that a state exists simply because the symbols of independence are there. States are not actors in and of themselves. They are shells—potentially powerful shells—but nevertheless hollow at the core. The machine of the state needs a "driver" able to use the stimulus provided by war to expand its reach and power. Without such a driver, whether it be state personnel, a dominant class, or even a charismatic individual, the political and military shell of the state has no direction. Without this direction, wars do not present opportunities for growth, but are mere challenges to survival. A fiscal system requires constitutional powers as well as a bureaucratic capacity to enforce them. This will not appear without an alliance between a political institution and a significant social sector. Without such an identification of interests, it is practically impossible for the state to grow, no matter the stimulus of violence.

4
Making the Nation

In previous chapters I have analyzed the scarcity of war in Latin America and the difficulties in establishing state authority on the continent. In this chapter, the discussion moves away from formal control and closer to consideration of other attributes associated with political development. Weber's famous definition of the state emphasizes not just the monopoly over the means of violence, but also the legitimacy thereof. Historically, state legitimacy has been at least partly based on the creation of nationalist sentiments that not only bound the population together, but also made the state the center and ultimate expression of that collective identity. This chapter's focus is the manner in which the forms of warfare and state authority helped create and were in turn shaped by particular forms of national allegiance.[1]

The events of the past decade have demonstrated that earlier reports of the death of nationalism were clearly exaggerated. Despite the confident predictions of modernization, convergence, and Marxist theories, nationalism has returned to political center stage with a vengeance. This nationalist renewal has generated a parallel renaissance in the academy. Beginning in the 1980s, leading scholars in a variety of disciplines returned to the study of nationalism and identity in general.[2] The new work marked a transition in how nationalism was perceived. While some holdouts still argue for the primacy of a common *ethnie*, the inventors and imaginers of nationhood have largely won the intellectual argument.[3] The focus has moved from how peoples unite themselves to how states invent nations. Yet, perhaps in part because of the limited range of cases cited, the conception and gestation of nations still remain the profoundest of social mysteries.[4]

This new literature largely ignores a very prominent exception to the global pattern of nationalism: the experience of Latin American states.[5] Much like the literature on the rise of the state, the discussion of nationalism often disregards the historical and geographical specificity on which much of theory is grounded. How to explain the Latin American anomaly? Following recent attempts at a conciliation of theoretical perspectives on nationalism,[6] I ask three questions. First, what is the content or iconographic vocabulary of the Latin American state's nationalist myths? Second, what kind of instruments or iconographic grammars are used? Finally, what do the media and messages tell us about the relationship between this state and its society? As in the other chapters, I analyze these questions through the prism of warfare.

Through the analysis of the role of war in the creation of national iconographies in Latin America, I make clear how much state-centered and state-created nationalism relies on history and shared experience, the mythic

1. For a wonderful description of the critical role played by war in the creation of ethnic community, see A. Smith, "War and Ethnicity."
2. Calhoun, "Nationalism and Ethnicity," 211–38.
3. A. Smith, "State-Making and Nation-Building"; Gellner, *Nations and Nationalism;* Hobsbawm, *Nations and Nationalism;* B. Anderson, *Imagined Communities;* Breuilly, *Nationalism and the State.*
4. Zelinsky, *Nation into State,* 230.
5. Even prominent treatments of this issue (e.g., Brading, *The Origins of Mexican Nationalism;* Mallon, *Peasant and Nation*) are mostly read by Latin Americanists.
6. Comaroff and Stern, "New Perspectives on Nationalism and War."

raw materials with which to construct communities. Emphasizing history does not mean a return to determinism or the supremacy of national character. History is malleable and partly the creature of power. Traditions are invented, but never completely. Nationalism, much like culture, is situationally grounded.[7] States are embedded in the societies from which they rise and they can only use those iconographic resources available to them. Each state might try to create its own myths, but because there are different histories, there will be different nationalisms. States may make their own history, but not entirely as they please.[8]

Nowhere is this clearer than in Latin America. The political appeal of war and its role in the development of nation building may be witnessed in a few cases on the continent. For example, much of Paraguayan identity is based on that country's fate in two wars. Similarly, a series of civil struggles culminating in the revolution consolidated state authority in Mexico. Finally, victory in an early international war may have been critical for the legitimization of the Chilean state. In general, however, wars did not make nations in Latin America. First, as was the case with the earlier discussion on taxation, there were not many wars, they were not suited for the task, and they came at the wrong time. More important, the class and caste divisions that helped define Latin America made the use of the symbols that did exist problematic. Moreover, many of the states were reluctant to create national pantheons that contradicted the composition and orientation of the elite. Not only did Latin America have the wrong tools and the wrong materials with which to build nationalism; those in charge were not that interested in building it in the first place.

Following a general discussion of nationalism in Latin America, I proceed to discuss the role of monuments in the construction of national memory. I then describe the general iconographic pattern in Latin America, followed by a detailed discussion of particular cases. To conclude, I offer an explanation for both the general Latin American exceptionalism and the differences within the continent.

Before proceeding it is important to clarify what is meant by nationalism. My use of the term is largely associated with nation building and integration.[9] State nationalism is characterized by the domination by a single political institution over a territory containing a population that believes it shares

7. Fine, "Small Groups and Culture Creation."
8. I borrow the paraphrasing of Marx from Eley and Grigor Suny, introduction to Eley and Grigor Suny, *Becoming National.*
9. Knight, "Peasants into Patriots."

an essential identity. The claimed common identity exists only as a collective and abstract aspiration whose most concrete expression is the state itself. This sense of communality is supported by a state-sponsored liturgy whose set of symbols and rituals support a form of secular religion in which the people worship themselves.[10]

Three characteristics help distinguish nationalist identity from others that I will argue are more salient on the Latin American continent, such as race or class. First, nationalism is associated with a specific and unitary institution, the nation-state. Second, it is continually and explicitly celebrated through a well-defined and elaborate canon. Third, the links between co-nationals are often abstract (unlike the concreteness of skin color or socioeconomic resources) and are most often defined by their shared occupation of a territory. Similar attributes serve to distinguish nationalism from patriotism.[11] Patriotism does not necessarily have anything to do with formal political institutions. The notion of *patria* does not imply any particular size or governmental arrangement; one's *patria* can be a valley, a region, an institution, or a country. Most important, patriotism does not necessarily imply obedience to either a collective will or its institutional representative. Patriotism is a faith; nationalism is a church.

Nationalism and Patriotism in Latin America

Latin America in the nineteenth century, and arguably the twentieth, had a great deal of regionalism, racism, and patriotism, but little nationalism. Two crucial characteristics helped define the general weakness of *official state* nationalism in Latin America; both contributed to the generic weakness of state authority. The first of these is the ethnic and racial divisions that dominate most societies on the continent and which have limited the development of panhistorical legends and ethnic identifications. The second is the absence of clearly identified external "others" that can be used to strengthen a sense of common identity. Thus, Latin American states' efforts to create nations worked under a double disadvantage: there were limits to the utility of the past and the present provided few opportunities with which to concoct a glorious heritage.

10. Mosse, *Nationalization of the Masses,* 2.
11. Hayes, *Essays on Nationalism;* Huizinga, "Patriotism and Nationalism in European History."

To these limits on historical invention we must add a sensitivity to the relationship between state and society. Central to much of the recent literature on nationalism is an assumption that all states will seek to integrate their populations and link them to political institutions. This has rarely been the case in Latin America, where masses were "organized, recruited, manipulated, but not politicized or included in the nation."[12] Finally, it is important to take into account that not all nationalist symbols and legends "work."[13] Some traditions may fall flat and some nationalisms may never resonate.

If a nation is a "materially and morally integrated society" characterized by the "mental . . . and cultural unity of its inhabitants" then few even mid-twentieth-century Latin American countries would qualify.[14] The continent's different identities have remained divided by layers separating classes and ethnic groups and do not appear to have developed the more "modern" layers dividing nations.[15] As discussed in Chapter 2, the absence of such sentiments helps explain why Latin America has been spared the military holocausts of Europe and illuminates the relative weakness of the Latin American state. The institutional bases of the nation-state never matched the cultural legitimating myths of the societies. Political rule was expressed territorially, but society and culture were both integrated and divided on different planes. The key to understanding the forms of political legitimacy that developed in Latin America is to keep in mind the fundamental misfit between formal organizational power (as expressed in the state) and the underlying social forms of authority that commanded more immediate loyalty.

Birth of a Nation?

The independence of Latin America has often been used as an example of the new nationalism associated with the nineteenth century. Yet Anderson is incorrect in claiming that the anticolonial movements were national, if by

12. Lynch, "Los caudillos de la independencia," 202.

13. For a discussion of the different attributes of "successful" cultural icons, see Schudson, "How Culture Works."

14. The definition is by Mauss as cited in E. Weber, *Peasants into Frenchmen*, 484. Weber notes that France also did not meet these criteria in 1870. But it did by 1914 and certainly by 1918. I argue that this is partly explained by the experience of war and subsequent elaboration of nationalist myths associated with it.

15. For a general discussion of these differences (but with no references to Latin America), see Calhoun, "Nationalism and Ethnicity," 1993.

that we are to understand that each new country was aware of its own particular identity prior to independence.[16] It is true that the administrative boundaries of the Spanish Empire and the daunting geographical challenges to communication and transport had begun to create some intracontinental differences. Simón Bolívar came to recognize the importance of these regional identities through the failure of his various federalist proposals.[17] But aside from a vague regional sentiment among a minute part of the elite, I know of no evidence that any large part of even the white population thought of themselves as a nation *separate from their creole neighbors*.[18] Criollos identified themselves as Americans—as opposed to Spaniards—but not as a specific subnationality.[19] The rules for indoctrinating schoolchildren in new patriotic values offered by Belgrano in 1813, for example, suggest an opposition between foreigners and Americans, but not between other Americans and Argentineans.[20]

The nationalism of Latin American independence was a product of the Enlightenment and sought a liberty grounded in (granted theoretical) universal rights. It sought recognition and defense of these rights, but never based them on claims to a special identity. The model was the French revolutionary fervor of 1789–92, not Napoleonic chauvinism. Bolívarian nationalism completely lacked references to ethnic or cultural dimensions; the ultimate criterion for nationality was political in nature.[21] Mexico and Brazil might represent exceptions, but at least in the former, nationalism remained "more creole than Mexican."[22] The Brazilians did express a feeling of superiority over Spanish America and there are indications that the Cisplatine War was perceived as one matching civilizations.[23]

Much more than in the European cases, identity and national consciousness had to be created after political boundaries had been drawn. States had to create the icons and liturgies that would support the "cultural revolu-

16. B. Anderson, *Imagined Communities*.

17. Collier, "Nationality, Nationalism, and Supranationalism."

18. Masur, *Nationalism in Latin America*; Mörner, *Andean Past*; Pagden, "Identity Formation in Spanish America"; Schwartz, "The Formation of Colonial Identity in Brazil"; Shumway, *The Invention of Argentina*; Collier, "Nationality, Nationalism, and Supranationalism." For an opposing view, see Vial Correa, "La formación de las nacionalidades hispanoamericanas como causa de la independencia"; Krebs, "Origenes de la conciencia nacional chilena."

19. Interestingly, in light of the themes of this book, we may detect the most coherent sense of a protoidentity within the various colonial militias.

20. Quoted in Szuchman, "Childhood Education and Politics," 114.

21. Collier, "Nationality, Nationalism, and Supranationalism."

22. Brading, *Origins of Mexican Nationalism*.

23. Seckinger, *Brazilian Monarchy*, 27–33.

tion" creating a nation.[24] They largely failed. More significant, they barely tried. Given the prerogatives from the colonial era that the dominant elites sought to maintain, the inclusion and integration of the masses was the last thing on their mind. They could not, did not, and had no desire to imagine a national community. This then brings up the question of why the unitarian project failed as well. By emphasizing the absence of nationalism, as defined earlier, I do not mean to ignore the existence of regional loyalties. Moreover, the caudillismo generated by independence also played an important role in the division of the continent. In the final instance, few elites were interested in creating strong national authorities.

Obstacles to Identity

As discussed in Chapter 2, one explanation for the Latin American pattern is the linguistic and even cultural homogeneity of the continent following the conquest. Without the competition between languages (and the states representing them), without the struggle between different elite cultures, there was no impetus for the subsequent conflict between political claims over territory.[25] Despite the differences between the various countries, one could argue that until relatively recently there was no such thing as a *national* culture in Latin America.[26]

Nor has Latin America produced the artistic and cultural environment that enshrines and has supported nationalist dogma in Europe. There are the many decades of patent self-hatred and European emulation. It is only much later in the nineteenth century or even well into the twentieth that literature (Benedict Anderson's favorite carrier of nationalist sentiments) begins to express a local as opposed to continental nationalism.[27] Latin American Romanticism did not serve as the basis for nationalism. Its practitioners spent much longer praising natural beauty than the ethnic purity or history

24. Corrigan and Sayer, *The Great Arch.*
25. See A. Smith, "State-Making and Nation-Building" for a discussion of how elite competition engenders nationalism.
26. Bermúdez, "Nacionalismo y cultura popular."
27. With rare exceptions (Hernández in Argentina), no Latin American author has played the role of Walter Scott, Fenimore Cooper, the Brothers Grimm, or Victor Hugo: creating literary traditions offering idealized and popular versions of a sanitized past. Martín Fierro is the only obvious example of a Latin American Lancelot (Monguió, "Nationalism and Social Discontent"; Díaz Ruiz, "El nacionalismo en la literatura latinoamericana"; Wetzlaff-Eggebert, "Literatura americana o literatura nacional." For a dissenting view, see Benítez-Rojo, "La novela hispanoamericana del siglo XIX").

of a particular country. When they did attempt to extol such characteristics, as seen in the work of José Enrique Rodó or Rubén Dario, it was on a pancontinental level. What was praised and extolled is *hispanidad*—or in other cases *indiginismo*—but it is not the intrinsic sacredness of a particular nation as defined by territory.[28] More-contemporary expressions of particularism have been of a very different sort from their post-1848 European counterparts: a revolutionary nationalism that does the opposite of glorifying the state.[29] A critical difference is that the nationalism of Latin American intellectuals has been almost exclusively from the Left. The gulf separating Pablo Neruda from Gabriele D'Annunzio or José Carlos Mariátequi from Martin Heidegger is measured in light-years. The Mexican "raza cósmica" may be the closest equivalent to the European brand of ethnic nationalism, but it developed relatively late and in drastically different geopolitical circumstances.

Some have suggested a strong link between the development of capitalism and the rise of nationalism.[30] The failure to develop a dynamic national capital in Latin America may have hindered, or at least not provided a necessary stimulus for, the rise of nationalist sentiments. Until the advent of import-substitution industrialization, production of consumption goods was extremely limited; the heart of Latin American economies was the extraction of basic commodities for the global market. Economic consumers were thousands of miles away, as were the most important sources of capital. Thus, competition for and protection of markets defined by territory did not exist until quite late in the twentieth century. Nor did Latin America develop a national bourgeoisie supporting a process of cultural differentiation and political separation. No class had an interest in creating a nationalist ethos or a political apparatus capable of defending its interests internationally—a local police force would do.[31]

I want to suggest another contributing factor that may help us better understand the nature of state-centered nationalism. If cultural identity is

28. Palacios, *La unidad nacional en América Latina.*
29. There are, of course, exceptions. Attempts to create *argentinidad,* for example, flourished in the face of the immigrations after 1880 (Vogel, "Elements of Nationbuilding in Argentina").
30. B. Anderson, *Imagined Communities;* Hobsbawm, *Nations and Nationalism;* and Mann, *States, War, and Capitalism.*
31. Yet this begs the question of causal order. The lack of nationalism may itself go far in explaining the absence of the developmentalist bourgeoisie bemoaned by Cardoso and Faletto. Rather than nations not flourishing because of the underdevelopment of capitalism, national markets could not congeal without cultural support. The nation had to precede the market.

based on collective remembering, there has to be narrative to recall.[32] Latin American states did not possess the historical capital necessary to construct national identities, as found in Europe. There were two sources for this nationalistic deficit, both grounded in historical experience.

While Europe had geographically defined ethnicities over which a new pattern of borders had been overlaid, in Latin America such regional distinctions were largely destroyed by the conquest. What the independence movement produced were not states overlapping distinctive groups, no matter how haphazardly, but states encompassing societies whose internal ethnic differences were greater than those between the various "nations" they sought to represent. The gulf between white, black, and Indian within countries was always greater than the differences between any of these groups across borders. This was true both for those on the bottom and for the respective ruling elites. The continental homogeneity of the latter was particularly profound. If we think of Latin America as having four "nations" at the time of independence—Spanish, Creole, Indian, and African—the first two were often united in their opposition to the last two.[33] Similarly, while there may have been deep differences between an Italian meatpacker of Buenos Aires, an Aymara miner in Bolivia, and a black peasant in Brazil, their respective superiors shared a considerable heritage and ideology. Since they were in charge of the state, there was little chance for the real differences to find official confirmation and support.

The presence of these varied ethnic groups necessarily blurred the boundaries of any imagined community.[34] What attachments were made were either to the specific geographical region, to members of the same racial group, or even to all the countries sharing a history and a common threat. But these did not represent nationalism as understood in the European sense. Perhaps most important, until well into the twentieth century for most cases, official, state nationalism ignored the non-European masses. It was purely an elite, white phenomenon.[35] When these populations sought to create their own version of the nation, they were often crushed by the state. In fact, in Peru state building involved the destruction of a nationalism from below.[36]

32. Gillis, *Commemorations,* 2.

33. Minguet, "El concepto de la nación, pueblo, estado y pátria." For a wonderful account of how the ethnic divisions helped define national identity, see Thurner, *From Two Republics to One Divided* and Ada Ferrer, *Insurgent Cuba.*

34. Dodds, "Geography, Identity, and the Creation of the Argentine State."

35. Thurner, "*Republicanos* and *la Comunidad de peruanos.*"

36. Mallon, *Peasant and Nation*; Stern, *Resistance, Rebellion, and Consciousness.*

In these circumstances, war would have provided an ideal iconographic solution.[37] Bolívar was well aware of war's symbolic power. He considered allowing Peru to remain loyalist "so as to provide Colombia with 'fearsome neighbors' to concentrate its mind."[38] War would have forged a sense of commonality while at the same time helping to construct an ever threatening "other" against which the nation needed to stand united. Without threats and dangers emanating from neighboring institutions, the sense of distinctiveness that is at the heart of nationalism failed to develop.

As discussed earlier, Latin American countries did not have the types of military experiences that formed so much of the basis of national allegiance in their countries, including the United States. These moments of shared sacrifice might have provided a new foundation for collective identification, a bridge across the racial gulfs. Latin America had no symbolic equivalents to the Hollywood war movie in which representatives of different ethnic groups, including African-Americans after the 1950s, meet and discover their common humanity and shared loyalties. The countries of the continent lacked the heroic legends, great exploits, and glittering conquests that are the raw material of national mythology. History created a particular form of national culture that in turn helped create a very different kind of narrative.[39]

How this narrative was used is an important consideration. Nationalism, whether democratic or totalitarian, implies state encouragement of the active participation of subjects. It may be nothing more than parade fodder, but the populace is integrated into liturgies requiring participation. Nationalism thus implies the mobilization of the masses. Yet Latin American history is characterized by the political marginalization of significant segments of the population.

The caudillos of independence were not interested in forming the kind of cultural or symbolic link associated with nationalism, but devoted much more attention to expanding their patronage networks.[40] The victory of Liberalism deprived nationalism of a political base as a secular state religion. Liberals disdained such particularisms, while the defeated Conservatives refused to organize the masses. Even in the immediate aftermath of wars, for example, Mexican elites were reluctant to use the discourse of nationalism, as traditionally understood in Europe. Mexican Liberals "rarely if ever ap-

37. A. Smith, "War and Ethnicity."
38. Collier, "Nationality, Nationalism, and Supranationalism," 60.
39. Silvert, "Nationalism in Latin America."
40. Lynch, "Los caudillos de la independencia."

pealed to the concept of the nation save in its constitutional sense. . . . [They] invited their fellow citizens to lay down their lives in service of 'la pátria,' which increasingly had less to do with a shared history and more with the ideology of liberal republicanism."[41]

In the twentieth century, Latin America did not experience the kind of political regime in which popular mobilization was paramount. The few democracies that have survived have often done so through the assurance of elite control—the integration of a nation of citizens has rarely been a goal. However, we certainly have no examples of the mass organization and ideology associated with fascism.[42] Latin America did experience periods of authoritarianism as lengthy as those of Germany, Spain, Italy, and the Balkans, but we have no instances of a state and a society establishing a bond through the worship of a common ethnic identity opposed to neighbors or some universal "other." Because of the relative stability of borders since independence, irredentism has never been a major political factor. The few mass movements that did arise, such as Peronismo, while borrowing elements from fascism, never achieved the totalitarian control associated with such regimes, nor did they engage in military adventurism, another critical characteristic. Moreover, Latin American mass movements depended on definitions of the enemy that were often couched in class terms, not ethnic ones.

What explains this lack of state interest? The popular engagement associated with nationalism is closely linked to a state's making greater demands on its subject population;[43] Latin American states, however, made surprisingly few. Large segments were not needed as soldiers, as workers, or even as consumers. Thus, there was relatively little incentive to homogenize and integrate them. To the perpetual question of "que hacer con el pueblo" (what to do with the people), answers usually involved exclusion, not mobilization.

The result of both the historical background and the nature of political institutions in Latin America has been a form of patriotism, sometimes tinged with chauvinism, lacking the coherence or institutional support of state nationalism. The "make-believe" sponsored by the government (to use Edmund Morgan's language) did not include venerating a link between state and nation. In fact, even as it celebrated the birth of the first, it tended to

41. Brading, "Liberal Patriotism and the Mexican Reforma," 28.
42. Payne, *A History of Fascism*. Note also that even among the extreme Right, xenophobia was relatively low. Deutsch, *Las derechas*.
43. Tilly, "States and Nationalism in Europe."

largely ignore the second. Before analyzing the specifics of the Latin American cases, I discuss the tools used to measure and compare the origin and extent of these sentiments.

Memories Are Made of This

A major difficulty in the research on nationalism is conceiving a common measure that allows comparative analysis. Estimates of which societies are more or less nationalistic and when they became so are often nothing more than subjective judgments. Similarly, nationalist beliefs are frequently both pervasive and amorphous, making definition of the various ideological and historical ingredients difficult if not impossible. In this chapter I use concrete manifestations of nationalist sentiments: monuments and street names. I have supplemented these data with the analysis of what we might call paper monuments: stamps and currencies. While these symbolic carriers lack the textual richness of other possible candidates such as political speeches and school textbooks, they have two important advantages.[44] First, information about them is relatively easy to obtain for our cases and they can be easily categorized and counted.[45] Second, they are on constant public display; they help define the public sphere. This is particularly important in societies characterized by low school attendance and high levels of illiteracy. We have no way of establishing how statues, stamps, and currencies are consumed, but we can certainly trace their production as a way to define *state-sponsored* nationalism.[46]

Monuments and street names express the attitudes and values of a nation through the choice of references and, more subtly, aesthetic style; they objectify the ideals for which the nation is supposed to stand. These memorials make the past not only bearable, but usable; they rewrite history as a glori-

44. Another potential resource are the guides including patriotic materials and speeches to be used in schools on national feast days. See, for example, Basurto, *México y sus símbolos*.

45. As in Chapter 2, I attempted to find public opinion data on nationalism, but was unsuccessful.

46. I do not mean to enter into a debate on the relative significance of nationalism from above or below (see Bonilla, "The Indian Peasantry and 'Peru' During the War with Chile"; and Mallon, "Nationalist and Antistate Coalitions in the War of the Pacific"). My argument is not meant as a refutation of the wonderful work being done in a very different tradition (e.g., Mallon, *Peasant and Nation;* and Joseph and Nugent, *Everyday Forms of State Formation*). Rather, I hope to complement the growing literature of nationalism from below with a more state-centered view.

ous beginning.[47] As understood here, monuments are largely a modern creation in that they mostly serve as a bridge between elite or institutional memory and popular remembrance. They do so by transforming historical figures into symbols and myths: they transform the political into the religious.[48]

Currencies and postage stamps also serve as leading carriers of political symbolism, providing an opportunity for the state to portray the glories of national history.[49] These paper monuments represent an unobtrusive pedagogical opening for emphasizing which heroes merit praise, which symbols are worth worshipping, which events warrant memory, and which national goals deserve greatest attention and effort. Because of their very ordinariness, "no other government artifact so symbolizes the nation's popular self-image."[50] No one who lived in Spain from the 1950s through the 1970s can ever forget that Francisco Franco was "Caudillo by the grace of God." No coin or stamp collector needs to be told that the British Commonwealth is ruled by a queen.

What kind of values do these "public classrooms" teach? They use history to diffuse politics by creating illusions of unity and solidarity. As has been said about patriotic literature, "they develop a narrative formula for resolving continuing conflicts."[51] Icons do not arise from a social vacuum; they reflect their social contexts. Because these symbols are built or printed by those with authority, they often serve to legitimize power. Monuments are merely the most visible aspects of the entire system of symbols and emblems that are designed to engender recognition of and acclamation for the political status quo.[52] They serve as an indication of what those who have enough power to construct such monuments want to remember or honor. They indicate the hierarchy of *official* memory. This may be nothing more than "lies about crimes," but the lies we tell can often say more than the truth we hide.

These symbols are not passive objects without their own role in the continual writing of history. They represent a "theory of the world" that both

47. Ignatieff, "Soviet War Memorials."
48. Mosse, *Nationalization of the Masses,* 50. While I consider Mosse to be the best analyst of this connection, see also Winter, *Sites of Memory, Sites of Mourning.* Related analysis might be Verdery, *The Political Lives of Dead Bodies.*
49. For currency, see Helleiner, "National Currencies and National Identities."
50. Skagg, "Postage Stamps as Icons," 198.
51. Sommer, *Foundational Fictions,* 12.
52. Agulhon, "Politics, Images, and Symbols in Post-Revolutionary France."

reflects and shapes social power distribution.[53] They remind and reaffirm and accordingly play a major role in the construction of what exactly is being remembered. Precisely because people are aware that monuments make history—they represent the most visible "text" of that history—their construction is often full of rancor and debate. We may even read monuments as indications of the victory of one group or vision over others.[54]

The presence of a monument does not necessarily speak to the society as a historical constant, but only to the time in which it was built. Without rituals and reminders, the significance of what was once held sacred is lost and forgotten. Yesterday's beloved general is today's neglected pigeon roost, and may be tomorrow's kitsch icon. Nor is the meaning of social symbols like war memorials rigid or stable.[55] Monuments such as the Völkerschlacht-denkmal in Leipzig could, at different times, symbolize democratic aspirations or collective authority. The monumental remnants of communism have been transformed into memorials of the victims of authoritarianism, reminders of political dangers, or advertisements for fast food. Nevertheless, the remnants of past mythologies form the basis for current ideologies, even if only in opposition to them.

The fashion and aesthetics of memory change across time. The column favored in antiquity has seen various cycles of popularity (as have the subset of obelisks popular in the early nineteenth century). The dynastic equestrian monument was born in the Classical era, was revived in the Renaissance, and reached its apogee in the era of absolutism. The Roman triumphal arch made a comeback as a temporary addition to parades and festivals in the eighteenth century and as a capstone to victory in the nineteenth.[56] The latter half of the 1800s saw a veritable explosion of "statuemania" in almost all Western cities. These monuments have been replaced by more "practical" memorials, such as schools and hospitals. Among war monuments, the trend has been to reduce the triumphalist bombast of previous efforts and replace it with an emphasis on sacrifice and loss. Thus, for example, cemeteries—the practice of marking battle graves is relatively recent—have often replaced monuments as centers of veneration.[57] National anthems, a form

53. Azaryahu, "The Purge of Bismarck and Saladin," 351.
54. See, for example, Harvey's account of the construction of Sacré-Coeur in Paris ("Monument and Myth").
55. Barber, "Place, Symbol, and Utilitarian Function in War Memorials."
56. It also seems to have been popular with authoritarian regimes in the twentieth. West-fehling, *Triumphbogen im 19. und 20. Jahrhundert.*
57. Curl, *A Celebration of Death.*

of musical monument, also date from the rise of nationalism as a political force in the nineteenth century.[58]

The use of paper monuments comes much later, since these required either a literate population, needing to buy postage stamps, or enough state control, in the case of currency, to ensure a monopoly. From the beginning, currency was an obvious carrier of political symbolism. The use of postage stamps as channels for propaganda was perhaps first recognized, or is at least most evident, after World War I. Fascist Germany, Italy, and Spain used them to clarify the message of the state, instill pride in the accomplishments of their regimes, and stoke the ardor necessary to achieve their goals. The opposing democracies soon followed suit.

The types of references also change. This occurs most radically when the nature of the regime is somehow transformed. In Haifa, Saladin gave way to Theodor Herzl; in East Berlin, Otto Bismarck gave way to Rosa Luxemburg.[59] The French Revolution marked a stark turning point. Not only did the Place Louis XV became Place de la Révolution, but the pool of possible honorees also changed: names honoring commoners had no place in the world's streetscape until after 1789.[60] This period also saw the rise of monuments honoring military heroes, Napoleon finding these a convenient way of pleasing his generals and promoting popular patriotism. The Third Republic, by contrast, was much more likely to honor artists.[61] Similarly, in Germany, poets and scientists were added to the usual cast of kings and generals.[62] Since World War I, monuments to illustrious individuals have been generally replaced by ones honoring anonymous symbolic representations or even whole collectives.[63] Some patterns are relatively constant, however. In most societies, the most important references are to formative periods. Origin myths play a central role in practically all forms of nationalism.[64] These are often seen as incarnate golden ages.[65] For the United States, for example, the Revolutionary War and subsequent decades appear as the central themes of national memory.[66] Zelinsky's exhaustive studies demon-

58. Sadie, *The New Grove Dictionary of Music and Musicians;* Cerulo, *Identity Designs.*

59. Azaryahu, "Purge of Bismarck and Saladin."

60. Baldwin and Grimaud, "How New Naming Systems Emerge," 157; Agulhon, "La 'statuomanie' et l'histoire," 147.

61. Hargrove, "Les statues de Paris"; Milo, "Le nom de rues."

62. Mosse, *Nationalization of the Masses,* 47.

63. Borg, *War Memorials;* Zelinsky, *Nation into State.*

64. Matossian, "Ideologies of Delayed Development"; Calhoun, "Nationalism and Ethnicity."

65. Eliade, cited in B. Schwartz, "The Social Context of Commemoration," 375.

66. B. Schwartz, "Social Context of Commemoration."

strate the central role played by George Washington, Andrew Jackson, and Abraham Lincoln in defining the American iconography.[67] Among nations that at least attempt to construct an unbroken link to some prenational ethnic group, references to these forebears are also common. The Hermannsdenkmal in Germany was one prominent example, as was Fascist Italy's Roman pretensions. The continuing popularity of Joan of Arc as a symbol in France is another.

Military references are a further popular motif. There is general agreement that war can and does often foster the kind of solidarity that is the basis of nationalism.[68] As many political leaders have found, war makes for votes. It is the fuel that allows the state to transform patriotism into nationalism. The early philosophers of the nation-state—G. W. F. Hegel, Johann Fichte, Johann Herder—appear to have been right: "war was the necessary dialectic in the evolution of nations."[69] There are few experiences that promote a sense of collectivity as well as war: "war creates a pathos and sentiment of community."[70] British nationalism, often cited as the first example of state-linked identity, was fed by the gore and glory of war.[71] Following recent work on nationalism, it would be difficult to imagine a more efficient genesis for *ressentiment* than war.[72] Nationalism can only be understood, in fact, within a geopolitical context. An isolated nationalism is impossible, since this sentiment is based on claims to distinctiveness vis-à-vis other nations.[73]

War created icons with which to teach nationalism. National anthems, for example, are notorious for their saber-rattling prose.[74] For some periods in some states, such references are central to the task of identity formation. In Israel, the poststatehood period saw considerable emphasis placed on military and heroic street names.[75] The heroism of Anzac forces in both world wars, and especially the disaster of Gallipoli, remain sacred symbols

67. Zelinsky, *Nation into State*. Washington, Franklin, Lincoln, and Jefferson also account for more than 15 percent of all stamps honoring individuals issued by the United States (Lehnus, *Angels to Zeppelins*, 157).
68. Zelinsky, *Nation into State*; Mann, "A Political Theory of Nationalism and Its Excesses."
69. Howard, *The Lessons of History*.
70. M. Weber, *From Max Weber*, 335.
71. Colley, *Britons*.
72. Greenfeld, *Nationalism*.
73. Calhoun, "Nationalism and Ethnicity."
74. Zikmund, "National Anthems as Political Symbols."
75. Cohen and Kliot, "Israel's Place-Names."

for Australia.[76] In the United States, memorials to various wars—and in the case of the Civil War, monuments to both sides of the same war—are a major part of geographical iconography.[77] The Soviet Union's fascination with war monuments and especially memorials to the "Great Patriotic War" is justifiably famous.[78] Germany also has a rich tradition.[79] War memorials became so common in France after World War I that they were mass manufactured.[80] Stamps with a victory theme were used by all the combatants in World War II. One Egyptian stamp from the 1960s made the Nasserite foreign policy crystal clear: it featured a dagger thrust into Israel.

We should not assume that war is automatically transformed into iconography, however.[81] Nor is it always defining. This pattern may be true for Wilhelmite Germany, but it certainly does not hold for pre–World War I Britain. For example, while Britain sought to honor those who defeated Napoleon, it largely did so through interior memorials not easily accessible to the masses, and as late as 1850 no public monument honored the duke of Wellington.[82] Even in modern Israel, biblical and Talmudic references made up nearly half the street names, compared with less than 10 percent for military/heroic ones.[83] Moreover, heroism can take several forms and does not necessarily imply military action.[84]

Stone and paper monuments thus provide a wonderful opportunity for the social scientist to study the very reflexivity that is part of identity construction. These phenomena provide insights into the way a society reads itself and its past. They allow us to read the writers of official history, to read the very process of mythmaking at its most basic level. In this particular instance, they allow us to measure the extent to which war and military heroism helped shape Latin American national identities.

Latin American National Myths

The national icons of Latin America do not appear to fulfill many of the functions assigned to such symbols. In particular, they fail to crystallize na-

76. Inglis, "Ceremonies in a Capital Landscape."
77. Savage, "The Politics of Memory"; Mayo, "War Memorials as Political Memory."
78. Ignatieff, "Soviet War Memorials."
79. Lurz, *Kriegerdenkmäller in Deutschland;* Weinland, *Kriegerdenkmäler in Berlin.*
80. Sherman, "Art, Commerce, and the Production of Memory."
81. Nor is military iconography always the same. European aesthetics may be unique in this respect (O'Connell, *Ride the Second Horseman*).
82. Colley, "Whose Nation?"; Yarrington, *The Commemoration of the Hero.*
83. Cohen and Kliot, "Israel's Place-Names," 245.
84. Levinger, "Socialist-Zionist Ideology."

tional identity and to draw the people into a moral communion.[85] In order to understand why, we need to analyze both their content and their context.

At first glance, the distribution of themes in Latin American monuments and street names would appear to follow the general pattern found in other countries: a strong emphasis on military and political themes (Table 4.1).[86]

85. Cerulo, *Identity Designs.*
86. I was able to obtain information for both monuments and streets for the following cities: Buenos Aires, Rio de Janeiro, Bogotá, Mexico City, Asunción, Montevideo, Santiago, and Caracas. For La Paz and Quito, I was only able to locate data on streets, while for Lima I had to limit myself to monuments. For Buenos Aires streets I used Municipalidad de la Ciudad de Buenos Aires, Secretaría de Cultura, *Barrios, calles y plazas;* and Cutulo, *Buenos Aires* (N = 2427). For monuments I used Baliari, *Los monumentos;* Vigil, *Los monumentos y lugares;* and Piccirilli, *Diccionario histórico Argentino* (N = 285). For La Paz, I relied on Viscarra Monje, *Las calles de La Paz.* This is not a complete listing of streets, but a sample selected by Viscarra Monje (N = 167). For Rio monuments, I used Amarente la Tarde, *Monumentos principais;* Diario de Noticias, *Monumentos da Cidade;* and Fontainha, *Historia dos monumentos* (N = 205). For streets, I relied on the ongoing work of Berger, *Diccionario histórico: Botafogo;* and *Diccionario histórico: V & VI regioes.* I have been limited to three regions in the city (N = 467). For Santiago the only source for monuments I could locate was Ossandón Guzmán and Ossandón Vicuna, *Guía de Santiago* (N = 54). Unsystematic information on street names was found in Thayer Ojeda, *Santiago de Chile.* For Bogotá streets I used M. Rosa, *Calles de Santa Fe de Bogotá,* and for monuments I relied on Cortazar, *Monumentos* (N = 196). I have a very limited sample of Quito streets. I used the listings found in Gómez, *Guía informativa de Quito* and checked with information available in Pérez Pimentel, *Diccionario biográfico del Ecuador.* This produced N = 61. I supplemented this information with the more anecdotal data found in Jurado Noboa, *Las calles de Quito.* I have not been able to locate a complete listing of monuments in Mexico City. My analysis is based on the most prominent landmarks of the city found in Mexico, Departamento de Turismo, *Guía de la Ciudad de México.* For streets I used Morales Díaz (N = 1171). For Asunción monuments I used Municipalidad de Asunción 1967 (N = 50) and for streets Municipalidad de Asunción, *Monumentos, parques, jardines y plazas* (N = 1035). I was not able to find a nomenclature for Lima streets. Data on monuments come from Cubillas Soriano, *Guía histórica biográfica* and Barra, *Monumentos escultóricos* (N = 258). Montevideo monuments are based on Casaretto (N = 41). Streets represent a random sample (N = 471) from Castellanos, *Nomenclatura de Montevideo.* I have not been able to find a systemic list of streets or monuments for Caracas. I have used the following: Misle, *Corazón, pulso y huella;* Gasparini and Posani; Valery, *La nomenclatura caraqueña.* For currency issues I have used two standard sources for the entire continent (Pick, *Standard Catalog;* Raymond, *Coins: Nineteenth Century Issues* and *Coins: Twentieth Century Issues*) and have supplemented these with individual country materials where possible. For Argentina, I have also used Banco Roberts, *Historia del papel moneda argentino* and Nusdeo and Conno, *Papel moneda nacional argentino;* and for Brazil, Violo Idolo, *Catálogo do papel-moeda do Brasil* and Casa da Moeda, *290 anos de historia.* For Ecuador I relied on Trujillo and for Mexico, Batiz Vázquez, *Historia del papel moneda.* Paraguayan and Uruguayan information came from Seppa, *Paper Money.* Zarauz Castelnau, *Billetes del Perú* was useful for Peru. For Venezuela I used Rosenman, *Billetes de Venezuela.* For stamps, I have largely relied on Scott's catalog. I counted all stamps featuring individuals and also noted those celebrating battles and military events as well as those marking special anniversaries. For some countries and periods I have also relied on Bushnell, "Postal Images"; and

As we will see, such aggregate portraits miss important differentiation. Yet even at this level of generalization we can find important distinctions between the Latin American pattern and that found in Europe and North America.[87]

First, Latin America tends to honor artists and scientists much more than European countries.[88] In her analysis of various cultural indicators in the United States and western Europe, Priscilla Clark finds much lower rates of artists on stamps, streets, and banknotes.[89] In several of the Latin American cities we can detect vestiges of the positivist fascination with creating a nation through progress exemplified by science, Mexico City and Rio being the clear leaders. A continental cult exists for such figures as Louis Pasteur, to whom there is a statue in almost every country.

Developmentalism is another major theme. In both currency and postal issues, Latin America shares a veneration of industry and progress far above anything seen in European or North American iconographies. Every country has at least some example of a symbolic smokestack. Prior to industrialization, currency issues prominently featured symbols of agricultural plenty. These icons may also be found in street names, as in the ubiquitous Progreso, or even monuments, especially those to the nationalization of industry. It might even be said that developmentalism has played a role usually assigned to military competition.

Such an emphasis on development faces three key problems at the heart

---

Reid, "The Stamp of Patriotism." Since these sources are almost all catalogs for dealers, they may not represent a complete sample. Through cross-checking for those countries where I found more than one source, I am fairly confident that they cover all major issues after 1900 and do a good job even before then. I have largely limited myself to a discussion of the persons featured on the bills and stamps and have mostly neglected the fascinating question of the nature of the allegorical figures often used (usually prior to 1900) and the graphic symbolism employed. For other national symbols, I relied on Helman and Serchio, *Las naciones americanas*.

87. Systematic comparisons are difficult because of differences in sampling, categorization, and so on. I am relying on the following as sources for comparison: Agulhon, "La 'statuomanie' "; Levinger, "Socialist-Zionist Ideology"; B. Schwartz, "The Social Context of Commemoration"; Cohen and Kliot, "Israel's Place-Names"; Zelinsky, *Nation into State;* Hargrove, "Les statues de Paris"; Ignatieff, "Soviet War Memorials"; Lehnus, *Angels to Zeppelins;* Milo, "Le nom de rues."

88. Religion retains some influence. Of the 299 Caracan *esquinas,* the largest number was religious in nature (45 for saints alone) or recalled some past event or figure from the local area. Among the countries of the Southern Cone, Paraguay is the only one with a significant religious presence in its iconography. Not surprisingly, given Ecuador's reputation for the strength of its faith (Bolívar reportedly referred to it as a convent), there is larger representation of religious figures in Quito than in any other city.

89. Priscilla Parkhurst Clark, *Literary France.*

Table 4.1 Distribution of references

STREETS AND MONUMENTS
(Percentage of biographical references)

| | MYTHIC THEME | | | MYTHIC PERIOD | | | | |
	Military	Political	Science/Art	Preindependence	Independence	National	Modern	N
Asunción monuments	60.0	44.4	17.8	10.8	13.5	45.9	29.7	50
Asunción streets	61.4	16.7	10.6	6.5	8.5	21.0	64.0	1035
Bogotá monuments	35.0	26.8	33.8	17.2	46.1	26.6	7.0	196
Buenos Aires monuments	37.9	41.9	27.4	4.8	37.1	42.7	3.2	285
Buenos Aires streets	42.9	27.3	32.2	7.6	30.3	30.0	26.4	2427
La Paz streets	41.5	35.2	31.4	2.4	10.8	21.6	56.9	167
Lima monuments	55.9	26.8	26.3	8.9	19.6	34.6	36.9	258
Mexico streets	29.5	26.3	52.5	15.6	9.9	50.9	22.8	1171
Montevideo monuments	12.1	36.4	69.7	3.7	25.9	33.3	37.0	41
Montevideo streets	31.6	29.0	33.0	15.5	33.0	40.9	23.1	471
Quito streets	11.5	36.1	55.7	11.5	13.1	50.8	44.3	61
Rio monuments	18.2	29.4	58.8	5.8	1.7	31.4	72.1	205
Rio streets	20.3	33.1	44.4	4.6	3.2	33.6	71.5	467
Santiago monuments	38.6	38.6	29.5	10.0	30.8	41.0	17.9	54

Note that categories are not exclusive and will total > 100%.

CURRENCY

Argentina	2 figures	San Martín and Belgrano; in nineteenth century, more than 20 different independence heroes
Bolivia	8 figures	5 independence and 3 postindependence military; 1 allegorical Indian
Brazil	28 figures	5 military, concentration on Empire and Old Republic
Chile	20 figures	2 military and O'Higgins; concentration on political figures
Colombia	9 figures	9 independence
Ecuador	4 figures	1 independence, 2 colonial, 1 Inca
Mexico	35 figures	2 purely military; concentrated on independence and Revolution
Paraguay	7 figures	5 military and one independence; 1 allegorical soldier
Peru	9 figures	4 military, 1 Inca; prior to 1968, allegorical representations of Liberty
Uruguay	2 figures	Both independence; gauchos and scene from independence
Venezuela	5 figures	3 independence; Bolívar dominates

POSTAGE

Argentina	San Martín dominant with other independence heroes
Bolivia	Independence dominates with isolated references to Pacific War
Brazil	Dispersed fields with no dominant figure
Chile	More than 100 different figures with no dominant field
Colombia	Independence dominates
Ecuador	Sucre and nineteenth-century political figures
Mexico	Independence and Revolution heroes dominate
Paraguay	Chaco War and López until 1970s then arts and scenery
Peru	Dispersed fields, but Miguel Grau most used—8 issues
Uruguay	Artigas dominant figure followed by artists (e.g., Rodó, Gardel)
Venezuela	Bolívar dominates with Sucre

SOURCE: See note 86, this chapter.

of a nationalist ethos. First, it very quickly brings into question precisely those issues of distribution and inequality that nationalism is often meant to quiet. Second, as the Cuban Revolution revealed, the enthusiasm of even the "new socialist man" for increasing productivity is rather limited. Production quotas do not appear to pack the same emotional punch of ethnic competition.[90] Finally, the battle between "civilization and *barbarie*," which is the antecedent to much of Latin American developmentalism, was inherently antipopulist. The advance of progress in Latin America more often than not has been seen as needing to defeat, control, and reshape *el pueblo*. As such, it made for a fragile base on which to build the worship of a common identity.

Political figures are less honored in Latin America, at least as compared with the United States. Interestingly, Latin America does share with the United States something of a flag fetish that is alien to Europe, but the continent does not venerate founding documents, nor has it created a liturgy of celebrating political institutions.[91] Nowhere do we see an equivalent to Mount Rushmore or the practice of honoring each and every president with a building or monument in Washington, D.C. With very few exceptions, such as Benito Juárez and Lazaro Cárdenas in Mexico and the oligarchs of the republic in Chile, few politicians are honored after their term in office.[92] In short, representatives of the authority of the state appear to play a relatively small role in Latin American national myths.

Latin American monumental iconography is characterized by enormous historical silences. While the same may be said of, for example, Germany and Russia, in these cases there are dramatic regime changes and collapses of political institutions on a scale not witnessed in Latin America. Yet again with some exceptions, among them Brazil, entire periods of independent life are forgotten.

The most dramatic example of historical amnesia is preindependence. As

90. The recent Cuban turn to prerevolutionary emblems and the traditional reliance on the threat of the United States also attest to the power of such symbols.

91. For a wonderful discussion of how these served to cement U.S. "nationhood," see Murrin, "A Roof Without Walls."

92. The pride in Chile's exceptional nineteenth century and the link between it and the current regime is perhaps most evident in the currency. From the very first national issue (1890s), Chile has honored not only a set of men, but practically a whole period and process of nation making. O'Higgins is featured, but so are the statesmen who created the Chilean state after the 1820s: Portales, Pinto, Montt, Prieto, and Santa María. This pantheon will remain surprisingly stable through the 1980s with some surprising additions (Balmaceda) and others to be expected (Prat).

noted earlier, origin myths are a common iconographic theme. In their search for historical symbols to appropriate, Latin American countries had two difficult choices. The first was to honor pre-Columbian civilizations. In some places including Mesoamerica and the Andes, this would have been, and has proven to be, quite easy given the accomplishments of these civilizations and their architectural legacy. This was the base for the earliest forms of Creole patriotism in Mexico.[93] Such a strategy would present a significant problem, however: how to glorify a past whose destruction came at the hands of the forebears of those who hold power? An Indian republic would have been able to do so and to have used an invented past to smash interethnic differences. For whites the task was difficult, since even if they desired to be compatriots of the Indians, they were descendants of those who had destroyed them.[94] The contradiction between historic and imagined community was too great.

The other option was to glorify the conquest. This is largely what the colonial regime did, and one may see vestiges of it in the older Latin American historiography. Such a strategy presented a mirror challenge. How to convince large parts of the population to honor those who had caused them to become an inferior caste?[95] In Brazil, the problem was perhaps even more difficult, given that for large parts of its history significant segments of the population were enslaved. Moreover, Brazil lacked a civil war and a figure such as Lincoln to legitimate the state for the black population.[96]

Of the two strategies discussed above, the worship of the conquest has been universally rejected. Early postal issues often featured Columbus and the local conquistador as well as images of Spaniards and Indians fighting, which have largely disappeared by the mid-twentieth century.[97] Ecuador is one of the few countries that still feature a conquistador on the currency, but this is balanced by another bill featuring the Inca general Ruminahui. None of the cities display significant references to the colonial era. Often there will only be a single monument to this period, usually honoring the

93. Brading, *Origins of Mexican Nationalism.*

94. I borrow this distinction from Francisco Antonio Pinto as cited in Vial Correa, "La formación de las nacionalidades hispanoamericanas," 130.

95. See Thurner, *From Two Republics to One Divided.* Despite early dreams that war would create (in Antonio Maceo's words) "no whites nor blacks, but only Cubans," preexisting racial differences were never gulfed (Ada Ferrer, *Insurgent Cuba,* 7).

96. A difficult paradox: Pedro II freed the slaves, but was ousted a year later. Should one celebrate the emancipator or the republic that replaced him?

97. The massive Columbus lighthouse in Santo Domingo is an exception, but it is somewhat idiosyncratic for many other reasons.

founder of the city or an even more distant Columbus. Mexico represents one extreme: it is impossible to find a single statue to Hernán Cortés in all of Mexico City.[98] Chile is at the other end of the spectrum: it completely ignores its Indian heritage. It is also the country that honors Columbus with the most stamps. Thus, in the process of creating their new national communities, the Latin American countries "forgot" hundreds of years of history.

The result of this general absence of origin myths is that Latin Americans feel, in Bolívar's words, like orphans divorced from any cultural parentage.[99] Further, orphans may not know their own kin; few Latin Americans necessarily feel an *ethnic* connection to their national compatriots. The same may be said of North Americans, but the United States has managed to construct a protoethnicity from a series of historical institutions such as the Constitution.[100] The limits of any imagined political community in Latin America were set long before the territorial boundaries of the respective countries.

The relative weakness of this sense of common identity is perhaps best indicated by the cosmopolitanism of Latin American iconography. The extent to which citizens of other countries—Latin Americans included—play a major role in public iconography is perhaps unique in the world. Despite its reputation for xenophobia, Latin America as a whole is very generous with its honors. It is difficult to imagine the United States or European countries devoting 15–30 percent of their monuments and street names to non-co-nationals.[101] (Stamps are less exclusive; currencies more so.) This reflects several historical legacies: the Enlightenment influence on independence struggles, later positivism, and the persistent pancontinentalism. The point here is not the source, but rather the implication: a state that often honors not itself or its citizens, but its neighbors. Even more remarkably, there are several cases of statues and street names honoring those against whom the nation fought at one time or another—Buenos Aires and Montevideo both have streets named after Mariscal López.

One characteristic that Latin America shares with North America and Europe is the almost complete absence of women from official iconography.

98. There are, however, two statues of Columbus. The only other public monument to the Spanish link is the *caballito* of Charles III in the city center.

99. Minguet, "Mythes fondateurs chez Bolívar."

100. Murrin, "A Roof Without Walls."

101. Montevideo is the most cosmopolitan city, with just more than 60 percent of street names accounted for by Uruguayans. Bogotá seems the most chauvinist, with 97 percent of monuments accounted for by Colombians. Most cities have 80–85 percent of monuments and streets honoring nationals.

Except for isolated cases of a few female heroines from the wars of independence, women are not to be seen, even in paper monuments. This begins to
change in the 1960s, but men still dominate the iconography, and when
women do appear, they are in traditional roles. For example, I counted thirteen statues or monuments to a generic *madre* in Buenos Aires alone.

Finally, despite its reputation for militarism, Latin American nationalism
appears much less based on bellicose claims and military heroics than European or North American examples.[102] The high percentage of military documents largely reflects the central importance of the founding fathers from
the independence period.[103] If we take into account other iconographic
sources such as stamps, currencies, and public festivals, the importance of
military symbols declines even further. Battle scenes or military heroes
rarely appear in stamps or currencies, again with the exception of indepen-
dence-related themes. In general, Latin America has not glorified a nation
at arms fighting to preserve political rule over a territory. After the wars
of independence, military conflict largely disappears as a source of state
legitimization. The only exception to this pattern is in national anthems.
These share a bloodthirsty martial air that is largely absent from other
iconographic genres. Five of the eleven relevant anthems feature some variant on the "liberty or death" theme, three others imply battle or conflict
against some oppressor, and almost all involve a call for the people to sacrifice or march toward some vaguely military goal.

The most exceptional aspect of the iconographic role of the military is
the drastic reduction in references to war beginning in the twentieth century

102. Considering how important wars have been as themes, or at least locales, for North
American and European literature, they play a surprisingly small role in Latin America (Sommer, *Foundational Fictions;* Merton, *The New Historical Novel in Latin America*). Clearly,
exceptions exist. The independence wars have given us several novels, including those by Gabriel García Márquez and Alejo Carpentier. A genre of odes to particular heroes, especially
Bolívar, has produced Juan Zorilla de San Martín's *La leyenda patria* and José Joaquín
Olmedo's "La victoria de Junín: Canto a Bolívar"; *Facundo* (1845) and *Amalia* (1854) take
place during the struggle against caudillism and Rosas in particular, while *Martín Fierro* (1872)
features gaucho against Indian. Civil wars and rebellions are highlighted in Euclydes da Cunha's *Os Sertões,* García Márquez's *Cien años de soledad,* and Mario Vargas Llosa's *La guerra
del fin del mundo.* The Mexican Revolution is portrayed, perhaps most famously, in *Los de
abajo* and *La muerte de Artemio Cruz.* Paraguay's Augusto Roa Bastos's *Hijo de hombre* is
another more contemporary contribution. An event as momentous as the War of the Triple
Alliance has called forth only relative unknowns such as Manuel Gálvez, while the Chaco War
has Augusto Céspedes.

103. Independence also dominates school curricula. In Colombia, for example, the independence conflicts are assigned a year of secondary school history, the same amount of study
given to the entire period after 1830 (Cacua Prada, "Proceso de socialización").

(Table 4.2). While such references account for nearly half of Argentine street names still surviving from the nineteenth century, for example, they are only 16 percent of those named after 1955. This trend, in part, reflects historical reality. Wars were concentrated in the nineteenth century. But there also seems to be a continentwide decline in references to war in general. Even the cult of independence was affected. By the 1980s, the importance of Argentine independence festivals was greatly reduced. In 1991, coverage of May 25 events merited only a small part of front pages of newspapers, whereas earlier these had monopolized entire sections.

Surprisingly, there does not appear to be any relationship between military rule and an increased use of bellicose icons. As opposed to the European cases, it is almost impossible to determine the nature of the regime, except in its broadest sense, by analyzing its public icons. There are, of course, some exceptions, such as the cult of Evita. Given Pinochet's goal to legitimate his regime with historical allusions, it may not be accidental that Portales first appears on Chilean stamps in 1975 and then reappears on the currency after an absence of several decades. But, authoritarian or democratic, civil or military, regimes have shared the same set of icons. Even more remarkable, it is impossible to tell when the country was at war.

Whatever the reason, Latin American states have been deprived of the kind of nationalist symbolism created after World War I. With few exceptions, Latin America lacks monuments to collective sacrifice, whether statues of anonymous individuals, such as those of U.S. Civil War privates or French World War I *poilus*, or intentionally faceless cenotaphs. In all my searches I found not a single statue celebrating the Latin American equivalent of the Minuteman. Almost all the monuments associated with war honor famous individuals. War is an affair of elites and the masses appear to have little to do with it. The Brazilian memorial to World War II is one of the few examples of anonymous monumental architecture reflecting more recent developments in honoring war dead. Others include the massive monument in Lima honoring the 1941 war with Ecuador, a similar monument for the dead of the Pacific, and that to the Roto Chileno in Santiago.

This aesthetic pattern is extremely important, for it indicates that the nationalistic "return" on even the relatively small number of war monuments is limited. These memorials do not serve to remind the nation of its hour of glory or of how *el pueblo* contributed to victory. Rather, they honor often generic men on horseback whose contemporary significance may be nil. Architecture combining nationalist aspirations and death is completely

Table 4.2 Changes in themes (percentage of biographical references)

	WAR			
	Pre-1920	1920–30	1930–60	Post-1960
Asunción streets		44.5	58.8	
Bogotá monuments	50.0	35.6		
Buenos Aires monuments		33.9	11.5	40.9
Buenos Aires streets	46.9	35.0	19.6	15.5
Lima monuments		23.8	33.3	16.7
Montevideo monuments		14.3	11.1	
Rio monuments	14.3	25.0		
Rio streets	15.6	8.6	18.5	11.4
Santiago monuments	60.0	38.5	25.0	

	POLITICS			
	Pre-1920	1920–30	1930–60	Post-1960
Asunción streets		22.9	11.4	
Bogotá monuments	14.3	26.7		
Buenos Aires monuments		54.0	59.3	30.2
Buenos Aires streets	32.1	28.7	23.6	23.5
Lima monuments		31.0	16.7	26.2
Montevideo monuments		28.6	44.4	
Rio monuments	44.4	42.5		
Rio streets	20.4	39.0	35.0	36.9
Santiago monuments	37.5	55.6	45.5	

	ART/SCIENCE			
	Pre-1920	1920–30	1930–60	Post-1960
Asunción streets		7.0	14.7	
Bogotá monuments	21.4	35.6		
Buenos Aires monuments		16.2	29.6	34.9
Buenos Aires streets	13.6	30.3	41.8	46.8
Lima monuments		23.8	41.7	21.4
Montevideo monuments		71.4	66.7	
Rio monuments	50.0	42.5		
Rio streets	32.6	45.1	43.0	52.5
Santiago monuments	0.0	11.0	36.4	

SOURCES: See note 86, this chapter.

absent, and so are the respective sentiments.[104] This has consequences. If a single hero is considered the only source of national pride,[105] how is it possible to construct a nationalist ethos broad enough to include large parts of the population?

In general, then, Latin American iconography is quite different from that of Europe and North America. It is much more focused on cultural and scientific figures, pays less attention to political symbols, and lacks the mythology of a people at arms uniting through sacrifice. As a whole, it lacks the sense of "great things done together" that is at the heart of national consciousness.[106] Within this pattern, however, we may detect important differences. Given their importance in the iconographies of nationalism, I have focused on the use of origin myths and military heroism.

The Question of Origins

Only Mexico and, to much lesser extent, Peru, have attempted the strategy of using the Indian past to create a sense of nation.[107] Perhaps the most interesting monument on the Avenida Reforma in Mexico City is that to Cuauhtémoc—the last Aztec ruler, who led the final resistance to Cortés. Unveiled in 1887, it marked the official beginning of a redefinition of Creole nationalism, establishing a link between the glories of the Aztec past and the current Mexican nation. In the dedication speeches, Cuauhtémoc was glorified as a "defender of the nation," founded in 1327 when the Aztecs settled in the Valley of Mexico. Cuauhtémoc also appears on Mexican currency, including the latest issues, which feature him on one side and on the reverse, a symbolic battle between a Spaniard and an Aztec.

Other attempts to consolidate this link between the current Mexican nation and the Aztec past are evident in the Monument to the Raza, Indios

104. For example, no Latin American university has the roll of dead that is a feature of every U.S. and British school. Nor are Latin American university students (no matter the prominence of their political rule) expected to courageously die for the fatherland on the orders of the state.

105. This statement appears in the official magazine of the Venezuelan armed forces, cited in Carrera Damas, "Simón Bolívar," 132.

106. I borrow the phrase from E. Weber, *Peasants into Frenchmen,* 110.

107. One iconographic genre where we do find much more continentwide attention paid to the question of race and the creation of a new *pueblo* is in literature. Works such as *El criollo* (1935), *María* (1867), *El Zarco* (1888), *Doña Barbara* (1929), and *O Guaraní* (1857) challenged accepted notions of race division and often called for the creation of a new unified nation transcending ethnic divides.

Verdes, the Plaza of the Three Cultures, the ongoing archeological site of the Templo Mayor and the National Archeological Museum, and the Fountain of Netzahualcóyotl in Chapultepec.[108] Since the 1930s, Mexico has made ample use of its Indian heritage in postage stamps.[109] Perhaps the most impressive expression of the theme of *mestizaje* that pervades Mexican political culture is the Basílica de Guadelupe outside Mexico City. Mexico is the only country where an explicit reference to pre-Columbian culture is made in its national symbols: the eagle and cactus have been a part of Mexican iconography since independence. The pre-Columbian presence is much less evident in street names. Roughly 5 percent of the people honored were explicitly Indian figures.[110] The conquest itself was not a prominent theme. However, Cortés, absent from monumental iconography, has several streets named in his honor.

Several features of "Aztec worship" are worthy of attention. First, according to Tenenbaum, the veneration of the Aztecs was meant to not only give the Porfiriato a historical link with which to legitimize itself, but also symbolically reassert the domination of Mexico City. A very specific Indian past was chosen, one that excluded the majority of non-European ethnic groups. Moreover, the chosen Indian dressed as a European—Cuauhtémoc's robe would not have looked out of place in fifth-century-B.C. Athens. For the Porfiriato, the Indians had to serve the same literal roles as Walter Scott's Highlanders or the generic Germanic tribes of the Kaiserreich. This required a complete switch in how the Indian past was perceived: "Barbaric Aztec society became noble, orderly, hierarchic, productive and civilized in the history painter's classical spectacle."[111] This perspective and inherent racism did not disappear with the Porfiriato, but could still be seen in history textbooks in the 1920s.[112]

Of all the other countries, Peru makes the strongest effort to include the large Indian majority into its nationalist mythology. This is so although, unlike Mexico, Peru also seems to honor the Spanish Conquest. A statue of Francisco Pizarro, only unveiled in the 1930s, stands in the center of Lima; as late as 1961, the old imperial capital of Cuzco dedicated a statue to him; and he appeared on a postage stamp as late as 1943. This aside, for Peru,

108. The architectural expression of this Indianist national ideology was the Mexican pavilion at the French World Fair of 1889. See Moyssén, "El nacionalismo y la arquitectura."

109. Reid, "Stamp of Patriotism," 46.

110. Thus, Juárez would not be counted as an Indian, but Cuauhtémoc would be.

111. Widdifield, "Dispossession, Assimilation, and the Image of the Indian."

112. Vaughn, *The State, Education, and Social Class in Mexico, 1880–1928.*

one Indian figure is especially prominent: Manco Capac fulfills the same role as Cuauhtémoc's in Mexico, the warrior defending a nation from some unspoken enemy. Manco Capac first appears on stamps in 1896, Atahualpa in 1917, and Huáscar in 1934; but the number of Indian iconic references increases after the 1968 military coup. More-recent Peruvian currency issues have also featured Manco Capac as well as other prominent indigenous figures: Inca Pachcutec, Garcilaso de la Vega, and Tupac Amarú.

Even through the 1960s, Bolivia had made no attempt to bridge its huge racial gulfs through the creation of a symbolic *raza*. The most striking characteristic of the La Paz nomenclature is who is *not* mentioned. Given the demographic profile of the country and its links to the Inca Empire and significant civilizations predating it, it is shocking to find only 2 streets out of 169 (in 1965) that made explicit mention of an Indian figure. Similarly, in Ecuador, I found only two references to pre-Columbian figures. Colombia and Venezuela were also lacking pre-Columbian icons. Perhaps the most surprising case, given its history of isolation and the legacy of the Jesuit missions, is Paraguayan public iconography. There is no attempt, for example, to "guaranize" national memory, and the figures represented are uniformly European, the only anomaly being that Paraguay, alone in the region, has an indigenous language on its currency. I was only able to identify one Afro-Brazilian among the figures depicted by the 205 statues in Rio. (Interestingly, the only major statue honoring a nonwhite is a gift from Mexico: an almost exact replica of the Cuauhtémoc statue.) The information for street names is less certain, but the biographical context makes it likely that the pattern is identical. The Brazilian government—or at least that part that is represented by the political geography of Rio—has not expended similar energy in creating symbols of this new "Brazilian."[113]

The Southern Cone may symbolize a third strategy for honoring national origins. While lacking the concern with a new *raza* similar to Mexico's, Montevideo does feature two statues that symbolize the mythological origins of the nation. The first is the monument to the gaucho, the other is the statue of a generic immigrant. Through these symbols, Montevideo attempts to unite the two central foci of its independent life: the pampas and the immigration that settled much of the country beginning in the late nineteenth century. Argentina's national identity is also closely linked to the

113. But a recent currency issue does allude to the multiethnic background of Brazil. Other Brazilian social myths support the idea of a multiracial society and certainly Brazilian religion has many examples of African figures.

legend of the gaucho and the pampas.[114] Both Argentina and Uruguay have used postage stamps to support the national legend of the gaucho, honoring this figure and symbols, such as maté gourds, that are associated with him, as well as authors, including José Hernández and Florencio Sánchez.[115]

How to explain these differences? In part, the Mexican and Peruvian emphasis reflects their archeological heritage. Machu Pichu and Teotihuacán are easier to glorify than civilizations that have disappeared leaving no remnants. Yet we should then see an equivalent myth in Bolivia and Ecuador. The answer partly lies in the historical timing of both of these iconographic turns to celebrating the indigenous heritage. In Peru it is particularly evident: only after 1968, with the first attempt by the Peruvian state to create a popular nationalism, do pre-Columbian figures assume a prominent role in official iconography. Similarly in Mexico, Porfirio Díaz's attempts to reestablish the centrality of Mexico City and his use of patriotic imagery in the rebellion of 1877 required an integration of at least parts of the population. More important, the 1910 revolution's concern with creating an inclusive authoritarianism helped shape the choices of nationalist myths. After 1876, Mexico opted to transform *dead* Indians into symbols, thereby easing its control over those still alive.[116] Moreover, Mexico had a long tradition— going back to the antecedents of independence patriotism—of recognizing the accomplishments of pre-Columbian civilizations.

Argentina's use of the gaucho was a reflection of political change. Certainly the Liberalism exemplified by Sarmiento would not have chosen it, but the populism that has marked Argentinean politics since the 1930s found the *barbarie* represented by the gaucho a convenient symbol in its fight against the Buenos Aires elite.[117]

Thus history helps determine national icons in two ways. First, the genesis of national symbols is partly a function of the available past, as in, for example, archeological remnants. Second, it is a product of a state's particular circumstances during the period of its creation. As we have seen, both presented problems for Latin America. The first required recognition of a national "original sin" that was too politically dangerous for the social and

114. Justo, *Pampas y lanzas*.
115. Reid, "Stamp of Patriotism."
116. For a wonderful discussion of the Porfirian attempt to create a new national history, see Morales Moreno, *Orígenes de la museología mexicana*. On the revolutionary regime, see Vaughn, *State, Education, and Social Class*. For a detailed discussion of the Mexican nationalist difference and its origins in the nineteenth century, see Mallon, *Peasant and Nation*.
117. Shumway, *Invention of Argentina*.

political status quo. The second involved an explicit attempt to resolve that sin through a new definition of the nation, but the vestiges of caste identity made it an unpopular alternative. A third path would have been through war, as the creation of an external other would have gone far to disguise or mitigate internal divisions. Yet as we will see, that avenue could only be partly utilized.

War

As will become clear, wars and nations may have a similar relationship in Latin America to what they have in Europe when the circumstances and the timing are similar. That is, when wars provide an opportunity for national mythmaking and when the relevant states are willing and able to exploit these opportunities, we tend to see the same process noted in other cases. However, such circumstances were rare indeed. I begin with a discussion of international wars, then move on to civil conflicts, and pay special attention to the wars of independence.

International

War dominates the Paraguayan nationalist imagination. No other Latin American country has experienced so much war, nor has any other state created such a cult around its military history. Through its use of both of its major conflicts, Paraguay has access to the two most powerful identity-building aspects of war: a catastrophic defeat that serves to unite the national "family" and a surprising victory that glorifies it. More than half the major monuments in Asunción are dedicated to remembering a figure or some aspect of a war. The War of the Triple Alliance alone accounts for eight public monuments.[118] The Chaco War is memorialized by three others. While some figures from independence, such as Francia, are honored, the focal point is not the creation of the nation, but its struggle to survive. The street names of Asunción reflect the same fascination, more than half the streets recalling a person or event associated with war. In this case, the Triple Alliance is not as significant as the Chaco War, which accounts for more

---

118. The elevation of Francisco Solano López to cult status only begins in the 1940s (Bushnell, "Postal Images").

than a fourth of all street names. The pattern continues in the currency, which features the only generic soldier seen in continental iconography as well as leaders of and heroes from the Triple Alliance and the Chaco Wars. Paraguay is one of the few countries that have used stamps for propaganda during a war. Stamps proclaiming the *chaco paraguayo* appeared during its conflict with Bolivia.

More than almost any other Latin American country after Paraguay, Bolivia owes its sense of national identity to wars.[119] Torn between its colonial administrative links to Buenos Aires and its economic and ethnic links to southern Peru, Bolivia as a nation-state only began to take shape following the defeat of its confederation with Peru and then the defeats of the Pacific and the Chaco. More than 40 percent of street names refer to war. Two generals associated with the Chaco are honored on the currency: Gralberto Villarroel and Germán Busch.[120] In the 1980s, they were joined by nineteenth-century heroes José Ballivián and Santa Cruz. The loss of territory in the War of the Pacific has been recalled in stamps and even the national seal which features an extra star symbolizing the missing littoral.

Peru is also concerned with making the remembrance of war a central part of its nationalist iconography. More than 40 percent of the sites identified and nearly two-thirds of major monuments celebrate a figure or an event associated with war. The great episode in this case is the War of the Pacific. Many of the monuments celebrating national military figures make explicit references to this war and the battles that took place around Lima (but there are no references to the guerrilla war against the Chileans in the sierra, and special stamp issues commemorate it). Several heroes from this struggle, especially Grau, are honored in most cities and in currency issues. Peru has also made a considerable effort to celebrate its one significant military victory in the nineteenth century, that against Spain in the 1860s; Francisco Bolognesi is a popular subject of statues. Both Grau and Bolognesi are among the most honored individuals in postal issues—the first is even more frequently pictured than Bolívar or San Martín! While references to the military appear to decline with time in most other Latin American cases, Peru has maintained the production of such institutional memories to the present day. Recent struggles such as the Ecuador war of 1941 receive their due. An

---

119. Ortega, *Aspectos del nacionalismo boliviano.*
120. The two were initially honored during the Villarroel dictatorship, but remained on currency through the 1960s.

air force pilot killed in this struggle is honored on a recent currency issue, one of the very few contemporary military men depicted. Several Peruvian stamps have featured Peru's disputed territory with Ecuador.[121]

Chile attaches a great deal of symbolic value to the military record of its armed forces. Especially after the War of the Pacific, Chilean nationalism had a clear martial air. The victory even created dreams of a Pacific hegemonism among parts of the political class.[122] Even before this triumph, some argue that Chile's sense of national consciousness was shaped by its experience as a "país de guerra."[123] But Chile's military veneration does not approach the levels of those of Peru or Paraguay. Such references account for only one-third of all monuments (although more than half of major ones). This is especially surprising given that Chile won all its wars. The War of the Pacific is largely represented by two sites: the monument to the martyr Arturo Prat and the Church of National Gratitude, built to commemorate the sacrifice of the Chilean dead.[124] Note that neither one is an example of the triumphalist architecture one might expect. Thus while Chilean national identity and governmental legitimacy owe a great deal to both episodes, there has been no attempt to glorify them in stone. What is also surprising is that there is little public memory of the war against the Indians and the expansion of the Chilean frontier, the subject of one of Chile's foundational texts, *La Araucana*.

To a greater extent than most of the other countries, Chile has preserved a liturgy surrounding its dates of military glory. The battle of Yungay, fought against the Peruvian-Bolivian Confederation, is celebrated in front of the Roto Chileno monument. On Navy Day, May 21, newspapers feature detailed biographies of Arturo Prat and descriptions of the battle of Iquique from the War of the Pacific. Army Day, the day following the celebration of Independence, is a time of military parades and exultation of martial glory. These festivities continued even through the Allende government and of course became even more central during the Pinochet years.[125]

Argentina honors those wars that are closest to independence: the conflict

121. Ecuador has responded with a series in which it asserts, "Ecuador has been, is, and shall be an Amazonian country," thereby announcing its long-standing claims in the region (Nussel, "Territorial and Boundary Disputes,"131).

122. Kiernan, "Chile from War to Revolution."

123. Krebs, "Orígenes de la conciencia nacional chilena."

124. For the Prat site, see the wonderfully detailed account of the creation of this national icon in Sater, *The Heroic Image in Chile*.

125. But even in Chile, such festivals have increasingly lost their luster. See *El Mercurio*, November 18, 1992, 1.

with Brazil in the 1820s and the English invasion of 1806–7. The latter's share of street names reflects an importance far beyond its actual historical significance. This in part is a remnant of the colonial nomenclature. More important, it indicates a need to celebrate a victory over a powerful enemy whose ethnic identity was so clearly different. The War of the Triple Alliance is barely mentioned, either in street names or in monumental icons. The Falklands/Malvinas war did bring about some changes in nomenclature, among them the erasure of English names.

Original plans to honor General Ignacio Zaragoza and other Mexican heroes of the French war were dropped during the Porfiriato and never reconsidered.[126] The outstanding monument to the American war is the "New" Monument to the Niños Heroes of 1847, in Chapultepec Park, commemorating the martyrdom of the cadets who died defending Chapultepec Castle from U.S. forces.[127] Among street names, however, references to these struggles are much more frequent. Currency issues give a much more prominent place to the war against the French. Cinco de Mayo (May 5), the date of a victory over the French, was for many years celebrated as a major holiday in Mexico and was one of the few times that the military played a prominent role: the annual cohort of draftees would parade in the *zócalo* (central plaza) and pledge their allegiance. Since the 1970s, however, this ritual has been generally downgraded and now appears to play a minor role south of the border (it has been appropriated by the Mexican-American population).

For several countries, postindependence wars play an even smaller role in their national iconography. While military and heroic statues dominate the major memorials of Montevideo, such figures account for less than 15 percent of total monuments. Roughly one-fourth of streets, however, do reflect military themes, and again, independence dominates. In Caracas, I was able to find only one geographical reference to a postindependence external struggle: Bloqueo, commemorating the blockade by the British Navy following a border dispute with British Guyana. Although in Colombia military figures are generally important, found in one-third of all monuments, they are again almost exclusively concentrated in the independence era. Only soldiers associated with that battle deserve honor. The only other mili-

126. Tenenbaum, "Streetwise History," 135; Casanova, "1861–1876," 129–30. Some of these were finally honored with station names in the Mexico City metro.

127. There is an older monument in the castle itself built by Díaz in 1880–81. Other monuments associated with that struggle include that found in Molino del Rey and a plaque honoring Irish volunteers who fought against the Americans in 1847.

tary reference I located was to the battle of Tarqui from the short war with Peru in 1828–29. One of the few references to a collective heroic experience, as opposed to veneration of an individual, is the Plaza of Martyrs (marking the Spanish reconquest in the wars of independence).

The political geography of Rio largely ignores the international and regional wars that consumed much of Brazil's military attention during two-thirds of the nineteenth century. Such monuments account for roughly 15 percent of the total (although they represent one-third of major monuments). Their representation in streets is equally low: 17 percent are named for military figures. Even among these references, war is not always celebrated. Several of the military men recognized in some form or another served during peacetime and were responsible for engineering or administration. Brazilian currency is more militaristic than the monuments and street names honoring several heroic figures.

The information from the very limited Ecuadorian sample would indicate that Quito has the least-martial geographical iconography. Just more than 10 percent of street names identified refer to a person or place with links to the military. I have not been able to find, for example, a reference to a monument to the war with Peru in 1941 that has produced a significant site in Lima.

Civil

While historical circumstance might help explain the relatively small role played by external wars in official iconography, there is even less mention of the many civil wars experienced by nearly all the countries. This is particularly surprising, since it was through these wars that most of the nations were forged. Certainly one would expect some icons in Argentina, for example. But while Buenos Aires honors some of those who fought against Rosas, there is nothing approaching the cult of the Civil War in the United States. The losing side, whether Federalist or Rosista, is largely ignored, while the Unitarian or Liberal victors claim a significant part of the urban nomenclature and monumental space. Rosas and Facundo Quiroga have yet to appear even on a stamp.[128] Thus, no attempt has been made to unify the nation through the elevation to cult status of heroes *from both sides*. Similarly, Colombia largely ignores its own violent history, Venezuela honors Bolívar,

---

128. Bushnell, "Postal Images." Rosas made it on to the currency after Menem's election.

but devotes much less attention to Páez. Bolivia barely mentions 1952, and Brazil ignores the rebellions of the nineteenth century.

Mexico is the exception to this pattern. Monuments in Mexico City are concentrated on the Avenida de la Reforma, extending from Chapultepec Park to the colonial center.[129] First laid out during the reign of Maximilian and subsequently elaborated by Juárez and then Porfirio Díaz, the avenue was Mexico's contribution to the "Hausmannization" of Latin American capitals during the last third of the nineteenth century.[130] Its name (and the monument to Juárez on the nearby Alameda) celebrates the victory of the Liberals during the last of the civil wars of the early nineteenth century as well as their leadership in the struggle against the French in the 1860s. More than half the statues lining the avenue are of men (no women) who played a military role while seven are of those whose role was political. Most distinctive of this series is the emphasis on an internal struggle. Almost half the statues portray men who gained their prominence during the almost half century of civil wars, whereas the American and the French wars receive much less attention. The struggle for the Reforma also receives considerable attention in Mexico's currency.

Not surprisingly, there is also a cult of the Revolution. The largest monument in Mexico City is devoted to it and occupies the site—and encompasses some of the materials—of Porfirio Díaz's proposed legislative palace. Along with the *zócalo*, this is the usual center of state ceremonies.[131] This monument includes the remains of the first and last presidents of the revolutionary war, Madero and Carranza. Madero and Álvaro Obregón also have their own statues elsewhere in the city. A monument to petroleum nationalization is an extension of this cult. Surprisingly, the Revolution is not so central to currency. Carranza and Madero were honored in the 1970s, but no other figure from this period has merited this attention. The most recent issue does feature Lazaro Cárdenas and the expropriation of petroleum. The murals of Diego Rivera and José Clemente Orozco are also part of this liturgy. They emphasize how the pre-Columbian past, the glory of independence, and the social injustice of the Porfiriato produced the Revolution and the social progress it brought. The history taught in schools culminates in the establishment of the postrevolutionary regime.[132]

129. The Reforma also serves as the focal point of ceremonies.

130. Duncan, "Political Legitimation and Maximilian's Second Empire"; Marroqui, *La Ciudad de México;* Needell, "Rio de Janeiro and Buenos Aires"; Tenenbaum, "Streetwise History."

131. Lorey, "The Revolutionary Festivals of Mexico."

132. Vaughn, *State, Education, and Social Class;* O'Malley, *The Myth of Revolution.*

Independence

The wars of independence stand out in the generally pacific history of Latin America. They represent a moment of martial glory, producing legends of heroism, sacrifice, and loyalty. They were the high point of Creole patriotism: the rise of a consciously American population challenging an easily identifiable enemy.[133] They remain the central icon in many national mythologies and are clearly the dominant expression of political consciousness on the continent. For example, only independence heroes such as San Martín, Sucre, and Bolívar—and their Mexican equivalents—have been honored with province names, and they have received the most numerous place-names. The flags of almost all the countries date from this period and many make references to this conflict, as seen in the *sol de mayo* on the Argentine flag, while national anthems refer to it almost exclusively.

Again, there are differences within this continental pattern. The discussion that follows begins with those cases in which independence plays a major role and then moves to those in which it is relatively minor.

At the center of Venezuelan iconography is Símon Bolívar—usually given such honorifics as Father of the Fatherland or Illustrious Hero of Independence.[134] The Plaza Bolívar (containing an equestrian statue) remains the symbolic center of Caracas. The elaboration of even such a central myth took a relatively long time to develop. Prior to independence, Venezuelan street names were almost all religious or, in a few cases, reflected local folklore. These were changed after the first declaration of independence in 1811 following the French revolutionary pattern of honoring the new republican virtues: Justice, Security, Confederation, Union, Fertility, and so on. The political confusion that ensued during the following decade produced conflicting names and city plans. By 1821, the republican references were finally victorious. That year also saw the addition of some battles and references to the military, such as in Street of the Brave. While there had been plans to honor Bolívar with the plaza as early as 1825, the statue was only finally obtained and unveiled in 1874, under Guzmán Blanco, who rebuilt much of the central city and attempted to create a new nomenclature around himself.

Other than the plaza and the monument commemorating Bolívar's battle

---

133. Brading, "Liberal Patriotism."
134. On the possible problems associated with this kind of cult (which apply to other countries in Latin America), see Carrera Damas, "Simón Bolívar."

in Carabobo, Caracas as a whole lacks monumental architecture.[135] This symbolic monopoly is even more evident in the national currency—called *bolivares* since the 1870s. Following some early appearances by Columbus, Bolívar completely dominates after 1890, sometimes joined by other figures from independence, including Francisco Miranda, Sucre, Páez, and Andrés Bello. Bolívar's is the only portrait featured on coins and is almost the only one to appear on more than one stamp, showing up in at least thirty designs. The only other individual enjoying even anything like this fascination is fellow independence hero Miranda. Major avenues are the only streets that are not numbered, and their names honor the standard independence troika of Bolívar, Sucre, and San Martín—plus O'Higgins and George Washington as well as specific Venezuelan icons such as Páez. All these figures also have statues or monuments, usually on the avenue that bears their name. Of the historical references among the Caracan *esquinas,* most were linked to the independence struggle, among them Sucre, Bolívar, and Junín.

The earlier colonial streets of Bogotá, whose names were either religious or recalled local folklore, were renamed by 1849, at which point we see the expected rise of names dealing with republican virtues. Perhaps even more than Venezuela, Colombia places Bolívar at the center of its nationalist mythology. In Bogotá alone there are at least three major monuments to him as well as at least four busts and innumerable plaques recalling biographical moments and heroic deeds. The Plaza Bolívar retains a strong political importance. In general, the independence period dominates the geographical iconography of Bogotá as in few other cities. Two-thirds of major monuments are devoted to this period. Of these, almost all have military or heroic connotations. The plazas and *puentes* of the city have retained their names, and these follow the monumental iconography described earlier: Bolívar, Santander, Libertador, and so on. Once again, Bolívar dominates the "paper" monuments. He is first featured in the 1860s, then joined by Washington and a group of independence heroes who will appear in practically every issue afterward: Franciso José Caldas, Antonio Nariño, Santander, Camilo Torres, Córdoba, and Ricuarte.[136] One of the few women so honored on the continent, Policarpa Salvarrieta, served as an independence guerrilla.

135. One possible exception (but not central) is the Arch of the Federation of 1895. The latter is the only example of a triumphal arch that I was able to find although temporary arches were a popular part of colonial and nineteenth-century celebrations throughout the continent.

136. Sometimes other figures "sneak in": nineteenth-century president Nuñez's wife served as a model for the Liberty head featured on coins during his term.

The Ecuadorian pattern is similar. Sucre and Bolívar dominate both paper and stone iconographies. The monumental center of Quito is the National Memorial, built to commemorate independence. Stamps give a different picture, with a wide assortment of figures honored. Until the 1950s issues are dominated by political and military figures, but no single one predominates.

The iconographic center of Argentine nationalism is the war of independence in general and José San Martín in particular. Independence brought about a general replacement of street names, previously dominated by religious imagery.[137] This "symbolic revolution" even included the renaming of streets celebrating the victory over the English. By 1811, a wooden obelisk, the "altar de la patria," had been placed in the Plaza de Mayo (then Victory Plaza) to celebrate the heroes of May 25. In 1856, the original obelisk was transformed into its present marble base surmounted by a statue of victory. In 1873, the obelisk was joined by a monument to General Belgrano, second only to San Martín in engendering nationalist mythology. Despite several attempts to create a more grandiose monument to independence,[138] the plaza remains the center of veneration of the birth of the state. Its companion is the Plaza of San Martín. The monumental statue there is merely the most visible of a truly national cult surrounding the general.[139] Buenos Aires alone possesses thirteen statues or monuments to the hero (who also has a major avenue named in his honor), while those provinces remotely touched by his life now honor their bit of history. This veneration began in the 1840s and achieved its climax through the works of Sarmiento and Mitre in the centennial celebration of 1878. Fought over by both Rosas and his opponents in their attempts to capture national legitimacy, San Martín became the representation of an Argentine nation finally dominated by Buenos Aires.

Most of the other plazas of the city also celebrate independence.[140] Politi-

137. Cutolo, *Buenos Aires.*
138. Gutiérrez, "La arquitectura como documento histórico."
139. Levy, "The Development and Use of the Heroic Image of José de San Martín."
140. The Plaza de Libertad (from 1822, with a statue of Adolfo Ansina, military leader in the civil wars of the 1850s and later a leading politician); Plaza Suipacha (battle of 1810, which had a statue of independence hero Viamonte replaced by yet another hero, Manuel Dorrego); Plaza del Congreso (honoring the two independence congresses of 1810 and 1816). For the centennial of the latter, twenty-five thousand schoolchildren congregated there to sing the national anthem and swear allegiance to the flag (Llanes, *Antiguas plazas,* 35); Plaza Dorrego (independence hero); Plaza Lavalle (independence hero); Plaza Primera Junta (honoring the first independence government and including statues of independence heroes Saavedra and Azacuenaga); Plaza Rodríguez (independence hero, and including a statue to O'Higgins); Plaza

cal and military/heroic figures from the period account for nearly 40 percent of the statues that can be associated with an individual or historic event. More than two-thirds of statues dealing with a military subject are based on independence heroes. Figures from that era account for nearly one-fourth of street names in Buenos Aires and nearly half of those with biographical references. More than half of these are military in nature.

The two dates celebrating independence, May 25 and July 9, were for many years the central festivals on the Argentinean political calendar. These featured military parades, visits to the Tomb of the Unknown Soldier, educational activities for children, and editorials proclaiming the links between past and present in the Argentine nation.[141]

Since the early twentieth century, San Martín and Belgrano have dominated the currency. Theirs are the only portraits featured until the 1980s, when they were joined by other early statesmen, among them Juan Bautista Alberdi, Sarmiento, and Rivadavia. The Argentine fascination with independence and San Martín in particular is more than adequately displayed in postage issues.[142] The great *procer* is featured on an outstanding 44 percent of stamps depicting political figures. Other independence figures such as Brown and Belgrano add to almost 60 percent of the total.

Montevideo lacks a central symbolic space along the lines of the Plaza de Mayo, but the Liberty Monument might serve as a close approximation.[143] The cult of independence is supported by several other sites in the city center: the Plaza de Libertad, featuring a statue of Artigas; Plaza Joaquín Suárez, featuring a statue of the independence hero; and the obelisk celebrating the Constitution of 1830. Other major figures honored for their role in the establishment and defense of the nation include Giuseppe Garibaldi, who fought for Uruguay prior to his Italian campaigns, and Eugenio Garzón, who fought for independence in several continental campaigns. Among street names, the independence struggle has the most references, but the later internal wars and fights against Brazil are also important.

Pueyrredón (hero of English invasions and independence); Plaza Belgrano; and Plaza Lorea (including a statue of Mariano Moreno, one of the leading intellectuals of independence). Other times (Plaza Garay, the only major reference to the colonial period), people (Carlos de Alvear, mayor in the 1880s), and places (Plaza Roma, Plaza Italia) are honored, but clearly the independence is the central historical act.

141. E.g., *La Nación*, July 9, 1951, 4.
142. Bushnell, "Postal Images."
143. The column has been the subject of considerable debate since its unveiling (Pedemonte, *Montevideo*). There have been discussions about the name (it was originally intended as a monument to peace, celebrating the end of one of the many civil wars) as well as about the objects held by the figure of liberty.

Much like those of Colombia and Venezuela, Uruguay's currency is dominated by a single figure: Artigas. With one exception, Juan Antonio Lavalleja, another independence hero, his has been the only face portrayed in paper or coin since the 1930s. He also is the dominant figure in postage stamps, with at least nineteen designs. Other independence figures, such as Joaquín Suárez, Lavalleja, and Fructoso Rivera, have also appeared in multiple issues.

As in most cases, Uruguayan iconography has developed over time. Independence and military heroes have become less important in monumental architecture. The most important shift occurred after independence when complaints that city streets had the appearance of a "grand temple of altars dedicated to saints" led to a massive renaming, featuring figures from independence; geographical allusions from the rest of the country; other independent republics; and "primary virtues of a republican state, order, peace, equality, union, etc."[144] The dominance of Artigas only dates from the 1880s.[145]

The famous Angel of Independence is arguably one of the most important icons of Mexican nationalism. Below the column topped with a gilded victory sit statues of independence heroes: Hidalgo (the most prominent), Morelos, Francisco Javier Mina, and Nicolás Bravo. There is a separate statue of Morelos near Bucareli Street, but no other for Hidalgo. The genesis for this monument goes back to Santa Anna's efforts to create historical cults—including the formal burial of his leg lost while defending Veracruz from the French. The inclusion of heroes was not without controversy as figures came and fell out of favor, such as Iturbide. Independence heroes, especially Hidalgo and Morelos, have been the most popular source for images for federal and provincial issues through the 1980s. This has also included the independence heroine Doña Josefa Ortiz de Domínguez. Hidalgo and independence in general are the most popular historical themes in early stamps, but themes since the 1930s have been more varied.

The use of the anniversary of independence as a means to legitimize the regime has a long history, including the emphasis placed on it by Maximilian in the 1860s.[146] On the night of September 15, the president gives the traditional *grito* of independence to the crowds gathered in the *zócalo*. The

144. Silva Cazet, "En torno a la nomenclatura de Montevideo."
145. Sommer cites the reading of Zorilla de San Martín's *La leyenda patria* at the dedication of the independence monument of 1879 as the turning point (*Foundational Fictions,* 242). Prior to this, Artigas had largely been seen through Argentinean eyes: as a rebel and a traitor.
146. Duncan, "Political Legitimation and Maximilian's Second Empire."

next day a huge military parade marks this institution's acceptance as a symbol of the nation. Yet even this political ritual does not have the solemnity usually attached to these affairs and the gathering at the *zócalo* has become more of a mass party than a celebration of national glory.

In Peru, independence does not exercise the iconographic domination seen in Argentina or in the northern Andes. While independence and its heroes are honored, the next half century plays a much more important role. This is also true for currency, in which not a single independence hero is portrayed throughout the nineteenth century. Bolivian currency and postage focuses on the independence period emphasizing Bolívar, Sucre, Pedro Domingo Murillo, and another of the few women, Juana de Padilla, but this period plays a less important role in street nomenclature. In Santiago de Chile, the independence struggle accounts for one-fifth of the monuments and nearly half of all the major sites. The equivalent of San Martín is O'Higgins, but he does not dominate the iconography, neither stone nor paper, nearly to the extent of his Argentinean counterpart.

Independence plays a relatively insignificant role in Rio's iconography and Brazil's currency and postage. The revolution of 1889 that toppled the monarchy and created the Old Republic does receive some attention, but again lacks any coherent theme, hero, or major monument dedicated solely to it. The two figures that appear to be revered in both stone and paper are José Bonifácio and Tiradentes. Brazil appears comfortable with the legacy of the empire. Nearly a fourth of the monuments and streets honor a person or an event associated with it. Both emperors, for example, have retained their monuments. While imperial references decline with time, the practice continues even well into the twentieth century. The empire also accounts for nearly two-thirds of the major monuments, but this very likely is a reflection of dominant aesthetic styles in the nineteenth and early twentieth centuries.

Conclusions: The Limits of History

How can we account for the Latin American pattern of military nationalism and the differences inside the continent? As I have argued, nationalist myths—or lack thereof—reflect historical experience. First, there has to be some historical narrative available, a symbolic skeleton around which to wrap nationalist legend. Second, there has to be a perceived need for the solidarity associated with nationalism. Many countries in Latin America lacked both the historical base and the kind of polity associated with nationalist integration.

Beginning with those who have not used military imagery, for Brazil to construct a national myth from independence would be practically impossible. According to Doris Sommer, the very "non-eventfulness" of Brazil's early history made it difficult to use this period as the basis for the romantic novels of the late nineteenth century. Yet the failure of the Brazilian state to use the other possible subjects of epic treatment remains puzzling. In the cases of Peru and Ecuador, independence was partly forced on often reluctant populations by external armies. While the birth of the nation is celebrated, there are limits to which one can mythologize an external liberation. Moreover, in the case of Peru, as in Chile, a subsequent struggle has partly supplanted the independence as a central theme. For Colombia, Venezuela, and Ecuador, there are no major external wars that could serve as the basis for a martial mythology. The internal wars that plagued all three countries did not produce clear enough winners to either allow for triumphalism or permit a nostalgic veneration of the loser.

At the other extreme, Paraguayan history would make neglecting war almost impossible. Yet the devastation of the Triple Alliance, and the success of the Paraguayans in holding off defeat for so long, could have produced either veneration or repulsion. Despite the massive loss of territory after the War of the Triple Alliance, Marshall López is not derided as a leader who sacrificed the nation (à la Santa Anna), but venerated as a martyr. (The fascination includes one of the few statues to a mistress in all of Latin America.) Interestingly, it was only following the defeat of the Liberals in the 1930s that we see the kind of bellicist nationalism arising in Paraguay. History mattered, but so did political necessity.

The cases of Peru, Bolivia, and Chile would indicate that the reverence of a war has little to do with the outcome. It would be nearly impossible to determine who won on the basis of the monumental evidence. The two major contestants have both created cults of single individuals—Prat and Grau—that closely follow a classic tradition. This suggests that it is the communal experience of shared danger and effort that makes the remembrance of war important. Defeats are recalled because they serve to link the community in a shared suffering. The survival of the nation despite the humiliation of defeat (and the ever important promise of revenge) works as well as a celebration of victory.

Argentina, Colombia, and Venezuela can claim "ownership" of the two great heroes of independence. For Argentina, independence itself was a relatively clean conflict not involving the regional and racial divisions seen in other countries. Yet that does not explain why it has not been supplanted by later wars. This is particularly interesting given the low level of national identification in Argentina prior to the late nineteenth century. It is also surprising given that such large parts of the Argentine population did not arrive until many decades after these events. Inversely, these same two conditions and the political chaos experienced by the country during its first half century may be precisely the reasons why it needed to create a cult around noncontroversial figures. During the first years of this century, at the time of the centennial celebrations of independence and when Buenos Aires was fully feeling the problems of assimilating large numbers of immigrants, the notion of using independence as a means with which to inculcate patriotism in new generations was widely discussed.[147]

Mexico's use of military themes perhaps comes closest to a European pattern: nonelite heroes (the *niños* of Chapultepec), the inclusion of civil and international wars, and a variety of icons and media. The key to the Mexican difference lies in precisely the kind of wars that were waged. More than in any other country, with the exception of Paraguay, Mexican wars were not matters of elites, but involved significant parts of the population. The independence, American, Reforma, French, and revolutionary wars did not hinge on one or two battles or the fate of a single general. Thus, much like the American and European examples after 1860, these wars could serve as symbols of a nation, because they did involve the nation.[148]

Yet even here, war has a limited role. The critical Mexican myth is how *mestizaje* contributed to a "cosmic race." In the apparently seamless progression from Tenoch through Cárdenas, the wars against the Americans and the French are like sideshows; they are distractions from the main story. Only two wars appear to be central to Mexican nationalism: the conquest, the seeds of *mestizaje;* and the Revolution, when the mestizos finally assume power over the nation. Mexican nationalism thus encapsulates both identity and "otherness" within its own frontiers. The French and American invaders do not represent the enemy against which the nation must struggle. Their place is symbolically occupied by the Spanish conquerors, the conservatives of the nineteenth century, and the economic oppression of the Porfiriato. This leaves Mexico with an almost insurmountable political paradox: the

---

147. Plotkin, "Política, educación y nacionalismo."
148. See, for example, Mallon, *Peasant and Nation;* and G. Thompson, "Federalism and Vantonalism."

enemy might be defeated in the iconography, but remains in control. The elite is still Spanish, and neither the dreams of Hidalgo nor those of Emiliano Zapata have been achieved.

This contradiction exemplifies the limits to the use of war in constructing a Latin American nationalism. Even those historical moments that would be expected to most easily contribute to the development of a nationalist consciousness lack the requisite symbolic depth. The colonial heritage of Latin America placed limits on what even these symbols could accomplish. This heritage, for example, weakened the ability of the Bolivian and Peruvian states to use war as a force for nationalist union. Recalling the war too much might bring back memories of elite betrayals and the sacrifice of the subaltern populations.

The icon of independence provides perhaps the best means with which to understand the constraints facing Latin American countries. First, there is the ambiguity of what exactly the criollos were fighting for. For each instance of San Martín's abolishing legal racial distinctions in Peru or Bolívar's use of black troops, there is a backlash against the fear of racial uprising. Although for the rebellious criollos the enemy was clearly the Spanish, this was not so obvious for the rest of the population.[149] Opposition to the independence cause was often found within the frontiers of the new "countries." Peruvian reluctance is well documented: out of nine thousand loyalists in the battle of Ayacucho, only five hundred had been born in Spain.[150]

Given these ambiguities, it was often difficult to choose what to celebrate. The Mexican experience, for example, has been the subject of considerable debate. Is 1810 the appropriate date? But this struggle was crushed within two years not by Spaniards, but by white Mexicans fearful of more Guanajuatos. Is Iturbide's 1821 entrance in Mexico City better? But he served in those armies that helped to defeat Hidalgo and Morelos. Thus, while the independence wars signaled the victory of the *pátria América,* the identity of the triumphant nation was and remains unclear.

A second difficulty with the use of the independence wars is that the enemy has largely disappeared. Despite some adventures in the 1820s and 1860s, Spain did not represent a significant threat to Latin America after independence. The independence wars represented too unequivocal a victory to be used by the state seeking to create a common identity. In the

---

149. Silva Michelena, "State Formation in Latin America."
150. Mörner, *Andean Past,* 116.

twentieth century, Spain's role was largely taken by the United States and it has served admirably as a basis for the legitimacy of revolutionary Nicaragua and Cuba. But there's the rub. Given that the Latin American state was more often than not allied directly or indirectly with the United States, fanning the flames of *anti-yanquismo* was a dangerous strategy. The Institutional Revolutionary Party (PRI) was one of the few that could master the art. (The anti-Americanism of contemporary military regimes such as in Guatemala deserves further study.) Moreover, as powerful as David-and-Goliath myths may be, it is important for the shepherd to win once in a while. Prior to the Cuban Revolution, this was almost unimaginable. The popularization of dependency theory was a double-edged sword. Given the asymmetry in power, resentment of the United States often degenerated into hopelessness rather than causing national devotion.[151]

A third obstacle to using the wars of independence as the basis for a *state-specific* nationalism is that they were fought by armies from various countries. Peru, Ecuador, and Bolivia were given independence by armies consisting of soldiers from the River Plate, Chile, and Colombia (often seen as outsiders by natives). Sucre won in Ayacucho with soldiers and officers from nearly every region of the continent. A person born in one state could become the president of another. It is only in those cases where regions sought to separate themselves from the traditional colonial boundaries that we find an early sense of difference. Paraguay is the best example here, but we might also include Uruguay.

Moreover, these wars left all the countries with a common set of images and references that would have made it difficult to completely demonize a neighboring enemy. The shared experience of the independence wars made all of the Latin American countries part of a single iconographic family. Ecuador, Venezuela, and Colombia fly practically the same flag, derived from Bolívar's standard during the wars of independence. Those of Argentina and Uruguay share images and colors. Every city except Montevideo and Asunción has a major statue to the Libertador, Simón Bolívar. This cult began almost with his death and continues—at least as measured by production of monuments—to this day evident not only in prominent places in capitals, but in small provincial cities as well.[152] What is most interesting

151. The use of the United States as a handy enemy was also mitigated by the fact that for most of the nineteenth century, it remained the model against which Latin American elites (and especially the victorious Liberals) judged their accomplishments (Aguilar Camín, "La invención de México").

152. While José de San Martín is also venerated, his is a more regional figure concentrated in the Southern Cone.

here is the phenomenon of having eleven separate nations sharing a common hero of such prominence. The only equivalent would be if Napoleon had somehow survived Waterloo and was a prominent feature of every European capital.

Thus, for a political institution interested in creating a sense of identity *bounded by territory,* the wars of independence represent potentially debilitating challenges. The same might be said of the two sides in the American Civil War, but arguably the states, if not the two regions, had created stronger senses of particular identity than had the Latin American countries. Moreover, given the early acceptance of boundaries based on colonial practice and on a policy of nonintervention, we see few examples of "crusaders" from one country attempting to liberate the other. Chile justifies its role in the war against the Peruvian-Bolivian Confederation in these terms, but Brazil and Argentina are reluctant to do so even with the War of the Triple Alliance. The sense of a shared heritage appears to have overwhelmed any sentiment of particularity.

What, then, does the Latin American experience tell us about the invention of nationalism in general? First, communities cannot be imagined out of the ether; they require some basis in the past. It is no accident that the countries with the most developed martial iconographies, Paraguay and Mexico, were ones whose struggles most involved the relevant populations. In these cases, allusions to the Triple Alliance or the Revolution could resonate with a shared experience. These countries constructed myths, but they did so on an experience with real connotations for their people.

The historical context in which the Latin American countries achieved independent statehood appears quite similar to that experienced by the European counterparts: the nineteenth century was the "springtime of nations" on both continents. The apparent similarity, however, hides two critical differences. First, the ethnic makeup of the population in Latin America was distributed in a very different way from in the European case. Second, with few exceptions, Latin American countries did not undergo the type of military struggles that have been used to construct imagined communities among even those of diffuse origins. Both these conditions placed limits on the development of nationalist symbols. The first because references to a collectivity were almost always exclusionary, the second because it limited the type of experiences that break down such segregation.

Lacking a common ancestor and shared trials, Latin American patriotism remained wedded to concrete places and people and did not develop into the institutionalized worship of an abstract identity that is at the heart of nationalism. Latin Americans such as the Chilean José María Núñez recognized that teaching history was "the ideal means to bind an individual's loyalties to his nation."[153] But in general, having lived a different history, they taught different lessons.

History is not merely given, but re-created through its portrayal. Not only did the Latin American countries have a different narrative from the standard Western state; they also had a different means with which to tell it. Nationalism made symbols the essence of politics, and in turn the aesthetic quality of these could be said to even shape some forms of politics, or at least reflect their basic qualities.[154] With a few exceptions, Latin American monuments fail to represent national identities. They do not embody an altar of the nation, but are elite icons whose hold on the popular imagination may not be very strong. To die for *el pueblo* is one thing, to do so for San Martín is another.[155] As a whole, historical traditions did not work to create a sense of national community.

The underdevelopment of Latin American national iconographies reflects the needs of the states. In general, since there were few threats of war, there was little need to create a population willing to sacrifice itself.[156] Since domestic markets were relatively unimportant, there was little need to integrate. Since there was no democracy, there was no need for citizens. Since there was relatively little war, there was no need for nationalism. Without the ideological glue of nationalism, the state developed with severe limits to its authority.

153. Quoted in Woll, "For God or Country," 24.
154. Mosse, *Nationalization of the Masses;* Berezin, "Cultural Form and Political Meaning"; Cerulo, *Identity Designs.*
155. Carrera Damas, "Simón Bolívar," 111.
156. While earlier observers blamed nationalism on war (Hayes, *Essays on Nationalism*), we may wish to reverse the causal order (A. Smith, "War and Ethnicity"). It may now be said that ever since the battle of Valmy, modern war and its dependence on conscription has made nationalism necessary (Hobsbawm, *Nations and Nationalism,* 83–84). This applies not only to the participants, but to the entire society evolved in treasuring their survival, resenting their defeat, or remembering the dead.

5
Making Citizens

Since the mid-nineteenth century and through the immediate

post–World War II period, European and North American armed

forces have often served as social institutions whose tasks included

not only national defense, but also the forging of young men[1] into

productive and responsible members of the community.[2] Through

mobilization, exposure to nationalist doctrine, and the cohesion

1. The gender specificity of these comments is not accidental. I will largely omit discussions of the role of women in the army (although these have often been critical, as in the *solderas* of the Mexican Revolution).

2. It is important to differentiate across cases and time periods. In the United States and Great Britain, the socializing role of the armed forces came in concentrated bursts during periods of conflict and then retreated after conscription ended. This pattern changed from 1945 to the 1970s when conscription became theoretically universal. Lester Pearson's comment that the Canadian soul could only be found during wartime speaks also to this effect. In the German and French cases, however, the role of the amed forces was much more consistent and constant.

encouraged by shared danger, armies made citizens and nations. For individuals, the transformation can be both dramatic and positive. The initiation into and training by the armed forces may improve the physical health of the recruit and teach him basic skills as well as discipline and self-respect. For the society as a whole, the collective experience could introduce previously isolated individuals to the variety of ethnic groups with whom they share a territory and build a camaraderie among all while exposing them to nationalist themes and a sense of patriotic duty.

In these ways, the military seems to fulfill almost every function one could ask of a public institution; it develops citizens and fosters community. Wars might arguably be worth their high costs in human destruction if they supported the promotion of such social bodies. In turn, the absence of such institutions, or the failure to properly make use of opportunities provided by war, would represent a significant potential loss for a society.[3]

As we saw in Chapter 2, participation in the armed forces has been historically very low in Latin America. Precisely when the mass armies were supposedly building the European states, sponsoring more democratic participation, and helping create a new nationalism, Latin American armies remained small and their social role was extremely limited. This is particularly noteworthy given the character of most continental armed forces. Latin American militaries have often seen themselves as the guardians of primordial national honor and have often accused civilian authorities of betraying national trusts. The self-image and presentation of these militaries resounds with patriotic language and symbols. Yet while ostensibly serving as the guardian of patriotic virtue, the continental militaries have been less successful in fulfilling one of the classic roles assigned to such institutions: instructors of the national youth in nationalism and patriotism.

How do we account for this Latin American exception? What were its implications? According to Alfred Vagts, each stage of social progress produces military institutions in conformity with its needs and ideas.[4] If the Latin American military often resembles its pre-eighteenth-century European counterparts more than its contemporaries, what does this tell us

3. The often heated discussion about the end of the mass army in Europe and North America would indicate that this institution was at least perceived as playing a major integrative role in modern societies (McArdle Kellerher, "Mass Armies in the 1970's"; van Doorn, "The Decline in the Mass Army in the West"; Janowitz, "The All Volunteer Military as a 'Sociopolitical' Problem"; Useem and commentators, "The Rise and Fall of a Volunteer Army").
4. Vagts, *A History of Militarism*.

about the Latin American state? The analysis of the Latin American coun-
terexample may help us better appreciate the role played by conscription
and mass participation in other regions. Most significant, it once again
points to the importance of taking into account the specific starting conditions of the Latin American republics and how these and subsequent events
altered the causal effect of war on state and nation building. Specifically, the
limited wars of Latin America and the low levels of conscription deprived
these societies of a critical stimulus for both democratization and the elaboration and legitimization of a broad-based citizenship. As was the case with
taxation and nationalist icons, Latin America's history did not provide the
circumstances under which the conscription-citizenship interaction could
develop.

The Rise of Conscription

Conscription understood as forced participation in a military is by no means
new or unique to modern western Europe. What distinguishes the European
pattern after the mid-nineteenth century is *theoretically* universal conscription including all social sectors, legitimated by a common membership in a
nation-state. It is this combination of bureaucratic application and nationalist legitimation that defines "modern" conscription, and it is precisely these
two characteristics—and their consequences—that I will argue were and
continue to be largely missing in Latin America.

While mass armies have a long history, their modern institutional structure may be traced to the sixteenth century. Beginning then, armies began
to require a greater imposition of the state on their societies. Sweden, in
1544, was the first country to organize a permanent army on the basis of
military obligation.[5] After the late seventeenth century, European states did
come to expect that their subjects had an obligation to serve in some vague
form. The Prussian state climbed from insignificance to minor-power status
in the eighteenth century on the basis of a modified version of compulsory
service. But resistance to conscription was practically uniform. To be in the
army still meant that one was a member of the rural poor, without money or
corporate sponsors able to remove the yoke of conscription.[6] It was widely

5. Corvisier, *Armies and Societies in Europe.*
6. Paret, *Understanding War;* Tallett, *War and Society in Early Modern Europe;* Cohen,
Citizens and Soldiers.

perceived that "the army must inevitably consist of the scum of the people, and of all those for whom society has no use."[7] Generals may have been exalted, but one has to look far to find an ode to the common soldier of Marlborough or Frederick. Before they represented "nations in arms," such forces were more likely to be considered armed hordes. Brutal discipline, not nationalist devotion, kept the troops literally in line.

This is not to deny the increasing professionalization of armies nor the administrative and technological innovations that mark the first two centuries of the "military revolution," but to note that the link between army and society was largely based on the coercive power of the first and rarely—the case of the United Provinces being one instance—depended on a sense of national identity within the second. Patriotic motivation had no role in this military organization.[8] Indeed, the idea of the armed masses was not one that the nobility or the monarchy could consider without apprehension. States could be as afraid of their own people as of the enemy.[9] Control over the means of violence would only be surrendered under the direst of circumstances and only in the face of an alternative worse than popular rebellion. The French Revolution and Napoleonic Wars provided a strong enough threat to require the radical rebalancing of military forces.[10]

The French National Assembly, when debating the policies through which it would reform the army of the ancien régime, was quite aware of the costs and benefits associated with universal conscription; with giving the army to the people and vice versa. The notions of soldier and citizen were seen as diametrically opposed. The revolution and its radicalization after 1791 bridged these two identities. The *levée en masse* of 1793 was inspired in part by external threat, but also by the need to mobilize the population for the revolution.[11] It represented a radical rupture with the past in that it called the "people" to defend their newly acquired status of citizen. The important break was neither technical nor strategic, but rather had more to do with the relationship between state and society. The state stopped legitimately being the possession of the few and came to represent the aspirations of the many. As such, it had the right and obligation to call on them to defend *their* property. We should not exaggerate the extent to which this

---

7. Tallett, *War and Society in Early Modern Europe*, 85.
8. Bartov, "The Nation in Arms."
9. Colley, *Britons.*
10. Vagts, *A History of Militarism.*
11. Paret, *Understanding War;* Preston, Roland, and Wise, *Men in Arms.*

redefinition mirrored an authentic and enthusiastic popular response.[12] Few human beings long to put themselves in mortal danger, no matter the cause. But an important change did take place. War stopped being a game of kings and queens and became the business of the people.

The various stages of conscription in Napoleonic France raised an army of one million men.[13] France's enemies had to respond in kind. The fear of a French invasion transformed the British military and the state.[14] If the army was to grow enough to counter the threat, administrative systems had to be established to count, select, coerce, arm, and transport men. Perhaps more important, the Napoleonic scare transformed the English, Welsh, Irish, and Scottish men who served by giving them a new sense of common identity with their fellow (British) soldiers, by showing them the larger island that existed past the boundaries of their shires, by granting them a new status within that society, and by inculcating them with a new sense of loyalty to it. War and the response to it made the "scum of the earth" (Wellington's term) into Britons in ways that had been unimaginable before the 1790s. Mass conscription resulted in a series of parallel and complementing processes that would arguably define the relationship between Britons and their state after 1815. On the one hand, the state came to demand more from the population than passive obedience. On the other, the population came to see themselves in the state and to demand more *from it* in part as recompense for their ultimate sacrifice.[15]

Not all Napoleon's enemies followed suit. Russia maintained its traditional form of conscription into what was anything but a "people's army."[16] Nineteenth-century conservatives such as Metternich were well aware of

12. French peasants being no more willing to die for a flag than any others. Conscription remained a divisive issue during the entire revolutionary period and was one source of anti-Parisian discontent.

13. Van Doorn, "Decline in the Mass Army," 149. But note that many who served in Napoleon's army were not French.

14. Colley, *Britons.*

15. In Germany, the transformation, while already debated in the 1790s, did not occur until the humiliation of 1806–7. Again, the remnants of the ancien régime were aware of the danger. To ask people to fight for their fatherland required that they be given a fatherland, one that they may not be willing to return to the Hohenzollern (Howard, *War in European History*). Frederick William III was not wholly won over to the new requirements of war (Paret, *Understanding War*). Following Napoleon's disaster in Russia, however, a patriotic fervor swept Germany, and Prussia instituted a limited form of conscription in 1814.

16. At the other extreme, the opposition in Spain did not come from a formalized authority, but from a popular rebellion—the first guerrilla. No matter their satisfaction at seeing Napoleon so militarily frustrated, this was not a precedent welcomed by the remnants of the ancien régime.

the potentially revolutionary influence of conscription and recommended its abolition.[17] Restoration France sought a return to the military status quo ante. The important point is not that all armies were transformed by the French Revolution—they were not. As their behavior in 1848 attests, the post-Napoleonic armies could still respond to the will of the ancien régime against the populace. What did appear was a potential new relationship between army, state, and people. No matter oligarchic resistance, the success of the Napoleonic armies, whatever the extent to which it was due to their "popular" base, offered a tempting strategy for imitation. In the struggle for mastery in Europe, once one player had decided to play by the new rules, all others had to follow.

The fifty years following Waterloo saw the resolution of several "technical" problems that had to be solved in order for mass armies to function properly. The first was the administrative challenge of moving and using so many men. These problems were mastered by the Prussian General Staff by the early 1860s, allowing the potential size of the new form of armed force to be used productively. Second, developments in the weapons used by the common soldiers, such as rifling and breech loading, made it possible to use men with relatively minimal training. There was also concern with the discipline of the new armies. Theorists had contended that those with short-term service—unavoidable with mass participation—could not be depended on in battle; however, the performance of Prussian troops in 1870 proved them wrong. If the military ardor or strict discipline of a conscript army was not the same as its professional equivalent, which was debatable, numbers and youthful verve made all the difference. A final obstacle was that a nation at arms required a more complex and demanding administrative state apparatus that had to manage and fuel this new armed force. The problems involved were considerable.[18] The increasing bureaucratization of the European state in the nineteenth century was both a reflection and a contributing element of the increased demands made by the new type of armies. States had little choice, since administrative efficiency was now required for their survival.

The American Civil War gave some indications of what was to come, involving as it did massive amounts of men (20 percent of the relevant population of the South, 10 percent of the North) and many new administrative and technological innovations.[19] But it was the surprising outcome of the

17. Andreski, *Military Organization and Society,* 69.
18. Woloch, "Napoleonic Conscription."
19. Preston, Roland, and Wise, *Men in Arms,* 218.

Franco-Prussian War, pitting a professional force against a conscript army, that altered the balance in favor of mass armies. After 1870, military powers or those who aspired to that role could no longer ignore the new means of doing war. Prussia had led the way in constructing a nation at arms and gave France its own version of Jena at Sedan. Within a decade, France, Italy, and Russia had borrowed the Prussian model. The two world wars of the twentieth century continued this pattern of universalized service. With some prominent exceptions, such as the peacetime United States and United Kingdom, this was to remain the standard until the 1970s, when volunteer armies returned.

Latin American Armies

As indicated in Fig. 5.1, Latin America, at least since the mid-nineteenth century, has had much lower levels of military participation than European countries or even contemporary counterparts. The differences are especially evident if we look at the decades of world war. On the one hand, these are exceptional moments. On the other, it is important to consider that for two, if not more, entire generations, their relationship to the state and their society was at least partly shaped through their experience in the military. Even during the nineteenth century, European countries tended to have a much higher percentage of their populations under arms. The differences are even more extreme when we take into account that the Latin American data are weighed toward those countries that did have wars (for others, the information is much sparser).[20] Even more important, longer terms of service in the Latin American armies meant that for any particular age cohort, the percentage actually having a link with military life was even extremely low (Table 5.1).

The absence of a large military has its roots in the colonial period. In part because of the efficiency of the conquest in eliminating external challenges and the demands of Spain's European wars, military presence on the continent was minimal before the nineteenth century. The combination of popular revolts and strategic threats during and after the Seven Years War did lead to more attention being paid to the formal defense of the colonies, but even in 1800, the Spanish military presence was minimal. As late as 1771,

---

20. The very uncertainty regarding the size of the different armed forces indicates the lack of attention paid to the role of the military in state formation.

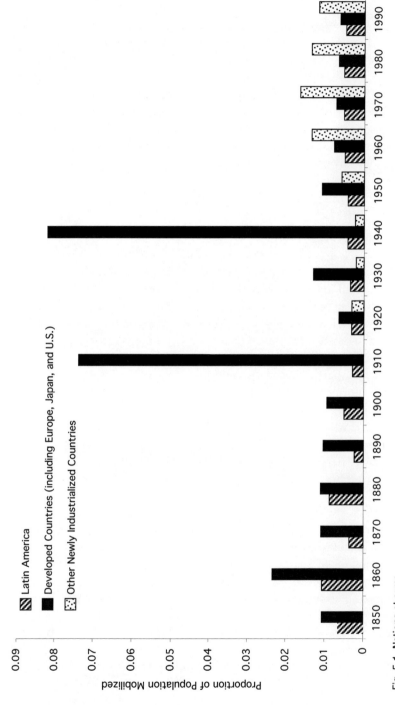

Fig. 5.1 Nations at arms

Legend:
- ▨ Latin America
- ■ Developed Countries (including Europe, Japan, and U.S.)
- ⬚ Other Newly Industrialized Countries

Proportion of Population Mobilized

Table 5.1 Latin American nations at arms (percentages)

	Argentina	Bolivia	Brazil	Chile	Colombia	Ecuador	Mexico	Paraguay	Peru	Uruguay
1850	0.8		0.2	0.2	0.0		0.3	1.5	0.3	1.4
1860	1.1		0.4	0.2	0.1	1.0	0.3	4.8	0.7	1.0
1870		0.2		0.2			0.4	0.5	0.3	
1880	0.3	0.7		0.9					1.5	
1890	0.4		0.1	0.2			0.3		0.2	
1900				0.5	1.0			0.3	0.1	
1910	0.3		0.2				0.3		0.2	
1920	0.3	0.3	0.2	0.5	0.1	0.2	0.5	0.3	0.1	0.5
1930	0.3	0.4	0.2	0.3	0.1	0.2	0.3	1.1	0.2	0.4
1940	0.8		0.3	0.4	0.5	0.2	0.3	0.5	0.4	0.4
1950	0.6		0.2		0.4	0.4			0.5	
1960	0.6	0.5	0.2	0.8	0.3	0.3	0.2	0.9	0.5	0.6
1970	0.6	0.4	0.4	0.9	0.2	0.4	0.2	0.6	0.6	0.7
1980	0.5	0.5	0.3	1.0	0.3	0.5	0.2	0.5	0.7	0.9
1990	0.2	0.5	0.2	0.7	0.4	0.5	0.2	0.4	0.6	0.8

for example, 2,500 men defended the entire La Plata province, which bordered on Portuguese Brazil and was already attracting the attention of British merchants. In Chile, the forces available to the viceroy prior to the independence wars were no more than 1,300 men.[21] Peru may have had 2,000, New Granada 3,500, and Mexico 6,000.[22] These numbers need to be supplemented by the presence of nonprofessional militias, including large sections of the Creole elite. If we include these men (for whom the military experience would be radically different), available armed forces were larger. In colonial Mexico, for example, Viceroy José de Iturrigay could count on roughly 16,000 men.[23] For the continent as a whole, Domínguez calculates 125,000 imperial forces *of all kinds* in 1808.[24]

The wars of independence of course brought about much larger military establishments. Nevertheless, the actual sizes of the armies involved remained small. In the first stage of his campaigns in 1812–13, Bolívar had no more than 500 men and the royalist army he faced fewer than 900.[25] Bolívar's ultimately triumphant Peruvian campaign began with 2,100 men and only grew to 4,900 over the course of the campaign.[26] San Martín's armies ranged from 4,000 to 6,000.[27] The Royalist army in Peru had 20,000 men, of whom 7,000 were Spaniards.[28] The battle of Ayacucho, arguably the largest and most decisive battle of independence, involved a combined total for both sides of no more than 17,000 men.[29] Armies were slightly larger in Mexico, but Iturbide's triumphant Army of the Three Guarantees, combining nearly all organized military forces in the area, had fewer than 40,000 men in 1821.[30] Malcom Deas says that it is in the end impossible to estimate the size of independence armies, but he believes that over the years, the various armed groups incorporated, disciplined, and indoctrinated many tens of thousands.[31]

21. Estado Mayor General del Ejército de Chile, *Historia del Ejército de Chile,* vol. 2, 14. This work hereafter referred to as *HEC*.

22. Loveman, *For la Patria,* 17.

23. Archer, "Army of New Spain," 705. Marcello Carmagnani puts the figure in 1810 as high as 24,462 ("Territorialidad y federalismo en la formación del estado mexicano").

24. Domínguez, "International War and Government Militarization," 1.

25. Tovar, *Historía de las fuerzas militares de Colombia,* vol. 1, 129. This work hereafter referred to as *HFAC*.

26. *HFAC*, vol. 2, 61.

27. *HEC*, vol. 2, 114, 167, 262; vol. 3, 15.

28. Fisher, "La formación del estado peruano," 466.

29. *HFAC*, vol. 2, 89.

30. Tenenbaum, "The Chicken and the Egg," 358.

31. Deas, "The Man on Foot," 5. Despite the relatively small size of the armies, the wars

Immediately following the independence wars, the new states drastically reduced their armed forces. The Argentinean army, for example, was down to 2,500 men by 1825, prior to the Cisplatine War with Brazil.[32] In Chile, the number was 3,500 by the same date.[33] By 1841, the Bolivian army was reduced to 1,500–2,000 men—this from a population of 1.8 million.[34] In Mexico, the decline took twenty years, with the army being cut in half from 1835 to 1846 alone.[35] In some countries, organized armies largely disappeared. The Colombian *Memoria* of 1843 is hesitant about the government's ability to recruit and manage an army of more than 500 men.[36] In Venezuela, the official armed forces fluctuated below 2,000 men with an occasional expansion during caudillo struggles.[37]

Clearly, these numbers grew during times of war. Latin American wars might have been relatively short and logistically nontaxing, but they did consume large numbers of men. During the Cisplatine War, for example, Brazil lost more than 8,000 men[38] implying a significant mobilization, while the Argentines sent 20,000 men to Uruguay.[39] The total forces available to Mexico in 1846 was at most 30,000, but Santa Anna only had roughly 11,000 at his disposal.[40] The Peruvian-Colombian War of 1828–29 included 8,000 Peruvians and 4,000 Colombians,[41] while Chile sent more than 5,000 men to Peru during its war with that country in 1838–39.[42] Santa Cruz commanded an army of perhaps 10,000 during the short-lived Peruvian-Bolivian Confederation. The War of the Pacific again involved battles between thousands, in which more than 500 could perish on either side (but note that these are still small numbers by European standards of the time). Chile mobilized perhaps 50,000 men during the entire war and its expeditionary force to Peru had at least 10,000 soldiers.[43] The War of the

---

were quite bloody. In Mexico alone, 250,000 to 500,000 (5 percent to 10 percent of the population) may have perished during these wars (Loveman, *For la Patria*, 32).

32. F. Best, *Historia de las guerras*.
33. *HEC*, vol. 3, 92.
34. Klein, *Bolivia*, 134.
35. Tenenbaum, "Chicken and the Egg," 358.
36. Deas, "Man on Foot," 7.
37. Ziems, *El Gomecismo*, 58.
38. McBeth, "The Brazilian Army and Its Role in the Abdication of Pedro I."
39. Rock, *Argentina, 1516–1987*, 102.
40. DePalo, Essay on Mexican army.
41. *HFAC*, vol. 2, 129–32.
42. *HEC*, vol. 3, 217, 240.
43. *HEC*, vol. 5, 153; vol. 6, 344. Loveman calculates that 25,000 Chileans served for some period in Peru (*Chile*, 190). Zeitlin claims even higher figures.

Triple Alliance was the high point of military mobilization. Brazil's army grew to 120,000–140,000 during the war, roughly 1.5 percent of the population,[44] while the Argentineans had roughly 25,000 men in the field.[45] Paraguayan figures are much harder to estimate, but probably reached more than 100,000 fighters and involved the virtual mobilization of the entire population. With losses of perhaps 300,000, representing 60–70 percent of the population, Paraguay was perhaps the only Latin American country that experienced the true ferocity of modern total war.[46] In the twentieth century, the only major interstate conflict was the Chaco War, between Bolivia and Paraguay, involving 400,000 men and resulting in more than 90,000 dead.[47]

Civil wars resulted in significant increases in mobilization. Although Colombia was not involved in any of the major international struggles of the nineteenth century, a government campaign in 1930 to provide pensions for veterans of the various civil wars produced 18,000 applicants—three decades after the last major conflict.[48] Throughout the nineteenth century, the official history of the armed forces lists a variety of Liberal and Conservative armies of 5,000 to 10,000 men. Colombia's civil wars were particularly violent. One estimate for the "War of a Thousand Days" lists 300,000 casualties[49] in a struggle involving armies of more than 75,000 men.[50] Chile's 1891 civil war involved armies of more than 10,000 men.[51] The first years of the Mexican Revolution saw the various rebel armies totaling 200,000 men fighting 50,000 federal soldiers. Later in the decade, the revolutionary army still stood at 100,000.[52] Caudillo armies in Argentina were also quite large when faced with threats. Rosas may have had 16,000–20,000 men under his command in the 1840s.[53] During his final campaign against Rosas in 1851, Urquiza could count on 10,000 men with 30,000 horses.[54] Cam-

44. Beattie, "Transforming Enlisted Army Service in Brazil," 89.

45. F. Best, *Historia de las guerras,* 251.

46. The debate over Paraguayan losses is a lively one. Reber, in "Demographics of Paraguay," represents the low end and Whigham and Potthast, in "Some Strong Reservations" and "Paraguayan Rosetta Stone," offer the higher figures quoted earlier. If the latter figures are correct, the old legend of 90 percent losses among males may just be true.

47. Rodríguez, introduction to *Rank and Privilege,* xvi. Another possible exception would be the mini-militarization of Peru during the 1930s as it fought small wars with Colombia in 1933 and Ecuador in 1941.

48. Deas, "Man on Foot," 7.

49. Bustamante, *Revisión histórica comparativa.*

50. HFAC, vol. 2, 276.

51. HEC, vol. 7, 237; Zeitlin, *Civil Wars in Chile,* 212.

52. Lieuwen, "Depoliticization of the Mexican Revolutionary Army, 1915–1940," 52.

53. Halperín-Donghi, *Guerra y finanzas,* 230.

54. F. Best, *Historia de las guerras.*

paigns against the Indians also required considerable effort. Argentina's Roca begins his "Campaign of the Desert" in 1879 with 6,000 soldiers and 800 Indian auxiliaries.[55]

One needs to also take into account the often larger number of men serving in a variety of civil militias. In some countries, such as Colombia and Venezuela, these appear to have been institutional fictions. In Argentina, however, the National Guard of the confederation in the 1850s theoretically included 120,000 men, whereas the army never went much beyond 4,000 men.[56] By 1863, the guard was up to 160,000 and 350,000 by 1880.[57] A similar discrepancy in size existed in Mexico, where Díaz's army was estimated at 40,000, but the National Guard reserve was 160,000.[58] But as discussed later, nowhere did the National Guard play a role closer to that envisioned by those proposing a nation in arms than in Chile. Not only, as seen in Table 5.2, was the guard much larger than the army, but it included close to 5 percent of the population.

Table 5.2   Chilean Men at Arms, Army vs. Guardia Nacional

	1830s	1840s	1850s	1860s	1870s*	1880s*
Guardia	25,000	47,738	62,311	40,696	66,000	53,000
Army	3,000	2,661	3,219	2,796	9,600	7,100

SOURCE: Estado Mayor General Ejército, *Historia del Ejército de Chile.*

* 1879 and 1885.

The peaceful twentieth century saw the establishment of generally small armies consisting of recruits through a system of—again theoretically—universal conscription and a professional core (see below).[59] As shown in Table 5.3, the armies have remained relatively small. It is difficult to compare the numbers of conscripts and the cohort percentages with European and North American counterparts, given the disappearance of the draft in the 1980s. One observer estimates that overall, 20 percent of young men on the continent will be affected by the draft.[60] The overall judgment on these armies, with the exception of special cases such as Cuba's, is that military experience is not generalized and affects a small part of the population.[61]

55. F. Best, *Historia de las guerras.*
56. Auza, "El ejército en la época de la confederación."
57. *Reseña histórica y orgánica del ejército argentino,* 86.
58. English, *Armed Forces of Latin America,* 304.
59. There appears to have been a relatively short "blip" of increasing military participation during periods of nationalist populism (e.g., Perón in Argentina and Vargas in Brazil).
60. Maldonado Prieto, "El caso de América Latina."
61. We should note that many armies (especially in the nineteenth century) suffered from

Organization and Recruitment

All the areas seeking independence from Spain had established constitutional claim to the citizenry in times of national emergency.[62] In the case of Argentina, for example, two battalions of local militia were organized in response to Indian and Portuguese threats.[63] The British invasion of 1806 led to a call for all able-bodied men to enroll in the militia.[64] It is not clear how much of the military force were official soldiers and how many were militiamen or untrained volunteers. The last were organized around a principle of noncontinuous service that the colonial administration raised purely in times of emergency.[65] The militias offered different incentives from armies and they made different demands. "They were essentially local, and the prospect that they might turn into something else did not enthuse the rank and file."[66]

Both sides of the independence wars sought to create armies through a variety of means. Areas under rebel control in Chile saw attempts to conscript all men ages sixteen to sixty by 1811 and the formation of citizen battalions in 1813.[67] Royalist armies in Mexico essentially kidnapped men, who were then "jailed under military orders to keep them from deserting and then marched in *cuerdas,* chained together like criminals on their way to the presidios."[68] One exception to this was Brazil, which did not see the mass mobilization that occurred in many parts of Spanish America.

It is important to note that the proindependence forces, while militarily effective, did not constitute "national armies." Although in some cases, their personnel shared geographical origins, they were organized as repre-

what Roquie calls "venezolanismo," in which the ratio of officers to men is too high. In 1900 Peru, for example, there were ninety-three men for every one hundred enlisted soldiers (Villanueva, *Ejército peruano,* 35). Too many officers were produced by the need to either co-opt provincial elites or give posts to allies and too many were kept in order to avoid conflicts over pensions. The result was that even the low numbers did not represent a large group united by common experiences, but often a stratified pyramid not promoting cohesion. The data indicates that this situation was resolved in the post–World War II period.

62. Fairly typical is the 1886 Colombian Constitution: "[C]iudadanos obligados a tomar las armas cuando las necesidades públicas lo exijan, para defender la independencia nacional y las instituciones pátrias."

63. J. Ferrer, "The Armed Forces in Argentine Politics to 1930."

64. *Reseña histórica y orgánica,* 1.

65. Ortiz Escampilla, *Guerra y gobierno,* 262.

66. Deas, "Man on Foot," 9.

67. *HEC,* vol. 2, 42.

68. Archer, "Royalist Army in New Spain," 76.

Table 5.3 Military service in 1995

	Armed Forces	Population Percentage	Conscripts	Percentage of Cohort (est.)	Duration (months)
Argentina	67,300	0.2	18,100	3	14
Bolivia	33,500	0.4	20,000	14	12
Brazil	295,000	0.2	132,000	4	12
Chile	99,000	0.7	31,000	11	12–24
Colombia	146,400	0.4	67,300	9	12–24
Cuba	105,000	0.9	74,500	28	24
Ecuador	57,000	0.5	30,000	14	12
ES	30,500	0.5	20,000	18	12
Guatemala	44,200	0.4	30,000	17	30
Honduras	18,800	0.3	13,200	13	24 +
Mexico	175,000	0.2	60,000	3	12
Paraguay	20,300	0.4	12,900	13	12
Peru	115,000	0.5	65,500	14	24
Venezuela	57,000	0.3	31,000	7	30

SOURCE: IISS, *The Military Balance, 1995–1996* (London 1995), 204–28.

Note: Cohort percentage is based on an estimate of the size of the male cohort of eighteen- and nineteen-year-olds in any year.

senting protostates.[69] In many ways, these armies never evolved past a provincial militia mode, with a few professionals leading often disorganized masses.[70] Rarely did these armies carry a national flag; they fought for a leader or for abstract notions of "liberty" or "America."

In the aftermath of the independence wars, most military establishments essentially ceased to exist. This was certainly true in Argentina after 1828. The efforts to get rid of the Bolívarian army left Colombia with almost no military by the 1840s.[71] Even wars had little permanent effect; in their aftermath armies were often smaller than for the prebellic status quo. The organizational capacities of armies or even their institutional stability were in doubt throughout the nineteenth century. A Brazilian officer *after* the Triple Alliance could say, "Everyone knows that our army doesn't exist, that it never had any form, that it never had organization, and that, therefore, it is rather soon for it to be reformed. What we need to take care of now, with urgency and tenacity is its *first organization.*"[72]

There appears to have been little enthusiasm for joining the military in any country. The army had a universally bad reputation, it offered no material incentives, and patriotism could not make up the difference. During the Paraguayan War, for example, Brazil made various attempts to increase recruitment and the government created status distinctions between the regular (pressed) army and the Voluntários da Pátria, but it was never enough to meet even the minimum needs.[73]

The faculties and force required by recruitment were often too much for the nascent states. Recruiting and conscription had costs—political, administrative, and financial. Just getting the soldiers ready, accounted for, moved, clothed, and fed was much more than most governments could handle.[74] Relations with the provinces were particularly problematic on this issue. The raising of the Argentine army for the Cisplatine War in 1825, for example, was delayed by provincial reluctance to part with men and with the continuing series of local revolts that seemed more urgent to the relevant

---

69. The larger armies were extremely heterogeneous and included a wide assortment of foreigners. At the battle of Ayacucho one could find representatives of every future state in South America, Spaniards, and even a few French veterans of the retreat from Moscow (Fisher, "La formación del estado peruano," 465).

70. Annino, "Soberanías en lucha," 252.

71. Bustamante, *Revisión histórica comparativa,* 24.

72. McCann, "The Nation at Arms."

73. Beattie, "Transforming Enlisted Army Service."

74. Deas, "Man on Foot," 15.

authorities.[75] In fact, efforts to recruit men often produced rebellions that necessitated even larger forces to be stationed locally. Even local militias had difficulties raising men and were often required to use the same dragooning tactics as the central governments.[76] Forced recruitment further increased hatred for the army and this forced the military to treat such efforts as a campaign of occupation.

Forced recruitment continued throughout the nineteenth century, but it was most often through nonstatal political means. Argentinean provincial caudillos would extract the human resources available to them in their region. Rosas certainly imposed such a "blood tax" on the Porteño population.[77]

Once one was in the army, it was often difficult to leave. The standard period for enrollment appears to have been six years (Brazilian terms were sixteen years!), and this was often extended through various means.[78] While those armies that existed were theoretically composed of "volunteers," their numbers were often supplemented by those who had been condemned to serve for one crime or another or had simply been at the wrong place at the wrong time. Peons found outside their haciendas, for example, could be press-ganged with impunity. Legends abounded of individuals being literally pulled off the street. Standing policies of sending such "recruits" to the frontier indicate that the governments knew the sources of their soldiers.[79] Men press-ganged in the Brazilian interior were chained together and then held in the holds of ships before being sent to Rio.[80] One source claimed that one-third to one-half perished during transport.[81] According to General Cunha Mattos, "[T]he worse disgrace in all the universe is to be a recruit in Brazil. It is a real punishment; a common soldier is considered a miserable slave."[82] Stories were rife of villages emptying upon word that the recruiting battalion was approaching.[83]

75. F. Best, *Historia de las guerras.*
76. G. Thompson, "Los indios y el servicio militar," 217–18.
77. Salvatore, "Reclutamiento militar, disciplinamiento y proleterización en la Era de Rosas," 30.
78. Given the difficulties in recruiting, it is not surprising that the armies wanted to keep all those they already had. In 1872, almost a third of recruits in the Argentinean army had served their four-year contract twice (J. Ferrer, "Armed Forces," 29).
79. Tenenbaum, "Chicken and the Egg," 357.
80. One finds references to chained men in almost all the cases.
81. McBeth, "Brazilian Army," 76.
82. Quoted in McBeth, "Brazilian Army," 81.
83. A popular lament went: "Água Preta, adeus, adeus / Não sei quando te verei / Vou recrutado p'ro sul / Catra la razão, contra a lei. Deixo esposa que me ama / Deixo filinhos menores / Muitos parentes e amigos / Deixo por teus arredores. . . . Em um colete de couro /

Desertion remained a constant problem. In part this was a response to the deplorable conditions under which the soldiers lived. Brazilian soldiers in 1905 were still the dregs of society and were treated as such. The men were poorly housed and rarely paid; illiteracy was general; many suffered from malaria, vermin, and inadequate diet; and discipline was harsh, even brutal (corporal punishment was allowed in most countries until the last quarter of the nineteenth century).[84] A further cause of desertion lay in recruits' concerns that their households would be unable to retain control of land or other resources in their absence.

The half century of military decline had its exceptions. Santa Cruz in the 1830s, for example, was able to resuscitate the Bolivian army in his efforts to create the Peruvian-Bolivian Confederation.[85] Elsewhere, the forces that had brought about independence remained the nucleus for the new militaries, as in Ecuador under Flores. In that country, the need to staff the army often dictated its purposes, and thus the army often focused on small actions that would produce booty with which to pay the men or their political sponsors.[86]

In the nineteenth century throughout most of the continent, the influence and significance of popular militias and national guards reached their zenith. In the Southern Cone and in Mexico, these groups were central actors in political developments. In Argentina and Mexico, they largely represented local and provincial interests, while in Chile the National Guard helped consolidate central power. Sometimes, membership in the militia was used to avoid "real" military service; sometimes they were the ones responsible for most of the fighting. The development of these alternative armies reflects two of the themes discussed in previous chapters and the associated limitations on state authority. National guards and militias, first, were frequently creatures of regional powers and explicitly intended to limit centralizing tendencies. Second, their makeup was often exclusive, demonstrating that citizenship—as indicated by its associated obligations—was restricted to the elite.

Regulations on militias were often the site of conflicts between central authorities and the provinces. In Mexico, for example, Liberals saw the civil militia as a locally controlled balance to a federal army. Central authorities

Preso no tirão comprido / Marcho de pé p'ra cidade / Comose for a um bandido" (from De, ed., *Folk-Lore Pernambucano* (1908), 323; reproduced in Joffily, "O Quebra-Quilo").

84. McCann, "Nation at Arms," 217.
85. Díaz Arguedas, *Fastos militares de Bolivia,* 150.
86. Bustamante, *Revisión histórica comparativa,* 45.

responded in kind. An 1827 law required that states maintain a ratio of one out of one hundred of the population under arms, but in 1835, the federal authorities tried to reduce this to one out of five hundred men in order to limit the size of provincial armies.[87] Guards and militias could also be used as a class weapon. In Peru by the 1830s, the guard was made up of citizens with relatively high social and economic status. By 1841 the National Guard was refusing entry to vagabonds and accepted only those with a known trade who lived in the capital. In later years, the same guard would be judged responsible for much of the oppression following the defeat by Chile; it was precisely the guard that provided the basis for stifling lower-class nationalist resistance.[88] The Brazilian National Guard, created in 1831, replaced the military in many places as the latter was moved to the frontier. The guard was more in tune with elite interests, as it was only open to the minority whose income would qualify them to vote.[89]

A country had different experiences with militias depending on the period. Prior to the war with the United States, the Mexican militias had resembled most of the autarchic and chaotic forces seen in other parts of the continent. After 1848, however, the Liberals were able to forge a national fighting force from local levies. It was the militia that defeated the Conservatives in the 1850s and the French in the 1860s. Such a powerful force represented a potential threat to later governments. Díaz, who had ridden to power on the militia, decided to abolish the National Guard in 1888 and returned to less potentially dangerous recruiting strategies.[90]

Recruitment for the guard was often easier than for the regular army, as various incentives were offered. In Mexico during the best years for the guard, service provided exemption from a special tax.[91] In Brazil, guard service provided an escape from army recruitment, an exemption that served as a foundation for the social control of regions by the *coronéis,* who would list their clients and, more important, their tenants, thereby protecting the local workforce.[92] Interestingly, these local powers opposed later efforts at universal conscription, since it would deprive them of this critical political good.

87. Santoni, "A Fear of the People," 272.
88. Villanueva, *Ejército peruano.*
89. McBeth, "Brazilian Army," 126.
90. G. Thompson, "Los indios y el servicio militar"; Mallon, *Peasant and Nation.*
91. G. Thompson, "Los indios y el servicio militar," 231.
92. Similar resistance by landowners to let go of their tenants is described for Mexico and Chile (G. Thompson, "Los indios y el servicio militar," 227–28; Collier and Sater, *History of Chile,* 138; Beattie, "Transforming Enlisted Army Service").

None of the South American countries had organized formal conscription systems until the end of the century. Argentina was arguably the first to establish a draft. An 1865 law made obligatory the enrollment of all Argentine citizens ages seventeen to forty in a national guard. Beginning in 1872, provinces were supposed to recruit conscripts through a lottery. This system was transformed in 1895 to a universal draft whereby all men were supposed to serve for sixty days.[93] One-fifth of these would serve for a whole year.[94] The Ricchieri Law of 1901 and its amendments in 1905 and 1907 established obligatory service for all Argentines beginning at twenty years old. This draft eliminated the volunteer army, now limited to specialized sectors and the office corps. Reforms included the elimination of the *personero,* or mechanism by which one could purchase a replacement. Yet only about half of a cohort could even be theoretically drafted, as the rest were "exempted for physical reasons, dependency considerations, participation in reserve programs, and budgetary factors that limited the number to be trained."[95] In 1920, for example, roughly 25 percent of the cohort was conscripted. During the following twenty years there was substantial growth in army size with a doubling of the cohort in the 1930s and an attempt during Perón to draft all eligible males.[96] After the fall of Perón, the army drew a consistently smaller cohort.

Chile established a conscription system in 1900. Stipulations were similar to those in Argentina, but the armed forces appear to have drawn a large percentage of the population, roughly nine thousand men, or one-third of the annual cohort in the 1910s.[97] In the postwar era, the percentage has been closer to 20 percent. Brazil saw an initial push for a draft law following each military disaster of the first half of the nineteenth century, culminating with the War of the Triple Alliance, which led to the introduction of a new draft law in 1874 that theoretically prevented the abuses and inefficiencies of the previous system. As in most Latin American countries, the poor, who had traditionally filled the army ranks, viewed the new system with much skepticism. The army's image was so bad that anything that smacked of potential recruitment was hated, and many of the "honorable" poor sought to avoid being linked to the "lumpen" that traditionally had made up the

---

93. J. Ferrer, "Armed Forces," 52–53.

94. Feijoó and Sabato, "Las mujeres frente al servicio militar," 5.

95. Potash, "Argentina," 90.

96. Rouquie, *Poder militar y sociedad política en la Argentina,* vol. 1, 305, 307; Potash, *Army and Politics, 1945–1962,* 83.

97. *HEC,* vol. 8, 26.

army.[98] Only in 1906 do the army and government begin accepting the notion of a nation at arms. The draft law remained imperfect, as authority rested on local authorities who would need both power and competence to carry it out—neither of which they possessed. Finally, Brazil has a first truly national draft in 1916, partly in response to World War I, using civil birth and voter lists for a lottery. Even then, the army only called up 2.5 percent of the cohort, of whom only half reported for the physical.[99] Paraguay appears to have established its draft in 1916. Colombia did not institute a draft until 1920 and Venezuela not until 1936. As we saw earlier, however, and will discuss in following sections, the draft did not make military service either universal or socially neutral. In the 1990s, all the Latin American countries with the exception of Uruguay had some form of conscription. While regulations regarding registration differed across the various countries, none utilized the full cohort available.

It is important to recognize the significant shift in military organization and comportment that occurs in the late nineteenth century. Beginning with the late 1880s in Chile, a series of European missions visited the major Latin American military powers to create more modern institutional establishments. Each country had its sponsors with subsequent legacies in military style and perspectives.[100] These missions encouraged and supported the professionalization of the militaries in general and helped regularize the forms of recruitment and the size of the armies, as discussed earlier. For our purposes, the important point is that while the missions were successful in creating institutional successors to caudillo armies, they did not create "schools for the nation." The very professionalization, when combined with the absence of geopolitical competition and tensions, argued against mass armies. What remained were organizations that now functioned much better and resembled their Weberian ideal types more closely. But they remained small and affected the lives of a relatively small minority of any country's population. Nationalism and patriotism were being taught, but the classrooms were largely empty.

Why Small Armies?

In summary, the armies of Latin America were often quite small in absolute numbers. As a percentage of the population, they never absorbed significant

98. Meznar, "The Ranks of the Poor."
99. McCann, "Nation at Arms," 234.
100. Loveman, *For la Patria*; Nunn, *Yesterday's Soldiers* and *Time of the Generals*.

segments of the relevant cohorts, nor did they serve as an institutionalized rite of passage for generations of men. The limited exceptions to this rule were episodic and never lasted long enough to create even a single generation of men with the institutionalized memory of service to the state. More important, on many of the occasions when men did take up arms, they did not do so under the sponsorship of the state, their period of service did not coincide with an inculcation into the virtues of the nation, and their services were not rewarded with a commitment to expanded citizenship rights. If the contemporary democratic state in Europe and North America owes so much to mass conscription, we should not be surprised to find that the Latin American institutions are so different from their European and North American counterparts in many regards.

Why were the armies so small? Why did these supposedly militaristic countries not include larger parts of the population? Why, despite elite concerns at the end of the century with creating a nation at arms, did these countries not use the draft?

There is, first, the absence of any clear need for large armies. Certainly in the twentieth century, it would be difficult to justify the political, social, and economic cost of large militaries. In the European cases, either wars or a semipermanent threat characterized the era of mass armies. No such environment existed in Latin America. Yet the instruments of war could create their own need much as the various mobilization strategies may have contributed to the start of World War I. Even in the absence of an external threat, arguments could have been made for the utility of the military as both a nationalist training ground and an economic repository for excess labor force. In this way, at least, the absence of perpetual military conflicts did deprive the Latin American states of the kind of developmental stimulus associated with war.

Yet once again, there is the question of whether the states would have been able to make use of these opportunities. There is, of course, the difficulty of organizing such an effort. As we have seen in previous pages, few Latin American states had the institutional capacity to monitor the progression of age cohorts; alert proper authorities to the coming of age of thousands, if not millions, of young men; coordinate their appearances before draft boards and the like; organize their transport to central depots; provide the basic materials required by training; and utilize them in some rational manner. Once again we note the causal conundrum in the utilization of war as an institution builder: such a strategy requires the a priori existence of an organizational foundation on which the building can occur.

Nor should we assume that an armed populace would be perceived as an unmitigated benefit. In part, the failure to create a larger army may be explained by the fact that such a strategy *could* have been detrimental to important economic sectors. A systematized removal of young peasant men would certainly not have been welcomed by agricultural elites. After 1900, the creation of urban labor shortages would also not have been in the interests of industrialists. When we consider that the army would provide opportunities for organization, the creation of friendship networks, and even the development of a class consciousness, the reluctance of elites is more easily understood.

Perhaps more important, the arming of potentially threatening races and classes represented an insurmountable political obstacle. It is worth noting that the nineteenth-century states, while largely unable or unwilling to create large formal armies in response to external threats, had no such difficulty organizing impressive and socially exclusive militias. The arming of those with something to lose from a change in social conditions was one thing, the arming of those who might potentially seek such a change was another. The demographic development of the Latin American armies was due to more than a simple race fear (but it was arguably the most important factor). The central issue is that a severely divided society was largely deprived of a mechanism with a proven record of sponsoring social cohesion. One example of success is Argentina's absorption of Italian immigrants, which points to how it might have worked. With the absence of a uniting army we again return to the question that haunted nation and state making since independence: whose nation?

Citizenship and Equality

In Europe and North America, the mass army also meant the creation of a nation where none had arguably existed before. The articulation of that nation is the most important aspect of the massification of war. Conscription encouraged a different attitude toward the state—one based on collective identity and shared citizenship. The link between military conflict and national loyalty is quite well known.[101] The historic consciousness that helps form a sense of "us" requires a "them," and war provides an excellent opportunity to emphasize this dichotomy. Simply put, the quickest way to

101. A. Smith, "War and Ethnicity."

make a nation is to make an army.[102] According to Best, armies served as schools of imperialist patriotism.[103] The case of Prussia may be the most extreme. The concept of Prussia only begins to develop during the wars of the eighteenth century.[104] The army then served to indoctrinate the population in the values that we now so commonly associate with nineteenth-century imperial Germany.[105] In this process, the contribution of the army as an institution was critical: after 1815 and especially after 1870, the army was entrusted even more with indoctrinating recruits to believe in a national identity defined from above. It was the funnel through which the Hohenzollern monarchy sought to secure its popular base.

A similar process occurred in states other than Prussia. Ralston describes how despite the harshness of the army, conscription did help create a greater sense of national identity among the Egyptian *fellahin*.[106] The army played a critical role in the development of Japanese nationalism following the Meiji Revolution. The French pattern was similar, but here the identification of the army with nation came more from below. Concern with a Napoleonic repetition and wary of traditional forces, the Third Republic sought to create an army in the image of the people.[107] The Israeli experience has been more along these lines; the army represents the institution in which most young Israelis crystallize their national identity.[108]

Armies and the experience of war helped create a unified identity that could obscure domestic divisions. Certainly the increased participation of the population made the continuation of a separate officer caste untenable— the professionalization of the military went hand in hand with greater popular participation and subsequently both signaled and might have contributed to greater civilian democracy.[109] The German officer corps might have aped the bearing and manners of the Junkers, but increasingly

102. Porter, *War and the Rise of the State,* 18.
103. G. Best, "Militarization of European Society."
104. Paret, *Understanding War.*
105. "Rather than reflecting attitudes already widely held in 1793 or 1814—loyalty to a cause, hatred of the foreigner, patriotism—conscription helped create and diffuse these attitudes. It constitutes one of several channels through which ideas, feelings, and energies flow to give substance to the new concept of the state and eventually to nationalism. . . . The army took on a new significance as an institution of popular education; in turn its position in the country benefited from the intensified patriotism that it fostered. . . . The army had come to symbolize cohesion and will of the national community" (Paret, *Understanding War,* 49–50, 73).
106. Ralston, *Importing the European Army,* 96–97.
107. Bartov, "Nation in Arms."
108. Orr, Liran, and Meyer, "Compulsory Military Service."
109. Huntington, *The Soldier and the State.*

they came from the middle class as did their British equivalents.[110] For Andreski, there is a close connection between the level of military participation and the degree of egalitarianism in the society as a whole.[111] Under certain conditions, the armed forces may offer the most equal access for disadvantaged members of a society. Certainly in the United States no other major employment sector has seen the rate of success of that of African Americans in the military.[112] In turn, success on the front required unprecedented social consensus at home. Without this kind of support, the sacrifices called for would be rejected.[113] Wars thus supported and demanded a new form of social cohesion.

Experience in the military also increased the scope of what Mann calls discursive literacy: the set of nationalist assumptions and myths that contribute toward the creation of a national identity.[114] In the former Soviet Union, socialization in the army played a major role for both ideological and nationalist indoctrination.[115]

Wars may have been the key to the creation of "imagined communities."[116] Through the absorption of elements of the newly arising bourgeoisie and petite bourgeoisie, armies may also have encouraged class cohesion during critical periods of early industrialization.[117] The veneration of discipline and order could not have been but appreciated by the bourgeoisie. Under these circumstances armies and war helped transform class societies into armed nations. Conflict was directed outward. According to Palmer,[118] war and military experience also helped break down provincial allegiances and networks and replace these with ones more centered on a national com-

110. But note that it is not merely being in the army, but the pressures of performance under fire that often drive the dismantling of signeurialism. See Markoff, *Abolition of Feudalism*.

111. Andreski, *Military Organization and Society*.

112. The extent to which the draft is racist or has a class bias remains a point of contention. For support of the view that the draft was relatively egalitarian, see Fligstein, "Who Served in the Military." For a perhaps overly celebratory discussion of race relations in the U.S. army, see Moskos and Butler, *All That We Can Be*.

113. Howard, "Total War in the Twentieth Century," 218.

114. Mann, *Sources of Social Power*, vol. 2.

115. Jones and Grupp, "Political Socialization in the Soviet Military." We should note that army service may also lead to the encouragement of regional hatreds (e.g., in the Soviet army, non-Russian nationalities often suffered at the hands of their Russian comrades, and in the U.S. Civil War, state identities were supported by regimental structure).

116. Anderson, *Imagined Communities*.

117. G. Best, "Militarization of European Society"; Mann, *Sources of Social Power*, vol. 2.

118. Palmer, *Age of Democratic Revolutions*.

munity. This point is certainly relevant for France, where the military played an important role in standardizing language and symbolic repertoires.[119]

Conscription in and of itself was not a nationalist panacea. Spain and Italy, for example, both tried it in the late nineteenth century without creating the kind of nationalist discipline seen in France or Prussia. In Spain, the absence of likely enemies made it clear that the military was largely there to suppress the very class from which the recruits had come. In Italy the "foreignness" of the Savoy monarchy made appeals to the Italian nation in arms somewhat disingenuous. Similarly, the acrimonious relationship between Russian peasant and lord carried over into their army.[120] Conscription could also lead to rebellion among ethnic groups within multinational empires.[121] Nevertheless, in almost all countries, military virtue and military liturgy had penetrated quite deeply into the popular psyche.[122] The very real enthusiasm that welcomed war in 1914 reflected in almost all countries an extremely successful (and considering the short time frame, a surprisingly quick) revolution in popular attitudes toward the state.[123] If the period after 1918 saw a requestioning of patriotism, World War II once again cemented the ties between people and state.

Conscription and citizenship were two sides of the same coin. Along with compulsory education and the right to vote, conscription was seen as a pillar of the democratic state.[124] This tradition has its roots in the Greek city-states and found considerable contemporary resonance.[125] Rousseau, for example, identified republican virtue with military service.[126] Engels saw compulsory military service as a more important instrument of democracy than suffrage.[127] The "proletarization" of the military gave the state a large capacity for violence, but it also armed the populace.[128]

119. Braudel, *The Identity of France*, 373–75; E. Weber, *Peasants into Frenchmen*, 299.
120. Kiernan, "Foreign Interests."
121. Peled, "Force, Ideology, and Contract."
122. Wilson, "For a Socio-Historical Approach to the Study of Western Military Culture."
123. During World War I, conscientious objection accounted for no more than .14 percent and .17 percent of the armed forces of the United States and Britain respectively. For World War II, the British rate was .448 percent and the United States experienced no more than forty thousand desertions in more than ten million soldiers. In Vietnam, on the other hand, the American army suffered a desertion rate of 7.34 percent (Mellors and McKean, "The Politics of Conscription in Western Europe," 26).
124. Kiernan, "Foreign Interests," 142.
125. Thanks to Barry Strauss for his introduction to this issue.
126. Cohen, *Citizens and Soldiers*, 117.
127. Janowitz, "Military Institutions and Citizenship in Western Societies," 186.
128. Tilly, in *Coercion, Capital, and European States,* provides an excellent summary of this process: "With a nation in arms, a state's extractive power rose enormously, as did the

One could see this as a form of political exchange: "Considered in purely mechanistic terms, the state needed unobstructed access to the citizen; in turn to gain his willingness to work and fight for the state, the individual had to be offered political power, or—if that was impossible—new psychological inducements and social opportunities to enable him to reach his full potential."[129] In exchange for the right to participate in war, citizens were rewarded with greater rights and more welfare services. According to Barkey and Parikh, "[W]hen states grew dependent on populations for crucial resources, they were forced to develop symbiotic relations with the latter."[130] For Ardant the pressure to extend the suffrage, increase national consciousness, give representation to the working classes, and generally draw the population into political life came to an important degree from the fiscal demands of the great military and administrative machines brought into being by the Napoleonic Wars.[131] The vote and national military service were corollaries.[132] What is perhaps most interesting here is the paradox of militarization and the encroachment on individual rights implied by conscription leading to democracy. William McNeill concludes that military service is the "ball and chain attached to political privilege."[133] Liberation from the nobility meant mobilization by the state.[134] "Military discipline meant the triumph of democracy because the community wished and was compelled to secure the cooperation of the non-aristocratic masses and hence put arms, and along with arms political power, into their hands."[135] The key may be that armies provided a basis for stability through repression *and* "counteracted social discontents by 're-educating' youth, year by year, by taking over the strength of the masses and enlisting it on the conservative side."[136] It has become clear from recent work on the social bases of democracy that war may also contribute to civil interaction and the construction

claims of citizens on their state. Although a call to defend the fatherland stimulated extraordinary support for the effort of war, reliance on mass conscription, confiscatory taxation, and conversion of production to the ends of war made any state vulnerable to popular resistance and answerable to popular demands as never before" (83; see also Downing, *Military Revolution,* 253).

129. Paret, *Understanding War,* 46.
130. Barkey and Parikh, "Comparative Perspectives on the State," 528.
131. Ardant, "Financial Policy and Economic Infrastructure of Modern States and Nations."
132. Preston, Roland, and Wise, *Men in Arms,* 159.
133. McNeill, "The Draft in the Light of History," 64.
134. Bartov, "Nation in Arms."
135. M. Weber, *General Economic History,* 325–26.
136. Kiernan, "Foreign Interests," 141.

of associations and other forms of social capital. The reverse image of the all-powerful state mobilizing resources for war is the society that solves all the subsequent problems generated by this commitment.[137]

As the examples of post-1870 France and Germany, czarist Russia, and the post–Civil War United States will attest, the creation of a mass army did not determine the nature of the political regime. But I would argue that no matter the precise degree of democratization, the conscript was a citizen, not a subject. Although in the twentieth century armed forces are commonly associated with the political Right, it is important to remember that at least until 1848, armies—especially those with some popular element—were seen as allies of liberalism. Conscription became an emancipatory measure; the conscript was seen as having a role in the nation.[138]

Armies also provide modern nation-states with a relatively disciplined and well-educated population ready and able to work in the new industrial order. Adam Smith appreciated the "regularity, order and prompt obedience to command" taught by the army and its importance to the new industrial workplace.[139] There is considerable evidence that this discipline is transformed into human capital that may significantly improve a nation's economic performance.[140] Further, the army was the school of the nation, primarily through the indoctrination of the young in the patriotic catechism, but also because it required literate conscripts who could read and follow orders. With regard to the first, it is important to remember that the large majority of recruits remained peasants and that the army was a means of teaching them "punctuality, good behavior, cleanliness and a sense of duty."[141]

The army was also seen as the "hospital of the nation" often providing the recruit's first exposure to modern medicine. Combined with the better diet available, this was said to add years to a soldier's life![142] Another factor is the well-known link between increased conscription and the creation of the welfare state.[143] At least in the case of Germany, the demands of the first and rewards of the second were explicitly tied in state policy and in the

137. Howard, "Total War in the Twentieth Century," 223.
138. Joenniemi, "The Socio-Politics of Conscription."
139. Cohen, *Citizens and Soldier*, 119.
140. Weede, "Military Participation Ratios, Human Capital Formation, and Economic Growth."
141. Kiernan, "Foreign Interests," 144.
142. Kiernan, "Foreign Interests," 145; E. Weber, *Peasants into Frenchmen*, 300–301.
143. Marwick, *War and Social Change in the Twentieth Century*; Skocpol, *Protecting Soldiers and Mothers*.

popular imagination. The need to muster significant numbers of men relatively quickly meant that states had to invest in improving the health of the population. In Britain during the 1850s, there was great concern that a large number of recruits were physically unfit for service,[144] and this encouraged initial expansion in public health. More recently, studies have found a significant relationship between military participation and basic measures of well-being.[145]

Certainly since 1793, armies have served as schools for the nation by training soldiers how to obey, but also inculcating them with a sense of identity and belonging. Armies have often served as a guarantee of political rights. Conscription represents the ultimate sacrifice on the part of a potential citizen and the granting of arms provides a means with which to defend those rights. In addition, armies may serve to promote economic and social development, providing services that future veterans may continue to demand in civilian life and supplying a rationale for producing more literate and healthier citizens. They train these citizens in precisely those attributes that are considered important in a modern labor force. In short, armies produce human capital and help consolidate a democratic contract between state and people.

Armies of Peons

Neither the informal nor the formal systems of recruitment and conscription were socially neutral in Latin America. As was the case in other regions of the world, the poor and those on the margins were much more likely to find themselves press-ganged. Since independence, the burden of bearing arms has fallen on the poor or those groups whom the society thought beyond the pale: "el grueso del reclutamiento se hacía por enganche. . . . Mal visto por el juez de paz, sospechoso a los ojos del comisario o simplemente sin trabajo, el gaucho era bueno para el servicio."[146] The vast majority of soldiers in the Rosista army had been itinerant workers or rural peons. A justice of the peace in 1857 Argentina noted that the "rural poor" bore the brunt of military service while even poor (but landholding) peasants could avoid it.[147] Still in 1870, the rank and file of the army was made up of the

144. Howard, *War in European History,* 107.
145. Dixon and Moon, "Military Burden and Basic Human Needs"; Bullock and Firebaugh, "Guns and Butter?"
146. Rouquie, *Poder militar,* 76.
147. Salvatore, "Reclutamiento militar," 33, 42.

poor and unemployed and the rich routinely avoided their obligations.[148] When different ends of the social hierarchy did meet, they do not appear to have succeeded in creating a common bond or identity; a vast chasm continued to separate the lumpenized ranks from the upper-class *señoritos* who made up the officer class. The European and North American armies were not exemplars of democratic recruitment, but the inequality found in Latin America made for a difference in kind, not just in degree. Moreover, selected conflicts outside Latin America required mobilization on such a scale that elites and masses shared the battlefield.

The various armies were explicitly told to search for their recruits among "the vice-ridden that can be found in gambling houses, taverns, and horse races." Other targets included the unemployed, "undisciplined sons," and those who had been sent to prison.[149] Brazil's penal code sentenced criminals to army service, and governors often protested against stationing armies full of criminals in their provinces.[150] Beattie concludes that during the nineteenth century, "the Brazilian army constituted the largest institutional bridge between the official Brazilian government and the criminal underworld."[151] During much of its existence, the Colombian military was a form of demoralized correctional institution and certainly not a fighting force.[152]

However, the army appears to have represented at least a limitedly democratic island in a sea of caste hierarchies. Argentinean colonial forces included *segregated* battalions of Indians, blacks, and mulattos, as did their Brazilian equivalents.[153] Significantly, nonwhite regiments were still restricted to the infantry and did not include cavalry. New Granada also had Indian militias.[154] Porteño government decrees during the independence wars added small numbers of newly freed slaves. According to one source, two-thirds of San Martín's army was nonwhite[155] and at the battle of Cuyo (1816) his forces included 780 freed slaves.[156] Even before San Martín's invasion, proindependence Chilean armies had recruited slaves and Indi-

148. Potash, "Argentina," 2.
149. *Reseña histórica y orgánica,* 294–95.
150. McBeth, "Brazilian Army," 72–73.
151. Beattie, "Transforming Enlisted Army Service," 73.
152. Bustamante, *Revisión histórica comparativa,* 24.
153. J. Ferrer, "Armed Forces"; Frigerio, "Con sangre de negros se edificó nuestra independencia"; Kraay, "As Terrifying as Unexpected"; Andrews, "Afro-Argentine Officers of Buenos Aires Province."
154. *HFAC,* vol. 1, 189.
155. Frigerio, "Con sangre de negros," 68.
156. F. Best, *Historia de las guerras.*

ans.[157] Bolívar recruited slaves by offering them liberty in exchange for their service.[158] Indians fought on both sides as royalist armies used the well-earned reputation of Creole racism against the rebels. The Royalist army in Peru was essentially Indian based, in part a result of some popular traditional loyalty, in part thanks to a form of the *mita* being used for recruitment.[159]

Others dispute the presence of lower-caste groups in the independence struggles. According to Villanueva, if these groups had participated, the independence wars would have yielded much more radical results.[160] Of course, a key question is how one defines "Indian" or "black." Díaz Arguedas claims that the majority of the *ejército libertador* of Peru was made up of *cholos* or mestizos and that Indians were not a significant presence.[161] The key point is that nonwhites were significant majorities in these armies. To what extent did nonwhite participation in the independence struggles make slavery unviable even had ideological conditions permitted it? The fate of slavery in nonbellic Brazil and the "ever loyal" isle of Cuba does suggest that the process of fighting for independence required at least de jure recognition of equality.[162]

After independence, nonwhites remained an important part of various militaries both as auxiliaries and as regular troops. Mexican armies often depended on Indian recruits, and their use often rose during times of intra-elite conflict. Perhaps the most dramatic effect of the military on race occurred in Brazil. Because of problems with recruiting during the War of the Triple Alliance, Pedro II ordered the manumission of government-owned slaves willing to serve in the army. He asked landowners to do the same, even offering government funds to help.[163] There is considerable dispute about how many slaves fought. The lower figure is four thousand, the higher twenty thousand. Whatever the number, the presence of black men on the frontlines and the expressed need of the country for their blood was a symbolic victory for the abolitionists.[164]

157. *HEC,* vol. 2, 45; vol. 3, 27, 65; Loveman, *Chile,* 123.

158. *HFAC,* vol. 1, 223.

159. Dobyns and Doughty, *Peru,* 145–51.

160. Villanueva, *Ejército peruano,* 20.

161. Díaz Arguedas, *Fastos militares de Bolivia,* 116.

162. But service was not a guarantee of postbellic rights as Afro-Cuban veterans found out after 1898. See Ada Ferrer, *Insurgent Cuba.*

163. Perhaps not surprisingly this led to the involuntary sale of the weakest and sickest slaves.

164. Beattie, "Transforming Enlisted Army Service," 95–96.

Within the army, of course, race order remained. The Bolivian army was organized by caste: "the whites were the officers, the cholos the sub-officials and the Indian peasants the troops."[165] In Peru, the same order prevailed.[166] In times of war, some of those distinctions would disappear. Segregation, for example, appears to have declined in the Brazilian army during the War of the Triple Alliance.[167] But race still determined one's likely rank, and as late as 1942, admission into the Brazilian military academies was under strict and explicit racial limits.[168]

There were differences in how various groups were treated, and distinctions were made between marginalized races. General Urbina of Ecuador, for example, freed slaves in order to include them in his army, but left many of the traditional controls over Indian peasants untouched.[169] Regional differences were also important. In Mexico, for example, Puebla appears to have had a stronger tradition of voluntary military service than had other provinces. There were also differences across time periods; after 1859, property restrictions on militia membership were removed in Mexico.[170]

There is also the significant Paraguayan exception. In 1864, Juan Bautista Alberdi noted the difference between the Paraguayans and the armies that were soon to defeat them: "[T]he Paraguayan army is numerous relative to the population because it is not different from the people. All citizens are soldiers, and since there is no citizen that does not own the property he cultivates, each soldier is defending his own interests."[171] While such a view may be an overly romantic reading of the almost totalitarian control that López exercised, it remains true that the Paraguayan population was mobilized and fought as no other before or since on the continent. Interestingly and in contrast to the case of Bolivia, sixty years later the Paraguayan elite fought in the Chaco.[172]

The view of the military as the nursery of the nation did have its ideologues. Perhaps this notion was strongest in early twentieth-century Brazil, where Olavo Bilac declared the draft an essential tool for national regenera-

165. Klein, *Bolivia*, 194.
166. Dobyns and Doughty, *Peru*, 209.
167. Beattie, "Transforming Enlisted Army Service," 108.
168. Beattie, "Transforming Enlisted Army Service," 509.
169. Bustamante, *Revisión histórica comparativa*, 50.
170. G. Thompson, "Bulwarks of Patriotic Liberalism: The National Guard, Philharmonic Corps, and Patriotic Juntas in Mexico, 1847–1888," *Journal of Latin American Studies* 22 (1990): 35–39.
171. Quoted in Vittone, *Las fuerzas armadas paraguayas en sus distintas épocas*, 217.
172. See Farcau, *Chaco War*, 55–56.

tion. The military would be "the school of order, discipline, cohesion; the laboratory of individual dignity and patriotism. It is obligatory primary instruction; it is obligatory civic education; it is obligatory cleanliness, obligatory hygiene, obligatory muscular and psychic regeneration. . . . For the dregs of society, the barracks are the salvation."[173]

The universal draft was meant to address some of these social inequities.[174] In several countries, especially Argentina and Chile, it was meant as an exercise in democracy and citizenship and as a meeting place for the divergent sectors of society.[175] In this sense, conscription performed unevenly. As late as the 1940s, Colombian soldiers were still common people, the great majority of them peasants of whom most were illiterate.[176] The Bolivian army that fought the disastrous Chaco War, for example, was made up of Indians, with few representatives of the white or even the mestizo population. It was well known that upper- and even middle-class sons could avoid service.[177] In Argentina's nineteenth century, few young men of wealth and education entered the military. Even after the 1905 universal-service Ricchieri Law (which Radicals explicitly intended to promote greater equality), membership in the military was still conditioned by social class. One officer disgusted by the social makeup of a particular cohort of draftees commented that it was strange that during the year in which these soldiers had been born, only the poor had given birth.[178] The contemporary Chilean case may be an exception; even here, however, class background is a significant predictor of likelihood of service.[179] Well into the 1990s the

173. Quoted in McCann, "Nation at Arms," 231.
174. "[L]as cargas públicas deben pesar con igualdad: el pobre como el rico debe pagar el tributo del patriotismo que exijan de sus personas la defensa de las instituciones, o la integridad, o la independencia, o el honor de la nación. Es así como la libertad es un beneficio común, es así también como el espíritu patriótico de un pueblo lo hace tan poderoso como puede serlo" (*Reseña histórica y orgánica*, 89).
175. According to Loveman, the idea of the nation at arms may have been fairly pervasive in principle throughout the continent. The army was meant to educate the indian (read black, poor, etc.) into a citizen who would then make the nation (*For la Patria*, 73).
176. *HFAC*, vol. 3, 62.
177. Díaz Arguedas, *Fastos militares de Bolivia*, 420–21; Farcau, *Chaco War*, 19; Saravia Ruelas, *Quienes perdieron sus pantalones en el Chaco?*
178. When they were drafted, representatives of "higher" classes had an easier time of it. For much of the twentieth century, regular conscripts in the Chilean army served nine months while university students only had to do three months (*HEC*, vol. 8, 27). Feijoó and Sabato, "Las mujeres frente al servicio militar," 5.
179. Based on educational background of recruits: 2.8 percent had university training, 24 percent had completed secondary school, 43 percent had attended secondary school, and 30 percent only elementary school (Maldonado Prieto). However, Chilean captain Tobías Barros could write in 1920 that "three fourths of the recruits are illiterate, poor peasants from the

correlation between class and conscription remained. The wealthy were universally able to avoid any kind of service. At present, depending on the country, middle-class youths sometimes participate, but it is not generally considered an elite rite of passage. For some working-class and rural youths, the army remains the most open means for social and economic mobility.

What was the source of this inequity? Under less institutionalized systems, the nonpoor had the protection that social status, and often race, could provide. It would not have occurred to a recruiting battalion to "invade" a wealthy neighborhood in the same manner as they did a rural village. The Brazilian term for those pressed into the army was eloquent: *desprotejidos,* or the unprotected.[180] Moreover, under almost all recruitment schemes, one could purchase exemptions from service. In Argentina, for example, the price for avoiding registration was five thousand pesos in 1864.[181] One could simply buy exemptions through a variety of mechanisms,[182] or they could be gained by membership in alternative organizations that, in turn, required social or economic status. For example, in the early years of the Brazilian draft, membership in a "shooting club" allowed middle- and upper-class boys to abstain from the forced and supposedly universal training required of even those on reserves.

Given the miserable conditions and the absence of a nationalist crusade either encouraging participation or sanctioning free riding, almost anyone who could get out of being in the military did so. This left the poor or those for whom the army was a step up socially. Social connections allowed wealthy young men to enjoy those few status privileges associated with military service. During the Chaco War, for example, these men could obtain a commission in the capital; this allowed them to parade around the plaza in a uniform without running the risk of dying in the desert.[183]

On some occasions wars and the emergencies they brought created situations not so dissimilar from the European pattern described earlier. The independence armies certainly included a wide social array of social groups. In Mexico, for example, the Trigarante army of 1821 was a heterogeneous

---

countryside or workers. . . . The rich . . . believe that the obligatory service law . . . was not meant to apply to them" (Loveman, *For la Patria,* 74).

180. Meznar, "Ranks of the Poor."

181. *Reseña histórica y orgánica,* 82.

182. In Brazil one could even buy insurance to pay for exemptions (Beattie, "Transforming Enlisted Army Service," 183–84).

183. Farcau, *Chaco War,* 43.

force that, at least momentarily, reflected many sectors of society.[184] In the War of the Pacific, once the first patriotic euphoria had tapered off, the military was forced to reach higher up the class ladder than usual, soliciting landowning peasants, artisans, and miners. The upper class, however, remained untouched.[185] On the Peruvian side, by contrast, large numbers of elite sons appear to have perished in the defense of Lima.[186] Yet in Brazil, even the very demanding victory in the War of the Triple Alliance did not require the mobilization of the wealthy.[187]

As previously discussed, national guards represented an exception to this pattern.[188] In Chile, officers came from the leading rural families, while the troops were made up of the middle sectors.[189] Prior to 1850, the Mexican militia appears to have been closed to *jornaleros,* or day workers; the militia required the relatively high income of two hundred pesos a year for admittance.[190] To qualify as a noncommissioned officer in the Peruvian national guard one had to be literate or own a business or some land—difficult qualifications for most of the population.[191] In Brazil, the "decent" people, even if poor, were in the guard, while the army was, or at least was perceived to be, filled with vagrants and criminals.[192]

The class contradictions of military service often made military effectiveness impossible. A confidential agent of U.S. president James Polk noted that the "class designated for enlistment is not to be found in this country; the rich have neither the patriotism or inclination to serve for nothing; the poor day laborer, excluded by regulation, could not be expected to perform the duty required of him without compensation."[193]

Of course, another viewpoint on the same situation might reveal not the

184. Ortiz Escampilla, *Guerra y gobierno,* 266–68.
185. Collier and Sater, *History of Chile,* 137–41.
186. Dobyns and Doughty, *Peru,* 196.
187. Beattie, "Transforming Enlisted Army Service," 203.
188. In the years prior to independence, military service appears to have been the province of those relatively well off. Militia service was usually reserved for men of property prior to 1810. The Argentine militias included *comerciantes,* professionals, and employees (Ribas, "Militarismo e intervenciones armadas"). Nevertheless, the troop sent from Spain were often the very dregs of recruits (Archer, "Army of New Spain," 707).
189. Cordero, "Chile, siglo XIX," 85–86.
190. Santoni, "Fear of the People," 282–83; Chavez, "Origen y ocaso del ejército porfiriano."
191. Villanueva, *Ejército peruano,* 85.
192. Meznar, "Ranks of the Poor," 335–51.
193. Quoted in Santoni, "Fear of the People," 282–83.

inherent inequality of service, but the opportunity for social mobility that it represented. Precisely because army service was not desirable, it remained an opportunity for those on the bottom of the racial pyramid to establish new claims or identities. This was certainly the case with the independence armies.[194] The Bolívarian army certainly represented a social innovation. Its officers, much less the troops, were not the children of the Creole aristocracy. In nineteenth-century Ecuador, the army facilitated elite circulation as veterans married into the old-guard families.[195] For Mallon, service in national guards represented a political space in which peasants could articulate their membership in the nation and make links with local and national politics. She also notes that those returning from military service often achieved a higher social status.[196]

There was clearly an awareness of the dangers that a popular army might represent. Bustamante compares the appearance of the independence army (at least as seen by an urban elite) to one made up of contemporary *favelados*—the appearance of armed marginalized masses would never bring calm to an isolated elite's heart. The armed poor and nonwhites were seen as potentially carrying out a social revolution. The hordes of *llaneros,* gauchos, and *huasos* represented a potential threat that had to be disarmed as quickly as possible.[197] A Rio newspaper in the early nineteenth century warned the government "not to put arms in the hands of a mass of men who either hate the system or have no interest in public order."[198] In Mexico, the "people of reason" were especially nervous at the sight of armed Indians, particularly in municipalities with small white populations.[199] Even when fighting for the nation, such groups were distrusted. Mallon has documented the terror occasioned by Indian fighting in the 1880s: "[I]t was one thing to resist the invader, but to create an armed, mobilized, and relatively autonomous peasantry and, even worse, to respect them as citizens—that was an entirely different story."[200]

Racial equality or even recognition of the disproportionate role played

194. We should not take too far the argument that independence armies were free of racism. For example, evidence indicates that mulatto or Indian officers were punished more harshly than their white counterparts (Bethell, *Cambridge History,* vol. 3, 377). Even prominent generals such as the *pardo* Manuel Piar could be executed if racial politics dictated it (Loveman, *For la Patria,* 33).
195. Bustamante, *Revisión histórica comparativa,* 47.
196. Mallon, *Peasant and Nation,* 313.
197. Bustamante, *Revisión histórica comparativa,* 17–21.
198. Quoted in McBeth, "Brazilian Army," 86.
199. G. Thompson, "Los indios y el servicio militar," 217.
200. Mallon, *Defense of Community,* 88.

by nonwhites in the military was especially problematic given the role of the armies during most of the nineteenth century. Protection of external frontiers against other nation-states was important, but so was protection of the "internal" frontier against Indians, urban *castas,* rebellious slaves, and so on.

In the twentieth century, while the inequities of recruitment remained, the officer class had become a route for social mobility or status consolidation in almost all the countries.[201] In Argentina, the officer corps was very much a middle-class institution. The social origin of officers in the 1960s was overwhelmingly the lower strata of the middle class.[202] Among children of upper-class parents, there appeared to be little interest in a military career. One social sector that was overrepresented was the military itself. In Brazil and Argentina in the 1960s, 40 percent of military academy recruits came from military families, and 26 percent of Chilean generals had military fathers.[203] In Mexico, the military since the 1940s has seen itself as part of the middle class—a kind of "uniformed, bemedalled bourgeoisie."[204] For lower-class youths, the military has represented an employer of last resort and a clear avenue for social mobility. Again, a military caste was clearly being developed as one-third of contemporary Mexican generals had military fathers.[205] In Bolivia, lower- to middle-class parents would send their sons to the military academy in order to provide them with a good career.[206] In Peru, the army was the home of the petite bourgeoisie and fairly meritocratic; it was considered a principal avenue for social mobility for middle-class boys.[207]

In the end, most regimes had ambiguous and contradictory policies vis-à-vis their militaries. Nineteenth-century Liberals distrusted the levy on which most armies depended and they were clearly aware that subaltern troops often served as cannon fodder. However, Liberals were attracted to the notion of military service making citizens as well as the promise of potential social mobility associated with it.

201. As do authors in most of the literature, I am concentrating here on the army. The much smaller navy tends to be more aristocratic in attitudes and origins. The air forces tend to look more like the larger service.

202. This overall trend was complemented by scholarships for military schools available to parents from poor households. Rouquie, *Poder militar,* 333.

203. Philip, *The Military in South American Politics,* 177–78.

204. Nunn, "On the Role of the Military in Twentieth Century Latin America," 40.

205. Camp, *Generals in the Palacio,* 127.

206. Corbett, *The Latin American Military as a Socio-Political Force,* 43.

207. McAlister, Maingot, and Potash, *The Military in Latin American Sociopolitical Evolution,* 33; Dobyns and Doughty, *Peru,* 236.

Service in the colonial militia may have been the strongest factor in generating and encouraging a specific territorial identity within the continent. Service in colonial armies and militias introduced soldiers and officers to those with whom they shared a place of birth and encouraged greater familiarity with the wider geography of their locale; in addition, it served to demarcate a clear institutional identity separate from the more generic and shared membership in the empire. The royal government consistently expressed concern with the "Creolization" of the military, even fearing that long service in the Americas might make Spanish officers "go native."[208] Experience in the royal military also tended to confirm a sense of persecution and resentment of the special privileges granted *peninsulares.* In many cases, while the Creoles made up the majority of the personnel, they were paid less than their European-born counterparts.[209] Service in the militia often also confirmed Creoles' faith in their ability to take on tasks, perhaps better than the Spanish authorities. The most extreme example of this came during the British invasions of Buenos Aires in 1806, during which the local militia saved the day despite the incompetence and cowardice of some Spanish officials.

Partly because of the distrust in their own population, partly because of logistical difficulties, various political authorities depended on foreigners and mercenaries to staff military institutions. The wars of independence certainly involved many soldiers fighting away from their immediate *patria,* clearly true in the cases of Ecuador and Peru. A Venezuelan army, however, liberated Colombia with few connections to the provincial neo-Granadian elite.[210] But it was not only Venezuelans fighting in Peru; significant numbers of Europeans fought—for a variety of reasons—throughout the continent. After independence, the significance of such foreigners declined, but did not disappear. Pedro I of Brazil, for example, did not trust Brazilian troops. In 1823, he attempted to transform all Portuguese-born prisoners into soldiers and later recruited mercenaries, importing two thousand German and three hundred Irish soldiers.[211] The reluctance of Argentines to fight in the War

208. Archer, "Army of New Spain," 707–11.
209. According to Loveman, Creoles made up 60 percent of the officer corps by 1800. In Argentina the figure was 90 percent. The majority of noncommissioned troops were also American born (*For la Patria,* 15).
210. McAlister, Maingot, and Potash claim that the post 1816 Bolívarian army included seventy-four Venezuelan generals and colonels, eighteen Colombian, and four Ecuadorian (*Military in Latin American Evolution,* 137; Bustamante, *Revisión histórica comparativa,* 20).
211. Bushnell and Macaulay, *Emergence of Latin America,* 155, 163; McBeth, "Brazilian Army"; Saldanha Lemos, *Os mercenários do imperador.*

of the Triple Alliance led the government to seek mercenaries in Europe, of whom at least several hundred served.[212] This was not a unique occurrence.[213] When volunteers joined the army it was often not in order to contribute to some social collective goal, but as a means with which to gain new social identities.

Wars were often unpopular and among recruits generated more resentment than patriotic fervor. This was certainly the case with the Cisplatine War and arguably true on the allied side of the Triple Alliance. The exceptions here would include the war against the French in Mexico (but arguably less the war with the United States) and, most significantly, the two wars fought by Chile over control of the Pacific Rim. The first war against the Peruvian-Bolivian Confederation served to consolidate the legitimacy of the Portalian state.[214] During the war, public demonstrations evidenced their support for the government's policies and the military in general. The military expedition was perceived as an expression of Chilean national identity. Certainly the official version is that the "Chilean people were the real victors [of the war]. The common citizen, worker, peasant, miner, fisherman, or artisan was transformed into a soldier and answered the call of the fatherland."[215] According to Loveman, "[M]ilitary service brought thousands of Chileans into a national institution, instructed them in the military's view of patriotism and national history, [and] deployed them in regions far from their homes."[216] The integrative role of the Mexican Revolution, as trains and strategy brought armies together from different parts of the country, has been widely noted.

Armies did attempt to fulfill their pedagogical roles. If nothing else, they served to "guard the symbols, fly the flag, [and] perform the national rituals."[217] In late nineteenth-century Brazil, officers attempted to indoctrinate their men in the ritual and cultural forms of nationalism. Officers, complaining that recruits could not sing the national anthem, produced songbooks that offered soldiers their first exposure to patriotic culture.[218] The Argentine army even prior to its consolidation in the 1860s succeeded in diluting provincial and racial identities; the segregation of regiments by

212. Rouquie, *Poder militar,* vol 1, 114.
213. Hanson, "Voluntarios extranjeros en los ejércitos liberales mexicanos, 1854–1867," 224.
214. Loveman, *Chile,* 141.
215. *HEC,* vol. 3, 228.
216. Loveman, *Chile,* 237.
217. Deas, "Man on Foot," 12.
218. Beattie, "Transforming Enlisted Army Service," 507.

color, for example, stopped in 1851.[219] Certainly in the Argentine case, the army was successful in helping to assimilate waves of immigrants, providing an institution in which the first generation could be educated in the rituals of Argentine nationalism and representing a legitimizing service as these individuals claimed their full right as citizens. The association of the army with immigrants continued well into the twentieth century. In the 1920s, one-third of all officers were immigrants' sons and in 1946, 50 percent of generals were.[220] Especially after the imposition of obligatory military service, the armed forces strengthened nationalism and popularized the notion that "to be a good Argentine was to be a good soldier."[221] The same may be said for Brazil, where military service appears to have been an important component of the nationalization of immigrant communities in the southern provinces.[222]

Colombia represents the other extreme, where the initial sense of nationhood arises from an explicit antimilitarism.[223] Similarly, in Ecuador, the very foreignness of the independence army made it difficult for the military to serve as a national symbol.[224] The role of the Indian population in the Mexican army is more ambiguous. A Prussian observer in 1848 noted that as oppressive as the *levas* were, they seemed to offer one of the few mechanisms with which to integrate Indians into the national collective.[225] Yet the same army was most often used in the late nineteenth century to destroy the last vestige of indigenist autonomy.

In the postwar era, anticommunism made the military's role as teacher of patriotism much more important. In the 1940s, for example, the Chilean armed forces undertook a campaign of "chileanidad" meant to educate the population in the values of the nation.[226] Throughout the continent, the armed forces came to see themselves as the warrior priests of the religion of a nation that faced innumerable external and internal threats. Again, these perceptions created very different organizational responses. First, they were not associated with concrete territorial enemies (unless we count Cuba). Second, in part because of limited resources, in part because of doctrine, in

219. Salvatore, "Reclutamiento militar," 43.
220. Potash, *Army and Politics, 1928–1945*, 22; *Army and Politics, 1945–1962, i, 5*.
221. García, *El servicio militar obligatorio*, 86.
222. Saldanha Lemos, *Os mercenários do imperador.*
223. Bustamante, *Revisión histórica comparativa*, 33.
224. Bustamante, *Revisión histórica comparativa*; Romero y Cordero, *El ejército en cien años de vida republicana, 1830–1930*, 151.
225. Cited in G. Thompson, "Los indios y el servicio militar," 212.
226. Loveman, *Chile*, 129.

part because of uncertainty of response, the solution to a national security crisis was not to include vaster amounts of the population in the state apparatus through conscription, but to use the armed forces to watch and repress the populace.

Unlike their European and North American equivalents, the Latin American militaries appear not to have played an important role in developing welfare states to provide them with better recruits. This is surprising given the generally low level of human capital that they had to confront. As late as the 1940s, for example, 60 percent of Brazilian draftees were illiterate and nearly half were declared unfit for duty for health reasons.[227] Nor did they generate an autonomous social sector demanding rewards for their service that subsequently evolved into welfare systems, as was seen in the United States and Britain.

The militaries seem to have had a very limited role in developing the human resources on which they depended, although here their record is a little better. For much of their early history, they treated their soldiers as pure cannon fodder. Not much was asked of them in terms of training or performance, nor was much given. The one possibly significant exception remains difficult to document. Allusions to the fiscal problems associated with the demands of veterans from the independence wars abound in the standard histories of the early national period. Yet we have few if any hard numbers to indicate the amounts involved or the penetration of the pension system. Interestingly, there are also many accounts of how independence veterans were defrauded out of the land grants and cash payments they had been promised.[228] The general impression is that some, with expected correlations by race, class, and rank, did receive significant economic advantages from participating in the war, but that they did so not through the bureaucratic apparatus of the state, but as a result of political booty. The situation differed by country. Certainly many of the veterans who settled in Ecuador appeared to have used their military experience to improve their lives, but few except the highest officers seem to have been able to preserve any benefits in Argentina.

As discussed in earlier sections, few of the Latin American militaries pos-

227. Beattie, "Transforming Enlisted Army Service," 501.
228. Loveman says that while leading generals of the independence wars often benefited grandly, the common soldiers received few, if any, of their promised benefits (e.g., the five-hundred–peso bonus promised by Bolívar) (41). Halperín-Donghi, *Contemporary History*, 105; Bushnell and Macaulay, *Emergence of Latin America,* 103.

sessed the institutional wherewithal[229] to significantly improve the educational and health profile of their recruits.[230] The *possible* exception is the Chilean case where some evidence indicates that the military was at least officially creating the infrastructure associated with modern armed forces.[231] The military had created an official health service by 1817 with associated hospitals by 1821 and even a vaccination program by 1831. A system of schools was established for the National Guard in 1843 and literacy programs were begun in the army by 1865. With the significant casualties and maimings of the War of the Pacific came protection societies (1880), a formal pension system (1881), and a reorganization of the health service (1880). As the army became increasingly professionalized after 1880, it began instituting courses in basic hygiene (1887). By the 1920s, recruits could count on literacy classes as well as basic health care.[232] Yet even in Chile we need to note the limitations. The wounded received at best superficial care on the battlefront. The infamous "pago de chile" for widows was a miserly three pesos.[233]

Participation in the Chilean military had important social consequences. As in many other wars, the relative shortage of men produced a temporary decline in crime and, on the other end of the social ladder, fewer eligible bachelors promenading in the *paseos*.[234] Service in the army during the War of the Pacific appears partly responsible for a move from the traditional countryside to the North. Veterans from the war were reluctant to return to the haciendas—and their subaltern positions—and became the nucleus of the politically active proletariat in the nitrate mines. The general migration to urban centers also led to much wider reach by public education.[235] According to Loveman, the educational training available in the military by the early twentieth century was even enough to provide some exiting sol-

---

229. One indication of the limited resources is that the contemporary Mexican military allows recruits to have second jobs! In Bolivia in the 1960s recruits were often dismissed before their terms were up for lack of money to pay them.

230. But because they came from such poverty, for many soldiers, service in the military still represents a significant improvement in educational, housing, health care, and dietary situations.

231. Based on *HEC*.

232. When Chilean recruits arrived for their service they were "subject to a rigorous disinfection, bathed, and shaved and incorporated into the army in conditions of absolute hygiene. . . . they slept in simple, but clean[,] beds . . . [ate] a basic, but nutritious[,] diet . . . [learned] table manners . . . and [received] a general education" (García, *El servicio militar obligatorio*, 65–66).

233. Collier and Sater, *History of Chile*, 138.

234. Collier and Sater, *History of Chile*, 141.

235. Loveman, *Chile*, 194–97.

diers with new trades.[236] Well into the second half of the century, the military still made it a policy that 10 percent of its incoming cohort be illiterate and receive a basic education from the military. Similarly, the twentieth-century wars in Peru, Ecuador, Bolivia, and Paraguay led to both the arming and radicalizing of rural Indians and urban workers who felt betrayed by their white leaderships.[237]

In the twentieth century, the educational mission of the various militaries was pronounced. In Argentina, for example, illiteracy was not considered cause for nonrecruitment, but these men spent a significant portion of their time of service in the classroom.[238] In Colombia in the 1960s new recruits received a basic primary education and some rudimentary vocational training.[239] The Bolivian army played an important role in teaching recruits basic Spanish and some literacy skills.[240] In Peru, the armed forces "operated a major educational system for conscripts, including the best vocational schools in the nation."[241] By the 1920s, the Brazilian army had more than fifty schools teaching reading and writing, with special attention paid to immigrant recruits whose families did not speak Portuguese.[242]

In general, the armed forces did not provide the Latin American states with opportunities for mass indoctrination in nationalist dogma. Nor did these bodies give significant segments of the population the political leverage needed to extract expanded citizenship rights. What were created were institutional islands of relative privilege explicitly divorced from a society perceived with distrust. Instead of being the school of the nation, the military became a guardian of abstract notions of patriotic values that had little to do with incorporating the majority of citizens into a more cohesive society.

Conclusions

We can identify four basic patterns among the militaries of the relevant cases. Paraguay during the War of the Triple Alliance represents perhaps a

236. Loveman, *Chile,* 237.
237. Loveman, *Chile,* 105.
238. *Reseña histórica y orgánica;* García, *El servicio militar obligatorio,* 82.
239. Ruhl, *Colombia,* 32.
240. García, *El servicio militar obligatorio,* 93.
241. The Peruvian army has had a very strong tradition of involvement in education. In the 1960s, an officer in the Peruvian army could expect to spend a third of his active career in school (McAlister, Maingot, and Potash, *Military in Latin American Evolution,* 35; Dobyns and Doughty, *Peru,* 236).
242. McCann, "Nation at Arms," 237.

unique case of total mobilization similar to what we see in some European cases during the past hundred years. Argentina during the first half of the twentieth century is an example of more limited extension of conscription. Originally meant to serve as a school for the nation—or more accurately a national school for immigrants—its reach was limited but did include segments of the middle class for at least some periods. Chile represents a related case where the military was not purely a reflection of the social order (nor was it perfectly democratic). The Chilean case is worth distinguishing because of the central role played by the National Guard during the early stages of state formation. That socially exclusive group does appear to have served many of the cohesive functions associated with the military, but it did so within a stratified environment. Finally, in the majority of cases, there is a huge gulf between the makeup of the armed forces and of the dominant classes. In Peru and Mexico, for example, the military, or at least the army, is a mechanism for social mobility for the lower working class. The enlisted mass came from if not the very bottom (as these might not be healthy enough to be useful), at best from the second quartile of the population. In general, the military was not only small, but also unrepresentative.

The same could be said of the European and North American militaries for the majority of their history. Even when aristocrats and elites served, they did so as officers, often not mixing with the men. But the experience of the world wars, no matter how recent, cannot be denied. No matter how segregated by class and race, the British, French, and American militaries certainly made a significant contribution to the creation not only of a nation, but a more equal one. There is no equivalent experience in Latin America. There the armies more resembled their eighteenth-century counterparts, held together by forced obedience, often used for internal control, and providing little by way of national coherence.

Before despairing at the "lost opportunity" for bellicist democracy, however, we should note that the Latin American experience and range of cases once again contributes to a healthy distrust of "necessary or sufficient" conditions in any social phenomenon. In the twentieth century, the country with the most enviable record of democracy, post-1948 Costa Rica, was also the one that abolished a formal armed service. The country with the highest rate of military participation, Cuba, was also the one that was able to resist all recent pressures to democratize. Armies did not guarantee democracy and social justice, nor did their absence make them impossible. Latin America, in general, however, was missing a potentially critical contributor to the development of contemporary politics.

6
Wars and Nation-States in Latin America

In this book I have been concerned with a double empirical puzzle:

why did the Latin American state fail to develop beyond its limited

organizational capacity, and why did international war occur so

infrequently on the continent? In the previous four chapters, I

have presented the linkages between these two questions and have

demonstrated how the absence of both institutional authority and

politically organized violence were bound in a circular, causal re-

lationship. The origins of this unique pattern of development are

found in the conditions under which the countries achieved inde-

pendence. We also need to consider other factors, however, such

as Latin America's actual military experience, the divisions within the societies and within the dominant elites, and the particular sequence of these developments, all of which helped to make the colonial legacy harder to escape. Throughout the book, I have noted both the general pattern observed in the continent as well as the variance within it. In this final chapter, I summarize the causal links between state capacity and war, and between rule and exceptions. I also discuss how these findings may improve our general understanding of the rise of the modern state.

Explaining Peace

We can begin with perhaps the most interesting empirical puzzle discussed in this volume: the relative scarcity of wars—but especially international ones—in Latin America. As I noted at the beginning, this certainly does not imply that Latin American political history has not been violent. The continent has not lacked bloodshed and cruelty in its history, but it has, somehow, skipped the *organized* exercise of violence that so defines other modern nations. It is the difference in political organization that helps account for both Latin American "exceptionalism" and differences within the continent.

I wish to emphasize a division between the micro or personal level of violence and that associated with war and necessarily involving social organization. Latin America is certainly not immune from the first. The animal instincts, Freudian impulses, rational estimations, and cultural socialization that help account for human violence are as present on the continent as anywhere else. Latin America has also had several examples of socially organized violence. These conflicts have often been between ideological, class, caste, or regional enemies, or combinations thereof. Class conflicts, peasant *jacqueries,* and revolutions of one sort or another have been common. However, the form of violence associated with war, that is, organized and connected with political units, has been much less common. This suggests an answer to our first empirical puzzle that has less to do with Latin America's relationship to violence and more with the form of political organization seen on the continent.

The absence of a strong centralizing state authority best explains the particular distribution and types of political violence observed on the continent. Because the state developed so late, generally only in the late nineteenth century and then only intermittently, social, political, racial, regional, and economic conflicts were rarely controlled from above. The Hobbesian function of the state was underdeveloped and what ensued was often the violence of all against all. There were simply too many conflicts occurring within each Latin American state for these countries to have much energy to fight one another.

These internal struggles and the never-resolved social and economic divisions produced a military that saw its major responsibility as the protection of an always ill-defined sense of nation from internal enemies. Whether these were Indians, class antagonists, or the supposed communist representatives mattered less than the fact that the military gaze was oriented inward.

By the time states had developed greater organizational capacity, the inertia of peace made it practically unimaginable to break with the geopolitical status quo. Moreover, strong international interests had already established their presence in the various economies and would not have necessarily benefited from dramatic alterations in the distribution of power. While there is little evidence of proconsular interference, the United Kingdom and the United States did appear to serve as the ultimate guarantors of the Latin American peace. This, combined with a military whose professional interest and ideological proclivities did not encourage international conflict, assured the continent its relative peace.

The exceptions tend to support the rule. For example, the flashes of conflict between Argentina and Brazil occurred at moments when state strength was either at a peak before a long fall (such as Argentina's Rivadavia in 1825) or at a peak after a long climb (both in the 1860s). Paraguay's capacity to withstand the War of the Triple Alliance owed much to its unique form of centralized autocracy. Chile's successes in its wars with its neighbors were partly a reflection of the administrative development of its state. Generally on the continent, where there were strong states, there was a higher probability of international war. Clearly, there remain mysteries or occasions that go beyond the explanatory capacity of any general model. The Chaco War is a perfect example, in which the two arguably poorest and least developed countries drove each other to collapse over a worthless piece of territory. In other cases, Latin American wars need no explanation, as a more powerful neighbor simply made use of an opportunity too good to pass up. The Mexican-American War of 1846 and even the Pacific War of 1879–1883 are good examples of this.

In general, we can answer the question of why major wars never developed by pointing to the inherent weakness of the state. Latin America does not necessarily contradict the first part of Tilly's famous dictum. Rather than attempting to imagine complex circumstances under which states might not fight wars, it seems more fruitful to question whether we really have states (defined rigorously) on the continent.

If the relationship between state capacity and violence is so strong, then contemporary institutional and political development may have darker sides than we have ever imagined. The iron cage of the modern state may represent a threat to human survival. Behind the apparent chaos of war lies organizational sophistication and bureaucratic rationality. Simultaneously, democracy entails in part the massification of politics, which in turn involves much larger numbers of people in political conflicts. Latin America's underdeveloped state and exclusive politics made it difficult if not impossible to create international killing fields. While very cognizant of the destruction and violence that has characterized Latin American political life, I contend that the absence of international strife makes the continent an interesting model. The foremost lesson is to concentrate on the institutional bases that allow hatred to degenerate (or develop?) into something much more violent. The questions we ask about conflicts should not be, Why do these people kill each other? but the infinitely more useful, How are they convinced to do so? and, How are they organized?

The Latin American experience represents a conundrum for policy makers looking to reduce political conflict in other parts of the world. Help develop political authority and you may reduce internal struggles and create the basis for better social infrastructures. But such states may also be more likely to engage in competition with one another culminating in massive slaughter. To maximize the likelihood of regional peace, one may choose to keep central political authority and capacity at a minimum, but this brings with it the injustices and petty violence of power vacuums. A very pessimistic reading of the comparison between Latin America and western Europe is that we may choose needless deaths through the whimper of injustice and inequality or through the bang of conflict, but suffering may be unavoidable. Moreover, the various paths followed by individual cases suggest that there are no absolute causal sequences to be found without appropriate attention paid to starting points. Given that complexity, we might well consider the advisability of political interference except in the most extreme circumstances.

Explaining the State

If we then accept the second part of Tilly's "law," could we not imagine that more war might have produced more state?

How do wars make states? In previous chapters we saw that they did so through three interrelated processes. Wars provide both the means and the incentive to centralize power. Given external threats, states seek to protect their internal situation by imposing their control over as much of their own territory as possible. The armies raised for external warfare may also be used to either threaten the autonomy of recalcitrant provinces or actually impose centralized order. The expansion of this direct control *may have* fiscal benefits as the government expands the pool of potentially extractable wealth. Wars are a critical half of "extraction-coercion" cycles whereby authority is used to extort resources that in turn are used to solidify or expand said authority.

Wars also help build nations. They do so by both providing the dramaturgical materials for nationalist liturgies and offering avenues and opportunities for the subject population to establish possibly more cooperative relations with the state. With regard to the first, wars are wonderful creators of national legends. The heroism of war is particularly well suited for elaboration and consecration by states. Wars are occasions when the "us" can appear more united and more homogenous in the face of a threat by "them." Victorious or not, wars are also moments of national unity when the collective fate of the nation at least theoretically overrides individualist imperatives. Celebrated in stone and in paper, the acts of war remind the people to whom their loyalty belongs. Finally, success in war (or even glorious defeat) can provide states with invaluable legitimacy, as these are public demonstrations of the capacity of political authority.

Through the massification of armies, wars also help define citizenship. Two mechanisms are involved here. By asking significant parts of the population to fight for the abstract cause of the nation-state, political authorities often need to offer something in return. If never explicit, the causal correlation between broad participation in the military and popular political rights seems quite significant. Conscription may historically have served as a prerequisite for democracy; it may even help in the development of "social rights." A state requiring that a significant number of young men be trained and be healthy enough for transshipment is a state that may be more willing to spend resources on education and public health. It may also be a state less willing to tolerate aristocratic prerogatives over its population. Finally, mass armies have tended to serve as schools of the nation. The process of turning young men into soldiers involves not only professional training, but also inculcating them with nationalist dogma. Content aside, this may even be the first time that these young men are taught the national lingua franca.

In general, the standard bellicist model assumes a relatively smoothly operating feedback loop (Fig. 6.1). External threats generate military needs. These include fiscal and personnel resources. The first are satisfied through some already existing administrative capacity (which in turn grows and makes fiscal extraction easier). The newly augmented organizational capacity and new funds further encourage and support the establishment of centralized authority. The personnel needs lead to conscription and to citizenship claims in exchange for granting the state such power. Meanwhile, the external threat gives rise to both elite unity and a broader sense of collective identity. The latter (along with the heroic deeds of the actual conflict) help develop an official nationalist ethos (which in turn helps consolidate elite unity). Both of these contribute to the legitimacy of centralized authority. The combination of institutionalized authority, citizenship claims, and nationalism are the essential components of a modern nation-state.

In Latin America, the process was generally quite different (Fig. 6.2). The fiscal response to military needs could not be met through an expanded administrative capacity, as one barely existed. The kinds of wars fought and the same limited state organizational capability precluded massive mobilization. Instead the professionalization following the 1890s produced socially isolated, small, and relatively privileged armed forces. External threats did not automatically translate into support or self-identification, but were precluded from doing so by social divisions. Given the absence of any core sense of nation, external threats often aggravated domestic divisions. These produced divided and isolated elites and a generally excluded majority without a sense of citizenship. The results of war on the continent were generally negative, in that it mostly brought about debt, economic breakdown, and political chaos. When it had a positive economic effect, it was too often in the form of providing a state with new "rents," but not forcing it to do more with what it already had undertaken. Positive political results, as in greater centralization, were usually accompanied by authoritarian rule and rarely with any parallel rise in popular participation.

What are the general conditions that help explain this difference? First, the sheer number of wars is much smaller on the Latin American continent and this may have an important effect on the actual political and social effect of the wars that did take place. We need to remember that it is not necessarily war itself, but the threat of war that often produces the positive state-building consequences discussed earlier. The Latin American countries did not arise in a geopolitically competitive world. When wars came, they

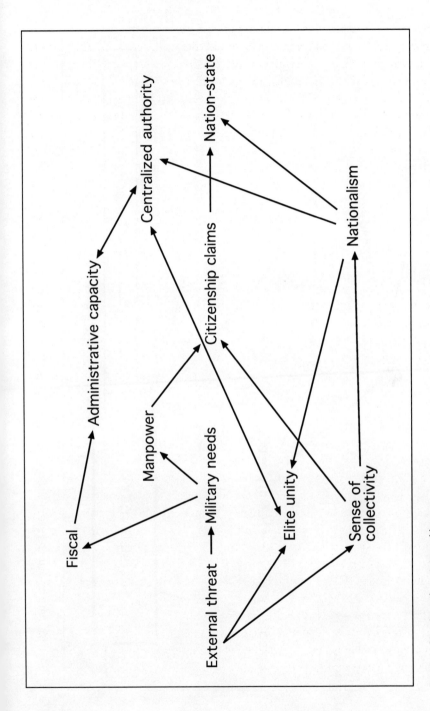

Fig. 6.1 Classic nation-state making war

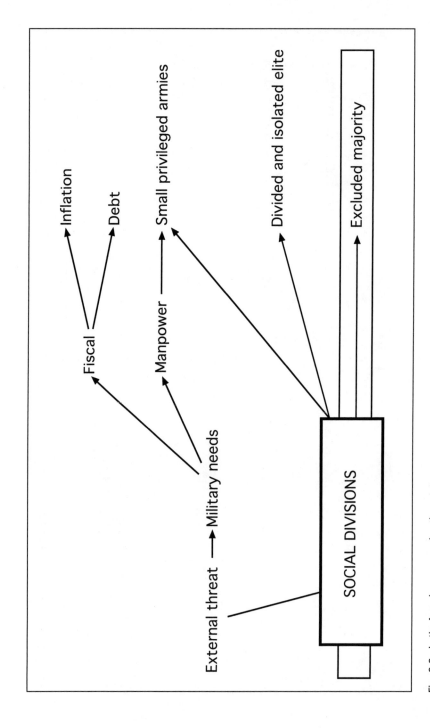

Fig. 6.2 Latin America wars and nation-states

often appeared epiphenomenal and not as part of a long-term set of relation-ships. Thus, wars may not have built states because they were too isolated in time and place to have the necessarily cumulative effect.

We also need to consider the kinds of wars that were fought. I have al-ready noted that the distinction between civil and international wars, while blurred, may be crucial in this regard. The kinds of civil wars seen in Latin America differed greatly from their European or North American equiva-lents. Namely, they rarely were fought by territorially cohesive and well-organized political entities. Instead they were often disorganized, geographi-cally dispersed, and multipolar. Moreover, rarely were these wars thor-oughly resolved in favor of one or the other sides. Civil wars were seldom moments when long-term conflicts were resolved and the nation moved into a new historical phase. Instead, they often did little but exacerbate internal hatreds and divisions. The international wars also left much to be desired from the point of view of political development. These were often of short duration and involved relatively simple logistical requirements. I have called these "limited wars," and it should not be surprising that they produced "limited states."

How to explain the particular interaction between violent conflict and state formation in Latin America? First, regionalism seems to have repre-sented more of a permanent obstacle to state formation and was often worsened through political violence. In part, this may be because of the daunting geographical challenges facing these countries. In the first half of the nineteenth century, the Latin American republics faced vast hinterlands demanding much more administrative and political capacity than any of the states could provide. They had limited resources with which to obtain the technologically constrained infrastructure needed for state formation. While the United States, Canada, and equivalent European states could "grow into" their frontiers, the Latin American republics were handed too much territory too soon. Combined with the acceptance of the old Spanish admin-istrative boundaries, this disallowed a more "organic" process of state de-velopment that could have used conflict to resolve disputes over authority. Paradoxically, the absence of stronger regional subidentities may have exac-erbated the regionalist problem. That is, an ethnically different core might have been more interested in stamping its identity on the provinces. The apparent homogeneity of the new nations (at least as defined geographically) made the maintenance of regional identities less of an apparent problem and a lower political priority.

We also need to keep in mind that in almost all these cases we are speaking of fairly poor societies made poorer still by the independence conflicts. Except perhaps in the case of Chile in the 1880s and *perhaps* Argentina and Brazil in the 1870s, we do not see bellic victors astride their territories as some form of colossus. Consider the conditions in which the United States finds itself after each of its most significant wars. Certainly in the late 1860s, the Northern economy provided the federal government with the resources it needed to expand and police its authority. Put another way, an economically devastated North might not have been up to becoming a Yankee Leviathan.

The main sources of wealth for the new states also represented questionable fiscal foundations. As discussed in Chapter 3, the availability of loans or easy commodity sales provided the state with an alternative to the much more challenging construction of internal markets and the development of a national infrastructure. The establishment and protection of *comprador* economies, in turn, required relatively little of the state. This indicates a critical distinction between Latin American and European states: the sheer amassing and control of territory was not as central for Latin America as it was for Europe. This distinction has already been made for Africa, where population was more valuable than land itself.[1] The situation in Latin America was not as extreme, and in some cases, such as the Pampas, land mattered a great deal. But for the states of nineteenth-century Latin America, what mattered most was control over the main port and access to some exportable commodity. Control over faraway hinterlands rarely led to geopolitical conflict.

Further, the new Latin American states arose in the wrong ideological environment. When one considers the basic tenets of the Liberalism that triumphed on the continent by the last third of the century, it was not the ideal philosophy on which to build an authoritative state. This was particularly true of the unfortunate (again, from the point of view of state making) congruence between Liberalism and federalism. While the Conservative project also had its obvious weaknesses—to say the least—it might have represented a better legitimizing ideology for the establishment of centralized authority.

Wars came at the wrong moments. For all intents and purposes, the major conflicts essentially preceded the establishment of nation-states. The greatest conflict of all involving a clear "us" and "them" occurred during the conquest in the sixteenth century. With notable exceptions, the frontier

---

1. Herbst, *States and Power in Africa.*

was not a threatening place where the state's support was needed or where the new nation could expand and grow into itself. Even in the nineteenth century, the capacities of any of the warring states to use violence as a stimulus for or as means to expand their control were severely limited. By the time states were established (in the 1890s), the warring years of the continent were over. Consider the development of Europe if the "hundred years' peace" of the nineteenth century had occurred one hundred years earlier. Would the subsequent political institutions have developed as they have?

The low level of geopolitical competition and its virtual disappearance after the 1890s also prevented the consolidation of the developmentalist dynamic of war. Wars did not occur because the states were unready for them and the countries remained unprepared, because war never came. It is perhaps this observation that best illustrates the historical specificity of the European cases and the importance of recognizing the indeterminate aspects of state formation. The evidence presented in this book should make us more aware of the central importance played not by the simple presence of one national characteristic or another, but *the interaction of these in specific causal sequences*. In other words, it is not just what happened, but when and in what order. In Latin America, wars and states did not engage one another in a productive harmonic, but appear to have canceled one another out.

If they had little role to play in defending their countries from external violence and were stymied in their imposition of control over their own territories, what roles did these states play? What were they there for? Whose interests did they serve? In my view, the independence period and immediately thereafter seems a very good example of John Meyer's notion of an isomorphic construction of a world polity.[2] There is no doubt about the very real anti-Spanish—or better yet, anti-imperial—sentiment in the American colonies in 1800. There is much less evidence for a need for, or even the perception of, the construction of nation-states. Can we speak of a nascent political class ready and able to occupy these new political institutions? Can we speak of core national interests that saw in the formation of the states new economic opportunities? With the possible exceptions of Chile, by 1830, and 1820s Brazil, few social groups identified their own survival with that of the central state.[3] Past a certain minimal policing func-

2. See Meyer, "The World Polity and the Authority of the Nation-State," 109–37; Meyer, Boli, Thomas, and Ramirez, "World Society and the Nation State." Thanks to Kieran Healy for first suggesting this point.

3. This is a standard interpretation of the Chilean case. For Brazil, see Carvalho, *A construção da ordem*, chap. 3.

tion, no group needed or wanted an institution that might impose a form of collective rationality on national interests. Except in Brazil, no monarchical family and allied factions so identified with the state as to make their individual and national interests congruent. The state was not where the action was, except when rents could be directly derived from it via loans or access to commodities.

If we cannot adequately answer the question of whose state, it is even more difficult to say whose nation was represented. Where was there a sense of a cohesive nation anywhere on the continent? One might ask the same question of Europe, where the state did help create its own citizenry. But on the European continent, we can identify crucial cores whose efforts to expand their authority and impose their nationality led to the eventual formation of a greater nation-state. In Latin America, the societies were so rife with caste and class divisions that the very process of independence created important fissures. If Latin America's external borders appeared peaceful, its domestic affairs were anything but, because the relevant frontiers were internal. Analyzing all aspects of potential war-led state development, we run into the same phenomenon: fear of the internal enemy prevented the consolidation of authority, the elaboration of all-encompassing nationalist mythology, and the incorporation of large parts of the population into the military apparatus.

Again, we need to remember that the Latin American countries were born as shards of an empire and that they retained the colonial race hierarchy. It is this, more than awkward borders or foreign intervention, that is the true postcolonial impediment to nation-state formation. The experience of Latin America leads us to examine the specific conditions under which states arose in western Europe. The racial and caste cleavages did not occur within the nation, but outside it. Transmaritime empires not only served to better define an "us" and bring civilization to the rest of the world, but also provided the kind of diverting wars (both with locals and with other imperial claimants) that drew attention away from internal conflicts. Latin American wars, but especially civil conflicts, accomplished the opposite.

Clearly, there are exceptions to these rules and considerable historical variations to be found on the continent. These occasions, however, tend to confirm the significance of the factors discussed earlier.

In terms of the centralizing effect of wars, I have already noted that those fought against the Indians on the Chilean, Mexican, and Argentinean frontiers did make important contributions. These were classic wars of conquest with few of the complications of other wars. Note that unlike other conflicts, these were fought against an unquestioned "other" and the wars brought about immediate benefits for the elite and, though to a much lesser extent, other parts of the population. The requirements of these wars were nicely calibrated to the capacities of the state, which was not overwhelmed by what it had to produce and could easily digest the new land through political alliances.

Chile's victory in the war against the Peruvian-Bolivian Confederation did not result in the kind of administrative growth predicted in bellicist accounts. It did, however, accomplish two critical goals. First, it helped consolidate an elite consensus, and second, it provided the central state with a much-needed degree of legitimacy. It did so, however, because of the particular imbalance between Chilean political development and that of its enemies, which was obvious even at this early date. The rise of the Porfiriato a decade after the Liberal victory over Maxmilian and his French allies may be another exception to the rule. Unlike most other civil wars in Latin America, this ended with the destruction of one of the contending sides. Much like classic state-making conflicts, this war provided the Mexican state with an ideological and organizational monopoly rare on the continent. Given that this conflict was a continuation of the almost constant fighting of the 1850s, it should not be surprising to find that significant parts of the population fought at one time or another. The veterans groups from these conflicts represented an important base for the early consolidation of the Porfirian regime.

The final exception is the early takeover of the Paraguayan state by Dr. José Francia prior to 1820. The exclusion—and sometimes elimination—of competing elites gave the Paraguayan state an enviable degree of autonomy. The relative homogeneity of the population (and the rare integration of Spanish and Guaraní) was further secured by the shared threat of Argentine domination. Francia's success in maintaining Paraguay ensured that no other power claimant would challenge the state. Of course, the success of this project was greatly assisted by Paraguay's small and compact population.

The most clear-cut pattern that emerges from these exceptions is the critical importance of *elite support*. In all four cases, the elite was bought off, was destroyed, or had achieved a rare moment of consensus. The preparation and occasion of war may have helped consolidate power, but the conditions were already present that would allow this process to proceed.

It is harder to discern any single variable that helps account for the exceptions to our findings on nationalism. Bolivia may be the weakest case in that well into the twentieth century, and arguably even today, this country most resembles an internal empire. It still maintains a clear ethnic hierarchy and excludes large parts of the population from meaningful political life. Nevertheless, it is undeniable that the loss of the Pacific littoral is a central element of Bolivian national mythology. The same might be said of Ecuador's loss of the Amazonian territory. Note again that in the latter case, a significant part of the population, defined by ethnicity, is functionally excluded. Thus, while war provided a basis for some sense of official nationhood, there are no signs that this led to progress in creating more inclusive societies. In both countries, conflicts continue over whose nation is represented by the state. Once again, the noncentrality of territorial boundaries and the inclusion of a coherent population within them may be both a reflection and a cause of this situation.

The central exception to the pattern of conscription is Chile. Unique among Latin American countries, it was able to create a form of military service that established a link between the state and a broadly defined elite. The National Guard was inclusive in its penetration of the upper reaches of society and exclusive in its definition of who was qualified to join. All the Latin American countries maintain a de facto (and some de jure) form of honorific reserved for the relative few. Chile's matter of signaling membership was more conducive to state building than other forms observed on the continent. How do we account for the Chilean exception? It might be more accurate to say that preexisting Chilean elite consensus made the guard possible rather than vice versa. Except for the civil war of 1851, the Chilean elite managed almost seventy years of relative social peace despite considerable differences in the role of the state, especially pertaining to religious life. It did not hurt that the elite was relatively small and geographically concentrated.[4] Perhaps more important, the Portales regime of the 1830s was able to impose a resolution to the Liberal-Conservative split that tore other nations apart.

Other possible exceptions include the residue of the Mexican war against the French and, of course, the Mexican Revolution itself. The Paraguayan experience in the 1860s is another. Here, once again, the particular conditions make it difficult to draw any generalizable lessons.

Making Nation-States

What can we learn about the general nature of state and nation making from the Latin American cases? Perhaps the most important lesson is that

---

4. Melquior, "State-Building in Brazil and Argentina," 265–88.

the formation of nation-states is not inevitable. The establishment of successful political authority over large territories is the exception and not the rule. This should have been more than patently clear after the African experience of the past forty years. Too often, however, the development of that continent has been explained away by the peculiarities of its history or the base societies. In the face of overwhelming evidence from much of the rest of the globe, however, political sociology has persisted in considering the western European pattern as a historical standard. We may have come a long way from the days when these cases were also considered normative, but we have not escaped a blinding empirical Eurocentrism. The sample selection bias of most social science research has allowed us to universalize the particular and to treat serendipity as inevitability. The question of state formation needs to be problematized much more broadly than it has been.

It is time that we turn the analysis of state formation 180 degrees. The process that occurred most successfully in northwestern Europe beginning in the sixteenth century and culminating in the nineteenth was the true exception.[5] Nation-states were created there with particular characteristics that owed a great deal to initial historical conditions. This principally applies to the contribution made by war to this process. We do not need to cross the Atlantic to see that the pattern was not repeated elsewhere. In the Balkan Peninsula and in eastern Europe in general, a great deal of civil and international conflict failed to create coherent and institutionally solid nation-states. Thus, the questions we have asked about respective regions need to be switched. The true exceptionalism of western European and North American cases needs to be much more appreciated and taken into account in the methodology of comparative historical work. The fate of Latin America needs to be normalized and reunderstood in the absence of an implicit other. This would allow us to better isolate and define the conditions that best account for the differential development of political structures.

The experience of "negative" counterfactuals points to three critical conditions that need to exist for the bellicist cycle of nation-state building to begin and develop successfully. First, *enough of an institutional/administrative core must exist prior to war for it to serve as a stimulus for administrative development*. Lacking this core, the chaos of war will not build, but will produce greater social divisions and institutional dysfunctions. Thus, the roots of states must be found in the slow buildup of authoritative institutions that might coalesce. It seems impossible, except in the most extreme geographical and historical situations, to create states where no authority

5. We may also add North America and Japan.

has previously existed. Second, *at least part of the dominant elite must see that the expansion of the state's authority is in their interest.*[6] One might even say that this same elite faction needs to perceive state expansion as imperative. Should elite segments be content with their provincial powers or should their political needs be limited to basic policing, then no social agent will arise to move the machinery to develop. Finally, *the institutional or elite core of the future state must be certain about the definition of the nation* and be willing to engage in the political actions required to achieve it.[7] The process is often less than attractive, as it involves conquest, the eradication of cultures, forms of ethnic cleansing, or even genocide. A nation-state may arise even with a significant part of the population excluded from it. For example, there is no denying white South African nationalism through the 1990s. What a nation-state cannot afford is uncertainty about the composition of its citizenship. The Latin American states seemed to be caught between the inclusivity of the Enlightenment ideology of independence and the exclusivity that their social structures required and imposed. Note that when the lines could easily be drawn, for example, with the Mapuche in Chile, efforts to define even heterogeneous population were more successful.

Perhaps we need to rethink the notion that wars make states. Wars best served as an accelerating mechanism for a process that had its origins somewhere else. States were not created in war, but emerged from it stronger than before. We cannot, for example, assume that states will arise and that they will have certain characteristics. Rather, we must reconsider the very problem of political authority and order, as well as the study of organized violence or war. Much of the literature on war focuses on the simple human capacity for violence. We have noted in various parts of this book that Latin America did not lack micro-level violence. What is missing and what needs to be much better studied in the general literature on war is how this personalized, individualized violence becomes organized and directed. It is certainly true that Europeans do not hold a monopoly on human violence or savagery; however, their particular experiences led them to live through many years of sustained and organized political use of violence.

6. John Hall on the success of the classic European states: "[L]arge sections of the powerful were prepared to give quite high taxation revenues to the crown because they realized that their own interests were usually being served" ("States and Economic Development," 164). On the critical importance of state-elite dynamics in explaining political institutional outcomes, see Lachman, "Elite Conflict and State Formation."

7. On the importance of an "ethnic core," see A. Smith, *The Ethnic Roots of Nations;* and "State-Making and Nation-Building," 243–52.

What is missing in the Latin American experience is organization. This is what links the infrequency of wars with the weakness of states. Latin American societies, again with the exception of Chile, appear to have lacked the capacity for the particular form of political organization associated with the state. As stated earlier, there is certainly evidence of micro-level capacity to organize institutions and to impose certain forms of violent behavior, so the explanation for the different development pattern does not lie in cultural predisposition. I do not believe that Latin America lacks a "disciplinary spirit," instead, it lacked the kind of disciplinary organizations associated with state building.

And it is the peculiarity of these organizations that needs to be emphasized. Because we have normalized and universalized the European and North American experience in our research, we have associated state building with a generic capacity for political organization. Yet is not state building merely one of the myriad forms that social organization can take? Instead of asking, Why no states? meaning why no political development, we should explain why one form of political organization as opposed to another. Again, the key may be in attitudes toward territorial control. In Europe, there existed a correlation between political organization and land, which was considered the most valuable asset. This particular constellation often produced a nation-state. But in a world without such organizations and where power was not always expressed territorially, the nation-state appeared to be a much more difficult institution to build.

The same can be said for the forms of social solidarity and cohesion that dominate a particular area. In general, and beginning in the seventeenth century, European communities congealed along isocultural lines, defined in a variety of ways, including language, religion, and geographical concentration. These identities either meshed well with relevant states or were subsumed through conquest. State and nation were relatively congruent. Faced with small minorities, the states were powerful enough to impose the centralizing rule or weak enough to be torn asunder.

The pattern was quite different in Latin America. There the central identities were not culture or nationality (as defined in Europe) but race, caste, and, beginning in the late nineteenth century, class. The point again is that there was no inherent quality that prevented the Latin Americans from adopting a national identity, but the existence of distinct historical processes that led to a different hierarchy of self-identification.

There are, therefore, two different questions we need to ask of the development of organizations and identities leading to a nation-state. First, did a process of herding, congealing, and organizing proceed? The answer for Latin America was yes. The second question concerns the form this process took. In this book I have sought to analyze why Latin America took a very different shape from that of the European standard.[8]

All these qualifications make me doubt the usefulness of any parsimonious model of state development. This is not necessarily an argument against the generalizing qualities of theoretical analysis, but one for expanding the examples that we consider worthy of study and relevant for our discussions. I do not believe, however, that we should graft the kind of modeling borrowed from mainstream social science onto comparative historical studies. Finding a single path through historical evidence is nearly impossible. This is true even forgetting the kind of subjective discovery and analysis of evidence from which even best-faith efforts suffer. We need to preserve and emphasize an appreciation for historical uncertainty and nonlinearity. This is not to argue for "pure" history, but to press for a better mixing of narrative and model. Perhaps even more important, we need to better understand—or visualize—the relationship between sociological structures and historical events. To explain a particular development we cannot focus exclusively on either one, but on the interaction. In our case, we might speak of the nascent political and social conditions of the continent as the underlying structure, and the wars that occurred as the events. Moreover, the relationship between these was partly articulated through an international environment (a metastructure?). For each of these—domestic conditions, forms of wars, and international environment, we can identify critical differences that help us formulate the question better. It's no longer, Why didn't Latin America develop a certain way? but, How do we explain the differences in European and Latin American evolutions?[9]

---

8. How might it have been otherwise? Consider some possible fictional counterfactuals. First a Latin America in 1850 consisting of only five macrostates: Brazil, a Confederation of the South (including most of the Southern Cone), a reborn (and Indian-led) Inca Republic along the Andes, a northern Caribbean Confederation (including parts of northeast Brazil and maybe some of the islands captured from colonial powers), and a Meso-American Empire. Or imagine a Latin America where Conservative-Liberal divisions crossed borders and where members of one party would seek to support confederants in other countries. Imagine then a continent divided between a Liberal North and a Conservative South (or vice versa). Any one of these conditions would have produced radically different states in the twentieth century. But are there any conditions imaginable where this might have occurred? I find it difficult to believe so. A change in even a single digit in the number of variables would have been insufficient. Hundreds of years of history would need to be overturned.

9. Perhaps the best example of how this may be accomplished (at least for Latin America) is found in Hirschman, *Development Projects Observed*.

We might call this spiral causation or path dependence, or simple historicism. This does not imply plain storytelling, however, but the identification of structural conditions that determine the relative probabilities of particular social and institutional outcomes, and an appreciation of how these conditions operate under a variety of constraints having to do with initial circumstances and historical sequences. We need not go as far as Clayton Roberts's rejection of "covering laws" to appreciate the appeal of what he calls colligation, or "the tracing of causal connections between events."[10] With enough sequences we may proceed to the classification of causal links and the analysis of respective probabilities. But the first step must be the collection of explanations.

To speak of necessary and sufficient conditions when explaining processes such as state formation is to engage in positivist hubris. Our task should not be the identification of any list of prerequisites, but rather the systematic analysis of the conditions of particular social structures and how these produce different outcomes. Such analysis may frustrate our professional fascination with model building, but it will produce a better understanding of the historical path to contemporary life and a richer conceptualization of the patterns observable in that history.

A focus on history will alert us to the critical importance of chronological order. An important lesson from the Latin American case is that not only did some things not happen (a significant number of wars), but that they often happened at the wrong time (before the consolidation of states). A more historical perspective would also allow us to accept the inherently circular logic of causation in such cases. The relationship between wars and states cannot be seen as occurring in just one cycle, but in a series of spiraling gyrations, with one causing the other. The cycle is not static, but moves, as a spiral, in a particular direction. The direction, speed of gyrations, and circumference of the cycles all depend on starting conditions, but the beginning of the cycle appears to be crucial. In Latin America, the circular causation between war and states began in the wrong places and in the wrong times, and that has made all the difference.

Johan Huizinga contrasted the perspectives of the sociologist and the historian by noting that the first searched for the result of what was already determined, whereas the second always needed to keep in mind the possibility of different outcomes.[11] I have suggested in this volume that much of the

10. Roberts, *The Logic of Historical Explanation.*
11. Huizinga, "The Idea of History."

Latin American path was already determined by the nature of its heritage. However, that is stating it too simply. I have also noted the critical importance of events and their ordering, not only for the particular fate of the Latin American state, but also for the development of its European counterparts. History is not a dice game in which historical probabilities can be calculated, for developments can be thrown off by specific events. In seeking to explain the past and its relationship to the present, we need to constantly keep both sides in mind.

In the end, I like the metaphor of fairy tale. Note that the best of these require two elements too often divorced in social science: a narrative and a broad moral. Latin America has millions of great stories. It is high time that we begin to appreciate the wider lessons it has to offer.

Bibliography

Abente, Diego. "The War of the Triple Alliance: Three Explanatory Models." *Latin American Research Review* 22, no. 2 (1987): 47–69.

Acevedo, Eduardo. *Notas y apuntes: Historia económica y financiera.* 2 vols. Montevideo: El Siglo Ilustrado, 1903.

Adelman, Jeremy. *Republic of Capital.* Stanford: Stanford University Press, 1999.

Adelman, Jeremy, and Miguel Centeno. "Law and the Failure of Liberalism in Latin America." In Bryant Garth and Yves Dezalay, eds., *Internationalization and the Transformation of the Rule of Law.* Ann Arbor: University of Michigan Press, 2001.

Aftalion, Florin. "Le financement des guerres de la Révolution et de l'Empire." In E. Aerts and Francois Crouzet, eds., *Economic Effects of the French Revolutionary and Napoleonic Wars.* Session B-1. Leuven: Leuven University Press, 1990.

Aguilar, Gustavo F. *Los presupuestos mexicanos.* Mexico City: Secretaria de Hacienda, 1940.

Aguilar Camín, Héctor. "La invención de México." *Nexos* (Mexico City), July 1993, 49–61.

Agulhon, Maurice. "Politics, Images, and Symbols in Post-Revolutionary France." In Sean Wilentz, ed., *Rites of Power: Symbolism, Ritual, and Politics Since the Middle Ages.* Philadelphia: University of Pennsylvania Press, 1985.

———. "La 'statuomanie' et l'histoire." *Ethnologie Française* 8, nos. 2–3 (1978): 145–72.

Alemann, Roberto. *Breve historia de la política económica argentina, 1500–1989.* Buenos Aires: Editorial Claridad, 1989.

Alonso Piñeiro, Armando. *Historia de la guerra de Malvinas.* Buenos Aires: Planeta, 1992.

Alvarez, Luis López. *Literatura e identidad en Venezuela.* Barcelona: PPU, 1991.

Amarente la Tarde, Antonia de. *Monumentos principais do Distrito Federal.* Rio de Janeiro: n.p., 1947.

Ames, Edward, and Richard T. Rapp. "The Birth and Death of Taxes: A Hypothesis." *Journal of Economic History* 37, no. 1 (1977): 161–78.

Anderson, Benedict. *Imagined Communities: Reflections on the Origins and Spread of Nationalism*. London: Verso, 1991.

Anderson, M. S. *War and Society in Europe of the Old Regime, 1618–1789*. New York: St. Martin's Press, 1988.

Anderson, Perry. *Lineages of the Absolutist State*. London: Verso, 1979.

Andreski, S. *Military Organization and Society*. Berkeley and Los Angeles: University of California Press, 1971.

Andrews, George Reid. "The Afro-Argentine Officers of Buenos Aires Province, 1800–1860." *Journal of Negro History* 64, no. 2 (1979): 85–100.

———. "Spanish American Independence: A Structural Analysis." *Latin American Perspectives* 12, no. 1 (1985): 105–32.

Anna, Timothy. *The Fall of Royal Government in Mexico City*. Lincoln: University of Nebraska Press, 1978.

———. *The Fall of the Royal Government of Peru*. Lincoln: University of Nebraska Press, 1979.

Annino, Antonio. "Soberanías en lucha." In Antonio Annino, Luis Castro Leiva, and François-Xavier Guerra, eds., *De los imperios a las naciones: Iberoamérica*. Zaragoza: IberCaja, 1994.

Arbulu, Javier Tantalean. *Política económico-financiera y la formación del estado: Siglo XIX*. Lima: CEDEP, 1983.

Archer, Christon I. *The Army in Bourbon Mexico: 1760–1810*. Albuquerque: University of New Mexico Press, 1977.

———. "The Army of New Spain and the Wars of Independence, 1790–1821." *Hispanic American Historical Review* 61, no. 4 (1981): 705–14.

———. "The Royalist Army in New Spain: Civil-Military Relationships, 1810–1821." *Journal of Latin American Studies* 13, no. 1 (1981): 57–82.

Ardant, Gabriel. "Financial Policy and Economic Infrastructure of Modern States and Nations." In Charles Tilly, ed., *The Formation of National States in Western Europe*. Princeton: Princeton University Press, 1975.

Auza, Nesto Tomas. "El ejército en la época de la confederación: 1852–1861." *Círculo Militar,* September–October 1971, 633–34.

Azaryahu, Maoz. "The Purge of Bismarck and Saladin: The Renaming of Streets in East Berlin and Haifa, a Comparative Study in Culture-Planning." *Poetics Today* 13, no. 2 (1992): 351–67.

Bach, Martin. *Studien zur Geschichte des deutschen Kriegerdenkmals in Westfales und Lippe*. Frankfurt: Peter Lang, 1985.

Baldwin, Lawrence M., and Michael Grimaud. "How New Naming Systems Emerge: The Prototypical Case of Columbus and Washington." *Names* 40, no. 3 (1992): 153–66.

Baliari, Eduardo. *Los monumentos*. Buenos Aires: Ministerio de Cultura y Educación, 1972.

Banco Roberts. *Historia del papel moneda argentino*. Buenos Aires: Banco Roberts, 1984.

Barber, Bernard. "Place, Symbol, and Utilitarian Function in War Memorials." *Social Forces* 28, no. 1 (1949): 64–68.

Barker, Nancy Nichols. *The French Experience in Mexico, 1821–1861: A History of Constant Misunderstanding.* Chapel Hill: University of North Carolina Press, 1979.

Barkey, Karen. *Bandits and Bureaucrats: The Ottoman Route to State Centralization.* Ithaca: Cornell University Press, 1994.

Barkey, Karen, and Sunita Parikh. "Comparative Perspectives on the State." *Annual Review of Sociology* 17 (1991): 523–49.

Barman, Roderick J. *Brazil: The Forging of a Nation, 1798–1952.* Stanford: Stanford University Press, 1988.

Barra, Felipe de la. *Monumentos escultóricos en Lima metropolitana y Callao y grandes ausentes.* Lima: Ministerio de Guerra, 1963.

Barraclough, E. M. C., and W. G. Crampton, eds. *Flags of the World.* London: Frederick Warne, 1978.

Bartlett, Robert. *The Making of Europe: Conquest, Civilization, and Cultural Change, 950–1350.* Princeton: Princeton University Press, 1993.

Bartov, Omer. "The Nation in Arms: Germany and France, 1789–1939." *History Today* 44 (9): 27–34, 1994.

Basurto, Carmen. *México y sus símbolos.* 8th ed. Mexico City: Editorial Avante, 1981.

Batiz Vázquez, José Antonio. *Historia del papel moneda en México.* Mexico City: Fondo Cultural Banamex, 1987.

Bazant, Jan. *A Concise History of Mexico from Hidalgo to Cardenas, 1805–1940.* Cambridge: Cambridge University Press, 1977.

———. *Historia de la deuda exterior de México, 1823–1946.* Mexico City: El Colegio de México, 1968.

Bean, Richard. "War and the Birth of the Nation State." *Journal of Economic History* 33 (1973): 203–21.

Beattie, Peter M. "Transforming Enlisted Army Service in Brazil, 1864–1940: Penal Servitude Versus Conscription and Changing Conceptions of Honor, Race, and Nation." Ph.D. diss., Department of History, University of Miami, 1994.

Bendix, Reinhard. *Kings of People.* Berkeley and Los Angeles: University of California Press, 1978.

Ben-Eliezer, Uri. "A Nation-in Arms: State, Nation, and Militarism in Israel's First Years." *Comparative Studies in Society and History* 37, no. 2 (1995): 264–85.

Benítez-Rojo, Antonio. "La novela hispanoamericana del siglo XIX." *Revista de Crítica Literaria Latinoamericana* 19, no. 38 (1993): 185–93.

Bensel, Richard Franklin. *Yankee Leviathan: The Origins of Central State Authority in America, 1859–1877.* New York: Cambridge University Press, 1990.

Berensztein, Sergio. "Rebuilding State Capacity in Contemporary Latin America: The Politics of Taxation in Argentina and Mexico." Working paper no. 24, University Torcuato Di Tella, Buenos Aires, 1995.

Berezin, Mabel. "Cultural Form and Political Meaning: State Subsidized Theater, Ideology, and the Language of Style of Fascist Italy." *American Journal of Sociology* 99, no. 5 (1994): 1237–86.

Berger, Paulo. *Diccionario histórico das Ruas do Rio de Janeiro: Botafogo.* Rio de Janeiro: Fundação Casa de Rui Barbosa, 1987.

———. *Diccionario histórico das Ruas do Rio de Janeiro: V & VI regioes*. Rio de Janeiro: Fundação Casa de Rui Barbosa, 1994.

Bermúdez, Egnerto. "Nacionalismo y cultura popular." In *El nacionalismo en el arte*. Bogotá: Universidad Nacional de Colombia, Facultad de Artes, Instituto de Investigaciones Estéticas, n.d.

Best, Felix. *Historia de las guerras de la independencia, internacionales, civiles y con el Indio*. 2 vols. Buenos Aires: Graficur, Biblioteca Nacional Militar, 1983.

Best, Geoffrey. Introduction to M. S. Anderson, *War and Society in Europe of the Old Regime, 1618–1789*. New York: St. Martin's Press, 1988.

———. "The Militarization of European Society, 1870–1914." In John Gillis, ed., *The Militarization of the Western World*. New Brunswick: Rutgers University Press, 1989.

Bethell, Leslie, ed. *The Cambridge History of Latin America*. 10 vols. Cambridge: Cambridge University Press, 1984–98.

———, ed. *The Independence of Latin America*. Cambridge: Cambridge University Press, 1987.

Bird, Richard M. "Land Taxation and Economic Development: The Model of Meiji Japan." *Journal of Development Studies* 13, no. 2 (1977): 162–78.

Black, Jeremy. *Why Wars Happen*. London: Reaktion Books, 1998.

Bonilla, Heraclio. "La crisis de 1872." In Heraclio Bonilla, ed., *Las crisis económicas en la historia del Perú*. Lima: Centro Latinoamericano de Historia Económica y Social, 1986.

———. "The Indian Peasantry and 'Peru' During the War with Chile." In Steve J. Stern, ed., *Resistance, Rebellion, and Consciousness in the Andean Peasant World, Nineteenth to Twentieth Centuries*. Madison: University of Wisconsin Press, 1987.

———. "The War of the Pacific and the National and Colonial Problem in Peru." *Past and Present* 81 (November 1978): 92–118.

Borg, Alan. *War Memorials: From Antiquity to the Present*. London: Leo Cooper, 1991.

Botana, Natalio R. *La tradición republicana: Alberdi, Sarmiento y las ideas políticas de su tiempo*. Buenos Aires: Editorial Sudamericana, 1984.

———. "Las transformaciones del credo constitucional." In Antonio Annino, Luis Castro Leiva, and François-Xavier Guerra, eds., *De los imperios a las naciones: Iberoamérica*. Zaragoza: IberCaja, 1994.

Bourke, Joanna. *An Intimate History of Killing: Face to Face Killing in Twentieth Century Warfare*. New York: Basic Books, 1999.

Bourne, Kenneth, and D. Cameron Watt, gen. eds. *British Documents on Foreign Affairs: Reports and Papers from the Foreign Office Confidential Print*. Pt. I, ser. D, vol. 2. Fredericksburg, Md.: University Publications of America, 1991.

Box, Pelham Horton. *The Origins of the Paraguayan War.* New York: Russell & Russell, 1967.

Brack, Gene M. *Mexico Views Manifest Destiny, 1821–1846*. Albuquerque: University of New Mexico Press, 1975.

Brading, David A. *Haciendas and Ranchos in the Mexican Bajío, León, 1700–1860*. New York: Cambridge University Press, 1978.

————. "Liberal Patriotism and the Mexican Reforma." *Journal of Latin American Studies* 20, pt. 1 (1988): 27–48.
————. *Miners and Merchants in Bourbon Mexico, 1763–1810.* Cambridge: Cambridge University Press, 1971.
————. *The Origins of Mexican Nationalism.* Cambridge: Centre of Latin American Studies, Cambridge University, 1985.
Braudel, Fernand. *The Identity of France.* Vol. 1. New York: Harper & Row, 1993.
Breuilly, John. *Nationalism and the State.* 2d ed. Chicago: University of Chicago Press, 1994.
Brewer, John. *The Sinews of Power: War, Money, and the English State, 1688–1783.* London: Unwin Hyman, 1989.
Brubaker, Rogers. *Citizenship and Nationhood in France and Germany.* Cambridge: Harvard University Press, 1992.
Buescu, Mircea. *Evolução económica do Brasil.* 2d ed. Rio de Janeiro: APEC Editora, 1974.
————. *História administrativa do Brasil.* Vol. 13, *Organização e administração do Ministério da Fazenda no Império.* Brasilia: FUNCEP, 1984.
Buisson, Inge. "El ejército libertador y la formación del estado boliviano, 1825–1828." In Inge Buisson, Günter Kahle, Hans-Joachim König, and Horst Pietschmann, eds., *Problemas de la formación del estado y de la nación en Hispanoamérica.* Special issue of *Lateinamerikanische Forschung* 13 (1984).
Buisson, Inge, Günter Kahle, Hans-Joachim König, and Horst Pietschmann, eds. *Problemas de la formación del estado y de la nación en Hispanoamérica.* Special issue of *Lateinamerikanische Forschung* 13 (1984).
Bullock, Brad, and Glenn Firebaugh. "Guns and Butter? The Effect of Military on Economic and Social Development in the Third World." *Journal of Political and Military Sociology* 18, no. 2 (1990): 231–66.
Bulmer-Thomas, Victor. *The Economic History of Latin America Since Independence.* Cambridge: Cambridge University Press, 1994.
Burgin, Miron. *The Economic Aspects of Argentine Federalism, 1820–1852.* Cambridge: Harvard University Press, 1946.
Burkholder, Mark, and Lyman Johnson. *Colonial Latin America.* New York: Oxford University Press, 1990.
Burns, E. Bradford. *Poverty of Progress.* Berkeley and Los Angeles: University of California Press, 1980.
Burr, Robert N. *By Reason or Force: Chile and the Balancing of Power in South America, 1830–1905.* Berkeley and Los Angeles: University of California Press, 1965.
Bushnell, David. *The Making of Modern Colombia.* Berkeley and Los Angeles: University of California Press, 1993.
————. "Postal Images of Argentine *Proceres:* A Look at Selective Myth Making." *Studies in Latin American Popular Culture* 1 (1982): 91–105.
————. "Regeneración filatélica." *Revista de Estudios Colombianos* 2 (1987): 27–31.
————. *The Santander Regime in Gran Colombia.* Newark: University of Delaware Press, 1954.

Bushnell, David, and Neill Macaulay. *The Emergence of Latin America in the Nineteenth Century.* New York: Oxford University Press, 1988.

Bustamante, Fernando. *Revisión histórica comparativa del temprano desarollo institucional del as FFAA. del Ecuador y Colombia.* Santiago, Chile: Documento de Trabajo programa FLACSO-Chile, no. 395, 1989.

Cacua Prada, Antonio. "Proceso de socialización en los programas oficiales." *Boletín de historia y antiguedades* (Bogotá) 72, no. 750 (1985): 617–32.

Calhoun, Craig. "Nationalism and Ethnicity." *Annual Review of Sociology* 19 (1993): 211–38.

Callaghy, Thomas. *The State-Society Struggle.* New York: Columbia University Press, 1984.

Calvert, Peter. *The International Politics of Latin America.* Manchester: Manchester University Press, 1994.

Camp, Roderic A. *Generals in the Palacio: The Military in Modern Mexico.* New York: Oxford University Press, 1992.

Campbell, John L. "The State and Fiscal Sociology." *Annual Review of Sociology* 19 (1993): 163–85.

Campbell, Leon G. "The Army of Peru and the Túpac Amaru Revolt: 1780–1783." *Hispanic American Historical Review* 56, no. 1 (1976): 31–57.

Canak, William. "The Peripheral State Debate: State Capitalist and Bureaucratic-Authoritarian Regimes in Latin America." *Latin American Research Review* 19, no. 1 (1984): 3–36.

Cardoso, Ciro, ed. *México en el siglo XIX: Historia económica y de la estructura social.* 2d ed. Mexico City: Nueva Imagen, 1992.

Cardoso, Fernando Henrique, and Enzo Faletto. *Dependency and Development in Latin America.* Berkeley and Los Angeles: University of California Press, 1979.

Cariola, Carmen, and Osvaldo Sunkel. *Un siglo de historia económica de Chile, 1830–1930.* Santiago, Chile: Editorial Universitaria, 1991.

Carmagnani, Marcello. "Finanzas y estado en México, 1820–1880." *Ibero-Amerikanisches Archiv* 9, no. 3–4 (1983): 279–314.

———. "Territorialidad y federalismo en la formación del estado mexicano." In Inge Buisson, Günter Kahle, Hans-Joachim König, and Horst Pietschmann, eds., *Problemas de la formación del estado y de la nación en Hispanoamérica.* Special issue of *Lateinamerikanische Forschung* 13 (1984).

Carrera Damas, Germán. "El nacionalismo latinoamericano en perspectiva histórica." *Revista Mexicana de Sociología* 38, no. 4 (1976): 783–91.

———. "Simón Bolívar, el culto heroico y la nación." *Hispanic American Historical Review* 63, no. 1 (1983): 107–45.

Carvalho, José Maria. *A construção da ordem: A elite política imperial.* Brasilia: Editora da Universidade de Brasilia, 1980.

Carvalho, José Murillo de. "Political Elites and State-Building: The Case of Nineteenth Century Brazil." *Comparative Studies in Society and History* 24, no. 3 (1982): 378–99.

Casa da Moeda do Brasil. *290 anos de historia, 1694–1984*. Rio de Janeiro: Casa da Moeda, 1984.

Casanova, Rosa. "1861–1876." In Eloísa Uribe, ed., *Y todo . . . por una nación*. Mexico City: INAH, 1987.

Casaretto, I. *Estatuaria urbana de Montevideo*. Montevideo: n.p., 1948.

Castellanos, Alfredo. *Nomenclatura de Montevideo*. Montevideo: Intendencia Municipal de Montevideo, 1977.

———. *Uruguay: Monumentos históricos y arqueológicos*. Mexico City: Instituto Panamericano de Geografía y Historia, no. 337, 1974.

Castro Carreira, Liberato de. *História financiera e orcamentária do Império no Brasil*. 2 vols. 1889; Brasilia: Fundação Casa de Rui Barbosa, 1980.

Cavalcanti, A. "Finances." In F. J. de Santa-Anna Nery, ed., *Le Bresil en 1889*. Paris: Librairie Charles Delagrave, 1989.

Cavarozzi, Marcelo. "Beyond Transitions to Democracy in Latin America." *Journal of Latin American Studies* 24, no. 3 (1993): 665–84.

Centeno, Miguel Angel. "Blood and Debt: War and Taxation in Nineteenth-Century Latin America." *American Journal of Sociology* 102, no. 6 (1997): 1565–1605.

———. "The Peaceful Continent: War in Latin America." In Gladys Varona-Lacey and Julio López-Arias, eds., *Latin America: A Panorama*. New York: Peter Lang, 1998.

———. "War and Memory: Symbols of State Nationalism in Latin America." *European Review of Latin American and Caribbean Studies* 66 (July 1999): 75–106.

Centeno, Miguel Angel, and Fernando López-Alves, eds. *The Other Mirror: Grand Theory Through the Lens of Latin America*. Princeton: Princeton University Press, 2000.

Cerrutti, Mario. *Economía de guerra y poder regional en el siglo XIX*. Monterey: Archivo General del Estado de Nuevo León, 1983.

Cerulo, Karen A. *Identity Designs: The Sights and Sounds of a Nation*. New Brunswick: Rutgers University Press, 1995.

Chavez, Alicia Hernández. "Origen y ocaso del ejército porfiriano." *Historia Mexicana* 9, no. 1 (1989): 257–98.

Chiavenatto, Julio José. *Genocídio americano: A Guerra do Paraguai*. São Paulo: Editora Brasiliense, 1987.

Child, Jack. *Geopolitics and Conflict in South America*. New York: Praeger, 1985.

Clark, Priscilla Parkhurst. *Literary France: The Making of a Culture*. Berkeley and Los Angeles: University of California Press, 1987.

Clissold, Stephen, and Alistair Hennessy. "Territorial Disputes." In Claudio Véliz, ed., *Latin America and the Caribbean*. London: Blond, 1968.

Coatsworth, John H. "Obstacles to Growth in Nineteenth Century Mexico." *American Historical Review* 83, no. 1 (1978): 80–100.

Cohen, Eliot A. *Citizens and Soldiers: The Dilemmas of Military Service*. Ithaca: Cornell University Press, 1985.

Cohen, Saul B., and Nurit Kliot. "Israel's Place-Names as Reflection of Continuity and Change in Nation Building." *Names* 29, no. 3 (1981): 227–48.

Colburn, Forrest D. "Crime in Latin America." *Dissent* 45, no. 3 (1998): 27–31.
Colley, Linda. *Britons: Forging the Nation, 1707–1837.* New Haven: Yale University Press, 1992.
———. "Whose Nation? Class and National Consciousness in Britain, 1750–1830." *Past and Present* 113 (1986): 97–117.
Collier, Ruth Berins, and David Collier. *Shaping the Political Arena: Critical Junctures, the Labor Movement, and Regime Dynamics in Latin America.* Princeton: Princeton University Press, 1991.
Collier, Simon. *Ideas and Politics of Chilean Independence.* Cambridge: Cambridge University Press, 1969.
———. "Nationality, Nationalism, and Supranationalism in the Writings of Simón Bolívar." *Hispanic American Historical Review* 63, no. 1 (1983): 37–64.
Collier, Simon, and William F. Sater. *A History of Chile, 1808–1994.* Cambridge: Cambridge University Press, 1996.
Collins, Randall. *Macrohistory: Essays in Sociology of the Long Run.* Stanford: Stanford University Press, 1999.
Comaroff, John L., and Paul C. Stern. "New Perspectives on Nationalism and War." *Theory and Society* 23, no. 1 (1994): 35–46.
Committee on Latin American Studies, University of California, Los Angeles. *Statistical Abstract of Latin America* (SALA). Vol. 35. Los Angeles: University of California, Los Angeles, 1997.
Corbett, Charles D. *The Latin American Military as a Socio-Political Force: Case Studies of Bolivia and Argentina.* Miami: Center for Advanced International Studies, University of Miami, 1972.
Cordero, Fernando. "Chile, siglo XIX: De la milicia a la Guardia Cívica." *Ibero-Americana, Nordic Journal of Latin American Studies* 22, no. 1 (1992): 83–97.
Coronil, Fernando. *The Magical State: Nature, Money, and Modernity in Venezuela.* Chicago: University of Chicago Press, 1997.
Corrigan, Philip, and Derek Sayer. *The Great Arch: English State Formation as Cultural Revolution.* Oxford: Oxford University Press, 1985.
Cortazar, Roberto. *Monumentos, estatuas, bustos, medallones y placas conmemorativas.* Bogotá: Editorial Selecta, 1938.
Cortés Conde, Roberto. *Dinero, deuda y crisis: Evolución fiscal y monetaria en la Argentina.* Buenos Aires: Editorial Sudamérica, 1989.
Corvisier, André. *Armies and Societies in Europe, 1492–1789.* Bloomington: Indiana University Press, 1976.
Cosío Villegas, Daniel. *A Compact History of Mexico.* Los Angeles: Media Production, 1974.
Cowley, Robert, and Geoffrey Parker, eds. *The Reader's Companion to Military History.* Boston: Houghton Mifflin Company, 1996.
Cubillas Soriano, Margarita. *Guía histórica biográfica e ilustrada de los monumentos de Lima metropolitana.* Lima: n.p., 1993.
Curl, James Stevens. *A Celebration of Death.* London: Constable, 1980.
Cutulo, Vicente O. *Buenos Aires: Historia de las calles y sus nombres.* 2 vols. Buenos Aires: Editorial Elche, 1988.

D.A.N.E. *Boletin Mensual de Estadística,* nos. 257–58 (December 1972–January 1973): 176–90.

Dalence, José M. *Bosquejo estadístico de Bolivia.* 1851; La Paz: Editorial Universitaria, 1975.

David, Lance E., and John Legler. "Government in the American Economy, 1815–1902: A Quantitative Study." *The Journal of Economic History* 26, no. 4 (1966): 514–52.

De la Torre Villar, Ernesto. "El origen del estado mexicano." In Inge Buisson, Günter Kahle, Hans-Joachim König, and Horst Pietschmann, eds., *Problemas de la formación del estado y de la nación en Hispanoamérica.* Special issue of *Lateinamerikanische Forschung* 13 (1984).

Deas, Malcom. "The Fiscal Problems of Nineteenth-Century Colombia." *Journal of Latin American Studies* 14, no. 2 (1982): 287–328.

———. "The Man on Foot: Conscription and the Nation-State in Nineteenth-Century Latin America." Paper presented at "Conference on Nation State in Latin America," University of London, 1999.

DePalo, William. Essay on Mexican army. University of New Mexico. Featured in http://www.pbs.org/kera/usmexicanwar/.June 2000.

Deutsch, Sandra Mcgee. *Las Derechas: The Extreme Right in Argentina, Brazil, and Chile, 1890–1939.* Stanford: Stanford University Press, 1999.

Diario de Noticias. *Monumentos da Cidade.* Rio de Janeiro: Diario de Notícias, 1946.

Díaz Arguedas, Julio. *Fastos militares de Bolivia.* 3 vols. La Paz: Editorial Don Bosco, 1971.

Díaz Ruiz, Ignacio. "El nacionalismo en la literatura latinoamericana." In Ignacio Sosa et al., eds., *El nacionalismo en América Latina.* Mexico City: UNAM, 1984.

Diehl, Paul, and Gary Goertz. "Territorial Changes and Militarized Conflicts." *Journal of Conflict Resolution* 32, no. 1 (1988): 103–22.

Dietz, Henry A., and Karl Schmitt. "Militarization in Latin America: For What? And Why?" *Inter-American and Economic Affairs* 38, no. 1 (1984) :44–64.

Dirección de Contabilidad (Chile). *Resumen de la hacienda pública de Chile, 1833–1914.* London: Spottiswoode, 1914.

Dixon, William J., and Bruce E. Moon. "The Military Burden and Basic Human Needs." *Journal of Conflict Resolution* 30, no. 3 (1986): 660–84.

Dobyns, Henry F., and Paul L. Doughty. *Peru: A Cultural History.* New York: Oxford University Press, 1976.

Dodds, Klaus-John. "Geography, Identity, and the Creation of the Argentine State." *Bulletin of Latin American Research* 12, no. 3 (1993): 311–31.

Domínguez, Jorge I. "International War and Government Militarization: The Military—a Case Study." In Linda Alexander Rodríguez, ed., *Rank and Privilege: The Military and Society in Latin America.* Wilmington, Del.: Scholarly Resources, 1994.

Downing, Brian Michael. *The Military Revolution and Political Change: Origins of Democracy and Autocracy in Early Modern Europe.* Princeton: Princeton University Press, 1992.

Duffy, Michael. Introduction to Michael Duffy, ed., *The Military Revolution and the State*. Exeter: Exeter Studies in History, University of Exeter, 1980.

Duncan Baretta, Silvio R., and John Markoff. "Civilization and Barbarism: Cattle Frontiers in Latin America." *Comparative Studies in Society and History* 20 (1978): 587–620.

Duncan, Robert H. "Political Legitimation and Maximilian's Second Empire in Mexico, 1864–1867." *Mexican Studies/Estudios Mexicanos* 12, no. 1 (1996): 27–66.

Dunkerley, James. *Power in the Isthmus: A Political History of Modern Central America*. London: Verso, 1988.

———. *Rebellion in the Veins: Political Struggle in Bolivia, 1952–82*. London: Verso, 1984.

Dupuy, R. Ernest, and Trevor N. Dupuy. *The Encyclopedia of Military History*. New York: Harper & Row, 1970.

Earle, Rebecca, ed. *Rumours of Wars: Civil Conflict in Nineteenth-Century Latin America*. London: Institute of Latin American Studies, 2000.

Ebel, Roland H., Raymond Taras, and James D. Cochrane. *Political Culture and Foreign Policy in Latin America*. New York: State University of New York Press, 1991.

Economic Commission for Latin America and the Caribbean (ECLAC). 1998. *The Fiscal Covenant*. Santiago: ECLAC.

———. "Public Insecurity on the Rise." *South America Report* 4 (1999): 11.

Ehrenreich, Barbara. *Blood Rites: Origins and History of the Passions of War*. New York: Metropolitan Books, 1997.

Eley, Geoff, and Ronald Grigor Suny. Introduction to Geoff Eley and Ronald Grigor Suny, eds., *Becoming National*. Oxford: Oxford University Press, 1996.

English, Adrian J. *Armed Forces of Latin America: Their Histories, Development, Present Strength, and Military Potential*. London: Jane's Sentinel Publications, 1984.

Ertman, Thomas. *Birth of the Leviathan: Building States and Regimes in Medieval and Early Modern Europe*. New York: Cambridge University Press, 1997.

Escude, Carlos. "Argentine Territorial Nationalism." *Journal of Latin American Studies* 20, no. 1 (1988): 139–65.

Estado Mayor General Ejército de Chile. *Historia del Ejército de Chile*. Santiago, Chile: Estado Mayor General, 1980–1986.

Evans, Peter. "Predatory, Developmental, and Other Apparatuses: A Comparative Political Economy Perspective on the Third World State." *Sociological Forum* 4, no. 4 (1989): 561–87.

Evans, Peter B., and James E. Rauch. "Bureaucracy and Growth: A Cross-National Analysis of the Effects of 'Weberian' State Structures on Economic Growth." *American Sociological Review* 64, no. 5 (1999): 748–65.

Evans, Peter B., Dietrich Rueschemeyer, and Theda Skocpol, eds. *Bringing the State Back In*. Cambridge: Cambridge University Press, 1985.

Faletto, Enzo. "The Specificity of the Latin American State." *CEPAL Review*, no. 38 (1989): 69–87.

Farcau, Bruce W. *The Chaco War: Bolivia and Paraguay, 1932–1935.* Westport, Conn.: Praeger, 1996.

Feijoó, María del Carmen, and Hilda Sabato. "Las mujeres frente al servicio militar: Una obligación cuestionada." Paper presented at the conference "La mujer en el mundo de hoy," Buenos Aires, 1982.

Ferns, H. S. *The Argentine Republic, 1516–1971.* New York: Barnes & Noble, 1973.

———. "Britain's Informal Empire in Argentina, 1806–1914." *Past and Present* 4 (November 1953): 60–75.

Ferrer, Ada. *Insurgent Cuba: Race, Nation, and Revolution, 1868–1898.* Chapel Hill: University of North Carolina Press, 1999.

Ferrer, Aldo. *The Argentine Economy.* Berkeley and Los Angeles: University of California Press, 1967.

Ferrer, José. "The Armed Forces in Argentine Politics to 1930." Ph.D. diss., Department of History, University of New Mexico, 1965.

Fine, Gary Alan. "Small Groups and Culture Creation: The Idioculture of Little League Baseball Teams." *American Sociological Review* 44 (1979): 733–45.

Finer, Samuel E. *The History of Government from the Earliest Times.* New York: Oxford University Press, 1997.

———. "State and Nation Building in Europe: The Role of the Military." In Charles Tilly, ed., *The Formation of National States in Western Europe.* Princeton: Princeton University Press, 1975.

Fisher, John Robert. "La formación del estado peruano 1808–1824, y Simón Bolívar." In Inge Buisson, Günter Kahle, Hans-Joachim König, and Horst Pietschmann, eds., *Problemas de la formación del estado y de la nación en Hispanoamérica.* Special issue of *Lateinamerikanische Forschung* 13 (1984).

———. *Government and Society in Colonial Peru: The Intendant System, 1784–1814.* London: University of London, Athlone Press, 1970.

Fishlow, Albert. "The Latin American State." *Journal of Economic Perspectives* 4, no. 3 (1990): 61–74.

Fligstein, Neil. "Who Served in the Military, 1940–1973." *Armed Forces and Society* 6, no. 2 (1980): 297–312.

Flora, Peter. *State, Economy, and Society in Western Europe, 1815–1975.* Chicago: St. James Press, 1987.

Fontainha, Alfonso. *Historia dos monumentos do Rio de Janeiro.* Rio de Janeiro: n.p., 1963.

Foreign Broadcast Information Service. LAT-96-207. Washington, D.C.: Central Intelligence Group, 1996.

Forero, Manuel José. "Nacionalismo y filatelia." *Arco* (Bogotá) 167 (1974): 77–80.

Friedman, Douglas. *The State and Underdevelopment in Spanish America: The Political Roots of Dependency in Peru and Argentina.* Boulder, Colo.: Westview, 1984.

Frigerio, José Oscar. "Con sangre de negros se edificó nuestra independencia." *Todo es historia* (Buenos Aires) 250 (April 1988): 48–69.

Fuentes Saavedra, Claudio. "Chile-Argentina: El proceso de construir confianza." Working paper no. 30, Universidad Torcuato di Tella, Buenos Aires, 1996.

Gallo, Carmenza. *Taxes and State Power: Political Instability in Bolivia, 1900–1950.* Philadelphia: Temple University Press, 1991.

García, Rubén. *El servicio militar obligatorio.* Mexico City: n.p., 1940.

Garrett, James L. "The Beagle Channel Dispute: Confrontation and Negotiation in the Southern Cone." *Journal of Interamerican Studies and World Affairs* 2, no. 3 (1985): 81–109.

Gasio, Guillermo, and María C. San Román. *La conquista del progreso.* Buenos Aires: Ediciones La Bastilla, 1977.

Gasparini, Graziano, and Juan Pedro Posani. *Caracas a traves de su arquitectura.* Caracas: Fundación Fina Gómez, 1969.

Geddes, Barbara. *Politician's Dilemma: Building State Capacity in Latin America.* Berkeley and Los Angeles: University of California Press, 1994.

Gellner, Ernst. *Nations and Nationalism.* Ithaca: Cornell University Press, 1987.

George, Larry N. "Realism and Internationalism in the Gulf of Venezuela." *Journal of Interamerican and World Affairs* 30, no. 4 (1989): 116–38.

Gereffi, Gary, and Stephanie Fonda. "Regional Paths of Development." *Annual Review of Sociology* 18 (1992): 418–48.

Giddens, Anthony. *The Nation-State and Violence.* Berkeley and Los Angeles: University of California Press, 1985.

Gillis, John R., ed. *Commemorations: The Politics of National Identity.* Princeton: Princeton University Press, 1994.

Gilpin, Robert. *War and Change in World Politics.* New York: Cambridge University Press, 1981.

Gochman, Charles, and Zeev Maoz. "Militarized Disputes, 1816–1976." *Journal of Conflict Resolution* 28, no. 4 (1984): 585–615.

Gomes, Gustavo Maria. *The Roots of State Intervention in the Brazilian Economy.* New York: Praeger, 1986.

Gómez E., Nelson. *Guía informativa de Quito.* Quito: Ediguias, n.d.

Gootenberg, Paul. *Between Silver and Guano: Commercial Policy and the State in Postindependence Peru.* Princeton: Princeton University Press, 1989.

———. *Imagining Development: Economic Ideas in Peru's Fictitious Prosperity of Guano, 1840–1880.* Berkeley and Los Angeles: University of California Press, 1993.

Gorostegui de Torres, Haydée. *Historia Argentina.* Vol. 4, *La organización nacional.* Buenos Aires: Editorial Paidos, 1972.

Gorski, Philip S. "Birth of the Leviathan: Building States and Regimes in Medieval and Early Modern Europe." *Contemporary Sociology* 27, no. 2 (1998): 186–89.

Goyer, Doreen S., and Eliane Domschke. *The Handbook of National Population Censuses : Latin America and the Caribbean, North America, and Oceania.* Westport, Conn.: Greenwood Press, 1983.

Grabendorff, Wolf. "Interstate Conflict Behavior and Regional Potential for Conflict in Latin America." *Journal of Interamerican Studies and World Affairs* 24, no. 3 (1982): 267–94.

Graham, Richard. *Patronage and Politics in Nineteenth-Century Brazil.* Stanford: Stanford University Press, 1990.

————. "State and Society in Brazil, 1822–1930." *Latin American Research Review*, 22, no. 3 (1987): 223–36.

Greenfeld, Liah. *Nationalism: Five Roads to Modernity.* Cambridge: Harvard University Press, 1992.

Grieshaber, Erwin P. "Survival of Indian Communities in Nineteenth Century Bolivia." Ph.D. diss., University of North Carolina, Chapel Hill, 1977.

Gurr, Ted R. "Polity II: Political Structures and Regime Change, 1800–1986." ICPSR study no. 09263, University of Michigan, Ann Arbor, 1992.

————, ed. *Handbook of Political Conflict.* New York: Free Press, 1980.

Gurr, Ted R., Keith Jaggers, and Will H. Moore. "The Transformation of the Western State: The Growth of Democracy, Autocracy, and State Power Since 1800." *Studies in Comparative International Development* 25 (1990): 73–108.

Gutiérrez, Ramón. "La arquitectura como documento: Histórico y valor simbólico." *Boletín de la Academia Nacional de la Historia* 64–65 (1992): 83–111.

Hale, Charles A. *Mexican Liberalism in the Age of Mora, 1821–1853.* New Haven: Yale University Press, 1968.

————. "The War with the United States and the Crisis in Mexican Thought." *The Americas* 14 (1957): 153–73.

Hall, John, ed. *States in History.* New York: Basil Blackwell, 1986.

Halperín-Donghi, Tulio. *The Aftermath of Revolution in Latin America.* New York: Harper Torchbooks, 1973.

————. *The Contemporary History of Latin America.* Durham: Duke University Press, 1993.

————. *Guerra y finanzas en los orígines del estado argentino, 1791–1850.* Buenos Aires: Editorial de Belgrano, 1982.

————. *Historia Argentina: De la revolución de independencia a la confederación rosista.* Buenos Aires: Paidós, 1972.

————. *Politics, Economics, and Society in Argentina in the Revolutionary Period.* Cambridge: Cambridge University Press, 1975.

Hamilton, Nora. *The Limits of State Autonomy: Post-Revolutionary Mexico.* Princeton: Princeton University Press, 1982.

Hamnett, Brian. "The Economic and Social Dimension of the Revolution of Independence, 1800–1824." *Iberoamerikanisches Archiv* 6 (1980): 1–27.

————. *Roots of Insurgency: Mexican Regions, 1750–1824.* Cambridge: Cambridge University Press, 1986.

Hanson, Lawrence Douglas Taylor. "Voluntarios extranjeros en los ejércitos liberales mexicanos, 1854–1867." *Historia Mexicana* 37, no. 2 (1987): 205–37.

Hargrove, June. "Les statues de Paris." In Pierre Nora, ed., *Les lieux de memoire II: La nation.* Pt. 3. Paris: Gallimard, 1986.

Haring, C. H. *Empire in Brazil: A New World Experiment with Monarchy.* New York: Norton, 1958.

Harvey, David. "Monument and Myth." *Annals of the Association of American Geographers* 69, no. 3 (1979): 362–81.

Hayes, Carlton J. H. *Essays on Nationalism.* New York: Macmillan, 1928.

Helleiner, Eric. "National Currencies and National Identities." *American Behavioral Scientist* 41, no. 10 (August 1998): 1409–36.

Helman, Osvaldo Manuel, and Juan Esteban Serchio. *Las naciones americanas y sus símbolos.* Buenos Aires: n.p., 1989.

Hensel, Paul R. "One Thing Leads to Another: Recurrent Militarized Disputes in Latin America, 1816–1986." *Journal of Peace Research* 31, no. 3 (1994): 281–97.

Herbst, Jeffrey. *States and Power in Africa: Comparative Lessons in Authority and Control.* Princeton: Princeton University Press, Forthcoming.

Hill, Christopher. "History and Patriotism." In Raphael Samuel, ed., *Patriotism: The Making and Unmaking of British National Identity.* Vol. 1. London: Routledge, 1987.

Hintze, Otto. "Military Organization and the Organization of Violence." In *The Historical Essays of Otto Hintze.* Edited by Felix Gilbert. New York: Oxford, 1975.

Hirschman, Albert. *Development Projects Observed.* Washington, D.C.: Brookings Institution, 1967.

Hobsbawm, Eric J. *Nations and Nationalism Since 1780.* London: Verso, 1991.

Holsti, Kalevi J. *The State, War, and the State of War.* Cambridge: Cambridge University Press, 1996.

Hooks, Gregory, and Gregory McLauchlan. "The Institutional Foundation of War-making: Three Eras of U.S. Warmaking, 1939–1989." *Theory and Society* 21 (1992): 757–88.

Howard, Michael. *The Causes of War.* Cambridge: Harvard University Press, 1984.

———. *The Lessons of History.* New Haven: Yale University Press, 1991.

———. "Total War in the Twentieth Century: Participation and Consensus in the Second World War." In Brian Bond and Ian Roy, eds., *War and Society: A Yearbook of Military History.* Vol. 1. New York: Holmes and Meier, 1975.

———. *War in European History.* Oxford: Oxford University Press, 1976.

Huber, Evelynne. "Assessments of State Strength." In Peter H. Smith, ed., *Latin America in Comparative Perspective: New Approaches to Methods and Analysis.* Boulder: Westview Press, 1995.

Huber Stephens, Evelyne, and John Stephens. *Democratic Socialism in Jamaica: The Political Movement and Social Transformation in Dependent Capitalism.* London: Macmillan, 1986.

Huizinga, Johan. "The Idea of History." In *Men and Ideas: History, the Middle Ages, the Renaissance.* Translated by James S. Holmes and Hans van Marle. New York: Meridian Books, 1959.

———. "Patriotism and Nationalism in European History." In Johan Huizinga, *Men and Ideas.* Princeton: Princeton University Press, 1959.

Hunt, Shane J. "Growth and Guano in Nineteenth Century Peru." Discussion paper 34, Woodrow Wilson School, Research Program in Economic Development, Princeton, 1973.

Huntington, Samuel P. *Political Order in Changing Societies.* New Haven: Yale University Press, 1968.

———. *The Soldier and the State: The Theory and Politics of Civil-Military Relations*. New York: Vintage Books, 1957.

Hurrell, Andrew. "An Emerging Security Community in South America?" 1998. Mimeographed.

———. "Security in Latin America." *International Affairs* 74 (3) 1998: 529–46.

Ignatieff, Michael. "Soviet War Memorials." *History Workshop* 17 (1984): 157–63.

Inglis, K. S. "Ceremonies in a Capital Landscape: Scenes in the Making of Canberra." *Daedalus* 114, no. 1 (1985): 85–125.

International Institute of Strategic Studies. http://www.isn.ethz.ch/iiss/mb10.htm.

Ireland, Gordon. *Boundaries, Possessions, and Conflicts in South America*. Cambridge: Harvard University Press, 1938.

Ivonne, Pini. "La reacción nacionalista en América Latina." In *El nacionalismo en el arte*. Bogotá: Universidad Nacional de Colombia, Facultad de Artes, Instituto de Investigaciones Estéticas, n.d.

Jackson, Robert H., and Carl G. Rosberg. "Why Africa's Weak States Persist: The Empirical and the Judicial in Statehood." *World Politics* 35 (1982): 1–24.

Jane's Information Group. *Jane's Sentinel, South America: Security Assesment*. Alexandria, Va.: Jane's Information Group, 1996.

Janowitz, Morris. "The All Volunteer Military as a 'Sociopolitical' Problem." *Social Problems* 22, no. 3 (1975): 432–49.

———. "Military Institutions and Citizenship in Western Societies." *Armed Forces and Society* 2, no. 2 (1976): 185–204.

Janson, H. W. *The Rise and Fall of the Public Monument*. New Orleans: Tulane University Graduate School, 1976.

Jaramillo Uribe, Jaime. "Nación y región en los orígenes del estado nacional de Colombia." In Inge Buisson, Günter Kahle, Hans-Joachim König, and Horst Pietschmann, eds., *Problemas de la formación del estado y de la nación en Hispanoamérica*. Special issue of *Lateinamerikanische Forschung* 13 (1984).

Joenniemi, Pertti. "The Socio-Politics of Conscription." *Current Research on Peace and Violence* (Helsinki), 8 (3–4) (1985): 137–42.

Joffily, Geraldo Irenêo. "O Quebra-Quilo: A revolta dos matutos contra os doutores (1874)." *Revista de Historia* 54, no. 107 (1976): 69–145.

Jones, Ellen, and Fred W. Grupp. "Political Socialization in the Soviet Military." *Armed Forces and Society* 8, no. 2 (1982): 355–88.

Joseph, Gilbert M., and Daniel Nugent, eds. *Everyday Forms of State Formation*. Durham: Duke University Press, 1994.

Jurado Noboa, Fernando. *Las calles de Quito*. Quito: Ediciones del Banco Central del Ecuador, 1989.

Justo, Liborio. *Pampas y lanzas*. Buenos Aires: Editorial Palestra, 1962.

Kagan, Donald. *On the Origins of War*. New York: Doubleday, 1995.

Kaiser, David. *Politics and War: European Conflict from Philip II to Hitler*. Cambridge: Harvard University Press, 1990.

Kallsen, Osvaldo. *Asunción y sus calles: Antecedents históricos*. Asunción: n.p., 1974.

Karsten, Peter. "Militarization and Rationalization in the U.S." In John Gillis, ed.,

The Militarization of the Western World. New Brunswick: Rutgers University Press, 1989.

Kaye, G. D., D. A. Grant, and E. J. Emond. *Major Armed Conflict: A Compendium of Interstate and Intrastate Conflict, 1720 to 1985*. ORAE Report no. R 95. Ottowa, Canada: Department of National Defence, 1985.

Keegan, John. *A History of Warfare*. London: Hutchinson, 1993.

Keeley, Lawrence H. *War Before Civilization: The Myth of the Peaceful Savage*. New York: Oxford University Press, 1996.

Kelly, Philip. *Checkerboards and Shatterbelts: The Geopolitics of South America*. Austin: University of Texas Press, 1997.

Kelly, Philip, and Jack Child, eds. *Geopolitics of the Southern Cone and Antarctica*. Boulder, Colo.: Lynne Rienner, 1988.

Kennedy, Paul D. *The Rise and Fall of the Great Powers: Economic Change and Military Conflict from 1500 to 2000*. New York: Random House, 1987.

Kiernan, Victor G. "Chile from War to Revolution, 1879–1891." *History Workshop* 34 (1992): 72–91.

———. "Conscription and Society in Europe Before the War of 1914–1918." In M. R. D. Foot, ed., *War and Society*. London: Elek Books, 1973.

———. "Foreign Interests in the War of the Pacific." *Hispanic American Historical Review* 35 (1955): 150–53.

Kinsbruner, Jay. *Independence in Spanish America*. Albuquerque: University of New Mexico Press, 1994.

Kiser, Edgar, Kriss Drass, and William Brustein. "Rule, Autonomy, and War in Early Modern Europe." *International Studies Quarterly* 39, no. 1 (1995): 109–38.

Klein, Herbert. *Bolivia: The Evolution of a Multi-Ethnic Society*. New York: Oxford University Press, 1982.

Kling, Merle. "Taxes on the 'External' Sector: An Index of Political Behavior in Latin America?" *Midwest Journal of Political Science* 3, no. 2 (1959): 127–50.

Knight, Alan. *The Mexican Revolution*. 2 vols. New York: Cambridge University Press, 1986.

———. "Peasants into Patriots: Thoughts on the Making of the Mexican Nation." *Estudios Mexicanos/Mexican Studies* 10, no. 1 (1994): 135–61.

Knight, Franklin W. "The State of Sovereignty and the Sovereignty of States." In Alfred Stepan, ed., *Americas: New Interpretive Essays*. New York: Oxford University Press, 1992.

Kolinski, Charles. *Independence or Death: The Story of the Paraguayan War*. Gainesville: University Press of Florida, 1965.

Kossok, Manfred. "Revolución, estado y nación en la independencia." In Inge Buisson, Günter Kahle, Hans-Joachim König, and Horst Pietschmann, eds., *Problemas de la formación del estado y de la nación en Hispanoamérica*. Special issue of *Lateinamerikanische Forschung* 13 (1984).

Kraay, Hendrik. "As Terrifying as Unexpected: The Bahian Sabinada, 1837–1838." *Hispanic American Historical Review* 72, no. 4 (1992): 501–27.

Krebs, Ricardo. "Orígenes de la conciencia nacional chilena." In Inge Buisson, Günter Kahle, Hans-Joachim König, and Horst Pietschmann, eds., *Problemas de la formación del estado y de la nación en Hispanoamérica*. Special issue of *Lateinamerikanische Forschung* 13 (1984).

Lachman, Richard. "Elite Conflict and State Formation in Sixteenth and Seventeenth Century England and France." *American Sociological Review* 54, no. 2 (1989): 141–62.

Langley, Lester D. *The Americas in the Age of Revolution, 1750–1850*. New Haven: Yale University Press, 1993.

Lecuna, Vicente. *Bolívar y el arte militar*. New York: Colonial Press, 1955.

Leff, Nathaniel. *Underdevelopment and Development in Brazil*. 2 vols. London: George Allen & Unwin, 1982.

Lehnus, Donald J. *Angels to Zeppelins: A Guide to the Persons, Objects, Topics, and Themes on United States Postage Stamps 1847–1980*. Westport, Conn.: Greenwood Press, 1982.

Levi, Margaret. *Of Rule and Revenue*. Berkeley and Los Angeles: University of California Press, 1988.

Levinger, Esther. "Socialist-Zionist Ideology in Israeli War Memorials of the 1950s." *Journal of Contemporary History* 28 (1993): 715–46.

Levy, Jack S. "The Causes of War and the Conditions of Peace." *Annual Review of Political Science* 1 (1998): 139–66.

———. *War and the Modern Great Power System*. Lexington: University Press of Kentucky, 1983.

Levy, James R. "The Development and Use of the Heroic Image of José de San Martín: 1840–1900." Ph.D. diss., Department of History, University of Pennsylvania, 1964.

Lieuwen, Edwin. "Depoliticization of the Mexican Revolutionary Army, 1915–1940." In David Ronfeldt, ed., *The Modern Mexican Military: A Reassessment*. Monograph Series , no. 15. La Jolla, Calif.: Center for U.S. Mexicana Studies, 1984.

Little, Walter. "International Conflict in Latin America." *International Affairs* 63, no. 4 (1987): 589–602.

Llanes, Ricardo. *Antiguas plazas de la Ciudad de Buenos Aires*. Buenos Aires: Municipalidad de Buenos Aires, 1977.

Lofstrom, William. "Attempted Economic Reform and Innovation in Bolivia Under Antonio José de Sucre, 1825–1828." *Hispanic American Historical Review* 50, no. 2 (1970): 279–99.

———. "From Colony to Republic: A Case Study of Bureaucratic Change." *Journal of Latin American Studies* 5, no. 2 (1973): 177–97.

Londoño, Juan Luis, and Rodrigo Guerrero. "Violencia en América Latina: Epidemiología y costos." Working paper R-375, Interamerican Development Bank, Washington, D.C., August 1999.

Looney, Robert E., and Peter C. Fredericksen. "The Effect of Declining Military Influence on Defense Budgets in Latin America." *Armed Forces and Society* 26, no. 3 (2000): 437–49.

López Cámarra, Francisco. *La estructura económica y social de México en la época de la Reforma*. Mexico City: Siglo XXI, 1967.

López Gallo, Manuel. *Economía y política en la historia de México.* Mexico City: Grijalbo, 1967.

López-Alves, Fernando. *Between the Economy and the Polity in the River Plate: Uruguay, 1811–1890.* Research paper no. 33. London: Institute of Latin American Studies, 1993.

———. *State Formation and Democracy in Latin America, 1810–1900.* Durham: Duke University Press, 2000.

———. "Wars and the Formation of Political Parties in Uruguay, 1810–1851." In Eduardo Posada-Carbó, ed., *Wars, Parties and Nationalism: Essays on the Politics and Society of Nineteenth Century Latin America.* London: Institute of Latin American Studies, 1995.

Lorey, David. "The Revolutionary Festivals of Mexico." Unpublished manuscript, University of California, Los Angeles, 1995.

Love, Joseph L., and Nils Jacobsen, eds. *Guiding the Invisible Hand: Economic Liberalism and the State in Latin American History.* New York: Praeger, 1988.

Loveman, Brian. *Chile: The Legacy of Hispanic Capitalism.* 2d ed. 1979; New York: Oxford University Press, 1988.

———. *For la Patria: Politics and the Armed Forces in Latin America.* Wilmington, Del.: Scholarly Resources, 1999.

Loveman, Brian, and Thomas M. Davies, Jr., eds. *The Politics of Antipolitics: The Military in Latin America.* Wilmington, Del.: Scholarly Resources, 1997.

Luna, Félix. *Historia integral de la Argentina.* 10 vols. Buenos Aires: Editorial Planeta, 1995.

Lurz, Meinhold. *Kriegerdenkmäller in Deutschland.* 5 vols. Heidelberg: Esprint-Verlag, 1985.

Lynch, John. "Bolívar and the Caudillos." *Hispanic American Historical Review* 63 (1983): 3–35.

———. *Bourbon Spain, 1700–1808.* New York: Blackwell, 1989.

———. *Caudillos in Spanish America, 1800–1850.* Oxford: Clarendon Press, 1992.

———. "Los caudillos de la independencia." In Inge Buisson, Günter Kahle, Hans-Joachim König, and Horst Pietschmann, eds., *Problemas de la formación del estado y de la nación en Hispanoamérica.* Special issue of *Lateinamerikanische Forschung* 13 (1984).

———. *Spanish Colonial Administration, 1782–1810: The Indendant System in the Viceroyalty of the Río de la Plata.* London: University of London, Athlone Press, 1958.

———. *The Spanish-American Revolutions, 1808–1826.* New York: Norton, 1986.

McAlister, Lyle N. *The "Fuero militar" in New Spain, 1764–1800.* Gainesville: University Press of Florida, 1957.

McAlister, Lyle, Anthony Maingot, and Robert Potash, eds. *The Military in Latin American Sociopolitical Evolution: Four Case Studies.* Washington, D.C.: American Institutes for Research, Center for Research in Social Systems, 1970.

McArdle Kellerher, Catherine. "Mass Armies in the 1970's: The Debate in Europe." *Armed Forces and Society* 5, no. 1 (1978): 3–30.

McBeth, Michael C. "The Brazilian Army and Its Role in the Abdication of Pedro I." *Luso-Brazilian Review* 1, no. 1 (1978): 117–29.

McCann, Frank D. "The Nation at Arms: Obligatory Military Service During the Old Republic." In Dauril Alden and Warren Dean, eds., *Essays Concerning the Socioeconomic History of Brazil and Portuguese India*. Gainesville: University Press of Florida, 1977.

McGreevey, William Paul. *An Economic History of Colombia, 1845–1930*. Cambridge: Cambridge University Press, 1971.

McIntyre, Colin. *Monuments of War: How to Read a War Memorial*. London: Robert Hale, 1988.

McIntyre, David. "The Longest Peace: Why Are There So Few Interstate Wars in South America." Ph.D. diss., University of Chicago, 1995.

McLynn, F. J. "Consequences for Argentina of the War of the Triple Alliance, 1865–1870." *The Americas* 41, no. 1 (1984): 81–98.

McNeill, William H. "The Draft in the Light of History." In Martin Anderson, ed., *The Military Draft*. Palo Alto, Calif.: Hoover Institution Press, 1982.

———. *The Rise of the West: A History of the Human Community*. Chicago: University of Chicago Press, 1963.

Mahon, James. "Reforms in the Administration of Justice in Latin America: Overview and Emerging Trends." 1999. Mimeographed.

Mahoney, James. "Path Dependence in Historical Sociology." *Theory and Society* 29 (2000): 507–48.

Mainwaring, Max., ed. "Security and Civil-Military Relations in the New World Disorder: The Use of Armed Forces in the Americas." George Bush School of Government and Public Service and the U.S. Army War College, Carlisle, Pa., 1999. Mimeographed.

Maldonado Prieto, Carlos. "El caso de América Latina." http://www.geocities.com/CapitolHill/7109/6-amelat.html, 1998.

Mallon, Florencia E. *The Defense of Community in Peru's Central Highlands: Peasant Struggle and Capitalist Transition, 1860–1940*. Princeton: Princeton University Press, 1983.

———. "Nationalist and Antistate Coalitions in the War of the Pacific: Junín and Cajamarca, 1879–1902." In Steve J. Stern, ed., *Resistance, Rebellion, and Consciousness in the Andean Peasant World, Nineteenth to Twentieth Centuries*. Madison: University of Wisconsin Press, 1987.

———. *Peasant and Nation*. Berkeley and Los Angeles: University of California Press, 1994.

Malloy, James, ed. *Authoritarianism and Corporatism in Latin America*. Pittsburgh: University of Pittsburgh Press, 1977.

Mamalakis, Markos. *The Growth and Structure of the Chilean Economy: From Independence to Allende*. New Haven: Yale Economic Growth Center, 1976.

Mann, Michael. "Capitalism and Militarism." In Michael Mann, ed., *States, War, and Capitalism*. Oxford: Basil Blackwell, 1988.

———. "A Political Theory of Nationalism and Its Excesses." Working paper 1994/57, Centro de Estudios Avanzados en Ciencias Sociales, Instituto Juan March de Estudios e Investigaciones, Madrid, 1994.

———. *The Sources of Social Power.* Vol. 1. New York: Cambridge University Press, 1986.

———. *The Sources of Social Power.* Vol. 2. New York: Cambridge University Press, 1992.

———. *States, War, and Capitalism.* Oxford: Basil Blackwell, 1988.

Mares, David R. "Securing Peace in the Americas in the Next Decade." In Jorge Domínguez, ed., *The Future of Inter-American Relations.* New York: Routledge, 2000.

Marichal, Carlos. *A Century of Debt Crises in Latin America: From Independence to the Great Depression, 1820–1930.* Princeton: Princeton University Press, 1989.

Markham, Clements. *The War Between Peru and Chile, 1879–1882.* London: Sampson, Low, Marston, Searle and Rivington, 1883.

Markoff, John. *The Abolition of Feudalism: Peasants, Lords, and Legislators in the French Revolution.* University Park: Pennsylvania State University Press, 1996.

Marroqui, José María. *La Ciudad de México.* Mexico: Jesus Median Editor, 1969.

Martin, M. W. "Postal Gallery of Our History." *Américas* 25, no. 3 (1973): 10–12.

Martín González, Félix. "The Longer Peace in South America, 1935–1995." Ph.D. diss., Columbia University, 1997.

Martz, John D. "National Security and Politics: The Colombian-Venezuelan Border." *Journal of Interamerican and World Affairs* 30, no. 4 (1989): 139–70.

Marwick, Arthur. *War and Social Change in the Twentieth Century.* London: Macmillan, 1974.

Marx, Anthony W. *Making Race and Nation: A Comparison of South Africa, the United States, and Brazil.* New York: Cambridge University Press, 1998.

Masur, Gerhard. *Nationalism in Latin America.* New York: Macmillan, 1966.

———. *Simón Bolívar.* Albuquerque: University of New Mexico, 1969.

Mathias, Peter, and Patrick O'Brien. "Taxation in Britain and France, 1715–1810." *The Journal of European Economic History* 5, no. 3 (1976): 601–49.

Matossian, Mary. "Ideologies of Delayed Development." In John Hutchinson and Anthony D. Smith, eds., *Nationalism.* Oxford: Oxford University Press, 1994.

Mayo, James M. *War Memorials as Political Landscape: The American Experience and Beyond.* New York: Praeger, 1988.

———. "War Memorials as Political Memory." *Geographical Review* 78, no. 1 (1988): 62–76.

Mellors, Colin, and John McKean. "The Politics of Conscription in Western Europe." *West European Politics* 7 (1984): 25–42.

Merquior, J. G. "Patterns of State-Building in Brazil and Argentina." In John Hall, ed., *States in History.* New York: Basil Blackwell, 1986.

Merton, Seymour. *The New Historical Novel in Latin America.* Austin: University of Texas Press, 1994.

Mexico, Departamento de Turismo. 1964. *Guía de la Ciudad de México.* Mexico City: Departamento de Turismo.

Meyer, John W. "The World Polity and the Authority of the Nation-State." In Albert

Bergesen, ed., *Studies of the Modern World System*. New York: Academic Press, 1980.

Meyer, John W., John Boli, George Thomas, and Francisco O. Ramirez. "World Society and the Nation State." *American Journal of Sociology* 103, no. 1 (1997): 144–81.

Meznar, Joan E. "The Ranks of the Poor: Military Service and Social Differentiation in Northeast Brazil, 1830–1875." *Hispanic American Historical Review* 72, no. 3 (1992): 335–51.

Migdal, Joel S. *Strong Societies and Weak States: State-Society Relations and State Capabilities in the Third World*. Princeton: Princeton University Press, 1988.

Migdal, Joel S., Atul Kohli, and Vivienne Shue, eds. *State Power and Social Forces: Domination and Transformation in the Third World*. Cambridge: Cambridge University Press, 1994.

Milo, Daniel. "Le nom de rues." In Pierre Nora, ed., *Les lieux de memoire II: La nation*. Pt. 3. Paris: Gallimard, 1986.

Minguet, Charles. "El concepto de la nación, pueblo, estado y pátria en las generaciones de la independencia." In Jean-Rene Aymes et al., eds., *Recherches sur le monde hispanique au dix-neuvième siècle*. Lille: Université de Lille III, 1973.

———. "Mythes fondateurs chez Bolívar: Quelques aspects." *Cahiers des Ameriques Latines* 29–30 (1984): 135–42.

Ministerio de Defensa. *Libro de la Defensa Nacional*. Santiago: Ministerio de Defensa, 1997.

Misle, Carlos Eduardo. *Corazón, pulso y huella de Caracas: Plaza Mayor-Plaza Bolívar*. Caracas: Ediciones de la Secretaría General, 1967.

Mitchell, Brian R. *International Historical Statistics: The Americas*. Detroit: Gale Research, 1983.

Mommsen, Wolfang J. "The Varieties of the Nation State in Modern History." In Michael Mann, ed., *The Rise and Decline of the Nation State*. Oxford: Basil Blackwell, 1988.

Monguió, Luis. "Nationalism and Social Discontent as Reflected in Spanish-American Literature." *Annals of the American Academy of Political and Social Sciences* 334 (March 1961): 63–73.

Moore, Barrington. *Social Origins of Dictatorship and Democracy: Lord and Peasant in the Making of the Modern World*. Boston: Beacon Press, 1966.

Morales Díaz, Carlos. *Quién es quién en la nomenclatura de la Ciudad de México*. Mexico City: Imprenta Barrie, 1962.

Morales Moreno, Luis Gerardo. *Orígenes de la museología mexicana*. Mexico: Universidad Iberoamericana, 1994.

Moreno de Angel, Pilar. "La estatua del hombre de las leyes en la Plaza de Santander en Bogotá." *Boletín de Historia y Antiguedades* 738–39 (1982): 623–34.

Morgenthau, Hans J. *Politics Among Nations: The Struggle for Power and Peace*. 5th ed. New York: Knopf, 1978.

Mörner, Magnus. *The Andean Past: Land, Societies, and Conflicts*. New York: Columbia University Press, 1985.

Morris, Michael, and Victor Millan, eds. *Controlling Latin American Conflicts*. Boulder, Colo.: Westview Press, 1982.

Morse, Richard. "The Heritage of Latin America." In Louis Hartz, ed., *The Founding of New Societies: Studies in the History of the United States, Latin America, South Africa, Canada, and Australia.* New York: Harcourt, Brace & World, 1964.

———. "Theory of Spanish American Government." *Journal of the History of Ideas* 15, no. 1 (1954): 71–93.

Moskos, Charles C., and John Sibley Butler. *All That We Can Be: Black Leadership and Racial Integration the Army Way.* New York: Basic Books, 1996.

Mosse, George L. *Fallen Soldiers: Reshaping the Memory of the World Wars.* New York: Oxford University Press, 1990.

———. "National Cemeteries and National Revival: The Cult of Fallen Soldiers in Germany." *Journal of Contemporary History* 14, no. 1 (1979): 1–20.

———. *The Nationalization of the Masses.* Ithaca: Cornell University Press, 1975.

Moyssén, Xavier. "El nacionalismo y la arquitectura." *Anales del Instituto de Investigaciones Estéticas* (Mexico) 14, no. 55 (1986): 111–31.

Municipalidad de Asunción. *Monumentos, parques, jardines y plazas de la Ciudad de Asunción: Historia y comentarios.* Asunción: n.p., 1967.

Municipalidad de Asunción, Seccion de Catastro. *Datos de la ciudad: Nomenclatura barrios, avenidas, calles pasajes.* Asunción: República de Paraguay, 1970.

Municipalidad de la Ciudad de Buenos Aires, Secretaría de Cultura. *Barrios, calles y plazas de la Ciudad de Buenos Aires: Origen y razón de sus nombres.* Buenos Aires: Instituto Histórico de la Ciudad de Buenos Aires, 1983.

Murrin, John A. "A Roof Without Walls: The Dilemma of American National Identity." In Richard Beeman, Stephen Botein, and Edward C. Carter II, eds., *Beyond Confederation: Origins of the Constitution and American National Identity.* Chapel Hill: University of North Carolina Press, 1987.

Navarro de García, Luis. "El orden tradicional y la revolución de independencia en Iberoamérica." In Inge Buisson, Günter Kahle, Hans-Joachim König, and Horst Pietschmann, eds., *Problemas de la formación del estado y de la nación en Hispanoamérica.* Special issue of *Lateinamerikanische Forschung* 13 (1984).

Needell, Jeffrey D. "Rio de Janeiro and Buenos Aires: Public Space and Public Consciousness in Fin-de-Siècle Latin America." *Comparative Studies in Society and History* 37, no. 3 (1995): 519–40.

Newland, Carlos. "La educación elemental en Hispanoamérica: Desde la independencia hasta la centralización de los sistemas educativos nacionales." *Hispanic American Historical Review* 71, no. 2 (1991): 335–64.

Noelle, Louise, and Daniel Schavelzon. "Monumento efímero a los héroes de la independencia." *Anales del Instituto de Investigaciones Estéticas* (Mexico) 14, no. 55 (1986): 161–69.

Nogueira, Denio. *Raízes de uma Nação.* Rio de Janeiro: Editora Universitária, 1988.

North, Douglass C. *Institutions, Institutional Change, and Economic Performance.* New York: Cambridge University Press, 1990.

North, Douglass C., and Robert Paul Thomas. *The Rise of the Western World: A New Economic History.* New York: Cambridge University Press, 1973.

Nugent, David. "State and Shadow State in Northern Peru Circa 1900: Illegal Political Networks and the Problem of State Boundaries." 1999. Mimeographed.

Nunn, Frederick M. "On the Role of the Military in Twentieth Century Latin America: The Mexican Case." In David Ronfeldt, ed., *The Modern Mexican Military: A Reassessment*. La Jolla: University of California, San Diego, Center for U.S.-Mexican Studies, 1984.

———. *The Time of the Generals: Latin American Professional Militarism in World Perspective*. Lincoln: University of Nebraska Press, 1992.

———. *Yesterday's Soldiers: European Military Professionalism in South America, 1890–1940*. Lincoln: University of Nebraska Press, 1983.

Nusdeo, Osvaldo, and Pedro Conno. *Papel moneda nacional argentino y bonarense, siglo XIX*. Buenos Aires: Editorial Hector C. Janson, 1981.

Nussel, Frank. "Territorial and Boundary Disputes Depicted on Postage Stamps." *Studies in Latin American Popular Culture* 11 (1992): 123–41.

Nye, Joseph S., Jr. "Old Wars and Future Wars: Causation and Prevention." In Robert Rotberg and Theodore Rabb, eds., *The Origin and Prevention of Major Wars*. Cambridge: Cambridge University Press, 1989.

O'Brien, Patrick. "The Political Economy of British Taxation, 1660–1815." *The Economic History Review* 41, no. 1 (1988): 1–32.

O'Connell, Robert L. *Ride the Second Horseman: The Birth and Death of War*. New York: Oxford University Press, 1995.

O'Donnell, Guillermo. "The Judiciary and the Rule of Law." *Journal of Democracy* 11, no. 1 (2000): 25–31.

———. "The State, Democratization, and Some Conceptual Problems." In William C. Smith, Carlos Acuña, and Eduardo Gamarra, eds., *Latin American Political Economy in the Age of Neoliberal Reform*. Miami: North-South Center Press, 1994.

O'Malley, Ilene V. *The Myth of Revolution: Hero Cults and the Institutionalization of the Mexican State, 1920–1940*. New York: Greenwood Press, 1986.

Ocampo, José Antonio, ed. *Historia económica de Colombia*. Bogotá: Siglo XXI, 1987.

Ocampo López, Javier. "La separación de la Gran Colombia en el proceso de la desintegración del imperio colonial hispanoamericano." In Inge Buisson, Günter Kahle, Hans-Joachim König, and Horst Pietschmann, eds., *Problemas de la formación del estado y de la nación en Hispanoamérica*. Special issue of *Lateinamerikanische Forschung* 13 (1984).

Organization for Economic Cooperation and Development (OECD). *Revenue Statistics*. Paris: OECD, 1997.

Organski, A. F. K., and Jacek Kugler. *The War Ledger*. Chicago: University of Chicago Press, 1980.

Orr, Emda, Edna Liran, and Joachim Meyer. "Compulsory Military Service as a Challenge and a Threat." *Israel Social Science Research* 4, no. 2 (1982): n.p.

Ortega, José. *Aspectos del nacionalismo boliviano*. Madrid: Ediciones José Porrúa Turanzas, 1971.

Ortiz, Juan Escampilla. *Guerra y gobierno: Los pubelos y la independencia de México*. Mexico: Instituto Mora, 1997.

Ossandón Guzmán, Carlos, and Ossandón Vicuna, Dominga. *Guía de Santiago*. 7th ed. Santiago: Impresora Nacional, 1983.

Oszlak, Oscar. *La formación del estado argentino*. Buenos Aires: Editorial de Belgrano, 1982.

———. "The Historical Formation of the State in Latin America: Some Theoretical and Methodological Guidelines for Its Study." *Latin American Research Review* 16, no. 2 (1981): 3–33.

Pagden, Anthony. "Identity Formation in Spanish America." In Nicholas Canny and Anthony Pagden, eds., *Colonial Identity in the Atlantic World, 1500–1800*. Princeton: Princeton University Press, 1987.

Palacios, Marco, ed. *La unidad nacional en América Latina: Del regionalismo a la nacionalidad*. Mexico City: El Colegio de México, 1983.

Palmer, R. *The Age of Democratic Revolutions*. Princeton: Princeton University Press, 1959.

Paret, Peter. *Understanding War: Essays on Clausewitz and the History of Military Power*. Princeton: Princeton University Press, 1992.

Parker, Geoffrey. *The Military Revolution*. Cambridge: Cambridge University Press, 1988.

Pastore, Mario. "State-Led Industrialization: The Evidence of Paraguay, 1852–1870." *Journal of Latin American Studies* 26, no. 2 (1994): 295–324.

———. "Trade Contraction and Economic Decline: The Paraguayan Economy Under Francia, 1810–1840." *Journal of Latin American Studies* 26, no. 3 (1994): 539–95.

Payne, Stanley. *A History of Fascism*. Madison: University of Wisconsin Press, 1995.

Paz, Julio. *Historia económica de Bolivia*. La Paz: Imprenta Artística, 1927.

Peacock, Alan T., and Jack Wiseman. *The Growth of Public Expenditure in the U.K.* Princeton: Princeton University Press, 1961.

Peceny, Mark. "The Inter-American System as a Liberal Pacific Union?" *Latin American Research Review* 29, no. 3 (1994): 188–201.

Pedemonte, Juan Carlos. *Montevideo: Hombres, bronce, marmol*. Montevideo: Barreiro y Ramos, 1971.

Peled, Alon. "Force, Ideology, and Contract: The History of Ethnic Conscription." *Ethnic and Racial Studies* 17, no. 1–2 (1994): 61–78.

Peloso, Vincent C., and Barbara Tenenbaum, eds. *Liberals, Politics, and Power: State Formation in Nineteenth Century Latin America*. Athens, Ga.: University of Georgia Press, 1996.

Pereira Fiorillo, Juan. *Bolivia, historia de su pasado económico: De la fundación a la guerra del salitre*. La Paz: Editorial Los Amigos del Libro, 1990.

Pereira Pinto, Juan Carlos. *Historia Política, Económica y Social de la Argentina*. Buenos Aires: AZ Editora, 1982.

Perez Pimentel, Rodolfo. *Diccionario biográfico del Ecuador*. 5 vols. Guayaquil: Universidad de Guayaquil, 1988.

Phelan, John Leddy. *The People and the King: The Comunero Revolution in Colombia, 1781*. Madison: University of Wisconsin Press, 1978.

Philip, George. *The Military in South American Politics*. London: Croom Helm, 1985.

Piccirilli, Ricardo, ed. *Diccionario histórico Argentino.* 6 vols. Buenos Aires: Ediciones Históricas Argentinas, 1954.

Pick, Albert. *Standard Catalog of World Paper Money.* 5th ed. 2 vols. Iola, Wisc.: Krause, 1986.

Pineda, Rafael. *Las estatuas de Simón Bolívar en el mundo.* Caracas: Centro Simón Bolívar, C.A., 1983.

Pinheiro, Paulo Sérgio. "Democracies Without Citizenship." *NACLA Report* 30, no. 2 (1996): 17–23.

Plotkin, Marinao ben. "Política, educación y nacionalismo." *Todo es Historia* 18, no. 221 (1985): 64–79.

Poggi, Gianfranco. *The Development of the Modern State: A Sociological Introduction.* Stanford: Stanford University Press, 1978.

Polachek, S. W. "Conflict and Trade." *Journal of Conflict Resolution* 24, no. 1 (1980): 57–78.

Pomer, León. "El estado nacional argentino." *Revista de Historia de América* 105 (1988): 53–88.

———. *La guerra del Paraguay: Estado, política y negocio.* 1968; Buenos Aires: Centro editor de América Latina, 1987.

Porter, Bruce. *War and the Rise of the State: The Military Foundations of Modern Politics.* New York: Free Press, 1994.

Potash, Robert A. "Argentina." In Lyle McAlister, Anthony Maingot, and Robert Potash, eds., *The Military in Latin American Sociopolitical Evolution: Four Case Studies.* Washington, D.C.: Center for Research in Social Systems, 1970.

———. *The Army and Politics in Argentina, 1928–1945: Yrigoyen to Perón.* Stanford: Stanford University Press, 1969.

———. *The Army and Politics in Argentina, 1945–1962: Perón to Frondizi.* Stanford: Stanford University Press, 1982.

Preston, Richard, Alex Roland, and Sidney Wise. *Men in Arms: A History of Warfare and Its Interrelationships with Western Society.* 5th ed. Fort Worth: HBJ, 1991.

Probst, Volker G. *Bilder vom Tode.* Hamburg: Wayasbah, 1986.

Puigbo, Raul. *Historia social y económica Argentina.* Buenos Aires: Ediciones Españolas, 1964.

Putnam, Robert D., with Robert Leonardi and Raffaella Nanetti. *Making Democracy Work: Civic Traditions in Modern Italy.* Princeton: Princeton University Press, 1993.

Quirk, Robert E. *Mexico.* Englewood Cliffs, N.J.: Prentice-Hall, 1970.

Quiroz, Alfonso W. *Domestic and Foreign Finance in Modern Peru, 1850–1950.* London: Macmillan, 1993.

Ragin, Charles. *Fuzzy-Set Social Science.* Chicago: University of Chicago Press, 2000.

Ralston, David. *Importing the European Army: The Introduction of European Military Techniques and Institutions into the Extra-European World, 1600–1914.* Chicago: University of Chicago Press, 1990.

Randall, Laura. *A Comparative Economic History of Latin America.* 4 vols. Ann

Arbor: University Microfilms; and New York: Institute of Latin American Studies, Columbia University, 1977.

Rasler, Karen, and William R. Thompson. *War and Statemaking: The Shaping of Global Powers.* Boston: Unwin Hyman, 1989.

Ray, James Lee. "Does Democracy Cause Peace?" *Annual Review of Political Science* 1 (1998): 27–46.

Raymond, Wayte. *Coins of the World: Nineteenth Century Issues.* New York: Wayte Raymond, 1947.

———. *Coins of the World: Twentieth Century Issues.* New York: Wayte Raymond, 1951.

Reber, Vera Blinn. "The Demographics of Paraguay: A Reinterpretation of the Great War, 1864–1870." *Hispanic American Historical Review* 68, no. 2 (1988): 289–319.

———. "Paraguayan State Budgets." N.d. Mimeographed.

Reed, Nelson. *The Caste War of Yucatán.* Stanford: Stanford University Press, 1964.

Reid, John T. "The Stamp of Patriotism." *Américas* 33, no. 8 (1981): 45–49.

Reseña histórica y orgánica del ejército argentino. Buenos Aires: Círculo Militar, 1971.

Resende-Santos, João. "Anarchy and the Emulation of Military Systems: Military Organization and Technology of South America, 1870–1930." In *Realism: Restatements, and Renewal.* Special issue of *Security Studies* 5, no. 3 (1996): 194–260.

Reyes Abadie, Washington, and A. Vázquez Romero. *Crónica general del Uruguay.* Vol. 3, *El Uruguay del siglo XIX.* Montevideo: Ediciones de la Banda Oriental, n.d.

Ribas, Gabriel A. "Militarismo e intervenciones armadas, 1810–1983." *Todo es historia* (Buenos Aires) 253 (1988).

Rippy, J. Fred. *British Investments in Latin America, 1822–1949.* Minneapolis: University of Minnesota Press, 1959.

Rivarola, Paoli, and Juan Bautista. *Historia monetaria de Paraguay.* Asunción: El Gráfico, 1982.

Roberts, Clayton. *The Logic of Historical Explanation.* University Park: Pennsylvania State University Press, 1996.

Roberts, Michael. *Essays in Swedish History.* London: Weidenfeld and Nicolson, 1967.

Rock, David. *Argentina, 1516–1987.* Rev. ed. Berkeley and Los Angeles: University of California Press, 1987.

Rodríguez O., Jaime E. *The Independence in Spanish America.* New York: Cambridge University Press, 1998.

Rodríguez, Linda Alexander. Introduction to Linda Alexander Rodríguez, ed., *Rank and Privilege: The Military and Society in Latin America.* Wilmington, Del.: Scholarly Resources, 1994.

———. *The Search for Public Policy: Regional Politics and Government Finances in Ecuador, 1830–1940.* Berkeley and Los Angeles: University of California Press, 1985.

————, ed. *Rank and Privilege: The Military and Society in Latin America.* Wilmington, Del.: Scholarly Resources, 1994.

Romero y Cordero, Remigio. *El ejército en cien años de vida republicana, 1830–1930.* Quito: Instituto Geográfico Militar, 1991.

Rosa, José María. *La guerra del Paraguay y las montoneras argentinas.* Buenos Aires: Hyspamerica, 1986.

Rosa, Moises de la. *Calles de Santa Fe de Bogotá.* Edición facsimilar. 1938; Bogotá: Colección Viajantes y Viajeros, 1988.

Rosenman, Richard. *Billetes de Venezuela.* Caracas: Corimon, 1980.

Rotberg, Robert, and Theodore Rabb, eds. *The Origin and Prevention of Major Wars.* Cambridge: Cambridge University Press, 1989.

Rouquie, Alain. *Poder militar y sociedad política en la Argentina.* 2 vols. Buenos Aires: Emecé Editores, 1981–82.

Rueschemeyer, Dietrich, Evelyne Huber Stephens, and John D. Stephens. *Capitalist Development and Democracy.* Chicago: University of Chicago Press, 1992.

Ruhl, J. Mark. *Colombia: Armed Forces and Society.* Syracuse, N.Y.: Maxwell School of Citizenship and Public Affairs, 1980.

Ruiz, Ramón. *The Mexican War: Was It Manifest Destiny?* New York: Holt, Rinehart, and Winston, 1963.

Rummel, R. J. *Death by Government.* New Brunswick, N.J.: Transaction, 1994.

Sadie, Stanley, ed. *The New Grove Dictionary of Music and Musicians.* Vol. 13. London: Macmillan.

Safford, Frank. "History, 1750–1850." In Paula Covington, ed., *Latin America and the Caribbean: A Critical Guide to Research Resources.* New York: Greenwood Press, 1992.

Saldanha Lemos, Juvencio. *Os mercenários do imperador: A primera corrente imigratória alemã no Brasil.* Porto Alegre: Palmarinca, 1993.

Salvatore, Ricardo. "Reclutamiento militar, disciplinamiento y proleterización en la Era de Rosas." *Boletín del Instituto de Historia Argentina y Americana,* tercer serie, 5 (1992).

Samuel, Raphael. "Continuous National History." In Raphael Samuel, ed., *Patriotism: The Making and Unmaking of British National Identity.* London: Routledge, 1987.

San Juan Victoria, Carlos, and Salvador Velázquez Ramírez. "La formación del estado y la políticas económicas." In Ciro Cardoso, ed., *México en el siglo XIX: Historia económica y de la estructura social.* 2d ed. Mexico: Nueva Imagen, 1992.

Santoni, Pedro. "A Fear of the People: The Civic Militia of Mexico in 1845." *Hispanic American Historical Review* 68, no. 2 (1988): 269–88.

Saravia Ruelas, Benjamin. *Quiénes perdieron sus pantalones en el Chaco?* La Paz: Editora Universo, 1986.

Sater, William F. *Chile and the War of the Pacific.* Lincoln: University of Nebraska Press, 1986.

————. *The Heroic Image in Chile: Arturo Prat, Secular Saint.* Berkeley and Los Angeles: University of California Press, 1973.

Savage, Kirk. "The Politics of Memory: Black Emancipation and the Civil War Monument." In John R. Gillis, ed., *Commemorations: The Politics of National Identity.* Princeton: Princeton University Press, 1994.

Schoultz, Lars. *Beneath the United States: A History of U.S. Policy Towards Latin America.* Cambridge: Harvard University Press, 1998.

Schroeder, John H. *Mr. Polk's War: American Opposition and Dissent, 1846–1848.* Madison: University of Wisconsin Press, 1973.

Schudson, Michael. "How Culture Works: Perspectives from Media Studies on the Efficacy of Symbols." *Theory and Society* 18 (1989): 153–80.

Schumpeter, Joseph A. "The Crisis of the Tax State." *International Economic Papers* 4 (1954): 5–38.

Schwartz, Barry. "The Social Context of Commemoration: A Study in Collective Memory." *Social Forces* 61, no. 2 (1982): 374–402.

Schwartz, Stuart. "The Formation of Colonial Identity in Brazil." In Nicholas Canny and Anthony Pagden, eds., *Colonial Identity in the Atlantic World, 1500–1800.* Princeton: Princeton University Press, 1987.

Scobie, James R. *Argentina: A City and a Nation.* New York: Oxford University Press, 1971.

Scott, James. *Seeing Like a State.* New Haven: Yale University Press, 1998.

Scott Standard Postage Stamp Catalogue. New York: Scott, 1973.

Seckinger, Ron. *The Brazilian Monarchy and the South American Republics.* Baton Rouge: Louisiana State Press, 1984.

SER en el 2000. Special issue of *Seguridad Estratégica Regional,* no. 8 (1995).

Seppa, Dale. *Paper Money of Paraguay and Uruguay.* San Antonio: Earl International, 1970.

Sherman, Daniel J. "Art, Commerce, and the Production of Memory in France After WWI." In John R. Gillis, ed., *Commemorations: The Politics of National Identity.* Princeton: Princeton University Press, 1994.

Shumway, Nicholas. *The Invention of Argentina.* Berkeley and Los Angeles: University of California Press, 1991.

Sikkink, Kathryn. "Las capacidades y la autonomía del estado en Brasil y la Argentina: Un enfoque neoinstitucionalista." *Desarollo Económico* 32, no. 128 (1993): 543–74.

Silva Cazet, Elisa. "En torno a la nomenclatura de Montevideo y a la formación de una conciencia nacional." *Revista Biblioteca Nacional* 24 (1986): 79–90.

Silva Michelena, José A. "State Formation in Latin America." *International Social Science Journal,* 23, no. 3 (1971): 384–98.

Silvert, K. H. "Nationalism in Latin America." *Annals of the American Academy of Political and Social Science* 334 (1961): 1–9.

Singer, J. David, and Melvin Small. *Resort to Arms.* Beverly Hills, Calif.: Sage, 1982.

Skagg, David Curtis. "Postage Stamps as Icons." In Ray B. Browne and Marshall Fishwick, eds., *Icons of America.* Bowling Green: Popular Press, 1978.

Skocpol, Theda. *Protecting Soldiers and Mothers.* Cambridge, Mass.: Belknap Press, 1992.

———. *States and Social Revolutions: A Comparative Analysis of France, Russia, and China.* Cambridge: Cambridge University Press, 1979.

Skowronek, S. *Building a New American State: The Expansion of National Admin-*

istrative Capacities, 1877–1920. New York: Cambridge University Press. 1982.

Skursi, Julie. "The Ambiguities of Authenticity in Latin America: Doña Barbara and the Construction of National Identity." In Geoff Eley and Ronald Suny, eds., *Becoming National*. Oxford: Oxford University Press, 1996.

Smith, Anthony. *The Ethnic Origin of Nations*. Oxford: Blackwell, 1986.

———. "State-Making and Nation-Building." In John Hall, ed., *States in History*. New York: Basil Blackwell, 1986.

———. "War and Ethnicity: The Role of Warfare in the Formation, Self-Images, and Cohesion of Ethnic Communities." *Ethnic and Racial Studies* 4, no. 4 (1981): 375–97.

Smith, David A., Dorothy J. Solinger, and Steven C. Topik. *States and Sovereignty in the Global Economy*. London: Routledge, 1999.

Smith, Peter H. "The Rise and Fall of the Developmental State in Latin America." In Menno Vellinga, ed., *The Changing Role of the State in Latin America*. Boulder, Colo.: Westview Press, 1998.

Sommer, Doris. *Foundational Fictions: The National Romances of Latin America*. Berkeley and Los Angeles: University of California Press, 1991.

Sosa, Ignacio. "De la patria del criollo a la idea de nación hispanoamericana." In Ignacio Sosa, ed., *El nacionalismo en América Latina*. Mexico: UNAM, 1984.

Stein, Arthur, and Bruce Russett. "Evaluating War: Outcomes and Consequences." In Ted Gurr, ed., *Handbook of Political Conflict*. New York: Free Press, 1980.

Stein, Stanley J. *Silver, Trade, and War: Spain and America in the Making of Early Modern Europe*. Baltimore: Johns Hopkins University Press, 2000.

Stepan, Alfred. *The Military in Politics: Changing Patterns in Brazil*. Princeton: Princeton University Press, 1971.

———. *The State and Society: Peru in Comparative Perspective*. Princeton: Princeton University Press, 1978.

Stern, Steve J. Introduction to part 3 of Steve J. Stern, ed., *Resistance, Rebellion, and Consciousness in the Andean Peasant World, Nineteenth to Twentieth Centuries*. Madison: University of Wisconsin Press, 1987.

———, ed. *Resistance, Rebellion, and Consciousness in the Andean Peasant World, Eighteenth to Twentieth Centuries*. Madison: University of Wisconsin Press, 1987.

Stoetzer, Carlos. *Postage Stamps as Propaganda*. Washington, D.C.: Public Affairs Press, 1953.

Stone, Lawrence, ed. *An Imperial State at War: Britain from 1689 to 1815*. London: Routledge, 1994.

Street, John. *Artigas and the Emancipation of Uruguay*. Cambridge: Cambridge University Press, 1959.

"Symposium on Historical Sociology and Rational Choice Theory." *American Journal of Sociology* 104, no. 3 (1998): 1520–1626.

Szuchman, Mark. "Childhood Education and Politics in Nineteenth-Century Argentina: The Case of Buenos Aires." *Hispanic American Historical Review* 70, no. 1 (1990): 109–38.

Tallett, Frank. *War and Society in Early Modern Europe, 1495–1715.* New York: Routledge, 1992.

Tenenbaum, Barbara. "The Chicken and the Egg. Reflections on the Mexican Military, 1821–1845." In Virginia Guedea and Jaime E. Rodríguez O., eds., *Five Centuries of Mexican History.* Mexico City: Instituto de Investigaciones, 1992.

———. *The Politics of Penury: Debt and Taxes in Mexico, 1821–1856.* Albuquerque: University of New Mexico Press, 1986.

———. "Streetwise History: The Paseo de la Reforma and the Porfirian State, 1876–1910." In William Beezley, Cheryl English Martin, and William E. French, eds., *Rituals of Rule, Rituals of Resistance: Public Celebrations and Popular Culture in Mexico.* Wilmington, Del.: Scholarly Resources, 1994.

Thayer Ojeda, Luis. *Santiago de Chile: Origen del nombre de sus calles.* Santiago: Guillermo Miranda, 1904.

Thomas, Hugh. *Cuba, or the Pursuit of Freedom.* New York: Harper & Row, 1971.

Thompson, Andrew. "Informal Empire? An Exploration in the History of Anglo-Argentine Relations, 1810–1914." *Journal of Latin American Studies* 24, no. 2 (1992): 419–36.

Thompson, Guy. "Bulwarks of Patriotic Liberalism: The National Guard, Philharmonic Corps, and Patriotic Juntas in Mexico, 1847–1888." *Journal of Latin American Studies* 22 (1990): 31–68.

———. "Federalism and Vantonalism in Mexico, 1824–1892: Sovereignty and Territoriality." In Eduardo Posada-Carbó, ed., *Wars, Parties, and Nationalism: Essays on the Politics and Society of Nineteenth Century Latin America.* London: Institute of Latin American Studies, 1995.

———. "Los indios y el servicio militar en el México decimonónico: Leva or ciudadanía?" In Antonio Escobar Ohmstede and Patricia Lagos Preisser, eds., *Indio, nación y comunidad en el México del siglo XIX.* Mexico: CEMC/CIESAS, 1993.

Thurner, Mark. *From Two Republics to One Divided: Contradictions of Postcolonial Nationmaking in Andean Peru.* Durham: Duke University Press, 1997.

———. "*Republicanos* and *la Comunidad de peruanos:* Unimagined Political Communities in Postcolonial Andean Peru." *Journal of Latin American Studies* 27 (1995): 291–318.

Tilly, Charles. *Big Structures, Large Processes, Huge Comparisons.* New York: Russell Sage Foundation, 1984.

———. *Coercion, Capital, and European States, A.D. 990–1992.* Oxford: Blackwell, 1990.

———. *European Revolutions, 1492–1992.* Oxford: Blackwell, 1993.

———. "Reflections on the History of European State-Making." In Charles Tilly, ed., *The Formation of National States in Western Europe.* Princeton: Princeton University Press, 1975.

———. "State-Incited Violence, 1900–1999." *Political Power and Social Theory* 9 (1995): 161–79.

———. "States and Nationalism in Europe, 1492–1992." *Theory and Society* 23, no. 1 (1994): 131–46.

———. "To Explain Political Processes." *American Journal of Sociology* 100, no. 6 (1995): 1594–1610.

———. "War Making and State Making as Organized Crime." In Peter Evans, Dietrich Rueschemeyer, and Theda Skocpol, eds, *Bringing the State Back In.* Cambridge: Cambridge University Press, 1985.

———, ed. *The Formation of National States in Western Europe.* Princeton: Princeton University Press, 1975.

Timmons Roberts, J. "Power and Placenames: A Case Study from the Contemporary Amazon Frontier." *Names* 41, no. 3 (1993): 159–82.

Torre Villar, Ernesto de la. "El origen del estado mexicano." In Inge Buisson, Günter Kahle, Hans-Joachim König, and Horst Pietschmann, eds., *Problemas de la formación del estado y de la nación en Hispanoamérica.* Special issue of *Lateinamerikanische Forschung* 13 (1984).

Tovar, Alvaro Valencia. *Historia de las fuerzas militares de Colombia.* Bogotá: Planeta, 1993.

Tovar Pinzón, Hermes. "La lenta ruptura con el pasado colonial, 1810–1850." In José Antonio Ocampo, ed., *Historia económica de Colombia.* Bogotá: Siglo XXI, 1987.

Treverton, Gregory. "Interstate Conflict in Latin America." In Kevin J. Middlebrook and Carlos Rico, eds., *The United States and Latin America in the 1980s.* Pittsburgh: University of Pittsburgh Press, 1986.

Trujillo B., Eduardo R. *Historia del papel moneda del Ecuador.* Guayaquil, Ecuador: S.N.

Tutino, John. *From Insurrection to Revolution in Mexico: Social Bases of Agrarian Violence, 1750–1940.* Princeton: Princeton University Press, 1986.

Ugarte, César Antonio. *Historia económica del Perú.* Lima: Imp. Cabieses, 1926.

United Nations, Statistics Division, Social and Housing Statistics Section. http://www.un.org/depts/unsd/social/watsan.html.

United States Department of State. *Foreign Relations of the United States.* Washington, D.C.: U.S. Government Printing Office.

University of Texas, Austin, Department of Sociology. "Rising Violence and the Criminal Justice Response in Latin America: Towards an Agenda for Collaborative Research in the Twenty-first Century." http://lanic.utexas.edu/project/etext/violence/memoria. July 2000.

University of Texas, Latin American Network Information Center (LANIC). "Trends in Latin American Networking." http://www.lanic.utexas.edu/project/tilan/statistics/internetinfra.html. July 2000.

Uricoechea, Fernando. *The Patrimonial Foundations of the Brazilian Bureaucratic State.* Berkeley and Los Angeles: University of California Press, 1980.

Useem, Michael, and commentators. "The Rise and Fall of a Volunteer Army." *Society* 131 (1981): 28–60.

Vagts, Alfred. *A History of Militarism.* 1959; Westport, Conn.: Greenwood Press, 1981.

Valencia Tovar, Alvaro, and José Manuel Villalobos Barradas, eds. *Historia de las Fuerzas Armadas de Colombia*. 6 vols. Bogotá: Planeta, 1993.

Valery S., Rafael. *La nomenclatura caraqueña*. Caracas: Ernesto Armitano Editorial, 1978.

Van Creveld, Martin. *The Rise and Decline of the State*. New York: Cambridge University Press, 1999.

van Doorn, Jacques. "The Decline in the Mass Army in the West: General Reflections." *Armed Forces and Society* 1, no. 2 (1975): 147–58.

Varas, Augusto, and Isaac Caro, eds. *Medidas de confianza mutua en América Latina*. Santiago: FLACSO, 1994.

Vaughn, Mary Kay. *The State, Education, and Social Class in Mexico, 1880–1928*. Dekalb: Northern Illinois University Press, 1982.

Vázquez, Josefina, and Zoraida Vázques. "El ejército: Un dilema del gobierno mexicano, 1841–1864." In Inge Buisson, Günter Kahle, Hans-Joachim König, and Horst Pietschmann, eds., *Problemas de la formación del estado y de la nación en Hispanoamérica*. Special issue of *Lateinamerikanische Forschung* 13 (1984).

Véliz, Claudio. *The Centralist Tradition of Latin America*. Princeton: Princeton University Press, 1980.

Verdery, Katherine. *The Political Lives of Dead Bodies: Reburial and Postsocialist Change*. New York: Columbia University Press, 1999.

Vial Correa, Gonzalo. "La formación de las nacionalidades hispanoamericanas como causa de la independencia." *Boletín de la Academia Chilena de la Historia* 33, pt. 2 (1966): 110–44.

Vigil, Carlos. *Los monumentos y lugares históricos de la Argentina*. Buenos Aires: Editorial Atlantida, 1948.

Vilas, Carlos M. "Incquality and the Dismantling of Citizenship in Latin America." *NACLA Report* 31, no. 1 (1997): 57–63.

Villanueva, Victor. *Ejército peruano: Del caudillaje anárquico al militarismo reformista*. Lima: Editorial Juan Mejia Baca, 1973.

Violo Idolo, Lissa. *Catálogo do papel-moeda do Brasil, 1771–1980*, 2d ed. Brasilia: Editora Gráfica Brasiliana Ltda, 1981.

Viscarra Monje, Humberto. *Las calles de La Paz, su origen y la historia de sus nombres*. La Paz: n.p., 1965.

Vittone, Colonel D. E. M. Luís. *Las fuerzas armadas paraguayas en sus distintas épocas: La infantería paraguaya y su patrono*. Asunción: Editorial El Gráfico, 1969.

Vogel, Henry P. "Elements of Nationbuilding in Argentina: Buenos Aires, 1810–1828." Ph.D. diss., University of Florida, 1987.

von Stein, Lorenz. "On Taxation" (1885). In Richard A. Musgrove and Alan Peacock, eds., *Classics in the Theory of Public Finance*. London: Macmillan, 1958.

Waisman, Carlos. *Reversal of Development in Argentina: Postwar Counterrevolutionary Policies and Their Structural Consequences*. Princeton: Princeton University Press, 1987.

Wallerstein, Immanuel. *The Modern World System*. Vols. 1–2. 1974; New York: Academic Press, 1980.

Waltz, Kenneth. *Theory of International Politics*. Reading, Mass.: Addison-Wesley, 1979.

Warren, H. G. *Paraguay: An Informal History*. Norman: Oklahoma University Press, 1949.

Weber, Eugene. *Peasants into Frenchmen: The Modernization of Rural France, 1870–1914*. Stanford: Stanford University Press, 1976.

Weber, Max. *Economy and Society*. 2 vols. Edited by Guenther Roth and Claus Wittich. Berkeley and Los Angeles: University of California Press, 1978.

———. *From Max Weber: Essays in Sociology*. Translated, edited, and with an introduction by H. H. Gerth and C. Wright Mills. New York: Basic Books, 1946.

———. *General Economic History*. New York: Free Press, 1950.

Weede, Erich. "Democracy and War Involvement." *Journal of Conflict Resolution* 28, no. 4 (1984): 649–64.

———. "Military Participation Ratios, Human Capital Formation, and Economic Growth." *Journal of Political and Military Sociology* 11, no. 1 (1983): 11–19.

Weinland, Martina. *Kriegerdenkmäler in Berlin 1870 bis 1930*. Frankfurt: Peter Lang, 1990.

Westfehling, Uwe. *Triumphbogen im 19. und 20. Jahrhundert*. Munich: Prestel-Verlag, 1977.

Wetzlaff-Eggebert, Christian. "Literatura americana o literatura nacional: Problemas de legitimación después de la independencia." In Inge Buisson, Günter Kahle, Hans-Joachim König, and Horst Pietschmann, eds., *Problemas de la formación del estado y de la nación en Hispanoamérica*. Special issue of *Lateinamerikanische Forschung* 13 (1984).

Whigham, Thomas. *The Politics of River Trade: Tradition and Development in the Upper Plate, 1780–1870*. Albuquerque: University of New Mexico Press, 1991.

Whigham, Thomas, and Barbara Potthast. "The Paraguayan Rosetta Stone: New Insights into the Demographics of the Paraguayan War, 1864–1870." *Latin American Research Review* 34, no. 1 (1999): 174–86.

———. "Some Strong Reservations: A Critique of Vera Blinn Reber's 'The Demographics of Paraguay: A Reinterpretation of the Great War.'" *Hispanic American Historical Review* 70, no. 4 (1990): 667–76.

White, Richard Alan. *Paraguay's Autonomous Revolution, 1810–1840*. Albuquerque: University of New Mexico Press, 1978.

Whitehead, Laurence. "State Organization in Latin America Since 1930." In Leslie Bethell, ed., *The Cambridge History of Latin America*. Vol. 6. Cambridge: Cambridge University Press, 1994.

Whittick, Arnold. *War Memorials*. London: Country Life Limited, 1946.

Wiarda, Howard J., ed. *Politics and Social Change in Latin America*. Amherst: University of Massachusetts Press, 1974.

Widdifield, Stacie G. "Dispossession, Assimilation, and the Image of the Indian in Late Nineteenth-Century Mexican Painting." *Art Journal* 49, no. 2 (1990): 125–32.

Williams, John Hoyt. *The Rise and Fall of the Paraguayan Republic, 1800–1870.* Austin: Institute of Latin American Studies, University of Texas, 1979.

Williamson, Edwin. *The Penguin History of Latin America.* New York: Penguin Books, 1992.

Wilson, Stephen. "For a Socio-Historical Approach to the Study of Western Military Culture." *Armed Forces and Society* 6, no. 4 (1980): 527–52.

Winn, Peter. "British Informal Empire in Uruguay in the Nineteenth Century." *Past and Present* 73 (1976): 100–126.

Winter, Jay M. *Sites of Memory, Sites of Mourning: The Great War in European Cultural History.* New York: Cambridge University Press, 1995.

Woll, Allen L. "For God or Country: History Textbooks and the Secularization of Chilean Society, 1840–1890." *Journal of Latin American Studies* 7, no. 1 (1975): 23–42.

Woloch, Isser. "Napoleonic Conscription: State Power and Civil Society." *Past and Present* 111 (1986): 50–100.

Wright, Quincy. *A Study of War.* Chicago: University of Chicago Press, 1965.

Yarrington, Alison. *The Commemoration of the Hero, 1800–1864: Monuments to the British Victors of the Napoleonic Wars.* New York: Garland, 1988.

Yepes del Castillo, Ernesto. *Perú, 1820–1920: Un siglo de desarollo capitalista?* Lima: Ediciones Signo, 1971.

Zarauz Castelnau, Anibal. *Billetes del Perú.* Lima: Imprenta Colegio Militar Leoncio Prado, 1979.

Zeitlin, Maurice. *The Civil Wars in Chile (or the Bourgeois Revolutions That Never Were).* Princeton: Princeton University Press, 1984.

Zelinsky, Wilbur. *Nation into State: The Shifting Symbolic Foundations of American Nationalism.* Chapel Hill: University of North Carolina Press, 1988.

Ziems, Angel. *El Gomecismo y la formación del ejército nacional.* Caracas: Editorial Ateneo de Caracas, 1979.

Zikmund, Joseph. "National Anthems as Political Symbols." *The Australian Journal of Politics and History* 15, no. 3 (1969): 73–80.

Zinnes, Dina. "Why War? Evidence on the Outbreak of International Conflict." In Ted Gurr, ed., *Handbook of Political Conflict.* New York: Free Press, 1980.

Zook, David. *The Conduct of the Chaco War.* New Haven: Yale University Press, 1960.

Index

administrative capacity, lack of, in Latin American states, 139–40, 275–80
African Americans, military mobilization of, 241
African culture, monuments and symbols in Brazil of, 196
African states: international conflicts and, 9; Latin American institutions' compared to, 3 n. 6, 270
agiotistas, Mexican reliance on, 132, 159–60
air forces in Latin America, 253 n. 201
Alamán, Lucas, 156
alcabala system, 131
Allende, Salvador, 200
Anderson, Benedict, 171–73
Anderson, M. S., 27
Anderson, Perry, 71, 107
Andinos movement (Venezuela), 109
Andreski, S., 241
Angel of Independence memorial, 208
Anglophobia, in Argentina, 88
Ansina, Adolfo, 206 n. 140
anticommunism: domestic strife and, 66 n. 31; military mobilization and, 256–57
Ardant, Gabriel, 103, 243
Argentina: battle for La Plata and formation of, 53–54; borrowing patterns in, 133; Brazilian conflict with, 152, 263; caudillo formation in, 156–57, 228; centralization of authority in, 113, 160–61; Chilean tensions with, 68, 87–88; civil militia formation in, 229–30, 234, 251 n. 188, 254; confederation struggle in, 128–29; conscription in, 236–37, 245–46, 249–50,

260; currency inflation in, 5; customs taxation in, 135–36; "Dirty War" in, 7; economic development in, 117; elite disagreements in, 151–52, 156–58; entente with Brazil, 54–56; export economy in, 114; Falklands/Malvinas conflict and, 72, 82; foreign loans to, 134; immigrants in, 239, 256; independence wars in, 49–52, 270; Indian wars in, 138, 229; military mobilization in, 80, 82, 94–98, 226, 228, 229 n. 59, 232–33, 253–57, 259; monuments and symbols in, 196–97; nationalism in, 214–15; racial/ethnic conflicts in, 65, 92; racial stereotyping concerning, 85; regional conflicts in, 62, 109, 113, 129, 145–46; state formation and capacity in, 11, 113, 160–61; taxation in, 118; war iconography in, 200–202, 206–7, 209–11
Argentine-Brazilian War of 1826–28, 134
arms manufacturing, 94 n. 109
arms races: economic limits and, 94–98; Latin American rejection of, 85–90
Army of the Three Guarantees, 48, 226
Artigas, José, 49, 208
artists, national myths in Latin America concerning, 185
Asia, authoritarian developmentalism in, versus Latin America, 5 n. 12
Atahualpa, 196
Australia, monuments and symbols in, 182–83
Austria-Hungary, war and statehood in, 116
authority structures: development of, in Latin America, 22–26; elite disagreements and,

Cuauhtémoc, 194–96
Cuba: internal conflicts in, 70; involvement in
  international conflict by, 52; military mobilization in, 98–99, 229, 260; national
  myths in, 188; political violence in, 8 n. 22;
  revolution in, 14, 65–66, 98–99; slavery in,
  247; U.S. relations with, 73, 213
cultural factors in state development: lack of
  nationalism in Latin America and, 168–70;
  militarism in Latin America and, 77–84,
  97–98; monuments in Latin America,
  178–83; national myths in Latin America
  and, 183–94; obstacles to nationalism in,
  173–78; war in Latin America and, 74,
  76–77
Cundinamarca, 145
currency: artificial wealth linked to printing
  of, 132–37; inflation in Latin American
  countries and, 5; national myths in Latin
  America and themes of, 184–94; origin
  myths expressed on, 196–98; political symbolism expressed in, 179–83; war iconography on, 199–203, 205–9
customs taxes, Latin American reliance on,
  135–37
"customs union," Spanish mercantilism and,
  131

D'Annuzio, Gabriele, 174
Dario, Rubén, 174
Deas, Malcolm, 226
debt crisis: intracontinental debts, 134 n. 86;
  limited war and, 23–26; in Paraguay, 126;
  state expenditure patterns and, 116–26;
  war's impact on, 127–40
democratic regimes: conscription and establishment of, 244–46, 265; lack of, as obstacle to nationalism, 177–78; nonbellic
  behavior and, 74
dependency theory: Latin American state
  and, 13–14, 25–26; war in Latin America
  and, 71–74
despotism: state formation and, 139–40;
  uniqueness of, in Latin America, 10–11
deterministic policies: independence movements in Latin America and, 52; war in
  Latin America and, 77
developmentalism, as national myth in Latin
  America, 185, 188
Díaz Arguedas, Julio, 247

domestic policy, military strategy in Latin
  America and, 83–84
drug enforcement, military spending and, 98

economic development: artificial wealth creation and, 130–37, 270; capacity for war
  and limits of, 92–98; military mobilization
  as threat to, 239; nationalism in Latin
  America and, 174–78; state institutional
  development and, 116–26; war as stimulus
  to, 106–8
Ecuador: Bolívar's presence in, 51; bureaucratic infrastructure lacking in, 140; economic crisis in, 131; ideological conflicts
  in, 63; military mobilization on, 234, 248,
  252, 254, 256–57, 259; monuments and
  symbols in, 189, 196, 198; nationalism absent in, 210, 213, 274; pacification and
  centralization of power in, 110, 114; Peruvian conflict with, 9 n. 23, 68, 72, 75 n. 62,
  85, 89–90, 92–93, 199–200; political instability in, 6; regional conflicts in, 62, 145;
  Rio accords criticized by, 86; war iconography in, 202, 206
educational infrastructure: Latin American
  state's failure regarding, 3–4; military conscription and creation of, 244–45, 257–59
Egypt: monuments and symbols in, 183; state
  development in, 28, 240
ejército libertador, 247
elites: civil conflict and role of, 73–74; conscription avoided by, 246–60; homogeneity of, in Latin America, 173–78; internal
  divisions among, 150–60; lack of government challenge to, 137; Mexican government and role of, 61, 137–38; military
  mobilization opposed by, 239, 252; nationalist sentiments among, 172; obstacles to
  nationalism from, 175–78; racism among,
  148–50; role of, in early independence
  movements, 51–52; state development and
  role of, 12 n. 34, 13–14, 164–66, 273–80;
  treat from masses to, 90–91; war as favorable option for, 76–77
El Salvador: military expansion in, 98; revolution in, 65
England. See Great Britain
Enlightenment, Latin American nationalism
  and, 172, 190, 276
equality, military mobilization as catalyst for,
  239–45

"governmental scope" measurements, centralization of government authority and, 110

Gran Colombia: debt crisis of, 134; formation of, 51

Grau, 89, 199, 210

Great Britain: militarism and statehood in, 103, 105–7, 128, 217 n. 2, 245, 260; monuments and symbols in, 182–83; peace in Latin America and role of, 263; political symbolism in currency of, 179

gross domestic product (GDP): debt crisis in Latin America and, 133 n. 84; international comparisons with Latin America, 6 n. 16

gross national product (GNP), military spending as portion of, 93

Guanajuato massacre, 35

guano revenues, Peruvian reliance on, 135, 136 n. 101

Guarani Indians: battle for La Plata and, 54; monuments and symbols of, 196; Paraguayan state formation and, 273

Guatemala: anti-Mayan campaign in, 7; military regimes in, 98, 213; racial/ethnic conflicts in, 65, 91–92

Guerra Grande, 72

guerrilla groups: Latin American military strategy and, 83 n. 77; pacification and centralization of power limited by, 110

Hall, John, 276 n. 6

Halperín-Donghi, Tulio, 147

health services, military mobilization and establishment of, 257–59

Hegel, G. W. F., 182

Heidegger, Martin, 174

Herder, Johann, 182

Hernández, José, 197

Hidalgo, Father Miguel, 48–49, 139, 148, 208, 212

hielos continentales: foreign policy and, 87; military strategy and, 82

Hintze, Otto, 101–2

hispanidad, pancontinental concept of, 174

historical analysis: lack of nationalism in Latin America and, 170–73, 175–78, 209–15; monuments and symbols in context of, 179–83, 188–94; state formation in context of, 14–20, 270–71, 278–80; taxation and war in context of, 105–8

Holsti, Kalevi, 86 n. 29

homogeneity of population, as obstacle to nationalism, 175–78

Howard, Michael, 74

Huáscar (Prince), 196

Huizinga, Johan, 279–80

Hunt, Shane, 135

Iberian culture, Latin American state development and, 12–20

iconography: absence of women in, 190–91; military role in, 191–94; monuments and symbols in Latin America and, 178–83, 213–15; national myths in Latin America and, 183–94; origin myths expressed in, 194–98

ideological conflicts in Latin America, 62–63

imagined communities, war and creation of, 30–31, 241–45

imports, taxation systems and, 159 n. 185

Inca Empire, monuments and symbols of, 196–98

Inca Republic, 278 n. 8

independence: artificial wealth creation and wars of, 130–37; elite divisions over, 152–60; equality and class structure influenced by, 250–59; Latin American wars for, 47–52; military mobilization and, 226–27, 230–37, 247, 254; monuments and symbols to, 191–94, 204–9, 212–15; nationalism in Latin America and, 171–78; sovereignty disputes and, 145–47; state formation in wake of, 138–40, 165–66, 270–74

Indian populations. *See also* specific Indian tribes: Argentinian campaigns against, 229; Bolivian taxation of, 118, 131; elites threatened by, 90–91; inequities of conscription, effects on, 246–59; marginalization, in Mexican independence movement, 49–52; Mexican origin myths and, 194–95; monuments and symbols of, 189–90; origin myths involving, 194–98; pacification and centralization of power resisted by, 110; racial/ethnic conflicts and, 64, 148–50, 272–74; Spanish Conquest and destruction of, 137–40; state-sponsored violence against, 109; support of Paraguayan state by, 113

indiginismo, pancontinental concept of, 174

Indios Verdes monument, 194–95

251–52; educational opportunities and service in, 258

national holidays, sharings of, among Latin American countries, 86

nationalism: defined, 169–70; lack of, in Latin America, 24–26, 29–32; limits of history and, 170–73, 175–78, 209–15; military mobilization and, 80–84; monuments and symbols as tools of, 178–83; obstacles to, in Latin America, 168–69, 173–78; patriotism and, 170–78; racism and, 148–50; war in Latin America and, 84–90, 140 n. 121, 167–70, 212–15, 265–74

naval forces in Latin America, 253 n. 201

neoimperialism, war in Latin America and, 71–74

Neruda, Pablo, 174

New Granada, 143, 145, 148, 226, 246

newspapers, public opinion reflected in, 85–90

Nicaragua, 65, 213

North Atlantic Treaty Organization (NATO): Latin American military analysis compared with, 80; Spanish entry into, 80 n. 68

Nuñez, José María, 215

Nunn, Frederick, 77

O'Donnell, Guillermo, 7 n. 19

O'Higgins, Bernardo, 188 n. 92, 205, 209

origin myths: Latin American iconography concerning, 189–94; nationalism in Latin America and, 194–98

Orozco, José Clemente, 203

Ortiz de Domínguez, Doña Josefa, 208

Ozlack, Oscar, 25

pacification, state-sponsored violence as, 109

"Pacific Union," creation of, 74

Padilla, Juana de, 209

Páez, José Antonio, 51, 149, 153, 156, 203, 205

Palmer, R., 241

pancontinental unity, absence of nationalism and, 86

Panteón de Héroes, 87

Paraguay: Brazilian support of, 82 n. 72; centralization of authority in, 109–13, 114 n. 34, 161–63, 273–74; Chaco war and, 58–59, 92, 228; church-state relations in, 151; concept of nationhood in, 24; financial and expenditure patterns in, 119–26; independence movement in, 49, 129, 213; military mobilization in, 237, 248, 259–60; monuments and symbols in, 196; nationalism in, 87, 169–70; racial stereotyping concerning, 85; regional conflicts in, 145; state expenditure patterns in, 116–17; war ideology and symbolism in, 198–99, 210–11; War of the Triple Alliance and, 55–56, 77, 87, 228, 263

Paraguayan War, 232

pardos, racial/ethnic conflicts and, 149

Paret, Peter, 103

Parikh, Sunita, 243

Pasteur, Louis, 185

Pastry War, 158

path dependence, 19 n. 57, 279

patrias bobas, 145

patrias chicas, 150

patriotism: citizenship and equality and, 240–45; in Latin America, 170–78, 214–15; monuments and symbols as tools of, 178–83

Paulismo movement (Brazil), 109

pax priiana (Mexico), 110

peace: coexistence with war, in Latin America, 66–68; Latin American state development and, 22–26; prevalence of, in Latin America, 9

Pearson, Lester, 217 n. 2

peasants: inequities of conscription and, 245–59; nationalist ideology among, 178 n. 46

Pedro I, 152, 158, 161, 254

Pedro II, 247

peninsulares: criollos and, 151–52, 157; independence movements in Latin America and, 49–52; military service by, 254

pension systems, military service and formation of, 258

per capita income levels, artificial wealth in Latin America and, 130–37

Perón, Evita, 192

Perón, Juan, 80

Peru: Bolivian relations with, 88; caudillo wars in, 129; Chilean relations with, 88–89, 114, 117, 134 n. 86; Colombian loans to, 134 n. 86; economic crisis in, 131; Ecuadorean conflict with, 9 n. 23, 68, 72, 75 n. 62, 85, 89–90, 92–93, 199–200; elite internal divisions in, 153, 157–58; foreign loans to, 134; guano revenues in, 135; independence movement in, 49–51, 210, 212–13; lack of domestic industry in, 136 n. 101; military mobilization in, 80–84, 97–98, 226, 228 n. 47, 235, 247–48, 251, 254, 259–60; monuments and symbols in, 192; origin myths in, 194–98; pacification and centralization of power in, 110; Peruvian-Bolivian Confederation, 56–58; racial/ethnic conflicts in, 64–65, 91, 148–50; regional rebellion in, 62, 129; sovereignty disputes and, 143; state viability in, 6, 11, 129–30; taxation system in, 135; war iconography in, 199, 209–10; war of 1864–66, 57 n. 18

Peruvian-Bolivian Confederation, 56–58, 114, 128, 200, 214, 227, 234, 255, 273

Peruvian-Colombian War of 1828–29, 227

Pinochet, Augusto, 80, 192, 200

Pizarro, Francisco, 195

Plaza of Martyrs (Colombia), 202

Plaza of the Three Cultures monument, 195

Poggi, Gianfranco, 15

Poland: decline of, as state institution, 103; state development in, 27

political capacity: conscription and citizenship and, 242–45; enforcement of social policies and, 3; lack of, as obstacle to nationalism, 177–78; militarism and statehood and, 103–8; state formation in Latin America and lack of, 138–40, 276–80; war in Latin America and, 92, 108–26

political figures, national myths in Latin America concerning, 188

political instability, in Latin America, 6

political sociology: Latin American statehood in context of, 14; war and state development and, 102–8

POLITY II data sets, centralization of government authority and, 110

Polk, James (President), 251

popular opinion: nationalism in Latin America and, 84–90; support for war and, 76–77

Porfirio Díaz, 109, 146, 160; civil militia formed by, 229, 235; elite divisions and, 155; formation of, 273; monuments and symbols under, 201, 203; origin myths used by, 195, 198; per capita income under, 130 n. 61; taxation during, 118

Portales, Diego, 57, 113, 161, 188 n. 92, 192, 255

Portalian Constitution, 113

Porteño regime, 246

Portuguese Royal House, presence in Brazil of, 52

postage stamps: national myths in Latin America and themes of, 184–94; origin myths expressed on, 195–98; political symbolism expressed in, 179–83; war iconography on, 199–200, 202–3, 205–9

Potash, Robert A., 77

power: border conflicts and balance of, 68–74; dilution of, in Latin American state governments, 7–11; fragmentation of, in early independence movements, 51–52; military conflict and centralization of, 103–8; monuments and symbols as legitimacy of, 179–83

Prat, Arturo, 89, 200, 210

pre-Columbian civilizations: Mexican monuments and symbols of, 194–95, 203; monuments and symbols of, in Latin America, 189–90, 196–98

Prieto, Joaquin, 188 n. 92

privatized protection, growth of, in Latin America, 6–7

protection, legitimation of war as provision of, 108–16

protection societies, formation of, 258

Prussia: conscription policy in, 219–20, 222; militarism and statehood in, 106–8, 116, 240, 242

public sector employees, corruption of, in Latin America, 5

Quiroga, Facundo, 156, 202

Quito revolt, 148

racial/ethnic conflicts: in Latin America, 64–65, 90–91; as obstacle to nationalism, 175–78; state formation and, 139, 164–66, 272–74

racism: conscription inequities and, 241 n. 112, 246–59; nationalism in Latin America and expressions of, 85–90, 170–71; regional conflicts and, 148–50

Ragin, Charles, 11 n. 29

Ralston, David, 240

"raza cosmica," 174

Reforma (Mexico), 203

ments and symbols of, 189–90; nationalism suppress during, 172; Peruvian iconography of, 195–98; social divisions in Latin America and, 141–43; state formation in Latin America and, 127–30
statecentric ideology, absence of nationalism and, 85–90
state formation and development: class divisions and, 28, 141–60; economic development in Latin America, 4–5; elites' role in, 160, 164–66; export economy and development of, 114–16; failure of, in Latin America, 2–11; foreign policy and development of, 114 n. 33; intra-Latin American comparisons, 160–63, 271–80; lack of war and, 262–64; longevity of, in Latin America, 9–11; military mobilization and, 238–45; monuments and symbols as legitimacy of, 179–83; origins of, in Latin America, 11–20, 275–80; provision of protection by, 108–16; racism as component of, 64–65; taxation and development of, 116–26; war and building of, 67–68, 101–8, 163–66, 262–74
Stepan, Alfred, 77
street names, national myths in Latin America and themes of, 183–94
Stroessner, Alfredo, 59
strong societies/weak state model, Latin American state development and, 12–20
Suárez, Joaquin, 207–8
Sucre, José de, 51, 145, 158, 204–5, 209, 213
symbolism: monuments in Latin America, 178–83; national myths in Latin America and, 183–94; of war, development of nationalism and, 176–78

Tacna, Peruvian loss and recovery of, 88
taxation: capacity for war and limits of, 92–98; customs taxation, 135–37; economic crisis in Latin America and, 131–37; elite divisions concerning, 158; failure of, in Latin American countries, 6, 133–37; inflation tax, reliance on, 132; military ideology and, 103–8; state institutional development and, 116–26, 139–40
Tejedor, Carlos, 113 n. 27
telephone service, shortcomings of, in Latin America, 4
Templo Mayor (Mexico), 195
Tenoch, 211

Teotihuacán, 197
Texas, Republic of, 59, 146
Thirty Years War, 21 n. 61, 27
Tilly, Charles, 15, 18–19, 104–5, 108, 127, 263–64
Tiradentes, celebration of, 86, 209
Torres, Camilo, 205
total war, examples of, 21–26
trade relations: customs revenues and, 136–37; in Paraguay, 126; state institutional development and, 114 n. 32; U.S. arms-sales policies and, 97–98; war in Latin America and, 70–74
transportation infrastructure, centralization of government authority and development of, 110
Treaty of Guadalupe Hidalgo, 60, 159
tribal conflict, absence of, in Latin America, 53
Trigarante army, 250
Tupac Amarú revolt, 148, 196

United States: arms sales to Latin America by, 97–98; geopolitics in, 163–64; independence in Latin America and, 212–15; military expansion in Latin America and, 98–99; military mobilization in, 102 n. 6, 217 n. 2, 218 n. 3, 241, 244, 246, 260; monuments and symbols in, 181–83, 185, 188, 190; peace in Latin America and role of, 263; regionalism in, 25 n. 66; taxation and war in, 104–8; war in Latin America and influence of, 71–74
universities, monuments and symbols in, 194 n. 104
urban migration, Latin American institutions' response to, 3
Urbina, General, 248
Urquiza, Justo José, 228
Uruguay: Argentinian involvement in, 152; in battle for La Plata, 54; centralization of political power in, 109; currency printing by, 132; debt crisis in, 133; elite divisions in, 154 n. 162; independence movement in, 49, 213; monuments and symbols in, 196–97; regional rebellion in, 62; state expenditure patterns in, 117; state formation in, 11, 128; telephone service in, 4 n. 8; war iconography in, 201, 207–8; War of the Triple Alliance and, 55–56